FOLLOW THE NEW WAY

Follow the New Way

AMERICAN REFUGEE

RESETTLEMENT POLICY AND

HMONG RELIGIOUS CHANGE

Melissa May Borja

HARVARD UNIVERSITY PRESS
Cambridge, Massachusetts
London, England
2023

First printing

Publication of this book has been supported through the generous provisions
of the Maurice and Lula Bradley Smith Memorial Fund.

Cataloging-in-Publication Data is available from the Library of Congress
ISBN: 978-0-674-98978-8 (alk. paper)

For Beata and Greg

Contents

FOLLOW THE NEW WAY

Introduction

Every year, the members of the Hmong Christian Church of God in Minneapolis, Minnesota, gathered for a cherished event: a "Thanksgiving celebration." Unlike other Thanksgiving observances in the United States, this day of worship, praise, and commemoration occurred in early May, in remembrance of the turbulent days in May 1975 when the US military evacuated thousands of people from Long Cheng, an airbase at the center of the CIA-backed Secret War. Nor did the celebration focus on the story of English Pilgrims seeking refuge in America. Instead, the church celebrated God's deliverance of a different group of people who came to America in search of safety and freedom: Hmong refugees.

If the *Mayflower* symbolizes the English Pilgrims' story, the Hmong Christian Church of God chose a more modern symbol of their passage: an airplane, which figures prominently on the cover of the 1991 program for the church's fifteenth annual Thanksgiving service. Superimposed on a globe, the oversized jetliner appears to depart from Southeast Asia, where the figure of a Hmong man stands proudly alongside the Christian flag. It heads toward North America, where another Hmong man bearing an American flag offers a simple greeting: "Welcome to U.S." The image offers a decidedly religious narrative of Hmong refugee migration. Above the airplane

Program cover for the Hmong Christian Church of God 1991 Thanksgiving celebration. Courtesy of the family of Rev. Young Tao.

and atop the globe is a large crucifix, under which we read the joyful declaration, "Thanks God for the saving of life," and emblazoned on the side of the airplane are well-known words from John 14:6: "I am the way."

The program cover uses a single image to tell three distinct stories about why this church set aside a day every year to offer prayers and songs of thanksgiving. First, it tells a providential narrative of Hmong resettlement in the United States. Looking back on their exodus from Laos, devoutly Christian Hmong refugees often describe their journey as the result of direct divine intervention. It was God, they say, who delivered the Hmong people to the United States, where they could enjoy a future of freedom and security. "Hmong never known that, [sic] they will come to America," declared Rev.

Young Tao, the church pastor, "but, by God's plan and His merciful [*sic*] we are here in wonderful country of the United States of America."

At the same time, the image of the airplane makes a second point: the American government and Christian churches worked together to resettle thousands of Hmong and other Southeast Asian refugees in the United States. After the Vietnam War, the government relied on religious voluntary agencies, congregations, and church-affiliated charities to provide abundant money, manpower, and material resources that were essential to national and local resettlement efforts. For this reason, the church gathered to thank not only God but also "the Government of the United States, the Governor of Minnesota and all those in authority under him, and the kind citizens of Minnesota who throug[h] their gracious generosity have assisted us to a happily resettle here in this wonderful State." The congregation also expressed thanks for "the agencies, Churches, sponsors, and friends who have shared willingly with us and have provided us with the necessities of the life such as food, clothing[,] furnitures, and housing." Concluding the statement of gratitude, which the celebrants read every year, was a simple declaration: "Thanks [to] the US government for the saving of our lives."[1]

The image tells one final story, perhaps less obvious but no less important. For many Hmong Americans, migrating to the United States was also an experience of spiritual crossing, one that introduced Hmong people to the belief that Jesus is "the way." Resettlement in the United States produced a wide array of changes in Hmong spiritual and religious life, including the decision by many Hmong people to join Christian churches and adopt Christian beliefs, practices, and identities. Not only do many Hmong Christians believe that they came to the United States because of God, but many also believe that Hmong people came to God because they had come to the United States. For these Hmong refugees, the two journeys were intertwined: making a new home in the United States involved making a new spiritual home in Christianity, a religion Hmong people have translated as *kev cai tshiab*—literally, "the new way."

That many Hmong Americans have embraced "the new way" of Christianity marks a significant shift. Of the 327,000 Hmong people who reside in the United States today, almost all trace their origins back to Laos.[2] There, the vast majority of Hmong people practiced a distinctive system of household-based rituals that affirmed their connection to ancestors and kin and facilitated spiritual well-being.[3] They continued these ritual traditions even as the Lao civil war uprooted them from their homes, forced them to flee to neighboring Thailand, and brought them to the United States. An analysis of the case files of refugees resettled by the International Institute of Minnesota indicates that only a fraction—about 16 percent—of Hmong refugees who arrived in the United States between 1976 and 1996 identified as Christian. The vast majority—about 84 percent—identified themselves as non-Christian, primarily as animist or ancestor worshipers.[4]

Four decades later, Christianity has a much greater presence in Hmong American life. In cities across the United States, there are Hmong Catholic, Lutheran, Episcopalian, Mormon, Pentecostal, Catholic, and Baptist churches.[5] The Christian and Missionary Alliance (CMA), an evangelical Protestant denomination, even has its own national "Hmong District," which counted 115 Hmong American CMA congregations by 2018.[6] The prominence of Christian communities is especially evident in the Twin Cities, the epicenter of Hmong America. There are dozens of Hmong Christian congregations in Saint Paul and Minneapolis, and the Saint Paul Hmong Alliance Church, which is affiliated with the CMA, counted nearly 3,000 members by 2005.[7] Hmong American Christianity is clearly thriving.

To be sure, estimates of the Christian share of the Hmong American population in the United States range widely, from as low as 30 percent in some communities to as high as 70 percent in others.[8] Precise figures about Hmong religious and spiritual life are not available, for several reasons. For one, counting the number of people in a particular religious group is always a difficult task, especially with a group like the Hmong, who have historically practiced their rituals at home rather than in formal religious institutions. The frequency of religious change and the fluidity of religious identity among Hmong Americans also make the task of tallying religious adherents a challenge.

But even if the exact number of Hmong American Christians is uncertain, this much is clear: Hmong Americans were often talking about—and troubled by—the religious changes that occurred in their community during the first two decades of their resettlement in the United States. In news media interviews, theatre, and film, they offered frank discussion about the "religious divide" that threatened the integrity of their families and their community.[9] Those who believed that survival in America required cooperation and cohesion feared that these religious schisms sowed dangerous discord and distrust. Tou Ger Xiong, a community activist in the Twin Cities, yearned for the days "before 'religion' became an issue," as he put it in an interview with the *Twin Cities Reader.* "Now, in America, because of rigid religious institutions, we're focusing our energy on difference instead of focusing on what makes us strong," he said.[10] In the eyes of some observers, religious divisions had consequences that reached far beyond how to handle a family funeral or wedding ceremony. As Wameng Yang, a Hmong Christian and social services caseworker, described it in the *St. Paul Pioneer Press,* these religious changes posed an existential crisis. "The Hmong are concerned that if we don't keep our traditional way, we will not trust each other," he said. "If that is gone, there is no more Hmong."[11]

How is it that "'religion' became an issue"? What caused Hmong refugees to experience such profound religious changes, and what did it mean for Hmong people to become Christian and follow "the new way"? As a historian with interests in both religion and immigration, I focus on American refugee resettlement policies and their religious impacts—in particular, how they facilitated Hmong people's adoption of Christianity at the same time they disrupted the practice of traditional Hmong rituals. This book tells the story of how the refugee policies of the US government unwittingly transformed the religious lives of Hmong people, despite the fact that the resettlement program appeared to affirm religious diversity and was administered by people who cherished commitments to religious freedom and pluralism. Put simply, this is a story about how the policies of refugee resettlement produced profound religious unsettlement.

I argue that American refugee resettlement policies changed Hmong religious life in two major ways. First, they deprived Hmong refugees of the human and material resources necessary for conducting their traditional rituals. Because American policies prioritized younger Hmong for admission, Hmong refugees were resettled in the United States without the elder traditional ritual experts, who were left behind in refugee camps in Asia. Moreover, because they were geographically dispersed across the country, Hmong refugees were separated from their kin and ethnic community, who were needed to conduct ceremonies.

At the same time, the administrative arrangements of refugee assistance facilitated the decision by many Hmong refugees to adopt Christianity. At the federal, state, and local levels, governments relied heavily on religious agencies and churches to provide essential resettlement services. This public-private, church-state system meant that Christian voluntary agencies and congregations were often the first point of contact for Hmong refugees looking for food, jobs, and housing. Because governments delegated much of the work of resettlement to Christian organizations, the refugee resettlement program produced close and dependent relationships between Christian resettlement workers and non-Christian Hmong refugees. The resettlement program thus helped introduce new religious alternatives to Hmong refugees while at the same time it rendered traditional religious options unviable.

Refugee resettlement policy set these religious changes in motion despite efforts by governments and voluntary agencies to make refugee assistance a religiously pluralistic enterprise. The people who envisioned and administered the resettlement program publicly championed ideals of pluralism and celebrated their commitment to serving refugees across boundaries of creed and culture. The pluralist intentions of the agencies and individuals who worked with refugees were often sincere. However, the ramifications of resettlement policies tell a different, more complicated story, and the religious changes experienced by Hmong refugees expose the difficulty of putting ideals of religious pluralism into practice. Even if governments and churches committed to respecting religious differences and protecting religious freedoms, an ambiguous definition of "religion" made these goals elusive. Uncertainty about what constituted religious activity in Christian resettlement work meant that religion was difficult to delimit and control. At the same time, uncertainty about whether Hmong beliefs and practices constituted a religion made Hmong traditions difficult to accommodate and protect.

The changes in Hmong religious life across the past five decades reveal not only the impact of American refugee resettlement policies but also the religious agency and innovation of Hmong people, who were highly responsive to changes in circumstances and often willing to adopt new practices or adjust old ways in order to ensure their spiritual security. While government policies helped introduce Hmong people to Christianity, Hmong people adopted Christianity on their own terms, and conversion was not binary. Many Hmong people continued to follow traditional Hmong rituals at the same time they practiced Christianity, or they switched back and forth between the two over their lifetimes. Significantly, the religious logic behind Hmong people's decision to become Christian reveals the endurance of their traditional cosmology and religious framework: Christianity, they believed, offered access to rituals and religious entities that facilitated harmonious relations with the spirit world. Put another way, for many refugees, conversion to Christianity allowed them to acquire new ways of managing old spiritual problems.

Furthermore, as Hmong refugees adapted to life in the United States, so, too, did they adapt their Hmong traditions to an American setting. Over time, they transformed Hmong beliefs, practices, institutional forms, and even language to align with American laws and customs and Protestant ideas of what constitutes a religion. Throughout this process, Hmong Americans have chosen to both claim and disclaim religion: they have at times categorized their traditions as religion, and other times as culture, and sometimes as both. Finding opportunity in the unsettled status of their native beliefs and practices, Hmong Americans have found ways to sustain their traditions and secure rights and respect in ways that reveal spiritual creativity and resilience.

To tell the story of the religious impact of refugee resettlement, I focus on Minneapolis and Saint Paul, the unofficial "Hmong Capital of the U.S."[12] It is a distinction the Twin Cities area was not supposed to have. When planning Southeast Asian refugee resettlement in the 1970s, officials from the US government and the voluntary agencies (also known as "volags") wanted to prevent the formation of ethnic enclaves. For this reason, they intentionally dispersed Hmong refugees across the country. To some degree the plan worked, and by 1983 Hmong Americans lived in seventy-two communities in thirty states. Nonetheless, some areas of the United States developed significant Hmong populations. California, in particular, emerged as the state with the largest number of Hmong residents, who lived primarily in the Central Valley. But it was Minneapolis and Saint Paul that emerged as the urban center with the

Metropolitan Areas with the Largest Hmong Populations in the
United States in 1983

Metropolitan Area	Number of Hmong Residents
Minneapolis/Saint Paul, MN	8,730
Fresno, CA	8,000
Merced, CA	4,500
Stockton, CA	4,000
Orange County, CA	3,000
San Diego, CA	3,000
Sacramento, CA	2,500
Providence, RI	2,300
Denver, CO	1,500–2,000
Los Angeles, CA	1,500

Source: Hmong Resettlement Study.

largest population of Hmong people. By 1983, the Twin Cities was
home to 8,730 Hmong Americans (see the table above).[13]

The rapid growth of the Twin Cities Hmong population owed
to several circumstances. First, Minnesota was a significant site of
primary resettlement due to energetic sponsorship and resettlement
efforts. Voluntary agencies and local churches began to resettle
Southeast Asian refugees as early as 1975 and started to sponsor
Hmong refugees in large number after 1978. Over time, the Hmong
refugees who had been resettled by the voluntary agencies and
churches began to sponsor their relatives, who further expanded the
Hmong population in the area. Significant secondary migration also
contributed to the dramatic growth of the Twin Cities Hmong community. By the early 1980s approximately 40 percent of the Twin
Cities Hmong population had relocated to Minnesota from over two
dozen states. Most of these secondary migrants had left their sites
of initial resettlement and moved to the Twin Cities in order to reunite with family, an essential source of economic, social, and ritual
support. In addition, Minnesota drew secondary migrants because
Hmong refugees spread word of the state's generous cash assistance
programs and educational opportunities. "Among the early arrivals
were some influential group leaders," wrote the authors of a 1984
government study about Hmong refugees in the Twin Cities. "They
were treated with kindness and felt that Minnesota was a good place
to be. They began persuading their relatives to come to Minnesota.

As more Hmong arrived in the state, Minnesota developed a reputation for being a good place to live."[14]

If Minnesota has been prominent in Hmong America, Hmong
Americans have also been prominent in Minnesota. Vietnamese,
Lao, and Cambodian refugees were also resettled in Minnesota, and
by 1980, between 12,000 and 14,000 Southeast Asian refugees
called Minnesota home. But Hmong refugees were the largest Southeast Asian refugee group in the state, with the majority living in
Saint Paul and Minneapolis.[15] The Twin Cities area was thus a unique
resettlement site: whereas other sites of significant Southeast Asian
resettlement tended to have multiethnic populations, as in California, the Hmong were the dominant Southeast Asian refugee
group in the Twin Cities from 1979 onward.[16]

«««‹›»»»

In this book, I make connections between the religious lives of
Hmong refugees and the American refugee resettlement system,
which produced complicated encounters between institutions and individuals with different beliefs, objectives, and experiences. To treat
these complex issues with nuance and compassion, I draw on a wide
array of sources that reflect different perspectives, including the archival records of national, state, and local governments; national voluntary agencies and their local affiliates; church-based charities and
individual congregations; and Hmong mutual aid associations and
refugee-serving community organizations. Finally, I make use of oral
history interviews with Hmong individuals, resettlement workers, religious leaders, and government officials. Oral history is valuable for
religion scholars seeking to understand how people participate in
and navigate unseen spiritual worlds.[17] Crucially, oral history centers
the stories and perspectives of Hmong people and treats them "as
authors and experts," as advocated by Hmong studies scholars Yang
Sao Xiong, Nengher Vang, and Chia Youyee Vang.[18]

I focus on "lived religion," which considers what religious people
do, not simply what they believe.[19] This book continues the work of
scholars who have begun to study how Southeast Asian refugees
have experienced the sacred in everyday life.[20] A focus on lived
religion offers the further advantage of understanding how Christian volunteers embraced refugee resettlement as a ministry and a

mission and an opportunity to express deeply held religion convictions through acts of service.[21] Most important, a lived religion approach is essential to understanding Hmong traditions, which have long centered on ritual practice. "When Hmong Americans talk about 'religion,' they generally tend to focus on what they do (practice), the ritual and ceremonial activities they hold in their homes," argued the anthropologist Vincent Her. "What's more, they accept these to be widely variable, different from region to region, community to community, and clan to clan."[22] Considering the rich array of ritual practices Hmong people have pursued at different times and in different places is central to understanding Hmong spiritual and religious life.

Hmong resettlement is a useful focus case for broader questions about religion, migration, and government in the United States, in part because Hmong experiences were representative of larger developments. The voluntary agencies that resettled the Hmong remain prominent in the work of refugee relief and resettlement.[23] Hmong resettlement also occurred at a pivotal moment, as refugee populations were changing and as the predominantly Christian voluntary agencies were adjusting to new religious diversity, new norms of pluralism, and new legal and political developments that reordered the relationship between church and state. Hmong resettlement tested the capability of Christian organizations to operate pluralistically and informed how these institutions handled subsequent Asian and African migrants who arrived in the 1980s and 1990s.

To be sure, the story of Hmong refugee resettlement and religious change is in many ways unique. Like other refugees, the Hmong had special challenges that complicated their adjustment to American life. They arrived traumatized by years of war, violence, and forced migration. Many struggled with injuries and both physical and mental health problems. Most had limited formal education and knowledge of the English language. Finally, those who arrived in the first years of resettlement had no previously established ethnic community to welcome them and ease the transition to life in the United States. Importantly, the difficulties of adjustment were not limited to economic, social, and political matters but also the spiritual and religious. Hmong ritual practices and spiritual beliefs, particularly those related to health, were difficult for many Americans to comprehend and to categorize. The fact that Hmong traditions do not conform to Christian-centric expectations of what constitutes a religion complicated the encounter between the Hmong refugees and their Christian sponsors.

But it is precisely because of Hmong people's uniqueness that their experiences offer an illuminating opportunity to explore the religious dimensions of refugee resettlement in an increasingly multireligious society. Suffering acute social and economic dislocation, Hmong refugees relied heavily on voluntary agencies and churches, while still pursuing rituals and beliefs that were often incomprehensibly foreign to the Christians who resettled them. As a case of extreme difference and dependency, Hmong refugee resettlement renders in sharp relief the consequences of using religious institutions to implement the refugee program, and it raises questions about the capacity of American individuals and institutions to accommodate religious difference. Even if individuals make genuine efforts to put pluralistic ideals into practice, the refugee resettlement system might still produce pressures for religious conformity, particularly on those who receive help, but also on those who give it.

Ultimately, studying the impact of refugee resettlement policy on Hmong religious life reveals the complex convergence of two tensions characterizing American religion and governance: first, the United States is both remarkably multireligious and deeply Christian; second, church and state are intertwined despite an expressed commitment to disestablishment and separation. Hmong resettlement experiences offer valuable lessons about how new religious diversity has challenged old ways of governing and how Americans have attempted to govern new religious diversity. The stories shared by Hmong refugees show us the power the state exerts on the spiritual lives of everyday people.

Refugee Resettlement as Church-State Governance

Although this book centers on the experiences of Hmong refugees in the United States, the story of how resettlement policies changed the course of their religious lives offers insights into several larger issues about religion, migration, and government in America. The first of these issues is the significance of Christian institutions in government efforts to aid refugees at home and abroad and the possibilities and perils that arise when government relies on faith-based voluntary agencies, church-based charities, and local congregations.

In the United States, refugee relief and resettlement are but one example of the many ways the government expands its capacity through partnerships with private institutions. The historian William Novak termed this phenomenon "public-private governance"; legal scholars Martha Minow and Jody Freeman called it "government by contract."[24] The overlap of public and private institutions is perhaps the most distinctive feature of American government, to the point that scholars have described the United States as an "associational state," a "subsidiarist state," and a "Rube Goldberg State."[25] This last term is particularly evocative in its representation of the complexity of the cooperation between public and private entities. The complicated connections between a dizzying number of institutions can make the entire system seem like a confusing contraption.

In these public-private collaborations, religious institutions have played an important role in efforts to care for vulnerable populations in both domestic and international contexts. Social service provision within the United States has long involved a mixed economy of government and private institutions, many of which have been religious.[26] Though government social welfare programs expanded and coincided with a reduction in the involvement of voluntary agencies in the 1930s, the role of private organizations generally increased throughout the twentieth century.[27] Government and religious organizations have also worked together to alleviate suffering around the globe. From feeding the hungry to caring for orphaned children, religious agencies have played a central role in international relief efforts, especially during moments of humanitarian crisis.[28] Although the United States does not have an official state church, the centrality of Christian institutions in many aspects of public life, from schooling to health care, amount to what the religion scholar Peter Beyer has described as a "shadow establishment," a phenomenon common in British settler countries.[29]

The organizations that have been most prominent in refugee relief and resettlement have been not only private but also religious.[30] At the peak of the Southeast Asian refugee crisis in the early 1980s,

religious voluntary agencies—and especially Christian agencies—
were responsible for resettling the majority of the Hmong, Lao,
Vietnamese, and Cambodian refugees who migrated to the United
States.[31] Even today, most of the voluntary agencies that hold official contracts with the federal government to offer refugee resettlement services are religious organizations. The close ties between
government and religious organizations characterize refugee resettlement not only nationally but also locally. Across the country,
state and local governments have collaborated with voluntary agencies and borrowed capacity by relying on congregations to serve as
sponsors who aid refugees during the first weeks after arrival. Particularly in the 1970s and 1980s, when Southeast Asian refugees
arrived in great numbers, congregational sponsorship was the resettlement model of choice.[32]

The scholarship on the conjoined relationship of church and state
has grown in recent years, but we need a better understanding of
how religious organizations have operated in the public-private,
church-state system in the United States.[33] In particular, we need to
know more about how these organizations have functioned not
merely as private contractors of the government but as religious
entities with distinctly religious beliefs, practices, organizational
structures, and identities. At first glance, religious voluntary agencies appear to provide nonreligious services within the understood
limits of the First Amendment. In reality, though, these organizations
and the individuals who work in and with them often understand
and carry out their work as distinctly religious in nature. By looking
at refugee resettlement not simply from the vantage point of the government but also from the perspective of the people who provided
and received resettlement services, we can better discern the unrec-
ognized religious character of these organizations and their work.
More broadly, we can gain a clearer view of what is at stake when
government and religion overlap—especially in seemingly secular
contexts, such as refugee resettlement, that appear to have nothing
to do with religion at all.[34]

In addition, we need a deeper understanding of the religious repercussions of this entanglement of church and state. The sociologist Robert Wuthnow, in his historical account of the influence of
government policies on American churches, likened his work to an
environmental impact study. That approach is similarly useful in

efforts to understand the religious consequences of the partnerships between government and religious institutions. When government delegates public work to private religious organizations, how does this arrangement shape people's religious beliefs, practices, and identities? In particular, what is the impact experienced by religious minorities? Much of the debate about providing public funding for religious organizations has focused on evangelicals, a reflection of the contemporary fascination with conservative political movements and controversial policy developments such as Charitable Choice and the creation of the White House Office of Faith-Based and Community Initiatives.[35] However, Catholics, mainline Protestants, and Jews all worked with government well before evangelicals did, though they have received less scholarly attention.[36] There is even less knowledge about how other religious groups—Muslims, Buddhists, Hindus, adherents of indigenous traditions—have experienced these partnerships.

The case of Hmong refugee resettlement brings all these issues together. I show how expanding public capacity through contracts with Christian organizations is a well-established strategy of governance in the United States. In Southeast Asian refugee resettlement, governments at the federal, state, and local levels depended on religious institutions to administer government programs and provide important social services. Put simply, religious organizations, including congregations, undertook the resettlement work for which government did not have adequate resources on its own. However, as we shall see, this public-private, church-state system had important religious consequences, especially for the non-Christian refugees who were on the receiving end of humanitarian aid and social services.

The Challenge of Religious Pluralism

This story of Hmong refugee resettlement and religious change matters for a second reason: it takes place during the last three decades of the twentieth century, a moment when the United States as a whole was undergoing significant religious change. During this period, Americans needed to adapt not only to the reality of an increasingly multireligious society but also to the prescriptive ideal of religious pluralism, which aims to manage this new religious diversity.[37] As Pamela Klassen and Courtney Bender defined it, religious pluralism is the "commitment to recognize and understand others across perceived or claimed lines of religious difference."[38] Pluralism is often connected to the goal of fostering peaceable relations between people who are religiously different because, as one refugee resettlement agency put it, showing respect to others "as human beings means respecting their beliefs as well."[39] Gaining currency in the United States throughout the twentieth century, the ideal of religious pluralism challenged Americans to learn more about their new religious neighbors and to strive to live harmoniously with them. However, as the case of Hmong refugee resettlement shows, these aspirations were sometimes difficult to put into practice.

Religious pluralism has had a significant impact on many areas of American public life, including refugee resettlement work. Historically, the religious voluntary agencies that administered refugee resettlement were either Christian or Jewish and were primarily responsible for resettling their own people—fellow Lutherans, Jews, and Catholics, for example. However, these circumstances changed in the 1970s, when the religious voluntary agencies faced the unprecedented task of resettling thousands of refugees who identified as Buddhist, Hindu, Muslim, and other faiths.[40] If the clientele of the resettlement agencies was changing, so too was the legal, political, and cultural terrain on which they operated. At the same time that the United States was becoming more multireligious, consequential Supreme Court decisions reconfigured the relationship between church and state and expanded the range of religious people who could benefit from the constitutional promise of religious freedom.[41]

I address two issues raised by these changing circumstances. First, I consider how Christian voluntary agencies in the 1970s and 1980s adapted to this new religious pluralism while also negotiating their dual roles as church charities and extensions of the state. Second, I assess the degree to which they were successful in accommodating religious difference, especially in their work with non-Christian groups. Attention to Hmong resettlement helps to inform these issues. Non-Christian groups comprise not only a growing share of the American population but also a growing share of the population that receives and provides social services. However, most of the religious freedom debate about contracting out government work to religious organizations has centered on the freedoms and needs of Christian service providers, not the freedoms and needs of Muslim, Hindu, Buddhist, and other non-Christian service recipients. This book remedies that oversight; while it considers the experiences of Christian service providers, it focuses on the issue of religious pluralism and freedom from the other end, bringing into the conversation the minority voices that have unfortunately received less consideration. At the center of this story are the Hmong, who experienced this church-state system of refugee assistance most directly, who felt the religious impacts of government resettlement policies most acutely, and who were the most spiritually and religiously vulnerable of all. In other words, at the center of this story are the people whose perspective matters most in assessing well-intentioned efforts to realize aspirations of religious pluralism and religious freedom.

The story of Hmong religious change demonstrates that new religious diversity posed important challenges to the public-private system of refugee resettlement. As Hmong experiences illustrate, the government's reliance on religious organizations to do the on-the-ground work of aiding refugees sometimes put people—particularly non-Christian people—in uncomfortable, and even coercive, situations. Some research suggests that by the start of the twenty-first century, religious resettlement agencies provided resettlement services in ways that were no different from their nonreligious counterparts.[42] But this book, by focusing on the early period of the 1970s and 1980s, offers a glimpse at how these organizations first attempted to understand and accommodate religious difference, which was important because refugee populations that arrived in subsequent decades would only become more racially, culturally, and religiously diverse.

I show that religious pluralism, as a prescriptive ideology, was—and continues to be—difficult to translate into action. Extolling American principles of religious freedom, government officials, private resettlement agencies, and lay volunteers often made genuine efforts to accommodate the beliefs and practices of the refugees whom they assisted. Even more, they considered affirming the religious and cultural background of refugee families to be more than a legal imperative and social expectation—it was a sacred obligation, informed by new developments in Christian thought. However, when face-to-face with Hmong refugees who practiced ancestor worship and shamanism, Christian resettlement workers sometimes found themselves engaged in encounters for which they were unprepared. Practicing religious pluralism in their refugee work was, like other aspects of resettlement, characterized by uncertainty, improvisation, experimentation, and sometimes error. Though focused on the specific experiences of a relatively small ethnic group, this book tells a much bigger—and deeply humbling—story about the politics and practices of religious pluralism and the difficulty of fulfilling the promise of religious freedom in modern America.

Religious Conversion and Spiritual Migration

Like the members of the Hmong Christian Church of God in Minneapolis, Hmong people have often spoken of their trans-Pacific crossing in relation to religious and spiritual crossing. These conversion narratives, so enmeshed in their experience of exodus, call attention to the intertwining of religion and migration. The case of Hmong refugees and religious change reveals two ideas: first, a religious experience can be understood as a form of migration; second, migration can be understood as a religious experience, with outwardly nonreligious migration policies nonetheless producing profound religious transformations.

Religion has long been recognized as vital to migrants as they undertake the challenge of creating new homes in new countries. Providing what Jewish studies scholar Shari Rabin described as a "mobile assemblage of resources for living," religion helps migrants to survive, offering them an array of critical forms of support.[43] Religion fosters connections to home but also creates a space where migrants create new American versions of themselves and participate in American civic life.[44] And while religion provides a sense of stability, it is anything but static. Like migrants themselves, religious beliefs, practices, and institutions change over time as they are adapted to new settings.[45] Scholars have even gone so far to use religion and migration as interpretive lenses for each other. The historian Robert Orsi wrote that migration is "a spiritual event," one in which "the outward journeying was matched by a changing inner terrain."[46] On the flip side, the religion scholar Thomas Tweed analyzed religion through the metaphor of migration and argued that religion is fundamentally defined by the experience of "crossing and dwelling."[47]

Building on these ideas, this book illuminates the importance of religion in the lives of one particular group of migrants: refugees. Social scientists have written about many aspects of Southeast Asian refugees' adjustment to American life, from employment and language acquisition to health and political engagement.[48] The development of the field of critical refugee studies has introduced new themes, calling attention to how empire, nation, and race have shaped not only refugee policies but also the cultural and political construction of the idea of the refugee.[49] But amid this scholarly literature, the importance of religion in the lives of refugees has received comparatively less attention. That religion is so often overlooked is not surprising. As we shall see, both government and voluntary agencies in charge of Southeast Asian refugee resettlement focused their attention on immediate concerns of housing, employment, and language. But Hmong refugees also had religious and spiritual needs, and they often turned to cherished rituals and beliefs when war, forced migration, and resettlement threw their lives into disarray. These traditions offered Hmong refugees a set of spiritual resources that enabled their survival in the present, connection to the past, and hope for the future. Centering religion in refugee stories changes not only how we view refugee migrations but also how we understand refugees themselves. "Acknowledging the spiritual dimension of Hmong refugee forced migrations frames the refugee as never really lost but always capable of returning to those who call upon the refugee's spirit and remind it to dwell in the present," argued the critical refugee scholar Ma Vang.[50]

The experiences of Hmong refugees also illuminate the importance of migration in the lives of religious people, whose beliefs and practices were shaped by state migration policies. Hmong refugee resettlement—both Hmong people's experience of refugee migration and the government policies that directed it—initiated important changes in belief, ritual, identity, and community. Historians of American immigration have long been attentive to the significance of religion in shaping public beliefs and attitudes about migration, though they have rarely considered how the laws and policies that manage migration might impact the religious beliefs and practices of migrants.[51] And yet this is what happened for the Hmong. American refugee policies hindered the practice of traditional Hmong rituals at the same time they established close relationships between Hmong refugees and Christian church volunteers, who introduced them to new religious beliefs and practices. American refugee policies thus set in motion a variety of changes, one of which was the decision by many Hmong refugees to convert to Christianity.

Religious conversion, I argue, is usefully understood not merely as a product of a migration experience but as a *form* of migration experience. Migration is a choice people make carefully and strategically, as individuals and as families, and in response to changing circumstances, practical needs, and material conditions.[52] Migration involves both change and continuity: migrants do not simply assimilate but retain aspects of their native culture while they adapt to a new one.[53] Finally, migration is a complex transnational phenomenon, and migrants often pursue lives that span national boundaries. Even though they live in one country, they often maintain social, economic, and political ties to another. They sometimes pursue multiple migrations throughout the course of their lives, moving from one country to a second country, and then to a third, and they sometimes return to their home country later in life, or migrate back and forth regularly, or live in a borderland area where the distinctions between one nation and another are blurred.[54]

Listening closely to Hmong stories makes clear that their conversion experiences shared much in common with migration. Conversion is often idealized as a neat, one-way journey, with full assimilation as the objective. In real life, though, conversion is far more complicated, much like the transnational lives of migrants. For Hmong people, conversion was a spiritual migration that people often pursued strategically and on their own terms, at times with ambivalence and sometimes with felt coercion. It was a decision shaped by the needs of their family and community, the power of the state, and the material conditions of their lives as refugees. Like migration, conversion was often multidirectional and involved several religious changes. Rather than being a one-time choice, conversion often involved a series of choices, and people sometimes pursued multiple conversions in the span of their lifetimes. Finally, like migration, conversion did not involve a clean break with past people, places, and practices. Rather, Hmong experiences reveal how religious conversion involved complex crossing and recrossing, or sometimes dwelling in religious borderlands, with converts making spiritual lives for themselves in the space *between* two worlds. If transnational migrants practiced what the anthropologist Aihwa Ong described as "flexible citizenship," religious converts often practiced flexible religious belonging.[55]

In truth, the language of "conversion" is itself somewhat misleading, and I use this term with no small discomfort. Hmong refugees became Christian in a process that involved both change and continuity. Exploring Hmong religious life as complex and hybrid, I show that conversion was not binary, and that newly acquired religious beliefs and practices did not supplant preexisting ones. Instead, the religious lives of Hmong people exemplified what the religion scholar Catherine Albanese has described as a process of contact and combination: they synthesized old and new and were selective about which elements of Christianity they chose to incorporate into their lives. For many, conversion was a process of encountering new practices—participating in church services and saying Christian prayers, for example—and adding them to the ritual tool kit from which they could draw in times of spiritual and physical distress.[56] To be sure, the additive dynamic of Hmong ritual life is not unique to the American setting. Hmong people have not necessarily seen their traditional beliefs and practices as exclusive of others, and in Laos they frequently incorporated Buddhism into their spiritual lives.[57] However, the convergence of multiple forces—the sharp dislocations produced by refugee migration, the disruption of traditional Hmong beliefs and practices, and the support of Christian missionary work through American resettlement policies— makes Hmong experiences in the United States a particularly compelling example of how encounter, exchange, and innovation characterize conversion and American religious life.

By thinking about how Hmong refugees saw conversion as an act of creative combination, I resist the powerful "collision of two cultures" narrative that has long portrayed Hmong Americans as tragically maladjusted migrants.[58] Stressing the incompatibility of Hmong ways with modern American life, this narrative centers on one key question: can Hmong people ever become American? These concerns animated much of the research about Hmong refugees in the early years of resettlement.⁵⁹ At the same time, cultural preservationists offered an alternative narrative of the Hmong as people who suffered profound cultural loss in an American setting that eroded an essential ethnic identity.⁶⁰ I seek to tell a more complex story about how Hmong people have pursued spiritual and religious lives that have been both very modern and very American, especially in their strategic efforts to institutionalize their traditional beliefs and practices and to use law and other tools to secure respect and accommodation for their traditions.

Today, the predominant narrative is not of Hmong refugees struggling to cope with life in modern America, but of Hmong Americans who have pursued new possibilities for what it means to be, and live as, Hmong people in diaspora.⁶¹ In keeping with the most recent scholarship exploring Hmong migration to the United States, I eschew the easy binaries of the older culture-clash narrative. Hmong or American, preservation or assimilation—it was, in fact, both and neither. I show how Hmong people in the United States have not simply stayed Hmong or become American, but have created something new altogether. Throughout the past four decades, they have used the material and spiritual resources at their disposal in their transition from Hmong refugees to American citizens and in their broader reinvention of themselves as Hmong Americans.

A close look at how Hmong people adopted Christianity invites a more expansive understanding of Hmong life, but also of religion, its purposes and practices, and its capacity for reinvention. For Hmong people—indeed, for all people—religious beliefs, practices, and identities are dynamic and evolving. Hmong Americans offer a compelling example of this reality, as they have often straddled religious boundaries, making Christianity their own without abandoning previous beliefs and practices, while also revisiting and refashioning their native traditions as circumstances changed and as spirits called them. I attend to the rich diversity and hybridity of Hmong religious life, paying attention to how the decision to become Christian was an undertaking they often pursued quite differently from how Christian missionaries and sponsors might have envisioned. There has never been a single, tidy way Hmong people have lived as Christians or animists or even, for a large and growing portion of Hmong Americans, "none of the above."

In telling this story about Hmong religious change, I must be clear about what this book is not. Many scholars have studied the phenomenon of Hmong conversion to Christianity, especially in the context of missionary encounters in the United States and Asia.[62] As these studies make clear, determining the extent to which any single event shapes individual religious change is difficult, if not impossible, as religious conversions are the product of multiple converging forces.[63] For that reason, I do not claim that resettlement alone caused Hmong adoption of Christianity. By no means was resettlement the sole cause of the growth of Hmong Christianity, even if it did contribute to it. Nor do I investigate the degree to which Hmong people fully converted and became "true" or "good" Christians.

My goal, rather, is to illuminate how American refugee policies facilitated this conversion and how Hmong people embraced conversion, along with many other spiritual and religious choices, in the context of their broader struggle to survive amid the turmoil of war, displacement, and resettlement. In making sense of the diverse religious lives pursued by Hmong refugees, I take a cue from Yang Sao Xiong, Nengher Vang, and Chia Youyee Vang, who have emphasized the importance of putting Hmong choices in the context of "the concrete situations of Hmong persons, families, and communities" and "the complex relationships among people and between people and states."[64] Because refugees experience a distinctive type of migration, we must interpret their religious lives in the context of the particular traumas and material conditions associated with war, forced migration, and resettlement.

The Hmong Way and the Category of Religion

The religious changes Hmong refugees experienced must also be interpreted in the context of their life in the United States, where Protestant Christianity is so predominant that it shapes the fundamental understanding of what counts as religion in the first place. For Hmong refugees, the vast majority of whom did not identify as Christian when they first arrived, the American context posed an important challenge: their traditional beliefs and rituals were not easily legible as religious. They faced the doubly daunting task of not only sustaining their ritual traditions in America but doing so in the context of a state and a society that praise religious belonging and protect the free exercise of religion while privileging those who conform to a Protestant-centric definition of religion. These issues point to the final matter I address: the limitations of the category of religion and the difficulties faced by those, like the Hmong, whose traditional beliefs and practices test the capaciousness of this category.

As many scholars have argued, religion is not a universal concept; rather, it is historically conditioned and culturally rooted in Protestant Christianity and Western imperial projects.[65] The religion scholar Winnifred Fallers Sullivan notes, for example, that after the Reformation, true religion was understood as "private, voluntary, individual, textual, and believed," and "public, coercive, communal, oral, and enacted religion, on the other hand, was seen to be 'false.'" However, she points out, this "false" religion "was, and perhaps still is, the religion of most of the world."[66] This Christian-centric definition of religion has had important implications for non-Christian groups in the United States, especially given the legal and cultural value Americans place on claiming a religion. For example, a substantial population of Asian Americans practice Buddhism and Hinduism, the beliefs and practices of which have not been as readily recognized as religious.[67] The situation has been particularly precarious for people who do not adhere to one of the "world religions." Native Americans, for example, have found that their indigenous traditions have not always been viewed and protected as legitimately religious.[68] For these groups, the issue is not simply that they have not been able to secure protection, respect, or accommodation for their beliefs and practices, but that they have been seen as having no religion at all.[69]

Like many Native Americans and Asian Americans, Hmong people have a set of beliefs and practices that utterly confound the Christian-centric definition of religion that remains so powerful in American society and law. Historically, these traditions—known simply by many Hmong practitioners as the "Hmong way" or "the old way"—have not been practiced in a temple, centered on a core text, or known by an official name. In nearly every aspect, the Hmong way runs counter to the type of institutionalized, individualized, textual, belief-centered religion that typically enjoys rights, respect, and recognition in the United States. Indeed, as a set of

beliefs and rituals centered on communality, practice, and oral
tradition, Hmong traditions fall precisely into the realm of what
Christians in the West—including Christian resettlement workers—
have long considered to be nonreligion or "false" religion.

The incommensurability of the Hmong way with Christian-
centric definitions of religion is further complicated by the fact that
"religion" is not a native category to Hmong people.[70] As Vincent
Her pointed out, "In Hmong, there is no word for 'religion,'" and
"a concise translation of this familiar term, from Hmong to English,
or English to Hmong, is difficult."[71] Given the foreignness of this
concept, the matter of applying the term "religion" to Hmong beliefs and practices has spurred debate. Some scholars have chosen
to describe Hmong traditions as a religion while acknowledging the
limitations of this etic term when discussing the Hmong way.[72]
Hmong people themselves have also been ambivalent about describing their traditions as "religion," and the words and categories
people have used to describe Hmong beliefs and practices have
produced controversy within the Hmong American community.[73]
Describing Hmong beliefs and practices in terms of "thought,"
"cosmology," "culture," and "custom," has offered a few work-
arounds.[74]

Whether their beliefs and practices were a legitimate religion was
not typically the most urgent question on Hmong people's minds as
they struggled to rebuild their lives in America, but it was an important one. Resettlement officials asked Hmong people to identify
their religion as they were applying for resettlement, before they even
set foot on American soil. Once they were in the United States,
Hmong people had to describe their native beliefs and practices to
Christian church sponsors, curious neighbors, and other people they
encountered at schools, hospitals, and funeral homes. The words
Hmong people chose to describe their traditions shaped their experiences at these American institutions, which promised protections
and privileges for people who had a recognizable religion. However,
Hmong people, like other non-Christian people, could not always
avail themselves of these advantages because, as Sullivan pointed
out, "in order to enforce laws guaranteeing religious freedom you
must first have religion."[75] Put simply, claiming a religion makes
it possible for people to claim rights, recognition, respect, and
resources.

Over the past four decades, Hmong Americans have often chosen
to describe their native beliefs and practices as religion. This choice
owes in part to important developments connected to Hmong refugee resettlement in the United States. First, non-Hmong people have
encountered Hmong beliefs and practices and tried to make sense of
them through familiar categories, one of which was the category of religion. Indeed, at times throughout the resettlement process, Americans
forced Hmong beliefs and practices into classifications—not just
"religion" but also "culture," "animism," and "ancestor worship"—
even if Hmong ways did not quite fit any of these categories. Second,
as more Hmong people have begun to believe, practice, and identify with Christianity, both Christian and non-Christian Hmong
people have recategorized Hmong ways as "religion." This move has
arisen from intense debates among Hmong people about which
Hmong beliefs and practices are religious and therefore forbidden
by Christianity and which are secular, nonreligious cultural traditions that converts are allowed to incorporate into their Christian
lives. Finally, as Hmong people have established themselves in the
United States—a country where claiming a religion carries legal, cultural, and political currency—they have found that claiming religion
brings practical benefits and accommodations. In the end, learning to
talk about their beliefs and practices as a religion has been an unfamiliar practice for Hmong Americans, but a necessary one. "Hmong
American practitioners are good at talking about what they do," said
Vincent Her. "What they are not used to doing is to explain precisely
what they do to people who are not familiar with Hmong culture.
They have never had to intellectualize Hmong religion, to piece together all its essential elements and to present these succinctly to
others. In the contemporary context of globalization, where Hmong
people are scattered around the world, this need is very pressing."[76]

This book sheds light on the challenges that have arisen when
Hmong Americans have needed "to explain precisely what they do"
and have been compelled to do so through the language of religion—
which, as a nonnative concept for the Hmong, often fails as a tool
of precise explanation. And yet, despite the limitations of the
Christian-centric category of religion, Hmong Americans have been
resourceful, practical, and flexible in making use of it. They have
translated their beliefs and practices as religion and invoked the First
Amendment to meet their material and spiritual needs. At the same

time, they have adapted and institutionalized their beliefs and practices to correspond to American and Christian expectations of religious life. To be clear, it is neither my purpose nor my position to claim that traditional Hmong beliefs and practices are a religion or not. Rather, my aim is to show that resettlement in the United States forced the category of religion and all its attendant questions on Hmong people, who have responded with creativity, canniness, and common sense.

Hmong Americans are of course not the first group of people to do all of these things in the United States. However, given the degree to which Hmong traditions unsettle assumptions about what counts as religious, understanding how Hmong Americans have navigated these issues offers a useful intervention into the scholarship on Asian American religion, and American religion more generally, which can sometimes take for granted that religion is a settled concept and a social characteristic people naturally have. For Hmong Americans, the meaning and applicability of religion in their lives have been anything but settled, and religion is something they have had to claim, intentionally and strategically. This book thus offers insights into the potential for religious pluralism in a nation where rights and respect are reserved only for those who have beliefs and practices seen as legitimately religious. More broadly, it reveals the shortcomings of the concept of religion, both as a means of communicating what people do and believe and as a basis for determining protections and privileges.

Ultimately, Hmong American experiences underscore the elusiveness of religious freedom, especially for those whose beliefs and practices are at odds with established understandings of religion. A religious history of Hmong refugee migration may indicate that Winnifred Fallers Sullivan is correct in her observation that religious freedom is impossible. But the stories told by Hmong refugees about their religious life offer a slightly different lesson: if one is not free and if one's soul is not at ease, then one can move, change, and adapt. That is precisely what many Hmong people did.

«««»»»

What language should scholars use in writing about a set of beliefs, practices, identities, and categories for which labels have proven to be so dynamic and, at times, contentious? A few basic choices guide the language I use as I describe the nuances and stakes of these issues. First, I reject the interpretation of Hmong beliefs and practices as a vague, primitive tradition; I begin with the assumption that Hmong beliefs and practices are a legitimate system that must be understood on their own terms and, when possible, described in their own terms.[77] For this reason, I use the word the Hmong people I interviewed most often used: "way." In general, I refer to Hmong beliefs and practices using the term "the Hmong way." Alternatively, I say the "old way" or the "traditional" way, as those were other terms Hmong people commonly used in our conversations.

In addition, I use the terms "religious" and "religion"—defined broadly—to describe Hmong beliefs and rituals when they involved Christianity and when the Hmong people whom I interviewed chose to use these terms themselves to describe their beliefs and practices. I acknowledge that some scholars and practitioners have applied "religion" to Hmong beliefs and practices whereas others have preferred the language of spirituality, custom, and culture. However, when Hmong people used "religion" to describe their beliefs and practices, I honor that choice and use the same term. Like many of the Hmong people who shared their stories with me and who chose to label their beliefs and practices as religion, I agree that the category of religion, while imperfect, can nonetheless serve as a useful interpretive aid in understanding patterns of Hmong spirituality and ritual life.

I choose to include *ua neeb,* or the set of traditions commonly known as shamanism, under the category of the Hmong way and Hmong religion for similar reasons. The application of the term "religion" to describe Hmong shamanism has provoked controversy, and people have described shamanism as religious in nature for a variety of purposes. First, both Hmong and non-Hmong Christians, particularly evangelical Protestants, have constructed shamanism as a set of deviant rituals that contradict core teachings of Christianity, and arguments that shamanism is religious has been used to justify prohibitions on its practice. At the same time, some American institutions—churches and hospitals, for example—have drawn parallels between shamans and Christian clergy in order to foster intercultural understanding. Finally, Hmong practitioners of shamanism have described its rituals in religious terms, demonstrating its equivalent status with Christianity. That Hmong Americans have argued that shamanism deserves respect and accommodation because it is religious demands that scholars, in turn, recognize, understand, and engage in these new labels and meanings, rather than deny and discipline them.

The book is divided into two parts. The first four chapters consider the policies and practices of refugee resettlement in the United States. In Chapter 1 I discuss events in Laos and Thailand that set the stage for Hmong migration from Asia and subsequent religious changes. I focus in particular on two twentieth-century developments: the encounters with Christian missionaries and the Lao civil war, which displaced Hmong people from their homes and forced their migration to refugee camps in Thailand. In Chapter 2 I examine the response of the federal government to the Southeast Asian refugee crisis and show that the resettlement of Southeast Asian refugees drew heavily on the contributions of religious voluntary agencies, much like refugee resettlement efforts earlier in the twentieth century. In Chapter 3 I turn to the local level and discuss church-based resettlement activities in the Twin Cities. I argue that for the Christian volunteers involved in refugee resettlement, the work of sponsoring and assisting refugees was a religious practice that expressed deep commitments to "welcoming the stranger" and pursuing missionary work. In Chapter 4 I discuss how the changing religious demographics of refugee populations in the 1970s introduced complications to the public-private, church-state resettlement system. Although resettlement workers made sincere efforts to understand Hmong beliefs and practices, these efforts were stymied by resettlement workers' unfamiliarity with Hmong traditions and, more fundamentally, by the incommensurability of the Hmong way with Christian-centric notions of religion.

The final three chapters focus on Hmong perspectives and the religious impact of American refugee policies. In Chapter 5 I show how American resettlement efforts disrupted the practice of the Hmong way by separating families and communities and depriving Hmong refugees of the most important resource for their traditional rituals—other Hmong people. In Chapter 6 I demonstrate how the American refugee resettlement system, with its heavy reliance on religious institutions, set up influential encounters between Hmong refugees and Christian resettlement workers. In the context of these resettlement relationships and the difficulty of practicing traditional rituals, many Hmong refugees chose to adopt Christianity on their own terms, often combining "the new way" with the Hmong way. Finally, in Chapter 7 I explore the various ways that Hmong people have preserved and adapted their Hmong traditions to an American setting. They have modified rituals, institutionalized their traditions, and deployed the flexible categories of religion and culture to secure recognition and accommodation. In the Conclusion I consider the impact of American resettlement policies on Hmong religious life by briefly considering two comparative cases. First, what if the Hmong had had a more recognizable religion? To answer this question, I compare the Hmong experience with that of Vietnamese, Cambodian, and Lao refugees, many of whom practiced Buddhism, a religion with which Christian sponsors were more familiar and therefore more accommodating. Second, what if the Hmong had been resettled in a country that did not rely on religious institutions? I turn to Hmong experiences in Australia, where the government administers the refugee resettlement program and has also made intentional efforts to support Hmong ritual practice. As a result, Hmong people in Australia have not experienced the same religious shifts toward Christianity.

Resettlement in the United States set in motion a great number of changes in Hmong beliefs and practices. Many of those changes centered on the adoption of Christianity. However, coming to America also changed the Hmong way and, more broadly, Hmong people. Not only did life in the United States compel Hmong people to modify their beliefs and rituals, but it also forced them to rename and reconfigure their traditional beliefs and practices to make them conform to the Western categories of "religion" and its nonreligious alternative, "culture." Their efforts to remake the Hmong way into an American religion thus suggests a fourth possible interpretation of the "I Am the Way" airplane. Resettling in the United States encouraged Hmong refugees to use the category of religion as a way to reorganize, describe, and protect their traditional beliefs and practices. In order to ensure the survival of their traditions, they claimed something they had not needed to claim before: a religion.

I

RESETTLEMENT

1

The Origins of Religious Unsettlement

MISSIONARY ENCOUNTERS, MILITARY ENGAGEMENTS, AND MIGRATION IN ASIA

At first glance, the biographical form included in every refugee case file looks like any other bureaucratic questionnaire. Neatly typed and in later years produced by a dot matrix printer, it includes the same mundane details as an application for a driver's license or a public library card: name, date of birth, address.

But much more was at stake for the thousands of people whose lives were summarized in these documents. Completed by representatives from the Joint Voluntary Agency (JVA) working in the refugee camps in Thailand, these biographical forms summarized the lives of thousands of Hmong refugees who had fled war-torn Laos and were applying for resettlement in other countries. By looking closely at the responses to each question and the brief notes occasionally included in each case, one can piece together stories of suffering, sorrow, and survival: "Badly injured in the war, reducing his ability to use carpentry skills"; "Has ceremony to carry out for dead father. Will be ready to go to USA in one month"; "His fa. and mo. are dead. 4 sibs are still in Laos"; "PA's [Primary Applicant's] 3 yr-old child was captured."[1]

The biographical form recorded a variety of details about refugees' experiences of war and dislocation, as well as information related to their potential resettlement—years of schooling, for example, and employment history. But one question on the form differed from the rest: the religion question. To the American officials processing applications for resettlement, a question that asked refugees to identify their religion may have seemed straightforward. But for some Hmong refugees, it was a strange and perhaps difficult question to answer. How do people identify their religion if they do not necessarily describe themselves as having a religion in the first place?

Nao Thao, a Hmong American shaman who resettled in the United States as a child, once explained to me the complexity of identifying Hmong people's religion. She and her family practiced traditional Hmong rituals, which was the "way" of the Hmong people. These rituals were the things that she and her ancestors *do,* she said, but not something they necessarily understood as a distinct aspect of their lives labeled "religion." When I asked what she *believes*—another Christian-centric way of making sense of religion— it became clear that Hmong people might "follow the traditional way" and at the same time adhere to beliefs associated with Christianity. For her part, Nao Thao said that she believes in her "ancestors," but she identified her religion—in her mind, the ritual practices that she does—as *ua neeb ua yaig,* or shamanism.[2]

Shamanism was not an option on the biographical forms, though, which reveals one of the fundamental problems with the religion identification question asked by JVA officials: its conceptual limitations. The biographical forms offered several possible checkboxes for this question: "Christian," "Protestant," "Catholic," "Buddhist," "Ancestral Worship," "Animist," and "None." Not only was *ua neeb ua yaig* absent from the list, but officials only selected one checkbox for each applicant. In reality, the practices of a Hmong refugee family could fall under more than one category, and "Animism," "Ancestral Worship," and even "Buddhism" are all terms that Hmong people have used to describe themselves. Hmong people were forced to fit their beliefs and practices into a foreign scheme of religious classification that made no sense to them, and "the traditional way" that Hmong people followed was more expansive than the biographical forms allowed.

When they had the option, Hmong people resisted the imposed categories. For several months in 1979, the JVA changed the interview forms, and the religion identification question became a free-response question that did not force refugees to conform to set check-boxes. During this brief period, one can see how Hmong refugees grappled with answering the religion question. For one, evidence of corrections suggest that people were confused about which category to choose. On several occasions, a respondent wrote "Buddhist," only to cross it out and replace it with "Animist." On other forms, people used two categories, writing "Ancestral Worship" or "Buddhist" and qualifying these responses by also noting "Animist" in parentheses. Still others answered the question without using any of the labels offered to them, choosing instead to identify their religion by using the simplest—and perhaps most accurate—term: "Hmong religion."[3]

Asking refugees to identify their religion may have seemed a simple matter to JVA officials, but for Hmong people it represented a more basic problem. Traditional Hmong beliefs and practices utterly confound American understanding of religion, and the range of ways in which Hmong refugees answered a single question on a biographical form tells a bigger story of the cultural encounter and mutual transformation that was unfolding well before Hmong refugees boarded the first airplanes for the United States. Hmong people and their ritual life challenged how Americans thought about religion and how they intended to manage it. At the same time, Americans challenged Hmong ritual life—through empire and war, through missionaries, and even through the bureaucratic paperwork of refugee resettlement.

«««‹›»»»

The story of how American refugee resettlement policies transformed Hmong spiritual and ritual life begins not in the United States but in Southeast Asia, with American military operations during the Lao civil war. In Laos, the United States engaged Hmong soldiers to fight as their allies in the Secret War. In addition to claiming the lives of thousands of people, the civil war displaced Hmong people from their homes and villages, destroyed their businesses and farms, and destabilized their communities and social structures. But lesser known is the fact that the war and the forced migration it produced also upended Hmong culture, beliefs, and ritual practices. In these traumatic circumstances, Hmong people turned to the traditions that had long offered spiritual and somatic support—and found that they, too, had been disrupted by empire and war.

In addition, another powerful foreign presence—Christian missionaries from Europe and the United States—shaped the trajectory of Hmong religious life. Missionary contact in Laos and Thailand contributed to the formation of a core group of Christians, particularly evangelical Christians, who would later establish influential Hmong churches in the United States. Even more significant was the long-term cultural and intellectual impact of the missionary encounter in Southeast Asia. Interactions with Christian missionaries in Laos and Thailand contributed to Hmong people's construction of Christianity as "the new way" and shaped how they responded to their Christian sponsors when they eventually resettled in the United States. Exposure to missionaries also changed how Hmong people themselves conceptualized and described Hmong traditions. As more people adopted "the new way" of Christianity, the Hmong way, in contrast, became understood as "the old way." And as Hmong refugees applied for resettlement overseas, government and voluntary agency bureaucracies forced Hmong people to reconfigure their beliefs and practices, fit them into a new set of categories, and claim a religion.

Encounters with Hmong people in Laos and Thailand also shaped American Christians and laid the foundation for how they would navigate the religious encounters of refugee resettlement. To begin, these early encounters in Asia introduced American Christians to Hmong rituals and spiritual beliefs. Christian missionaries in Asia struggled to make sense of Hmong traditions, and their responses to Hmong beliefs and practices varied. The most curious and open-minded missionaries eagerly documented Hmong rituals, which they interpreted as colorful cultural practices and, implicitly, as examples of primitive superstition. Other missionaries, feeling more threatened, condemned Hmong rituals as an abhorrent form of demon worship and undertook aggressive campaigns to burn and dismantle objects associated with Hmong ceremonies. Although the approaches of missionaries differed, what they had in common was the fact that they analyzed Hmong beliefs and practices through an imperialist and Christian-centric lens.[4] As a result, their understanding of the Hmong way was often conceptually flawed and, in some cases, literally destructive. The limitations of missionaries' understanding mattered immensely, not only in Asia but beyond. Most significantly, the ideas that developed through these midcentury encounters would find continued life in the 1970s and 1980s, when they would shape how American Christians would make sense of the beliefs and practices of the Hmong refugees whom they felt called to resettle.[5]

"You Must Have Respect for the Others That We Do Not See"

Although today they reside on nearly every continent, Hmong people for most of their history lived in East and Southeast Asia. In the nineteenth century, several factors—including war, taxation, and pressures to assimilate—compelled significant numbers of Hmong people in China to migrate to Vietnam, Laos, and Thailand. Since most Hmong people were farmers, the promise of more land also drew them further south. In the Indochinese peninsula, the Hmong lived in small highland villages, where they practiced swidden agriculture and moved frequently in search of fertile soil. But their migrations owed not only to their need for good land but also their desire for their own land. As a stateless ethnic minority group, Hmong people have a long history of oppression and forced migration in Asia, where they often moved in order to elude state governance, ensure their autonomy, and seek safety from colonial violence.[6]

Most Hmong people who live in the United States today trace their origins to those Hmong migrants who had settled in Laos, where, as elsewhere, they were an ethnic minority. Throughout the nineteenth and early twentieth centuries, the Hmong in Laos lived mostly in small communities in the isolated mountain regions of the north. There, the Hmong maintained a distinctive culture defined by a unique language, artistic tradition, and kinship-based social structure that remains important to Hmong communities around the world today. In this system, Hmong people are born into one of eighteen clans. The clan is considered to be a Hmong person's extended family, and clan membership is indicated by one's surname. Male elders serve as clan leaders, who are responsible for resolving conflicts and ensuring the well-being of all families and individuals in the clan.

Hmong people have historically had a distinctive set or "way" of beliefs and rituals that constitute "the main core" of Hmong culture.[7] Central to the Hmong way is a cosmology that organizes existence into two worlds: the visible realm of *yaj ceeb,* the "Land of the Light," where human beings, material things, and nature live; and the unseen *yeeb ceeb,* the "Land of the Dark," where gods, ancestral spirits, and nature-based spirits reside. Negotiating life between the "seen" and "unseen" realms, Hmong people have historically held a deep sense of "sacred presence" and understood the world to be richly populated by a wide array of spirits, including the spirits of ancestors and the spirits of nature—for example, those dwelling in animals, mountains, forests, waterways, and rocks.[8]

Foundational to the Hmong way is an awareness that humans exist in an interdependent relationship with these different spirits. Hmong people have strived to live harmoniously with the unseen world in the belief that troubled relations with spiritual beings can give rise to bodily harm and other calamities. The Hmong American writer Mai Neng Moua observed that in Laos, "the lines between the spirit world and human world seemed more permeable," and as a result, "people were afraid of spirits," especially those "who believe dead ancestors can still communicate with you and have the power to affect your everyday life."[9] Fearing the negative repercussions of angering the unseen world, Hmong people have aimed to honor the spirits of the *yeeb ceeb,* whose goodwill can ensure health, peace, and prosperity. As the anthropologist Dia Cha put it, "You must have respect for the others that we do not see."[10]

Rituals have been the primary means through which Hmong people have maintained peaceful, reverent relationships with the spirits whom they traditionally believe determine their health and well-being. These rituals fall into two broad categories: *ua dab,* which are the household-based rituals that maintain good relations with the spirits, and *ua neeb,* which are the rituals of Hmong shamanism.[11] Both these terms begin with the verb *ua,* which means "to do," a fact that illuminates the importance of *doing* the Hmong way. In contrast to Christianity, which has tended to focus on individual faith, the Hmong way has centered historically on community ritual practice. The anthropologist Vincent Her observed that Hmong people "place as much emphasis on 'practice' (ways of doing) as on beliefs, if not more so."[12] In other words, what Hmong people *do*—which ceremonies they conduct, which songs they sing, and which offerings they make to the spirit world—matters as much as, and perhaps more than, adherence to a creed. Moreover, it is not only important that Hmong people do these rituals, but that these rituals do useful and helpful things for Hmong people. The expectation is that rituals, when conducted properly, will offer direct and immediate benefit in the seen world. Hmong people have thus traditionally looked for observable signs—manifested in an improvement in physical health, in particular—that their rituals can solve real problems. These signs serve as evidence of the rituals' power and efficaciousness.[13]

Household-based rituals, known collectively as *ua dab*, vary by clan, community, and region, but they share a few common features. First, they are united in common purposes: maintaining balance and peaceable relations with kin, ancestors, and the natural world; safeguarding the health and well-being of both body and spirit; honoring and remembering deceased relatives; and securing the continuity of the generations and the safe passage of the soul from the physical life into the afterlife. Through regular offerings of food and incense, Hmong people have shown reverence to ancestral spirits who can intervene in the affairs of the living. Through seasonal and life-cycle rituals, they have affirmed their spiritual ties with family. Finally, through home rituals, they have conveyed their hopes for prosperity and abundant harvests. As an earth-centered tradition that recognizes the omnipresence of spirits in the natural world, the Hmong way has expressed the aspirations of a people whose livelihood has historically been tied to agriculture and dependent on the forces of nature. Moreover, as a kinship-centered tradition, the rituals of the Hmong way are specific to one's household, lineage, and clan.[14]

In addition to these household rituals, Hmong people have traditionally practiced shamanism, known in Hmong as *ua neeb*. According to the anthropologists Gary Yia Lee and Nicholas Tapp, Hmong shamanism is "a system for curing illness and other forms of social unhappiness and disharmony." Offering the ritual tools to cope with a wide range of bodily, social, and natural calamities, shamanism serves a variety of legal, medical, political, and social purposes. At the center of *ua neeb* is the Hmong shaman, or the *txiv neeb*. Shamans play a principal role in the Hmong spiritual community as the only humans who can communicate and negotiate with the unseen world on behalf of the living.

Shamanism has been particularly important for Hmong people as a means of maintaining spiritual and bodily health. Hmong people have traditionally understood illness to have a spiritual cause, usually related to one of the many souls that Hmong people believe humans possess. According to this view, health problems can be the result of the loss of one or more souls, which can wander off, become lost or frightened away, or even captured by another spirit. In these circumstances, the lost soul must return to the body in order to restore the well-being of the afflicted person. In some cases, it is sufficient to perform a *hu plig* ceremony, in which a shaman or an elder call the soul home, coaxing it to return with chants and offers of food. In more serious cases, a *txiv neeb* must chase and recapture the lost soul so that the sick person can be made spiritually whole again. In these rituals, the *txiv neeb* enters a trance and journeys into the spirit world to search for the lost soul. After finding it, the shaman bargains or battles with the spirits that captured the soul, sometimes bartering the soul of a sacrificed chicken or pig in exchange for that of the sick human.[15] Paja Thao, a Hmong shaman who eventually resettled in Chicago, described his work as follows:

> Saub gives you power to help the soul
> To catch and protect the soul
> If you follow this way
> Truly you can catch the soul
> And the sick one will feel better
>
> You go to catch the soul with your two hands
> And with your heart
> And you grip the soul
> After that, the sick one feels better too[16]

As Paja Thao's words reveal, the goal of the shaman's ritual is simple: that "the sick one feels better." Acknowledging that the rituals are not always effective, shamans have often discussed the likelihood of success with Hmong families. "If they cannot bring [the soul] back they usually tell the family that it may not work," said Dia Cha.[17] The key word here is "work." Hmong people who have practiced shamanism, and the Hmong way more generally, have expected its rituals to do work in their lives and bring immediate and observable impact. A shaman's work, in other words, should have a discernible effect on both the body and the soul. According to Mai Lee, a Hmong American woman in Minnesota, the goal of the healing ceremony is to ensure that "there's happiness, and you live peacefully, with no medical problems."[18]

Aside from performing rituals and serving as the primary liaisons between the *yeeb ceeb* and *yaj ceeb*, shamans have also functioned as respected community leaders and teachers. "Shamans are important individuals in Hmong society," said Boua Neng Moua, a Hmong American man in California. "They give us guidance and advice. When Hmong people move, they ask a shaman to tell them where to go and how to get there safely. Shamans are very powerful individuals because they influence many people who act on the basis of what they say."[19] Keith Vang, whose father was a shaman in Laos, recalled that his father "wore many hats" and served as a "spiritual healer" and a source of "marriage counseling." "In any sort of dispute, he was considered a person to go to," Vang said.[20]

Shamans are only one of many individuals who play an important role in the proper practice of Hmong rituals. Traditional Hmong ceremonies have typically required the contributions of a great number of people in the Hmong community. Clan members, in particular, are necessary because rituals are specific to each clan. Moreover, because rituals can be labor-intensive and long in duration, Hmong people benefit from having numerous clan members available to help. The traditional funeral, which is the most important and elaborate of all Hmong events, illustrates the importance of having a network of knowledgeable clan and community members. Chong Thao Xiong, a Hmong elder who was born and raised in Laos but later resettled in Wisconsin, listed the variety of ritual experts needed for a proper Hmong burial:

1. A Funeral Guide (to direct the spirit of the dead person to recover the placenta and to go to meet with the predecessors)
2. A Qeej Player (to play the Death Songs)
3. Two Funeral Directors (to help the family make decisions, decide which relatives to invite, and give thanks for gifts received)
4. Two Arrangers (to kill and clean the animals and to see that the Qeej Player and the Drummer get their shares—the Qeej Player gets three ribs)

5. Two Rice Cooks (to prepare food)
6. A Master of Ceremonies (to set things up and set times and places for each task)
7. [A] Quartermaster (to provide water and fire)
8. [A] Tablemaster (to provide utensils)[21]

As this list makes clear, Hmong people are not able to do the Hmong way without other Hmong people, and they are particularly dependent on Hmong people who have ritual expertise. These ritual experts include shamans as well as elders, who serve as the community's repository of ritual knowledge and who ensure that ceremonies are performed properly. In addition, elders are vital to the ritual education of younger generations. Traditionally, Hmong people have passed down the details of Hmong rituals through oral tradition.[22] Chong Thao Xiong, for example, recalled that he "began to work with the older men in religious ceremonies, wedding negotiations, and funeral services."[23] His education centered on an apprenticeship with these elders because, as he explained, "Our Hmong ways are not written down on paper but are passed on by word of mouth."[24] More importantly, Hmong people transmitted knowledge of the Hmong way through doing. In Laos, where many rural Hmong people did not have any formal schooling at all, participating in work—whether farming or housekeeping or doing rituals—was the primary form of education, and true expertise in Hmong ceremonies required years of direct experience. As Mai Neng Moua explained, "In order to really know, you have to work (and sometimes fight for work) and get your hands dirty."[25] This type of rigorous, hands-on training often occurred in the context of families, which took pride in passing on expertise from one generation to the next. For example, Nao Xue Vang, a Hmong American man in Wisconsin, recalled that he "didn't have formal schooling" but "learned how to perform Hmong religious services," especially for weddings and funerals. "I studied with my father, and, because of what my family members knew, I quickly learned Hmong sciences and skills."[26] These rituals reinforced Hmong people's relationship with clan and community as well as with the rural mountain region they historically called home.

For the vast majority of Hmong people in Laos, the beliefs and rituals of the Hmong way were woven into the practices of daily life, and being Hmong meant practicing Hmong rituals. Moreover, Hmong people did not organize their society into separate spheres of the religious and the secular. Rather, a religious establishment of sorts existed in Hmong communities in Laos, where ritual, political, social, cultural, and medical activities were conjoined.[27] Nao Thao recalled how her parents, who were shamans, understood their spiritual beliefs and practices when they were living in Laos before the war. There, her family felt no need to label different aspects of their lives as "religion" or "culture" or to draw distinctions between the ritual traditions of Hmong people and those of other ethnic and religious groups. "Back then, I didn't compare too much about these things— [as in] 'Oh, this is what we do, this is not what we do,'" she said. Rather, she saw ritual life in Laos as more straightforward than what she would later experience in the United States. Hmong rituals were the essential and timeless "way"—kev—of Hmong people. As Nao Thao put it, "This is what we did, and this is what we do."[28]

"Follow the New Way"

Although Hmong people in Asia often lived in remote highland regions, they nonetheless encountered Christian missionaries from Europe and the United States. At the end of the nineteenth century, for example, Roman Catholic missionaries from the Paris Foreign Missions Society and China Inland Mission worked with Hmong people in Guizhou and Yunnan provinces and in northern Vietnam. Most notably, Samuel Pollard of the Bible Christian movement distributed the first Hmong translation of the Bible, created a script for the Hmong language, and built churches, schools, and medical clinics in Yunnan. Foreign missionaries also interacted with Hmong communities in Laos. In 1934 Pope Pius XI revived missionary activity in the region and sent Catholic priests of the Oblates of the Order of Mary Immaculate. The Christian and Missionary Alliance (CMA) also dispatched missionaries to Laos, especially to the mountain provinces where Hmong people resided.[29] Through their outreach to the Hmong and other highland ethnic groups in Laos, the CMA missionaries helped set in motion what Rev. Timothy Vang, a Hmong CMA pastor, described as the era of a great "people movement," a moment in the 1950s and 1960s when substantial numbers of Hmong people in Laos adopted Christianity.[30]

These Christian missionaries included people of different theological, denominational, and cultural backgrounds, which shaped how they engaged with Hmong people. Catholic and mainline Protestants tended to approach the Hmong with an anthropological and comparative religions framework, and they often drew on the paradigm of world religions, which involved classifying different beliefs and practices and placing them on a scale that ranged from primitive to civilized.[31] On the one hand, this approach to Hmong ritual life meant that they sometimes viewed the Hmong way as backwards and dismissed Hmong spirits as figments of a premodern imagination. On the other hand, the curiosity of missionaries in Laos led them to study and document Hmong stories, beliefs, and rituals.[32]

The evangelical missionaries associated with the CMA had a more uncompromising approach. To illustrate, it is useful to consider the recollections of Ted and Ruth Andrianoff and Malcolm and Helen Sawyer, two married couples who served on the CMA's Southeast Asia field team. Like other evangelical Christians, the Andrianoffs and the Sawyers drew a sharp distinction between Christian truth and the forces of Satan, and they believed that Hmong people inhabited a complex, dangerous supernatural landscape populated by the evil spirits. Hmong rituals, as the CMA missionaries saw them, were thus a form of devil worship—or, as Malcolm Sawyer described it, "appeasing the evil spirits by doing."[33] However, the missionaries believed that the evil spirits were rarely ever placated and that Hmong people were forever enslaved to these demons. For this reason, the Sawyers and Andrianoffs saw the work of introducing Hmong people to Christianity as a great spiritual battle against Satan, with the ultimate goal of liberating Hmong souls. As John and Ruth Andrianoff put it, the conversion of Hmong people in Laos was a moment when "the God of Grace did indeed step into Hmong history to deliver these people from bondage to the spirits, just as He had promised."[34] The missionary understanding of Hmong spirits as Satanic had an important impact on Hmong people, even those who did not convert to Christianity. For example, Hmong people did not historically consider the spirits of the unseen world to be "demons," although the arrival of the missionaries influenced their thinking. "Prior to contact with Christian missionaries, Hmong didn't perceive Ntxwg Nyug [one of the Hmong deities] as the 'Devil,'" explained Dia Cha. "It's the missionaries who labeled him as such. He is just an important figure in the Other World."[35]

Viewing Hmong people as devil-worshipping heathens, the CMA missionaries pursued a distinctive style of missionary work. One of their strategies was to win Hmong converts through a visible demonstration of the superior power of their Christian god. As the Andrianoffs recounted in a pamphlet about their missionary work in Laos, an assistant to the missionary couple named Nai Kheng decided to live in a house that was famous in the village for being "possessed by evil spirits." The Andrianoffs advised Nai Kheng that living in the spirit-possessed home would demonstrate to the other Hmong villagers "that our God is stronger than any evil spirits." And, according to the Andrianoffs, the plan worked: a powerful shaman named Moua Yia was impressed that Nai Kheng was able to stay in the haunted house and had not been scared away by the spirits. "Their God must be more powerful than the spirits," Moua Yia reportedly said. "If there is a God that mighty, I want to worship him, too." The Andrianoffs explained that even the spirits to which the Hmong were held in bondage sometimes "announced the truth of the Gospel."[36] Malcolm Sawyer, too, described how he regularly did battle with the evil spirits, not only in Laos but even in the United States. "I've had occasions here in the United States to cast out evil spirits out of people," he said. In Laos, he and his wife "always threw out evil spirit worship in the name of Christ, and prayed constantly."[37]

That the Sawyers "threw out evil spirit worship" points to another common practice of CMA missionaries in Laos: the systematic and often public destruction of Hmong ritual objects. For example, when Moua Yia said that he was ready to become a Christian, the Andrianoffs sprang to action. "Nai Kheng and Moua Yia began removing the spirit fetishes from the chief's home," they wrote. "They threw them into a pile behind the house and began going from house to house, taking down all the fetishes and collecting spirit-related ornaments people were wearing. Flames from the fire rose five meters into the air. Afterward the people returned joyfully to their homes, free from the spirit bondage under which they had been living."[38]

Both the aggressive destruction of Hmong sacred objects and the use of the term "fetish" reflect the fact that the missionaries saw

Hmong rituals not simply as a form of devil-worshipping heathenism but as a false religion. The term "fetish," the religion scholar David Chidester argued, derives from the Latin *facere*—"to make or to do"—and thus refers to an item of "uncertain meaning or unstable value" that is "artificial, illicit, or evil making."[39] The CMA missionaries' decision to deploy the term "fetish" was an act of denying the legitimacy of Hmong rituals and, more broadly, to assert that the Hmong do not have a true religion.[40] More broadly, it reflected the hierarchical framework of twentieth-century world religion scholars, who categorized the beliefs and practices of ethnic groups like the Hmong as one of the "little traditions" or "primitive religions," rather than any of the great "Western" or "Eastern" traditions. These efforts to classify the religions of the world have been part and parcel with European and American imperial projects.[41]

Christian missionaries and Western religion scholars were not the only ones who viewed Hmong beliefs and practices with contempt; Lao Buddhists, who comprised a majority of the population in Laos, also dismissed Hmong traditions, which they saw as mere superstition. According to Helen Sawyer, the Lao Buddhists "said they had a religion, Buddhist religion," whereas "the others didn't have a real religion."[42] In her observation, this distinction was central to how Lao Buddhists made sense of the comparative willingness of Hmong people to adopt Christianity. "The tribal people were spirit worshippers," said Helen Sawyer, "so when the tribal people became Christians, the Lao people themselves laughed at 'em and said, 'Well, they don't have a religion really. All they do is fear evil spirits. They don't really have a religion. We have Buddha, the Christians have Christ. They have nothing, so they've taken the Christian's Christ.'"

In distinguishing themselves from Hmong people, Helen Sawyer said, Lao Buddhists used the world religions paradigm to their advantage. By identifying themselves as people who had a "real religion," and by drawing a parallel between the Buddha and Christ, Lao Buddhists asserted the equivalence of their religion. As Helen Sawyer recalled, Lao people said "that Buddhism was older than the Christian religion, Buddhism was the national religion of the country, that we should not be trying to make converts out of the Lao people, because they already had a religion and it was a good religion, the same as ours."[43] Making this claim offered Lao Buddhists a way to counter Christian missionaries and to redirect them toward Hmong people, who allegedly had "nothing" in the way of religion. To be sure, it is not clear what Helen Sawyer herself actually believed about the Lao Buddhist and Hmong populations. On the one hand, she may have agreed that Buddhists were less in need of conversion because they had "a good religion" that was as legitimate as Christianity. On the other hand, it is possible that she and the other CMA missionaries shared this narrative to explain their failure to convert the Lao Buddhist population, whom she saw as an intransigent people who "tolerated" Christians but "also did not accept the religion very easily."[44]

In either case, Helen Sawyer's recollections emphasized an important theme: that Christian missionaries in Laos had their greatest success among the "spirit worshippers"—that is, ethnic groups such as the Hmong and the Khmu. The CMA missionaries recalled facilitating hundreds of conversions among the Hmong. Many of these conversions involved dramatic and symbolic acts that expressed a "complete break with the spirits."[45] "When they become Christian, all that stuff is thrown away," Malcolm Sawyer said. "The objects in their house are thrown away. They're burned. The altars outside the villages burned and [others were] . . . cut down and thrown away. And the strings are cut off. We've cut off many [laughs] hundreds and hundreds and thousands of strings from people and taken the paraphernalia off their necks and so forth. And they become Christian."[46]

In narrating this great "people movement," CMA missionaries emphasized the power of divine intervention, but they also acknowledged that there were practical reasons why Hmong people adopted Christianity. For one, the animal sacrifices necessary for Hmong rituals were expensive and burdensome for poor Hmong families. "Sometimes they would sacrifice meat and cattle that they ought to be having for food," explained Helen Sawyer. "They sacrificed to please spirits, which kept them poor all the time, they said."[47] In addition, she observed that many Hmong people considered Christian conversion a strategy to gain access to schools and other practical advantages. "Some I know became Christians because they wanted education for their children, wanted a better way of life," Helen Sawyer said. "I'm sure that was in the minds of some of the people, especially ambitious, aggressive Hmong tribal people, who wanted to better their standard of living and everything else."

To be sure, this narrative of a vast "people movement" obscures the important fact that Christian missionaries had limited impact in Laos, where the great majority of Hmong people continued to follow the traditional way. Geography was an important factor: given their location in remote highland villages, most Hmong people had little contact with missionaries. "They never reach out to our place," recalled Houa Vue Moua, a Hmong American woman who lived in Laos as a child and later made a home in Minnesota. "We never heard about them, we never saw them. . . . The priests, the Christian, were able to reach out to the Hmong [in the city], but not our people, not our area."[48] Similarly, Wang Her, a Hmong man in the Twin Cities, recalled that in Laos, it took several days of travel to encounter any Christians at all, as most of the missionary activity was concentrated in Xieng Khouang province. "It took us two days to reach Xieng Khouang," he said. "There were not any nice flat roadways, only small trails up and down mountain ranges. If we wanted to go to the church in Xieng Khouang, we had to travel one whole day and by nightfall we would reach and sleep at the village of Cahum. From there to Xieng Khouang was still another day of walking."[49] Hmong encounters with Catholic missionaries were similarly limited. For example, the Hmong anthropologist Gary Yia Lee recalled that he had attended a Catholic church and school as a child but was only able to do so in the capital city, Vientiane.[50]

Nonetheless, Hmong encounters with Christianity in Asia did have a long-term impact on Hmong religious life, most notably by establishing a small but influential Hmong Christian population. Why some Hmong people chose to adopt Christianity is a difficult question to answer, and there are many possible explanations. For one, the clan-based, patrilineal social structure encouraged mass baptism among Chinese Hmong and, later, Lao and Thai Hmong. Following the example of village leaders and clan heads, whole families adopted Christianity, as did entire villages on occasion. The messianic elements of Christian doctrine also appealed to those who believed that the Hmong people had lost their literacy upon the disappearance of *Vaj*, an ancient king. These Hmong converts accepted Jesus Christ as the long-lost *Vaj*, whom they had hoped would return to earth. Finally, circumstances of poverty and oppression may have functioned as a crucial catalyst for Christian conversion.

The plight of the Hmong compelled some missionaries to do more than establish churches and distribute Hmong translations of the Bible; they also built schools and medical clinics, led campaigns for Hmong land rights, and organized mass smallpox inoculations. These efforts drew thousands of Hmong to the missionary headquarters. Critics of Christian missionary efforts described these converts pejoratively as "rice bowl Christians" who changed religion purely for material reasons. Setting aside the question of whether these converts were genuine Christians—a question that is impossible to answer—the broader point remains that Hmong converts may have viewed conversion to Christianity as offering some relief to the political, social, and economic marginalization they suffered as an ethnic minority group.[51]

In sharing stories of their Christian conversion, however, many Hmong people emphasized one common theme: healing. Hmong people who encountered missionaries in Laos often saw Christianity as a means of finding a cure to an illness or protection from bodily affliction. For example, Rev. Timothy Vang, a Hmong American CMA pastor, explained how a visiting relative introduced his father to Christianity when they were still living in Laos:

> He said, "Uncle, your family has been sick all the time. This one is well, the other is sick, and repeating like that, year in, year out. Why don't you try Christianity? Why don't you try Jesus? Jesus is the Son of God. (Or they call *Yexus*.) *Yexus* is the Son of God. He came from heaven to earth, and he healed people who were sick, just like your family. I have become a Christian, so why don't you try?"

Vang's father thought about what his relative had suggested, and he gathered his sons, to whom he said, "*Yexus* came to earth to help people, and if we accept Jesus, we do not have to do this kind of shamanism, spiritism anymore." The father was enthusiastic about adopting Christianity, and his sons agreed to follow him. "So we just called that man again to come and pray for us, and he came to pray for us," Vang said. "He took away the altar, the fetishes, everything outside and burned them."[52]

Like Timothy Vang's father, the parents of Shong Yer Yang, a Hmong man who later resettled in the Twin Cities, believed that adopting Christianity would offer security against sickness. "Even after killing all the pigs and all that stuff [for Hmong rituals], it still didn't help our family," Shong Yer Yang said. "So, finally, at that time—I would say I was about six years old—we heard about Christians, about converting, and so my parents decided that they were going to convert because it doesn't matter how much animals we killed—to do the rituals, it doesn't seem to help." His parents had long been frustrated with the inefficacy of shamanism. "Doing the rituals always had failed us so many times because everybody was sick all the time, and we would use so many sets of baby pigs that were slaughtered for numbers of years, and it has never helped," he said. "And so they just had enough of it. . . . If it doesn't help, then why should we even continue?" For this reason, Shong Yer Yang said that his parents were eager to find a new, more effective way to guarantee the health of their family: "When they heard of Christianity and [people] saying that when you become Christian, you're going to get better, you're not going to be sick, and you don't have to do things in that [ritual] order anymore, that's when my parents decided that we were going to be converted—for that purpose, so that we're not afraid of being sick."

From Shong Yer Yang's story, it is not clear if becoming Christian also brought increased access to modern medicine, better food, or other material benefits that could have had a positive impact on health. Nevertheless, the causal link between adopting Christianity and becoming well, spiritually and bodily, was certain to Shong Yer Yang. "After we were converted," he said, "we were a lot healthier."[53]

When Hmong Christians enjoyed improved health, their well-being confirmed the rightness of the decision to convert to Christianity. Bee Yang, a Hmong woman who converted to Christianity in Laos, believed that her children were healthier after her family became Christian. Before her conversion, she had lost six of her fourteen children—"my children kept dying," she emphasized—and she converted to Christianity for the sake of saving her remaining family. "As soon as I was converted to being a Christian, then my other children that I had after had survived," she said. Christianity gave her a new set of rituals, a direct way to intervene in her children's health, and a greater sense of agency. "My kids, they were sick, but after we prayed for them, they get better," she said. She also found that she herself "felt a lot better" and "wasn't having so much deep sorrows" after becoming Christian.[54] Similarly, Wang Her attributed the great improvements in his health to his decision to become Christian. "Before I was a Christian, I constantly had fevers," he explained. "After becoming a Christian my fevers were gone, and I was not allergic to certain types of food anymore. To this day I have not experienced the same type of fevers or food allergies I used to experience before I became a Christian."[55]

These early encounters between Hmong people and Christian missionaries in Laos produced enduring ideas about Christianity and religious change. Not only did they introduce Christianity as an alternative means of addressing spiritual and bodily problems, but they constructed it as "the new way," an idea reflected in the Hmong term for Christianity, *kev cai tshiab*. Even decades after the first missionaries arrived in Laos, Hmong Americans continue to talk about Christian beliefs and rituals using the language of "new." For example, when asked to identify her religion, You Vang Yang, a Hmong American woman in Minnesota, declared, "I believe in the new religion." Her daughter, May Hang, pressed for more specific information and responded, "You believe in the Christian religion now?" You Vang Yang clarified her earlier statement, saying, "I believe in Christ, believe in God, and believe in Jesus."[56]

Half a century ago in Laos, the presence of missionaries concerned Hmong leaders, who believed that the "new way" challenged the "old way" of the Hmong. "In our village, my parents would not want to hear anything about Jesus' name or anyone carry a Bible," said Rev. Joua Tsu Thao, a Hmong American pastor in the Twin Cities. "Matter of fact, if they know that whoever carry a Bible to our village, the elder people will not even allow them to walk through our village." Joua Tsu Thao attributed this hostility to anxiety that the introduction of Christianity would disrupt Hmong rituals and, more broadly, Hmong society. "I think the fear [was that] the Christian interrupt the belief in the altar that they have," he said. Christians were forbidden from bringing their Bibles inside Hmong homes, which housed the sacred household altar at which Hmong people made offerings to ancestral spirits and performed other rituals. "They're afraid that Jesus's [spirit] might scare their spirits in some way," he said.[57]

"In Laos There Was Much Magic"

Despite the local opposition to Christian missionaries, Joua Tsu Thao ultimately did develop a relationship with a Christian person—and this person was actually his commanding officer during the Secret War. As Joua Tsu Thao recalled, joining the military meant that he was "far away from home" and unable to visit his family on his precious few days off work. Instead, he spent those days with his commander, who came from the "first family that became Christian in Laos." Visiting his commander's family was transformative for Joua Tsu Thao. "So when I was in vacation in the city, I went to church with them," he said. "And that was my first time hearing the Gospel."[58] The war changed Joua Tsu Thao's life not only by making him a soldier and separating him from his family but also by introducing him to new people, new communities, and "the new way."

Joua Tsu Thao's story reveals an important point: that while Christian missionary presence set in motion some important changes in Hmong beliefs and practices, during this period it was the Lao civil war that caused the greatest disruptions in Hmong life, including in Hmong spiritual life. Concerned that Laos would fall to the Communist Pathet Lao, the United States began to send military and humanitarian aid to Laos as early as 1955. In 1961 the CIA approached General Vang Pao, a nationalist and anti-Communist Hmong officer in the Royal Lao Army, to propose the idea of recruiting Hmong soldiers to fight against the North Vietnamese and the Pathet Lao. Vang Pao agreed to ally with the United States on the condition that the Americans supply Hmong people with military and humanitarian aid.[59] Thus, despite the fact that Laos was supposed to be a neutral country under the Geneva agreement of 1962, Laos became the site of extensive military operations supported by both the United States and North Vietnam. By 1963 the United States was dropping forty tons of supplies daily to aid Hmong and Lao troops as they fought on several fronts of the Secret War: in the cities, where the Royal Lao Army fought Communist troops; in northeastern Laos, where Hmong guerrilla units battled the Pathet Lao; in northern Laos, where Hmong soldiers coordinated the ground war with American B-52s overhead; and in the south, where Hmong soldiers supported an air war along the Ho Chi Minh Trail. With the assistance of the CIA and the Green Berets, Vang Pao and the tens of thousands of Hmong soldiers whom he commanded were the frontline defense responsible for warding off the Communist advance until the American evacuation in 1973.

The human cost of years of fierce guerrilla warfare was staggering. Though precise statistics are not available, an estimated 17,000 Hmong soldiers died during the decade and a half of war. The war also disrupted Hmong society as a whole. An untold number of Hmong civilians faced displacement from their villages, suffered catastrophic injury and illness, or died. Seeking refuge in the forest and mountains and deprived of the land that had long been the foundation of their self-sufficiency, they subsisted on air-dropped rations and spent years fleeing from the Communists, often relocating several times in a near-constant search for safety. This uncertainty only increased in 1973, when the Vientiane Accords established a cease-fire in Laos. Hmong soldiers who had fought with the United States faced uncertain future and feared for their lives as Communists gained power in the region. When Saigon fell to Communist forces in 1975, Hmong and American people in neighboring Laos began to prepare for evacuation. The CIA airlifted Vang Pao and other officers from Long Cheng in May 1975. However, most Hmong people were less fortunate; of the thousands who flooded the headquarters at Long Cheng, only a small fraction—about 2,500—were evacuated by the United States.[60]

Hmong people were angry at the United States for abandoning them and leaving them to suffer. Tong Pao Xiong, a Hmong American man in California, recalled how the Americans showed "no remorse" when they left. "Our men died horribly, leaving widows and orphans," he said. "Parents died, leaving their children alone. Children died, leaving parents with nothing. The Americans threw everything away as if our country was of no value to them. They had a country which they went back to, and they threw us away like their baggage. They left us in misery."[61]

Amid this misery, Hmong people turned to a traditional source of healing, comfort, and support: their rituals. Throughout the war, they continued the Hmong way as much as they were able. Nao Kao Xiong, for example, recalled how he had used spiritual healing practices of *khawv koob* to heal soldiers wounded in war. "I helped cure

a lot of General Vang Pao's soldiers," he said. "There were so many
soldiers with broken arms, legs, nonstop bleeding, torn skin."[62] Amid
the violence, suffering, and danger, the rituals of the Hmong way also
offered comfort, courage, and a means to communicate with spirits
that could offer hope and wise counsel. "When our country was in-
vaded by outsiders, fear gripped everyone in the villages," said Pang
Yang, a Hmong man in California. "In Pernong, news of the invasion
spread like wildfire. Everyone was scared." As the troops closed in,
the Hmong Christians in the village prayed and sang hymns, while
others turned to traditional Hmong rituals. "People also called on
the shamans and sought the spirits' guidance in making their decisions about where to move," he recalled. "They offered sacrificial
chickens to the spirits."[63]

However, practicing Hmong rituals became increasingly difficult as
violence and destruction forced people to seek refuge in the jungle or
the mountains. Living constantly on the run made it difficult to do
rituals. "We never held our traditional New Year's celebrations during
those long, hard years when we were constantly on the run," said Pang
Yang. "We were afraid that holding the celebrations would enable
the Vietnamese soldiers to find us."[64] The dislocations of war also
forced Hmong people to leave behind animals and sacred items that
were necessary for traditional ceremonies. For example, Shoua Vang,
a Hmong American man in Minnesota, recounted how his family
had a sacred drum that they used for funeral ceremonies. "When my
family fled Laos in 1975, we prayed that, if everyone was protected
on the journey and we reached a safe place, we would rebuild our
sacred drum," he said. "The drum in our home was too big to carry,
so we only took the ceremonial hoop that framed its wooden barrel
shaped body." They promised to rebuild the drum but were not able
to do so until seven years later, when they were resettled in the United
States.[65] As Shoua Vang's story indicates, it was difficult to practice
Hmong rituals during war, but the war also made it more important
than ever to seek the protection and guidance of the spirits. As Ma
Vang argued, the war and the flight from Laos "disrupted the spirit-
body balance" of Hmong people. "Upon leaving each temporary
place of refuge along their escape path, the refugees must remember
to not only gather their bags but also gather spiritual strength by
calling their ntsuj pligs to follow and ancestral spirits to protect their
journey," she wrote.[66] But doing so was not always possible.

When the war eventually forced Hmong people to flee Laos, it was not only the leaving of animals and sacred items that unsettled Hmong souls but also the leaving of the land itself. Indeed, Hmong beliefs and rituals historically had deep connections to the land—its rivers, its trees, its mountains—and for Hmong people, the Lao highlands were a unique and powerful spiritual milieu. The war was thus a double tragedy, one that not only displaced Hmong people but also devastated their beloved spiritual home. Stories told later by Hmong refugees revealed a deep longing for the mountains where their people, their ancestors, and their gods once dwelled in peace and spiritual harmony. "In Laos there was much magic," recalled Doua Vang, a shaman who resettled in California. "For instance, in Seng Tong there was a god whom we offered gifts to yearly. This ensured us that everyone in the village would have a good harvest season and everyone would be in good health. This god, Dab Phuaj Thaub, used to live in the mountains of Phuaj Thaub, but that is all gone now because of a landing strip for airplanes [that] has been built on the mountain."[67]

"God's Grace Shown in Loving Service by Volunteers"

It was at one of those airplane landing strips where Neng Xiong, a Hmong American woman in Minnesota, began her harrowing escape from war-torn Laos. American and Hmong forces had been defeated, and she and her children found themselves on the chaotic tarmac, engulfed by a crowd of other Hmong refugees desperate to evacuate. "A huge fight broke out at the airport there," she said, "[and] it was hard to get into the plane." Pushing through the crowds, she managed to climb into one plane, but she was separated from her children in the process. "They were crying, looking for me," she said. "I was crying, looking for them." The door of the airplane closed, and she saw some of her children, terror-stricken, pound on the window to catch the attention of the pilot. The pilot allowed these children to board the plane, but as he began to steer the aircraft down the runway, Neng saw that some of her other children, left behind, were chasing the airplane on the tarmac. "There were a couple of my kids still running after the plane," Neng recalled, "and so I said, 'Please stop the plane. I still have kids outside—please stop!' And they stopped the plane and got my kids inside the plane."[68]

She was one of the lucky ones. Thousands of other Hmong people, abandoned in Laos, were forced to flee by foot and embark on the treacherous westward exodus to Thailand. Carrying their possessions on their backs and sometimes subsisting on little more than insects and tree bark, families trekked through the jungle and journeyed at night to avoid capture by enemy soldiers. Once at the Mekong River, which marked the border with Thailand, the Hmong families faced the dangerous waters as well as the gunfire of troops directed by the Thai government to prevent refugees from crossing.

By 1979 nearly 30,000 Hmong refugees attempted to make the dangerous crossing each month, and the mass of refugees from Laos, as well as from Cambodia and Vietnam, overwhelmed Thai officials. The sheer scale of the refugee outmigration was one reason: 25,000 Hmong had fled immediately after the evacuation at Long Cheng, and several waves of Hmong refugees continued to enter Thailand throughout the second half of the 1970s and the 1980s. But Thailand did not want any refugees in the first place. Having signed neither the 1951 Geneva Convention nor the 1967 Protocol, the Thai government had no category for "refugee" as defined by the United Nations High Commission on Refugees (UNHCR); in its view, Hmong, Cambodian, and Vietnamese people who had been displaced by war were illegal immigrants. The first group of Hmong, who arrived between 1975 and 1978, benefited from the support of the Carter administration, but with the arrival of refugees from Cambodia, Laos, and Vietnam, the Thai government instituted a policy of deterrence and directed troops to push refugees back at the border and coerce repatriation. By 1981 Western nations had accepted 93 percent of the refugees in Thailand for resettlement, but the refugee crisis was far from over: between 1982 and 1986 an additional wave of refugees, many of whom were difficult to classify as political refugees, entered Thailand. Despite these hostile circumstances, the United Nations managed to initiate humanitarian operations in Thailand and established several refugee camps for Southeast Asian refugees. The most significant of these camps for Hmong refugees was Ban Vinai, which sheltered tens of thousands of Hmong refugees until its closure in 1995.[69]

In the camps, refugees were in a desperate physical and mental state. Jean Carlin, a physician from the University of California, Irvine, traveled to Ban Vinai refugee camp in 1979 and reported on the experiences of severe violence, trauma, hunger, and loss endured by the refugees there. "The refugees arrive in Thailand exhausted, sick, malnourished, perhaps wounded and often emotionally stunned after their incredible marches through Cambodia or Laos and their ultimate escapes across the borders," she wrote. Ban Vinai offered some measure of safety and security, but it was inadequately prepared to meet the extreme needs of Hmong refugees. At the time of Carlin's visit in 1979, Ban Vinai sheltered 42,000 Hmong refugees and was, in her view, "the most inaccessible, most overcrowded and worst camp in all of Thailand (and perhaps all of Southeast Asia)." The camp lacked proper sanitation, sufficient food, and adequate medical care. Camp physicians labored without adequate supplies and access to hospitals, and refugees shrewdly recognized the futility of seeking medical help. "I was told that many many more sick and profoundly malnourished children and adults were in the camp who would not come to the 'hospital' because nothing was done to help them there," Carlin wrote. She reported that infants and children were "starving to death" and that the Hmong population was generally "apathetic, listless, unable or unwilling to smile, reticent, [and] lacking in energy and initiative," as well as "severely anemic." On top of that, she noted that the Hmong were "culture shocked" and "simply bewildered by it all."

Carlin argued that unless the government took action, living in the refugee camps would cause refugees both immediate and long-term suffering. "The disruption of Hmong families, the competitive society in the camps, the hot climate, lack of useful work, starving children and racial prejudice have and will continue to erode the Hmong culture and resilience," she wrote. "Long stays (up to 4½ years or more) in incredibly poor camps will demoralize even the strongest Hmong eventually; hope for a future begins to grow dim." She urged government and voluntary agency officials to expedite resettlement, coordinate services, and provide more humanitarian aid. "It is *urgent* that medical care and food sufficient to save lives reach refugees *immediately!* More meetings and more task forces to 'study' the problem further are 'cop outs.' PEOPLE ARE DYING NOW! What good is a study of how and when they die, when we know they are *starving to death*." Writing that "few people leave except by dying," she declared, "the Hmong, as a people, may become extinct! *This is genocide*."[70]

As Carlin's report revealed, the situation in the refugee camps was dire—so dire, in fact, that both government and private voluntary agencies sprang to action and worked together to aid refugees. At Ban Vinai and other refugee camps throughout the region, providing relief to refugees was a collaborative, public-private project. This approach to refugee work reflected some general patterns in international humanitarian aid throughout the twentieth century. For one, international humanitarian work often involved both government and nongovernment institutions. These private institutions included many Christian organizations, which were motivated by both a commitment to humanitarian work and a vision for Christian missions that focused on social concerns as much as saving souls. Christian groups had long been involved in international humanitarian work, but the crises produced by the global Cold War in the second half of the twentieth century created new contexts for Christian humanitarian missions.[71]

Religious voluntary agencies from around the world and across the theological and denominational spectrum powered much of the refugee relief efforts. Typically affiliated with Christian denominations and often staffed by missionaries, these organizations provided refugees with food, shelter, medical care, educational programming, and agricultural support. In addition, they performed critical responsibilities in screening, interviewing, and preparing refugees for third-country resettlement. At Ban Vinai, for example, Christian churches and agencies were involved in almost every aspect of aiding Hmong refugees. The CMA ran a handicraft sales program, a small pig raising project, and a rice mill. Catholic Relief Services operated an in-hospital patient feeding program and a sewing and tailoring school. Finally, World Vision, an evangelical Christian organization, was one of the "lead" agencies and was responsible for relief and emergency supplies, educational and vocational training, English-language instruction, agriculture projects to support home gardens, camp development and maintenance, and family development programs. Most importantly, World Vision was in charge of medical care in the camp. With the American Refugee Committee (ARC) and the Free Finnish Mission seconded to it, World Vision provided all the inpatient and

Hmong man in front of a World Vision health center at Ban Vinai refugee camp. Courtesy of Timothy N. Castle.

outpatient services for the tens of thousands of Hmong refugees at Ban Vinai.[72]

The Christian churches and voluntary agencies were not only relief organizations responsible for refugees' health and safety—they were also religious organizations that were often deeply committed to refugees' salvation. To be sure, Christian voluntary agencies understood and practiced evangelism differently, depending on their theology and denominational affiliation. However, evangelical agencies, churches, and volunteers had a significant presence in the refugee camps, and they were particularly enthusiastic about combining relief work with missions. Evangelical leaders from around the world encouraged this approach. For example, at the peak of the Southeast Asian refugee crisis, the Consultation on World Evangelization (COWE) chose Thailand as the site of its 1980 meeting and made refugees a central agenda item. In a special report about "reaching refugees," COWE acknowledged the importance of addressing "social concerns" and encouraged Christians to resist the systems of oppression that produced forced migration in the first place. At the same time, COWE emphasized the "Biblical Mandate" for sharing

the gospel and urged Christian aid workers to incorporate evangelism in relief and resettlement work. In COWE's view, the refugee
population offered unique opportunities for Christian witness
because "under conditions of extreme stress, refugees tend to seek
God more intensely." COWE acknowledged that "Christians have
sometimes been criticized for taking advantage of and even ex-
ploiting refugees for evangelistic purposes" and maintained that
"neglecting the physical and social needs of refugees, or of using
them as leverage, for religious ends is deplorable." However, COWE
declared that evangelizing refugees should be Christian aid workers'
highest priority. "Refugees have spiritual needs during each phase
of their traumatic pilgrimage, and insensitivity to those needs would
be equally irresponsible for concerned Christians," the report said.
"Sensitive, timely sharing of the gospel alone can meet the deepest
needs of refugees."[73]

World Vision, one of the most prominent Christian voluntary
agencies in the refugee camps, exemplified this approach to missionary humanitarian work.[74] As a Christian agency, World Vision
provided its staff the following guidelines about the organization's
"Christian Role":

1. As a Christian agency ministering to the whole man; World
   Vision policy is to provide assistance to all displaced persons
   equally; without reference to religious belief.
2. As a Christian agency; World Vision expects staff to reflect
   the teachings of Jesus Christ in their everyday lives so as to
   provide a powerful, loving example to all.
3. As a Christian agency; World Vision prohibits and does not
   endorse any form of proselytism. However, World Vision
   does provide assistance and support to Christian churches in
   the camp.
4. As a Christian agency; World Vision encourages staff to engage in Christian evangelism and witness to non-Christians in
   ways which do not hinder specifically authorized World Vision
   projects. (The Thai Ministry of Interior policy is that VOLAGS
   are requested to assist in the camps for specific medical and
   development problems. Furthermore, religious activities are allowed in secondary importance, in ways which do not hinder
   the specific authorized projects and programs.)[75]

For the individuals on the staff of World Vision and other Christian agencies, evangelism was often a central objective of their work. Lois Visscher, for example, was a Presbyterian medical missionary who aided Cambodian refugees at Khao I Dang and Hmong refugees at Ban Vinai. A devout woman who began each day with Bible study, Visscher saw her work as a physician as a unique form of Christian witness and deliberately chose to affiliate with Christian hospitals and voluntary agencies. To Visscher, the refugee camps were the product of human sin, sites of suffering that originated "in the diabolical inhumanity of man to man." But she also viewed the refugee camps as sites of God's love, expressed in the work of Christian volunteers like herself. Khao I Dang, she wrote, "reflects God's grace shown in loving service by volunteers, cheerful endurance by Khmer, and world-wide liberality by God's chosen who support voluntary agencies and the United Nations High Commissioner on Relief."[76] Visscher was a physician, but she saw herself first and foremost as one of "God's chosen" who provided "loving service" for refugees.

However, Visscher's particular role as a medical missionary complicated the work of evangelism. At Ban Vinai, World Vision was responsible for overseeing the camp's medical center, and Christian missionary physicians often had their most intense encounters with Hmong people in hospital settings. There, Visscher and other physicians worked with Hmong staff and cared primarily for Hmong patients, who often desired to conduct traditional healing rituals that Western doctors sometimes considered strange, exasperating, and even demonic. As a devout Christian and a dedicated missionary, Visscher understood the importance of belief and ritual. However, she was also a staunch practitioner of Western medicine, and she understood that being an effective physician demanded that she earn the trust and cooperation of her patients and her staff. Publicly burning fetishes and denouncing Hmong rituals as demon worship as the Sawyers and Andrianoffs had done in Laos would have compromised her ability as a physician to care for her Hmong patients.

Visscher had conflicted feelings about Hmong rituals and beliefs. On the one hand, she and other Western medical practitioners made efforts to accommodate traditional practices. Voluntary agencies established a traditional medical center at Ban Vinai, for example.[77]

Individual physicians like Visscher acknowledged the significance of these practices to her Hmong patients and tolerated them. "They by no means are ready to give up their old ways," she wrote in a letter to a friend. And like the Christian missionaries who preceded her in Laos, Visscher was clearly fascinated with Hmong rituals, which she took care to document in a detailed photo album chronicling her work in Thailand. But even if she was affectionate toward Hmong people and curious about their beliefs and practices, Visscher remained skeptical of shamanism, which she regarded as a hindrance to the practice of scientific Western medicine and a sign of Hmong people's lack of modernity. "Non-Christian Hmong of all ages retain their faith in Shamans or Spirit Healers," she wrote. "The Hmong may even interrupt our 'scientific' modern medicine treatment to have 'ceremonies' to appease whatever spirit (of ancestor, usually) is displeased and has brought on the patient's illness."[78] Visscher expressed her deep frustration that Hmong beliefs about the spiritual origins of illness may have discouraged the sick from seeking Western medical care. "The Hmong do not like much to come to the hospital, when they are sick," she wrote. "At first they should ask the shaman and he asks the spirits. Sometimes is our help then too late."[79]

Though candid about her distrust of Hmong shamanism when communicating with her friends and family, Visscher generally appears to have kept her opposition to Hmong practices to herself. Serving as a medical missionary in the 1970s and 1980s, she straddled the boundary between old and new missionary styles. Like the Sawyers and Andrianoffs before her, she prayed regularly that the unsaved souls in her hospital ward would accept Christ as their savior, and like other Western Christian missionaries, she considered Hmong beliefs and practices to be little more than primitive superstitions. However, she permitted shamans in her hospital and accommodated requests by Hmong patients to practice their traditional rituals.

Finding a way to understand and respond to Hmong beliefs and practices was only one challenge that Christian relief workers faced. They also struggled with the call to share the gospel and provide humanitarian aid at the same time. In truth, Christian relief workers who aspired to mix missionary work with relief work sometimes found it uncomfortable and inappropriate to do so. Rudolph

Skogerboe, another Christian physician who worked at Ban Vinai, served as part of World Vision's medical team in 1982. In its staff guidelines, World Vision emphasized that Christian evangelism should be a priority, but Skogerboe admitted that sharing the "Good News" sometimes seemed ill advised in the face of such urgent need. "One beautiful Hmong woman was suffering because of attempted suicide," he recalled. "She was depressed and felt hopeless because her family had been killed in Laos." At that moment, though, he realized that the care she needed was not necessarily a religious message. "I felt it would be a little out of place to preach about the love of God. What she needed was someone to care for her even if it was just a little."[80]

Skogerboe's concern that sharing the gospel might "be a little out of place" reveals an important shift: compared to the more forceful style of evangelism pursued by the Sawyers and Andrianoffs in Laos, missionary physicians like Skogerboe and Visscher tended to tread more carefully when working with a non-Christian population. A few factors may have contributed to the change in approach. For one, Visscher and Skogerboe worked in a different capacity: as medical missionaries, they were responsible for pursuing Christian witness primarily through the delivery of medical care to the indigent, whereas the Sawyers and the Andrianoffs had different responsibilities and obligations. In addition, Christian ideas about missionary work were different. Skogerboe and Visscher served as medical missionaries in Southeast Asia a full three decades after the Andrianoffs and Sawyers first arrived in Laos. By the 1970s, the practice of openly seeking Christian converts was, in the eyes of many people working at the refugee camps, a violation of UNHCR rules, an inappropriate practice for medical professionals serving refugees, and an outdated, culturally imperialistic mode of missionary work.[81] Even organizations that made the most passionate calls for combining missionary work with relief work acknowledged the potential abuses of power that can occur with this approach.

To be sure, not all Christian missionaries in the camps shared Skogerboe's concern that evangelism could be "a little out of place"; accounts of Christian missionary work in the refugee camps reveal that other Christian aid workers readily mixed evangelism with humanitarian aid. Skogerboe was also a musician, and one day he was invited to play the horn at the Sunday services of a Hmong church that met at the camp. Skogerboe recalled that though the Hmong preacher was passionate and used a "public address system that was so loud that it could wake the dead," it was difficult to hear over the noise of people clamoring for food. "The 600-plus listeners weren't listening too well," he recalled. "Through the open windows, hundreds of children were being treated to fresh milk and gifts from the Overseas Christian Relief people." The scene was so chaotic that, in his view, "it all seemed more like a circus than a church service."[82]

If Skogerboe was uncomfortable with the mixing of relief work and missionary work, he was not alone; other relief organizations also criticized how Christian agencies and church groups intertwined aid and evangelism. Doing so, they pointed out, contradicted official policy. For example, voluntary agency officials discussed recent reports of proselytizing in the camps at one meeting of the Committee for the Coordination of Services to Displaced Persons in Thailand (CCSDPT), a consortium of the voluntary agencies providing refugee relief services. The CCSDPT's leader at the time, Robert Van Leeuwen, responded by reading the guidelines for religious activities set forth by the UNHCR:

Organizations active in the delivery of emergency relief may also have a religious aspect in their normal work. Some are traditional partners of UNHCR, with the separation between these two roles long established and well understood, but for others it may be useful to recall the basic principle. Religious activities by those outside the refugee community, where permitted by the authorities, must be clearly disassociated from the delivery of assistance and services to refugees. In particular, no proselytizing should take place in association with the provision of such general community services as education, health and social welfare, or in connection with the employment of refugee workers.

Van Leeuwen urged the member organizations of the CCSDPT to modify their activities in accordance with this policy.[83] Still, nonreligious organizations sometimes complained about the persistent proselytizing in the camps, especially by World Vision. One report noted that a physician associated with the ARC, which worked with World Vision to run the hospitals at Ban Vinai, "was very down on the 'evangelical' agencies, saying they didn't provide enough medical care—that those agencies which provide medical care without prosethizing [*sic*] do a better job."[84]

In addition to the contentious matter of proselytizing in refugee camps, religion complicated how Christian and nonreligious agencies related to each other. At Ban Vinai and other refugee camps, Christian agencies such as World Vision worked closely with nonreligious organizations such as the ARC. However, the officials at World Vision international headquarters in California at one point demanded that their Christian organization no longer employ or work with non-Christian groups.[85] Religion even complicated how the agencies participated in meetings with one another. When a religious voluntary agency representative wanted to begin the CCSDPT meetings with prayer, officials from the other voluntary agencies protested. The nonreligious agencies insisted that they must operate with "religious neutrality" and suggested that the group begin each meeting with a moment of silence rather than prayer.[86] The small compromise of a moment of silence offered a veneer of secularity, which was a comfort for some people. Nevertheless, given the central involvement of organizations like World Vision in the daily operation of the camps, the reality was that refugee relief in Thailand ran on religion, which provided money, manpower, and motivation to address the humanitarian crisis.

"[In] Laos, They Don't Have Church, but Thailand, They Have Big Church"

When Hmong refugees encountered groups like World Vision in the refugee camps, it was not the first time they had contact with Christian missionaries. However, their contact with Christian missionaries increased in both frequency and intensity in Thailand. For a variety of reasons, the refugee camps offered more advantageous conditions for missionary work. In contrast to the remote Hmong villages in rural Laos, the refugee camps in Thailand gathered together tens of thousands of people in one place. This high population density made it easier for missionaries to evangelize a larger number of people. Refugees also arrived at the camp regularly, giving missionaries a new audience almost daily. Finally, Shong Yer Yang observed that Hmong refugees had more "motivation" in Thailand;

amid the upheaval of war and forced migration, Hmong people, he believed, had a greater "understanding that we need to change."[87]

Most significantly, contact with missionaries increased in Thailand because Hmong refugees depended on Christian voluntary agencies and churches for essential aid. Looking back on their lives in the refugee camps, Hmong people recalled visiting religious organizations to obtain food, medical care, education, and other assistance. For example, True Xiong, a Hmong American woman in Minnesota, remembered how churches provided medicine. "There was a Catholic church where, if you got sick, if you needed a shot, they would give you a shot," she said, and "if [you] needed some meds, they would give you medications."[88] Another Hmong woman, Neng Vang recalled that churches gave her the chance to receive an education. Her daughter, Paj Ntaub Lis, said, "They teach you Hmong there—the Hmong language—and there were other opportunities for children at the church, and that's why she liked it."[89]

Because Christian voluntary agencies and churches administered so many aid and educational programs in the refugee camps, Hmong people began to identify Christian organizations as generous sources of help—an association that shaped their relationship and response to Christianity not only in Thailand but also later, in the United States. One Hmong man, Yong Kay Moua, recalled his first interactions with Christians in the 1970s. "We still believed and still practiced in the traditional Hmong way, but because the World Vision [was] coming to Laos, they had little service for the refugees, so we learned about that a little bit, and then when we crossed to Thailand, the World Vision also come to serve the refugees, so we learned a little bit about that," he said. "So we know that the church, many different church, extend their help to the refugees."[90] For many Hmong refugees like Yong Kay Moua, these early encounters with Christian humanitarian workers were their very first introduction to Christianity, and they arrived in the United States already seeing Christian churches as benevolent and charitable.

Receiving help from Christian relief organizations did encourage some Hmong refugees to adopt Christianity, a decision perhaps motivated by material needs. Cziasarh Neng Yang, who lived in Ban Vinai as a teenager, emphasized that the dire conditions of the refugee camps shaped how Hmong people responded to Christian missionaries. "I think people are looking for a way out—a way out, meaning, if we become Catholic, maybe we would get supported by the outside world for material good," he said. In his memory, Christian missionaries "brought many valuable goods to distribute to the church members," and he believed that Hmong people's "economic wish" was "one way that people [were] attracted to the religion, to the practice, to the belief."[91] In his view, Hmong refugees were what other observers pejoratively described as "rice bowl Christians"— people who converted to Christianity to gain a bowl of rice and other material help.[92]

Stories shared by other Hmong refugees reveal that, indeed, many people did not necessarily have religious objectives in mind when they visited a church or spoke with a missionary. Many Hmong people explained that they were rather uninterested in Christianity and were simply looking for tangible things that were essential for survival, such as food, medicine, and resettlement opportunities abroad. "During that time, I believe it was just people wanting to go and get free stuff," said True Xiong. "Even though they were practicing the Hmong ritual, the practice—healing, and all that stuff—they still went and got medicines." In fact, she believed that Hmong people saw the churches in the refugee camp as another source of aid, not as a religious institution. "They were just another program there to help," she said.[93]

Part of the reason why Hmong refugees were uninterested in the missionaries' beliefs and rituals was because Hmong people were satisfied by their own beliefs and rituals. The Hmong American writer Kao Kalia Yang was a child when she was at Ban Vinai and remembered how churches reached out to children. "There were a lot of missionaries, so they were trying to recruit," she said. "They gave candies." But even if she longed for a lollipop, her family was lukewarm about the religious message that came with it. "The funny thing was we never felt like we didn't have a belief system in place, so we weren't looking," she said. "We were looking for a home, so when they came, we were more interested in the homes, potentially, on the other side of the ocean, than the actual religions." Not only was her family primarily interested in securing passage to America, but they were not even sure what value Christianity had to offer them. "It wasn't so fruitful for my family," she said."[94]

The fact that Kao Kalia Yang and her family were satisfied with their own beliefs and rituals and "weren't looking" to replace them

Hmong man playing a *qeej* at Ban Vinai refugee camp. Courtesy of Timothy N. Castle.

illuminates an important point: that despite all of the upheaval and dislocation during the years of war, Hmong refugees remained committed to their traditional beliefs and practices. Dennis Grace, who served as the International Rescue Committee (IRC) representative to the JVA in Thailand, observed that other Southeast Asian refugees were often "thinking 'West'" and adopting the habits, language, and clothing of the places where they hoped to eventually resettle. In contrast, Hmong refugees "may as well have been in a location inside Laos" and were eager "to preserve, to remain the same as where they'd come from."[95] Indeed, General Vang Pao and other Hmong leaders had intentionally organized Ban Vinai to suit traditional Hmong living patterns.[96]

At Ban Vinai and other refugee camps, Hmong refugees continued to practice the Hmong way. Shamanism flourished, in part due to the high density of shamans. Anthropologists counted thirty shamans in ninety Hmong refugee camp households, with seven shamans living in a single building in Ban Vinai.[97] "The fabric of camp life is suffused with shamanic performance," recalled Dwight Conquergood. "As I walked daily through the camp, I could often stand in one place and hear three shamanic performances coming from different directions. Most mornings I was awakened before dawn by the drumming and ecstatic chanting of shamans."[98] The vibrant ritual life of the camp left a similarly strong impression on Ginny Ascensao, a nurse who worked at Ban Vinai. "When I first arrived the sound of the Shamans (Hmong witch doctors) chanting and banging their bells and pots would be heard all night long, all through the camp," she said. As part of the camp medical staff, she noted that Hmong refugees resisted visiting the hospital unless they were extremely ill and preferred "to utilize their own Shamans initially for treatment."[99]

Life in the refugee camp was not always amenable to Hmong rituals, though. Camp residents had reduced access to livestock necessary for ritual sacrifice. "In the camps, everything very strange," said Soua Sue Lee, a Hmong man who later resettled in Minnesota. "We cannot kill any cows, any pigs." For rituals that involved killing animals, he said that he had to buy the meat from Thai restaurants.[100] However, even if animals were available for purchase, the money to pay for them frequently was not. Neng Vang and her daughter recalled that camp poverty and scarce resources caused Hmong people to scale back the size and scope of their rituals. "In Thailand, because you're limited as far as food, you only call your immediate family and/or just the six people who would help watch the shaman as they go into the trance," they said.[101] High shaman fees in the camps also made rituals prohibitively expensive for some Hmong refugees.[102]

In addition to the lack of money and ritual resources, Hmong refugees worried that practicing their traditions would imperil their chances of being sponsored for resettlement in the United States. To be sure, the cultural orientation materials created by the voluntary agencies to prepare Southeast Asian refugees for resettlement stated that "people are allowed to practice whatever religion they choose in America," that "success in the U.S. does not depend on the acceptance of American religious values," and that refugees "do not have to attend their sponsor's church or convert to the religion of their sponsors."[103] However, a 1986 report by the Minnesota State Refugee Advisory Council examined the conditions of health care in the refugee camps and discovered that Hmong refugees avoided being treated at the traditional medicine center for fear that resettlement workers would see them there. "A very large traditional medicine center operates in Phanat Nikhom and it houses the traditional healers of all ethnic groups except the Hmong shaman," the report found. "The Hmong in the camp will not visit the shaman when located in the TMC for fear of ridicule and the suspicion that they may not be able to go [to] the US if they are seen visiting the shaman."[104] Although no available evidence substantiates the claim that voluntary agencies prioritized Hmong refugees who identified as Christian, the possibility that Christian Hmong refugees might receive greater assistance or gain earlier admission to the United States was enough to persuade some Hmong refugees to abstain from practicing traditional rituals in public.

It is not surprising that Hmong refugees worried that their religious identity would affect their opportunities for resettlement, given what they likely knew about the admission process. As discussed earlier, officials with the JVA, which processed refugee cases and handled the interviews in the camps, explicitly asked Hmong refugees to identify their religion on the biographical forms that they were required to complete when they applied for resettlement. Precisely why the JVA asked this question is unclear. Government and voluntary agencies may have surveyed and identified the religion of every refugee who applied for resettlement because of the desire to accommodate religious differences and to match refugees with sponsors of the same religion.

Whatever the reasons, though, the fact that JVA officials directly asked Hmong refugees to account for and identify their religion was curious and complicated, for several reasons. For one, questions about religious identification on official government forms are rare. Since the US Bureau of the Census began surveying the American population in 1790, it has never included a question about religion on its decennial census. The reluctance was due, in part, to practical concerns that asking such a highly personal question would reduce census participation rates. More fundamentally, the Bureau of the Census believed that asking a religious identification question would run afoul of the First Amendment. In the middle of the twentieth century, with the Holocaust fresh in their memory, Jewish Americans campaigned aggressively against the inclusion of a religious identification question on the census on the principle of "religious privacy." This idea gained traction, and in 1976, the same year that Hmong refugees first gained entry into the United States under the Lao Parole Program, Congress passed a law prohibiting the Census Bureau from including any mandatory questions about "religious beliefs or to membership in a religious body" on its surveys.[105]

Refugee resettlement interviews, however, were an exception to the commitment to "religious privacy." That resettlement officials asked a religious identification question of all Hmong refugees who were applying for resettlement underscores the degree to which refugee resettlement was not simply a government undertaking but a public-private effort that itself blurred the boundaries of church and state. If Census Bureau officials and Congress worried that Americans would find a question about religious identification to be intrusive and in conflict with the First Amendment, refugee resettlement officials did not hold the same concerns for refugees, whose lives were subject to government intervention and social engineering in numerous ways.

Asking Hmong refugees to identify their religion was complicated, partly because the biographical forms were poorly conceived but more fundamentally because, as noted earlier, the category of religion was a foreign construct to them. The foreignness of this category is evident in the difficulty of translating the word "religion" and equating Hmong people's practice-centered spiritual traditions with a Christian conception of religion that is centered on belief and faith. One Hmong translation for the word "religion" is *kev ntseeg,* a compound of the word *kev,* which means "way" or "path," and the word *ntseeg,* which means "belief"; together, *kev ntseeg,* the term preferred by many Hmong Christians, is understood to refer to "faith." Another translation for "religion" is *dab qhuas,* which is, variously, a generic term for religion, a description of ancestral and lineage-specific household spirits, and a catch-all word that some Hmong people have used to describe all elements of their ritual traditions—ancestor worship, spirit worship, shamanism. *Dab qhuas* unites the word *dab,* which translates as "ghost," "spirit," or "demon," and *qhuas,* which means "to praise"; put together, *dab qhuas* suggests an emphasis on worship and ritual practice rather than belief and is a term frequently used by those who practice the traditional Hmong way.[106] Thus, the two translations for the word "religion"—*kev ntseeg* and *dab qhuas*—are commonly understood to mean, respectively, "faith" and "praise and worship of spirits." These terms might seem very similar in the eyes of many Christian Americans, but this is not necessarily so for Hmong refugees asked to identify their religion on government forms. It is not clear whether resettlement officials used the term *kev ntseeg* or *dab qhuas* or possibly another term altogether when they interviewed Hmong refugees applying for resettlement, but the choice may have mattered.

The problems with the religion identification question notwithstanding, the biographical forms still offer invaluable information about the religious lives of Hmong refugees before they resettled in the United States. In the case files for 3,276 Hmong refugees assisted between 1976 and 1996 by the International Institute of Minnesota, an agency affiliated with the American Council for Nationalities Service, the biographical forms included the section that provided religious identification information. These records reveal a couple important details. First, some Hmong refugees identified as Christian, Protestant, or Catholic before resettling in the United States—about 16 percent of the 3,276 Hmong refugees for whom religious identification information is available. In fact, most Hmong were not Christian, which leads to the second important finding that emerges from these records: the vast majority of Hmong people—about 83 percent—identified their religion as Ancestral Worship, Animism, Buddhism, or Hmong Religion (see the table below).[107]

Religious Identification of Hmong Refugees Resettled by the International Institute of Minnesota between 1976 and 1996

Religion	Number	Percentage
"Ancestral Worship"	287	8.8
"Ancestral Worship/Animist"	6	0.2
"Animist"	2,238	68.3
"Animist/Buddhist"	2	0.1
"Buddhist"	180	5.5
"Hmong"	10	0.3
"Hmong Religion"	3	0.1
"Catholic"	148	4.5
"Christian"	214	6.5
"Protestant"	164	5.0
"Invalid Code"	9	0.3
"None"	5	0.2
Response Left Blank	10	0.3
Total	3,276	
All Non-Christian	2,726	83.2
All Christian	526	16.1

Source: International Institute of Minnesota.

Though the question of religious identification was both difficult to answer and deeply personal, almost every single one of the individuals answered the religious identification question during the resettlement interview. This high response rate may have been due to the particular context of the resettlement interview. In general, Hmong refugees saw the resettlement interview as a high-stakes event and worried that incorrect answers would imperil a future in the United States. Hmong men recalled, for instance, that the inability to correctly identify a weapon used in combat could call their claims to military service into question and compromise their priority status in resettlement.[108] Admission of a medical problem could hold up a family in Thailand for weeks or months, and any tiny discrepancy between forms—about ages and birth dates, for example—could cast doubt over applicants' honesty and the legitimacy of their claim to refugee status.

In the end, how Hmong refugees responded to the religious identification question may not have had any impact at all on their resettlement prospects. It is not clear how voluntary agency or government officials used any of this information or if there was an advantage to identifying as Christian, as some Hmong refugees believed. But the experience of being asked to identify their religion to resettlement authorities—and to present their traditional beliefs and practices as "religion"—was new to Hmong people, who, until that moment, had not been forced to organize their lives according to these categories. How Hmong refugees defined their religion as they were applying for resettlement was but a precursor to what they would later experience once they were living in the United States, a country where practicing, preserving, and ensuring First Amendment protections for the Hmong way would hinge on describing it as "religion."

«««««»»»»»

The story of Hmong religious change begins first with the story of American empire. The Secret War—financed by the United States but fought by Hmong soldiers—resulted in the traumatic loss of life and land and the forced migration of thousands of Hmong people to Thailand. Amid this anguish and upheaval, Hmong refugees sought healing and guidance through the rituals of the Hmong way, only to find that the war had disrupted a critical source of stability and support—their spiritual traditions.

The Secret War intensified religious transformations produced by another arm of American empire: Christian missionaries, whose early encounters with Hmong people laid the foundation for future religious changes when Hmong refugees resettled in the United States. For one, pre-migration missionary contact shaped American knowledge of Hmong ritual life. American resettlement workers, having little knowledge of the Hmong refugees whom they had sponsored, relied on the writings of missionaries who had worked in Laos decades earlier. In this way, missionaries in the mid-twentieth century guided how resettlement workers in the 1970s and 1980s understood Hmong people and attempted to accommodate—and often change—Hmong beliefs and practices.

Hmong encounters with Christian missionaries in Asia also influenced Hmong religious choices in the United States. To be sure, relatively few Hmong people had direct contact with missionaries in Laos. However, foreign missionaries in Laos did introduce Christianity to some Hmong communities and helped establish an influential, if small, Hmong Christian population. These Christians, particularly those associated with the CMA, would later serve as the nucleus for Hmong Christian communities in the United States.

More than anything, these encounters in Asia generated new categories that Hmong people applied to bring order to their increasingly complex ritual lives. No longer were Hmong beliefs and practices simply the Hmong "way." Missionaries introduced Christianity, which became "the new way" in the Hmong cultural and religious imagination. Traditional Hmong rituals, in contrast, became "the old way." And, through the bureaucratic interactions with aid workers and government officials processing their paperwork in the refugee camps, "the old way" began to become something else entirely: a religion.

Well before they had even set foot in the United States, the transformation and reorganization of Hmong ritual life was already underway.

2

Administering Resettlement

REFUGEE RESETTLEMENT AS
CHURCH-STATE GOVERNANCE

On October 24, 1979, a priest, a rabbi, and a minister set out on a mission. Their destination was the White House, and their target was the president himself. Their goal was to convince President Jimmy Carter to increase the government's commitment to aid Southeast Asian refugees abroad and at home. They knew that the stakes of their mission were high. Halfway across the world, Southeast Asia was mired in a humanitarian crisis. Vietnamese refugees were fleeing by boat and perishing at sea; Hmong and Lao people displaced by war and persecution were making dangerous journeys to seek safety in Thailand; malnourished victims of the Khmer Rouge were languishing in refugee camps after surviving a genocide that had killed nearly a quarter of Cambodia's population.

As these events unfolded, a diverse coalition of American people—religious communities, trade unions, civic organizations, and more—refused to avert their eyes from the suffering. They appealed to the public to support resettlement projects and organized fundraisers to support international relief efforts. They also lobbied the government to establish a generous, long-term refugee program to aid Southeast Asian refugees. The United States, they argued, had a responsibility to do what it could to ease the human misery that it had played a part in creating.[1]

On that fall day in 1979, the people charged with delivering this message to the White House were those who specialized in calls to conscience: religious leaders. Each individual appeared on behalf of a key sector of "tri-faith America."[2] Representing Catholic Americans were Father Theodore Hesburgh and Cardinal Terence Cooke; representing Protestant Americans were Rev. Harry Haines and Patricia Young; and representing Jewish Americans was Rabbi Bernard Mandelbaum. If at one point in American history Protestants, Catholics, and Jews had been at odds with each other, the Cold War and the crisis in Southeast Asia compelled these religious leaders to meet with the leader of the free world to show that they and the faithful Americans they represented were united in benevolence. The delegation emphasized that they believed action on refugee issues was a shared moral imperative that transcended religious boundaries.

The delegation accomplished its mission. After a morning of conferences, President Carter announced that the United States would "act swiftly to save the men, women and children who are our brothers and sisters in God's family." He promised $3 million in refugee aid funds for UNICEF and the International Committee of the Red Cross and $9 million in refugee assistance funds to support food relief efforts in Thailand. He urged Congress to appropriate $20 million for a supplemental "Food for Peace appropriation." Finally, he pledged support for congressional authorization of $30 million for other relief programs for refugees.

President Carter emphasized that the response to the Southeast Asian refugee crisis was not merely a government response but a unified effort powered by the moral and material resources of both church and state. He praised the commitment of different religious organizations to "match the government effort," and he appealed to the American public to rally their local congregations to contribute to the cause. "I ask specifically that every Saturday and Sunday in the month of November, up until Thanksgiving, be set aside as days for Americans in their synagogues and churches, and otherwise, to give generously to help alleviate this suffering," he said.

Shortly after the president's announcement, the religious leaders spoke passionately about the importance of tri-faith America united in religious benevolence. "I think it says something about America of 1979 when so many different religious groups, often in conflict in the past, stand together as brothers and sisters representing about 150 million Americans and are willing to pool their efforts, their enthusiasm, commitment and zeal to do something about this horrendous situation," Hesburgh said. In Hesburgh's view, there is power in cooperation, compassion, and shared convictions. "I think it's good for America that all of us stand together in this prime response of religion which is 'Love your neighbor as yourself,'" he said.[3]

In appealing to Christians and Jews to give generously to relief efforts, President Carter was perhaps preaching to the choir. By 1979 a global legion of faithful do-gooders had already mobilized to aid refugees displaced by the wars in Vietnam, Cambodia, and Laos. In Washington, DC, clergy lobbied government officials for increased refugee admissions and generous funding for refugee relief programs. In small towns and large cities across America, congregations collected furniture and clothing to give to newly arrived refugee families. And on the other side of the Pacific, religious voluntary agencies and missionaries provided emergency food aid, medical care, and education programs in refugee camps.

As these examples show, the American response to the Southeast Asian refugee crisis was not a job that the government undertook on its own, but rather one in cooperation with an array of voluntary agencies, churches, and individual volunteers. By the 1970s this public-private approach was well established, having developed in response to other humanitarian crises earlier in the twentieth century. During World War II, the federal government worked closely with private voluntary agencies to aid European war victims, and the collaborative approach forged during this period endured. Government and private agencies cooperated in efforts to resettle Hungarian Freedom Fighters in the 1950s and Cuban exiles in the 1960s. When the United States was faced with the daunting task of resettling hundreds of thousands of Southeast Asian refugees in the 1970s, the government once again turned to its trusted partners, the voluntary agencies, which were experienced, organized, and prepared to mobilize an army of resettlement workers that had been active for decades.[4]

Importantly, the American effort to aid and resettle refugees was a public-private effort powered largely by religious resources.[5] The church-state cooperation celebrated by Carter, Hesburgh, and

Mandelbaum characterized all levels of refugee assistance, from overseas humanitarian aid to domestic resettlement services. This collaboration was sometimes visible and official, most notably in the arrangements between the federal government and the national voluntary agencies, which received public funds to provide both immediate and long-term assistance to refugees. At the state level, too, government officials worked with church-affiliated voluntary agencies to coordinate social services for refugees. But a look at re-settlement activities at the local level indicates that the government also relied on religious groups in other crucial, if less conspicuous ways. As the challenges of refugee resettlement and the limited reach of public services became clear, churches and local religious chari-ties filled the gap by providing a variety of support services—English classes, job skills workshops, and programs for children and elders—to help their new refugee neighbors.

Several factors explain the central involvement of religious organ-izations in Southeast Asian refugee resettlement. Like other private voluntary agencies, religious voluntary agencies were well established by the 1970s, with decades of experience in refugee work. Structural reasons also explained the significance of religious groups. As trans-national institutions with a global presence, religious organizations were well positioned to respond to an international refugee crisis that spanned continents. In addition to their breadth, religious organ-izations had depth. Through its affiliated congregations, they were able to marshal rich human and material resources at the local level, making them ideal to support long-term, labor-intensive resettlement efforts. Finally, religious people brought a moral commitment to ref-ugee work that sustained their involvement, even when newspapers no longer covered refugee crises on their front pages.

Ultimately, the "shadow establishment" of religious voluntary agencies and their affiliated congregations helped make it possible for the United States to admit and resettle over one million South-east Asian refugees.[6] It was an enormous effort and one that we should not take for granted. As Carl Bon Tempo argued, it is a wonder that the United States resettled any Southeast Asian refu-gees at all.[7] The Southeast Asian refugee crisis erupted at a moment when unemployment was high and Americans were both weary of war and wary of refugees. In this context, the role of religious groups was especially important because throughout the twentieth century, the US government agreed to admit refugees only when it was confident that refugees would be able to adjust to American life effectively and with minimal negative impact on American society.[8] The system of church-state refugee resettlement allowed for that confidence by offering the powerful resources of religious people who felt a deep responsibility to care for refugees. Voluntary agencies and their partnering congregations were a critical reason why government officials were willing to undertake a politically unpopular resettlement project of unprecedented size and complexity.

"Sons and Daughters of the American Revolution"

The humanitarian disaster that compelled the religious delegation to visit President Carter in 1979 had been years in the making. War in Vietnam, Laos, and Cambodia had displaced millions of people and had produced several phases of refugee migrations. The first occurred during the US military involvement in the Vietnam War, which began in 1965 and lasted a decade. The fall of Saigon and the withdrawal of American military forces from Vietnam in the spring of 1975 produced another group of refugees. In response to this crisis, President Gerald Ford gave the green light to use parole powers to admit 200,000 Vietnamese refugees, some of whom had been evacuated by the US military, and others who had fled on their own and were later taken into protective custody by the United States.[9] These Vietnamese refugees stayed in four refugee camps located at military bases throughout the United States until sponsors could assist their resettlement elsewhere.[10] In the same year, the Khmer Rouge took control in Cambodia, and the Pathet Lao assumed power in Laos. While Vietnamese refugees were the overwhelming focus in 1975, the United States that year also admitted 4,600 Cambodians considered vulnerable to persecution and approximately 300 highland people from Laos, including the Hmong.[11]

Americans may have believed that the crisis was resolved when the last military-run refugee camp in the United States closed, but violence and political conflict in Southeast Asia continued to cause mass displacement of people in the late 1970s and early 1980s. In

1979, after the downfall of the Khmer Rouge, Cambodian survivors of Pol Pot's genocidal regime sought refuge in neighboring Thailand.[12] Meanwhile, new groups of refugees began to escape Vietnam by sea. Some of these "boat people" had been political, military, and cultural leaders in South Vietnam recently freed from reeducation camps.[13] Others were members of the Hoa ethnic group fleeing persecution in Vietnam.[14] Finally, Hmong and Lao refugees fearing for their safety under the new government continued to cross into Thailand.[15]

Due to a well-organized advocacy campaign in support of refugees, the US government eventually admitted Southeast Asian refugees for resettlement to a degree that far exceeded expectations. Between 1975 and 2010, the United States resettled 1.2 million Southeast Asian refugees in what was the most extensive, expensive, and institutionally complex refugee resettlement project in American history.[16] It was also, at times, a haphazard and chaotic effort that many planners initially predicted would last only a year. In fact, it lasted three decades.

The effort to resettle Southeast Asian refugees in the United States developed in several stages. The Indochinese Migration and Refugee Assistance Act of 1975 outlined the first plan to assist Vietnamese and Cambodian refugees. In these initial efforts, the federal government gravely underestimated the needs and numbers of Southeast Asian refugees, and in the years that followed, a series of stopgap measures allowed for the admission and resettlement of more refugees, including Lao and Hmong refugees. By 1979, President Carter had raised the quota of incoming refugees to 14,000 persons per month to allow for the resettlement of Vietnamese, Cambodian, Lao, and Hmong refugees.[17] But even if more Southeast Asian refugees were admitted, there remained the challenge of supporting these refugees as they adjusted to life in the United States.

To address these needs, Congress passed the Refugee Act of 1980, which created admission procedures that facilitated the efficient resettlement of refugees, provided funding and institutional support for refugee resettlement programs, and imposed a cap on the number of refugees admitted annually. Most significantly, the act aligned the US definition of "refugee" with the standards of United Nations conventions and protocols and defined a refugee as any person who is outside his or her own country, unable or unwilling to return to that country, and unable or unwilling to avail of the protection of that country out of fear of persecution due to race, religion, nationality, or political opinion. These changes were a response to criticism that, until that point, the United States had aided only refugees who were anti-Communist allies; refugee policy, critics argued, should not be driven by Cold War geopolitics but by international laws and norms.[18] But while the Refugee Act of 1980 introduced several landmark changes, it also maintained much of the previously existing system. Most notably, it continued a system in which the federal government relied heavily on voluntary agencies to implement its resettlement programs.[19]

While lawmakers agreed to adjust refugee policy in response to the ongoing refugee crisis, the broader American public was polarized on the matter of whether the United States should welcome refugees in the first place. Reasons for supporting refugee admissions varied, but arguments in favor of Southeast Asian refugee resettlement emphasized a few central themes. First, there was the idea that the United States is a "nation of immigrants." Many Americans rooted their support for Southeast Asian refugees in the notion that the United States has special status in history as a refuge for persecuted and downtrodden immigrants. This exceptionalist narrative obscures the fact that throughout history, many people became American through enslavement and colonial conquest. Nonetheless, the enduring mythology that the United States is an immigrant nation powerfully shaped Americans' self-imagination and, in turn, their openness to refugees. One 1975 survey found that the leading reason why Americans supported the admission of Southeast Asian refugees was the "tradition [of the United States] as a sanctuary for Europeans fleeing oppression of their homelands." The same poll found that a plurality of respondents agreed with the statement that the United States "began with people of all races, creeds and nationalities coming here to escape religious or political persecution, so we ought to let the refugees from Vietnam in."[20]

The context of the Cold War caused Americans to feel a special obligation to aid people who faced retribution and persecution at the hands of Communists. Here, too, an American exceptionalist narrative shaped public opinion. The idea that the United States was a bulwark against evil and oppression motivated many Americans to open their doors to Southeast Asians fleeing Communist regimes.

A 1986 poll found that a majority of respondents agreed that the United States should accept political refugees who were specifically fleeing Communist-controlled countries.[21] Indeed, by the end of the Vietnam War, rewarding the loyalty of Cold War allies was a well-established principle in American refugee policy. From the anti-Soviet Hungarian refugees in the 1950s to the Cuban asylum-seekers in the 1960s, the United States had welcomed "freedom fighters" who had taken a stand in the global war against Communism. Admitting these anti-Communist refugees was not merely an expression of American benevolence, but rather an act of "calculated kindness" that was politically advantageous, both domestically and internationally. Similarly, Americans felt a special responsibility to assist the Vietnamese, Lao, and Hmong people who faced Communist regimes in their own country.[22]

The fact that Southeast Asian refugees were fleeing a region where the United States had been directly involved in years of brutal warfare also heightened many Americans' sense of responsibility. Americans were particularly committed to admitting Southeast Asian refugees who had worked closely with the US military, and individuals in the military or diplomatic corps insisted that the United States should not abandon their Southeast Asian allies. Some officials even threatened to resign from the Foreign Service in protest if the United States deserted their Asian colleagues.[23] Other refugee advocates argued that Americans must aid and admit Southeast Asian refugees because their suffering was the consequence of US military action. Speaking before the Senate Foreign Relations Committee shortly after the fall of Saigon, David Stickney of the American Friends Service Committee appealed to Americans to acknowledge their role in producing the refugee crisis in Southeast Asia. In his view, it was the moral duty of the United States to show a generous response.

> Our war actions and our military support to the wars in Indochina are directly responsible for enormous amounts of human, social and environmental damage in Indochina, amounting to the proportions of a great human catastrophe. There have been calls from high United States levels to put the Vietnam war behind us. Can we in good conscience put out of sight and out of mind the enormous damage we caused or helped to cause? Can we put out of sight and mind the declarations of two Presidents that we must help to repair the terrible

damage to Vietnam and the Vietnamese? We believe that Americans cannot in good conscience do that.[24]

Just as powerful as American guilt was the idea of American goodness and the idea that the United States must be a world leader in supporting human rights. In the 1970s commitments to human rights provided a new framework for responding to refugees. President Ford made the well-established argument that Southeast Asian refugees should be admitted because they were America's anti-Communist allies, much like Hungarian and Cuban refugees. In contrast, liberal pro-refugee advocates like Senator Ted Kennedy argued that Southeast Asian refugees deserved American help because the nation had the responsibility to address human suffering, not just reward Cold War loyalties. With Southeast Asian refugees, as with Soviet and Chilean refugees during the same period, the 1970s witnessed what the historian Carl Bon Tempo described as "the human rights revolution in refugee affairs."[25]

The notion that the United States was the benevolent leader of the free world also drew on religious ideas. As one Senate resolution put it in 1975, "the Good Samaritan lives on in the minds and hearts of the American people and is a part of their character."[26] The inclusion of this language reflects not only that religious rhetoric and beliefs animated pro-refugee sentiment but also that religious groups were prominent voices in the campaign to support refugees. Global religious leaders like the pope, for example, urged government officials around the world to open their doors to refugees and offer "increased aid and compassion."[27] In the United States, national religious leaders like Hesburgh and Mandelbaum lobbied for more generous humanitarian aid to care for refugees overseas and called for government to increase the number of Southeast Asian refugees paroled into the United States for resettlement. Just as important were efforts at the local level, where congregations urged communities to support resettlement projects and welcome Southeast Asian newcomers.

Finally, refugee advocates argued that Americans should admit refugees not only because Americans are good but also because refugees are good for America. As the 1975 Senate resolution declared, "This period influx of refugees and exiles can serve to keep us humble, saving us from the sins of arrogance, pride and self-righteousness."[28] Supporters of refugee resettlement emphasized that refugees reinvigorated American democracy and reminded the nation of its own best ideals. For example, Hakon Torjesen, an aid worker in Ban Vinai refugee camp, believed that Southeast Asian refugees helped twentieth-century Americans reconnect with the aspirations and values that are foundational to the American project. "Here by harsh rules of succession, are sons and daughters of the American Revolution," he wrote. "Here, as unlikely-looking as all their predecessors, are more 'giants of the earth.' Here, in its traditional wrapping, is the gift."[29]

Not all Americans saw refugees as a "gift," however. Despite the lofty ideals and passionate advocacy of refugee supporters, the majority of Americans consistently opposed the resettlement of Southeast Asian refugees. This sentiment was by no means a new development in American culture; public opinion polls indicate that Americans have usually been reluctant to admit refugees and were sometimes even hostile toward them. For example, in the wake of Kristallnacht in late 1938, a Gallup poll found that only 21 percent of Americans surveyed believed the United States should welcome a larger number of Jewish exiles fleeing Nazi Germany; 72 percent said it should not.[30] Public opinion polls after the Vietnam War showed similarly low support for resettling Southeast Asian refugees. One national Gallup poll conducted in May 1975, just one month after the fall of Saigon, found that only 36 percent of Americans surveyed favored the resettlement of Southeast Asian refugees; 54 percent of Americans surveyed opposed it.[31] Although attitudes toward Southeast Asian refugees warmed somewhat over time, American reluctance to admit Southeast Asian refugees remained consistent throughout the 1970s and 1980s. Even a full decade after the end of the Vietnam War, a plurality of Americans believed that the United States had accepted too many refugees.[32]

Although opposition to admitting refugees was fairly consistent throughout the twentieth century, public attitudes about Southeast Asian refugees must be put into the specific context of the 1970s. First, the Southeast Asian refugee crisis occurred at a moment when economic, political, and social forces converged to make Americans particularly wary of refugees. The 1970s found the United States mired in a swamp of economic troubles, including inflation, high levels of unemployment, rising energy costs, increased foreign competition, disruptions in the industrial sector, recession, and sluggish growth. At the same time, Americans debated the cost of government spending on social programs, a matter that drew on a long history of racialized discourse about poverty and deservedness. Popular media disseminated sensational stories about "welfare queens"—a term frequently associated with Black women—who were accused of being overly dependent on public aid, abusing the welfare system, and robbing the government and the American people. During the same period, Black, Latino, Native, and Asian American activists continued their long-standing push for political, social, and economic justice, and their efforts were met with fierce and sometimes violent pushback—for example, in response to battles over busing and de-segregating public schools. Southeast Asian refugees thus entered into a complex political landscape in which white supremacy pro-foundly shaped public opinion about aiding refugees, a matter that was part of the broader debate about allocating public resources to support people in need. Finally, the context of the Cold War contrib-uted to public hostility toward refugees. Many Americans saw South-east Asian refugees as indebted to the United States because Americans had rescued them and given them "the gift of freedom."[33] While the idea of American benevolence encouraged some Americans to wel-come refugees, this narrative simultaneously fostered resentment against refugees by lending support to the view of the United States as an overburdened benefactor giving generously to an ungrateful and undeserving world.

The views of residents in Niceville, Florida, reveal the scope and intensity of anti-refugee sentiment. Niceville is located near Eglin Air Force Base, which was the site of one of the four military-run camps that housed newly arrived Vietnamese refugees. Despite the proximity to refugees—or perhaps because of it—the people of Niceville revealed the limits of American niceness. When the local radio station polled area residents about the 1,500 Vietnamese being airlifted from Saigon, 80 percent of the people said that they did not want the military to bring refugees to their town. At one point, resi-dents circulated a petition demanding that refugees be sent to a different place, and schoolchildren made jokes about shooting refu-gees. "Far's I'm concerned, they can ship them all right back," one woman told the New York Times. This woman's support of sending refugees back to Vietnam reflected broader national sentiment. In one national poll in spring 1975, 85 percent of surveyed Americans believed that the United States was too panicked when Saigon fell and that the government should arrange to send refugees back to Vietnam if they want to go.[34]

In Valparaiso, a town close to Niceville, anxiety about refugees reflected a broader anxiety about the nation's stagnating economy and weakening social safety net. "We got enough of our own problems to take care of," said Grady Tomberlin, a local barber. A barbershop customer declared, "They don't even have enough money to take care of Social Security now—and they want to bring in more people." Tomberlin agreed that refugees would burden a nation that was already stretched thin. "I don't see why I ought to work and pay taxes for those folks who wouldn't work over there," said Tomberlin. "They ought to have stayed on over there."[35]

The economic concerns expressed in Tomberlin's barbershop were the most common reason Americans gave for opposing Southeast Asian refugee resettlement. Many Americans believed that refugees would impose an economic burden on the United States. A survey in May 1975 found that 62 percent of surveyed Americans believed that immigrants take jobs away from Americans; only 28 percent believed otherwise.[36] In another poll, a plurality of respondents agreed with the statement that "refugee immigrants to the United States take more from the US economy through social services and unemployment than they contribute to the US economy through taxes and productivity."[37]

Geography also shaped public opinion on the feared economic burden brought by Southeast Asian refugees. Especially in states and cities where large numbers of refugees resettled, Americans worried about refugees living in communities where resources were already stretched thin. For example, Jerry Brown, governor of California, worried that Southeast Asian refugees would take the jobs of Californians, one million of whom were already unemployed, and urged Congress to change refugee legislation so that it offered "jobs for Americans first." That Governor Brown voiced particularly strong opposition to refugees was part of a larger pattern confirmed by a May 1975 poll, which found that opposition to refugees was strongest in regions of the country where unemployment and economic anxiety were high.[38]

Americans were opposed to resettling Vietnamese refugees for reasons beyond economic matters. With the United States still mired in the Cold War, people expressed concern about security against Communists slipping in among the refugees. Robert Carr, a realtor in Valparaiso, Florida, feared that Vietnamese refugees would bring Communist influence. "How do you know we're not getting the bad guys?" Carr asked. "You can't say for sure. Nobody can, and Lord knows we got enough Communist infiltration now."[39] He was not the only one to raise this issue. After years of war in Asia, many Americans were uneasy about resettling people who not only looked like the enemy but were feared to actually be the enemy. Some members of Congress expressed concern that security screenings did not vet refugees adequately and that Communist subversives lurked among the refugees accepted for resettlement.[40]

Americans opposed to refugee resettlement also argued that Southeast Asian refugees were culturally unassimilable and a danger to American well-being. In multiple ways, anti-refugee discourse harked back to the anti-Asian fears of the "Yellow Peril" that animated the era of Asian Exclusion. For example, the president of the Commission Council of Plaquemines Parish, outside New Orleans, declared, "What we have here is a group of people who have been dumped in our area who are totally unaccustomed to our ways, our manner of living, our mores and our laws."[41] His views were widely shared. In one public opinion poll in 1977, a majority of respondents agreed with the statement that "many Indochinese refugees just can't adapt to living in this country, and after they come here will want to go back to Southeast Asia to live, so it is wrong to let them in."[42]

In addition to expressing concerns about refugees' cultural adaptability, opponents of refugee resettlement portrayed Southeast Asian people as vice- and germ-ridden people who threatened public health and safety. "There's no telling what kind of diseases they'll be bringing with them," said Vincent Davis of Niceville. When asked by the reporter to identify which diseases the Vietnamese refugees carried, Davis replied, "I don't know," and then added, "but there's bound to be some of those tropical germs floating around."[43] One worried woman described Vietnamese refugees as "people that have got the dough and have been selling heroin for the last 10 years" and "people that shove women and children off planes."[44]

Hostility to Southeast Asian refugees sometimes boiled down to simple overt racism. At Fort Walton Beach High School, near Niceville, students discussed plans to establish a "gook klux klan." Anti-Asian racism was manifest in subtler ways, too—for example, in the relative reluctance to support resettlement efforts. Rev. Fredrik Schiotz, president emeritus of the American Lutheran Church, for example, observed that enthusiasm for refugee work was not as high among some congregations as they had expected. "Perhaps the fact that they are Orientals instead of Europeans has made for some resistance," he noted.[45] Given the fierce white opposition to school desegregation plans, the vitriolic racism faced by Southeast Asian refugees is perhaps not surprising. Refugee resettlement, after all, was in many ways a form of government-mandated integration.

Finally, lingering resentment due to the war in Vietnam caused some Americans to be wary of refugees. Clare Boothe Luce, who had commended the work of the International Rescue Committee (IRC) in a television broadcast and received numerous angry letters in response, reflected on anti-refugee hostility in an article for the *New York Times*. In her view, the opposition to Southeast Asian refugee resettlement was "rooted in a suppressed sense of guilt, shame and frustration over the Communist victory in the Vietnam war."[46] Luce's point about American responsibility for the plight of refugees may have some truth. One 1977 poll found that a plurality of Americans agreed with the statement that "this country was built on the humane principle of being a place where oppressed people could come to live, and Indochinese refugees should not be an exception." However, the same respondents expressed far less enthusiasm for admitting refugees when they were asked to consider the issue in light of American failure in the war on Vietnam. Only 17 percent agreed with the statement that "the US was at least partly responsible for non-Communist people wanting to leave their home countries, so we should let all 100,000 of these refugees come to this country to live"; in contrast, 71 percent disagreed.[47]

As a result of all these forces, Americans were not merely unenthusiastic about Southeast Asian refugees—they were sometimes outright hostile to them. Southeast Asian refugees recounted numerous instances when they were targeted in acts of harassment, discrimination, vandalism, and violence. One employee of a local resettlement agency in Saint Paul recalled how a Hmong family was "harassed weekly" by a neighboring white couple, whose acts of intimidation warranted several reports to the police: throwing bottles at the family, kicking and throwing eggs at the family's car, running over the family's garbage can, and shattering the glass on the family's back door. Many other incidents went unreported, including when the white couple stuffed underwear into the Hmong family's mailbox, yelled insults at them, and threatened them while appearing to hold a gun. "I am particularly concerned since the previous occupants of this house (also Hmong) experienced the same harassment eventually resulting in their evacuation," the caseworker wrote. "The neighbors have clearly established a very repulsive pattern."[48] News reports suggest that this "repulsive pattern" of hatred and violence against Southeast Asian refugees erupted elsewhere in the county. In Montana, vandals destroyed the community garden tended by Hmong refugees.[49] In Indiana, a union booted Southeast Asian refugees from its membership, reportedly for working too hard.[50] And along the Gulf Coast, the Ku Klux Klan harassed Vietnamese fishermen and the white people who sympathized with them.[51] Hmong refugees experienced so much violence and harassment in Philadelphia that hundreds of Hmong families left the city en masse.[52] In 1986 the US Civil Rights Commission included some of these incidents in its report, which confirmed that racist acts of discrimination, intimidation, and violence against Asian Americans, including Southeast Asian refugees, was a national problem.[53]

Even when Southeast Asian refugees were doing the very things demanded of them—learning new skills, applying for jobs, and striving for economic self-sufficiency—they were the target of hate. The opposition to Hmong refugees in Minnesota flared in 1983 when Church World Service (CWS) developed a plan to relocate around a dozen Hmong families to a farm near Winona, Minnesota.[54] Local residents expressed strong opposition to the proposal in a series of public events, where they shared several reasons why they wanted to keep Hmong refugees out of their town. Richard Frickson feared Hmong refugees as potential criminals. "Who's going to handle a rape case or a murder case up there?" he told the *St. Paul Dispatch*.[55] Meanwhile, the local leaders of the Anti-Christ Information Center of the International Christian Ministries accused a supporter of the Hmong farm of being a Communist agent and believed that the refugee program was an attempt by Communists "to use them

(Hmong) to gain power and control in our country, and specifically in our area."[56] Sometimes opponents of the farm project gave no specific reason at all—only that they did not like Hmong people. As Richard Roraff, a Winona farmer, explained to the *St. Paul Dispatch,* "The question is not whether we want them; the question is just very simple—we don't want them. And if that's going to get me to the gates of hell, I'll go, because I'm going to be with a lot of nice, good people."[57]

"The Government Alone Cannot Do the Total Job"

Such widespread animosity toward Southeast Asian refugees made clear to government officials that they faced a daunting task in undertaking a resettlement effort that the majority of Americans did not support. Eager to prevent public backlash, they centered their plans on a primary goal: to minimize any negative effects that Southeast Asian refugees might have on the communities where they were resettled. This vision for resettlement focused on reducing three types of impact: economic, cultural, and geographic. As Representative Hamilton Fish put it in congressional hearings in May 1975, they wanted to ensure that Southeast Asian refugees "would not be very noticeable."[58]

Minimizing refugees' economic impact was resettlement planners' highest priority. As L. Dean Brown of the Interagency Task Force on Indochina Refugees stated in a hearing before the Senate Foreign Relations Committee, "The aim is to integrate these people into the fabric of American society, without displacing American workers, in such a manner that the refugees quickly become self-supporting and productive tax paying citizens of this country."[59] Government reports and congressional debates scrutinized all aspects of refugees' economic lives and drew on detailed data about refugees' employment levels, vocational training, and use of public assistance. Officials acknowledged that Southeast Asian refugees were eager to work and sometimes were quite educated; as one military spokesperson put it, they were not mere "rice paddy types."[60] Nonetheless, the fact that one-third of Southeast Asian refugees used public assistance worried resettlement officials.[61] On this matter, there was some disagreement about how to view refugees' use of public assistance. Wells Klein of the American Council for Nationalities Service (ACNS), one of the leading voluntary agencies, viewed public assistance pragmatically and argued that while "the use of public assistance tends to be viewed as an index of failure," it was also "an essential ingredient of the total program."[62] However, the use of any amount of public assistance was enough to worry government officials preoccupied with the problem of welfare dependency.

Secondary to facilitating the economic integration of refugees was the goal of cultural assimilation. Resettlement planners acknowledged that Southeast Asian refugees hailed from very different cultural, racial, and religious backgrounds than previous refugees, who had come primarily from Europe. They openly discussed how this new group of refugees might struggle to adapt to American culture. In her testimony before the Senate in 1975, Julia Taft, director of the Interagency Task Force on Indochina Refugees, emphasized that Southeast Asian refugee resettlement was unprecedented in its cultural challenges. "This has truly been an historic undertaking," she declared. "Never before in the history of this country, Mr. Chairman, have so many people from such different cultures, ethnic and religious backgrounds been introduced into American society in such a short time." After noting the resettlement successes achieved by the government and its private partners, she recognized that given the scope of the challenges, "the full assimilation of the refugees into American life will be a long journey."[63]

Government officials drew on lessons from the past to emphasize the importance of promoting refugees' assimilation into American culture. Senator S. I. Hayakawa—who represented the state of California, home to the largest population of Southeast Asian refugees—spoke of his concern about "the ultimate assimilation of Indochinese" and "their being interwoven not just in the fabric of California life, but in the fabric of the Nation as a whole." Hayakawa praised the relocation of Japanese Americans after their incarceration during World War II and suggested that it might offer a model for resettling Southeast Asian refugees. According to Hayakawa, when the War Relocation Authority orchestrated their migration to cities throughout the United States, Japanese Americans found that "their assimilation into the overall American life was shortened perhaps by a generation."[64]

Hayakawa's support for the organized relocation of people to scattered sites throughout the country points to the third type of impact that government officials hoped to minimize: geographic impact. In order to equalize the "burden" that refugees imposed on cities and states, resettlement planners endeavored to scatter refugees throughout the country. During a Senate hearing about Southeast Asian refugees in 1975, L. Dean Brown acknowledged "the fear that large numbers of people were going to be dumped on one community or another without any planning." His solution was to have a clear policy that "the new arrivals should be dispersed as evenly and as equitably as possible through the United States, avoiding, in particular, resettlement in economically hard-pressed areas."[65] At the same hearing, Julia Taft assured senators that all efforts were being made "to insure a wide distribution of the refugees throughout the United States."[66]

This scatter policy represented both a continuation of and a departure from previous policy. Other Western nations have embraced dispersal plans in their resettlement programs.[67] In the United States, the federal government made an effort to disperse Cuban asylees in the 1960s. Initially, most Cuban asylees arrived and stayed in Florida. Concerned about the local burden that ethnic enclaves posed on communities like Miami, the government offered incentives for Cuban asylees to move to other locations.[68] Southeast Asian refugee resettlement, however, was different in that it involved a more concerted effort to disperse refugees. Unlike Cuban asylees, Hmong, Lao, Vietnamese, and Cambodian people secured refugee status while still outside US borders. The federal government thus had more control over the entire course of their refugee migration because it directed it from the refugee camps until their resettlement and placement with American sponsors.

In dealing with Southeast Asian refugees, refugee resettlement officials pursued the scatter policy for a variety of economic, cultural, and political reasons. For one, because they aimed to promote participation in the workforce, they believed that it would be more advantageous to relocate refugees to communities where there were ample opportunities for employment. They also hoped to facilitate cultural assimilation and to prevent the formation of ethnic enclaves. As L. Dean Brown argued, government policies that deliberately suppressed the formation of "new ethnic communities" would help refugees assimilate more quickly and minimize the burden that refugees would impose on communities that already had significant immigrant populations.[69] Knowing that some cities and states were more heavily impacted by refugee arrivals than others, resettlement officials believed that dispersal would allow states to share the responsibility of resettlement evenly and fairly and decrease the possibility of local backlash against refugee populations. Finally, the government depended on volunteer sponsors to help carry the financial responsibilities of resettlement and to undertake much of the day-to-day labor of assisting refugees. By the middle of the 1980s, Southeast Asian refugees already resettled in the United States were able to serve as sponsors for their relatives. In the 1970s and early 1980s, however, the federal government relied heavily on volunteer sponsors, often congregations, that were located throughout the country.[70]

Ultimately, refugee resettlement officials considered dispersal to be the best way to meet the needs of both refugees and the communities where they would be resettled. To be sure, some resettlement experts at the time warned of the potential problems of splitting up families and communities.[71] But many voluntary agencies and government officials emphasized the benefits of dispersal. John McCarthy, representing the United States Catholic Conference (USCC), explained his plan for dispersing Southeast Asian refugees in a congressional hearing in May 1975: "We are going to work our darnedest that these communities are scattered throughout the land—not to isolate these people, but in turn not to affect our economy, our socioeconomic development, the community life, or anything else," he said. "These are a beautiful people. We hope to settle them in a beautiful way." "Very nicely expressed," responded Senator Ted Kennedy.[72]

Significantly, it was McCarthy, a private citizen representing the Catholic Church, who assured senators that Southeast Asian refugee resettlement would be a "beautiful" process—not the other way around. The exchange between McCarthy and Kennedy reveals another important aspect of the American system of refugee resettlement: that it was a joint enterprise between public and private, and especially church and state. Put simply, providing humanitarian relief and resettlement services for one million refugees traumatized by war was an undertaking deemed too big, too expensive, and too complex for the government to do on its own. According to William Guttieri, executive director of USCC-affiliated Catholic Charities in Stockton, California, resettlement introduced problems that were "beyond the ability of our government to solve.[73] Facing an overwhelming task of unprecedented magnitude, government thus joined forces with private voluntary agencies—in particular, religious voluntary agencies—to implement its refugee policies at the national, state, and local levels. As the leaders of the Interagency Task Force explained it, voluntary agencies were the "keystone of the refugee resettlement program," the institutions that did "the main tasks" of resettling the refugees.[74]

The groundwork for this cooperative arrangement was laid well before the Vietnam War. Since at least the nineteenth century, the federal government borrowed capacity through partnerships with private religious organizations in aid projects both at home and abroad.[75] In particular, federal American Indian policy was a sphere that saw significant church-state collaboration. During the nineteenth and early twentieth centuries, the federal government provided funding for churches and missionaries to undertake projects aimed at assimilating Native Americans.[76] Later in the twentieth century, church-state cooperation in both domestic and international programs continued to increase, especially during the Cold War.[77]

These developments set the stage for the nation's public-private resettlement system, which became gradually more complex throughout the twentieth century. Voluntary agencies first worked with the federal government to provide aid to refugees overseas in the 1930s, and during World War II the War Relief Control Board united the efforts of the voluntary agencies and the federal government to assist war victims abroad. But a particularly crucial event occurred in 1945, when President Harry Truman signed an executive order that allowed refugees admitted to the United States to be sponsored not only by individuals but also by humanitarian organizations. This new rule helped to solidify the role of the private voluntary agencies, and public-private collaboration expanded over the course of the coming decades as Cold War conflicts uprooted more people around the world and brought more refugees to the United States. For example, when 202,000 European refugees arrived under the Displaced Persons Act of 1948, the federal government covered the cost of transatlantic transportation and the voluntary agencies cared for refugees upon their arrival. When 35,000 Hungarian refugees arrived after the Hungarian uprising in 1956, the federal government began to give payments—about $40 per refugee—directly to the voluntary agencies to cover the cost of resettlement. And when 100,000 Cubans arrived in 1959 and 1960, the federal government's commitment to refugee resettlement increased substantially. The Department of Health, Education, and Welfare established the Cuban Refugee Program, and Congress passed the Migration and Refugee Assistance Act of 1962, which appropriated funds to assist Cuban refugees. But while the federal government spent $260 million on refugee assistance between 1961 and 1967, the government's refugee program still operated through the voluntary agencies, as well as the states.[78]

When the Southeast Asian refugee crisis erupted, it is not surprising, then, that the federal government and the voluntary agencies collaborated from the very beginning. In 1981 David North, Lawrence Lewin, and Jennifer Wagner prepared a report for the Bureau of Refugee Programs and identified the following rationale for the government's collaboration with the voluntary agencies:

1. The volags [voluntary agencies] are *there* and likely to stay, providing capacities and continuity lacking in public agencies.
2. They are more flexible in size and in function than units of government.
3. They bring private resources to bear, as governmental agencies cannot.
4. They attract, and keep, dedicated staff people.
5. They avoid a potential bias towards welfare, which might be found in the human resources agencies.
6. They are knowledgeable about, and sensitive to, ethnic differences and the special problems of refugees.[79]

Having directly served refugees for decades, voluntary agencies had developed a specialized knowledge of refugee and immigrant affairs, which the government lacked. For this reason, representatives from the agencies often appeared before Congress to offer information and guidance. Voluntary agencies were valued not only for their expertise but also for their direct knowledge of activities on the ground and their representation of diverse American constituencies.[80]

For all these reasons, expanding capacity through partnerships with voluntary agencies appealed to government officials, especially in a project as ambitious as Southeast Asian refugee resettlement. As Stanley Breen of the American Refugee Committee observed, "It is our contention that the government alone cannot do the total job, and the private sector including the voluntary agencies, the churches, and the business community will really get the job done with the proper support of government services that are needed."[81] In such a cooperative effort, the boundary between government voluntary agencies was blurry. One participant at a refugee resettlement planning meeting in San Francisco put it most succinctly: in resettlement, "private is public."[82]

In this system, the voluntary agencies received funds from the State Department to provide a range of resettlement services. Overseas, they helped refugees apply for resettlement and arranged for travel. In the United States, they received a per capita government grant, which ranged from $300 to $500, to provide housing, groceries, dishes, beds, pillows, blankets, warm clothing, and pocket money for new arrivals. In addition, they enrolled children in schools and adults in language and job training; assisted refugees in locating employment; and identified sponsors, often families or churches, that could assume these responsibilities after forty-five days, the initial period of resettlement and the window of time for which voluntary agencies were responsible for the newly resettled. These agencies also received grants from the newly formed Office of Refugee Resettlement, under the Department of Health and Human Services, to provide long-term programs such as English as a Second Language (ESL) classes, job training, and mental health programs.[83]

The agencies that contributed most to Southeast Asian refugee resettlement in the United States were not only private but also religious. The following figure shows the distribution of refugee cases and illuminates the significance of religious involvement. The agencies that held contracts with the federal government to resettle refugees represented diverse communities, and nonreligious agencies such as the IRC and the ACNS were actively involved. However, religious organizations resettled the lion's share of Southeast Asian refugees. The religious voluntary agencies varied in theological orientation and operational structure, but their collective contributions were so significant that members of Congress made a point of in-

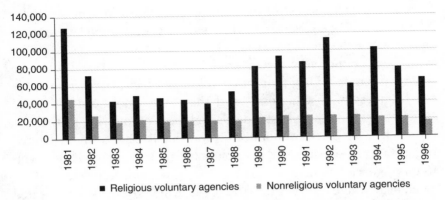

Annual refugee caseloads of religious and nonreligious voluntary agencies,
FY 1981–1996. *Data source:* Office of Refugee Resettlement.

quiring specifically about the support of faith communities. For example, in the first month after the fall of Saigon, Representative
Hamilton Fish asked L. Dean Brown about "the cooperation of the
affiliated churches" in refugee resettlement efforts. "Every church
group in the United States is with us," assured Brown.[84]

While the federal government found it financially and institutionally practical to rely on private agencies, resettlement planners
saw the involvement of religious agencies as bringing special advantages. Indeed, some voluntary agency leaders urged Congress
to see the religiousness of voluntary agencies as a distinctive asset.
As Rev. John Schauer, representing CWS, testified before Congress,
"The churches and Christians provide distinct and unique services to refugees that no organization not dedicated to religious
ideals and to the teachings of Jesus Christ, who suffered also, could
provide."[85]

These voluntary agencies, with their role in refugee resettlement for-
malized by law and supported by millions of dollars in federal funds,
functioned as an extension of the state but at the same time enjoyed a
considerable degree of autonomy. As Naomi and Norman Zucker argued, voluntary agencies were "integral to the formulation and execu-
tion of refugee policy in general."[86] And the federal government, intent
on ensuring the most efficient use of public funds, wanted to ensure
that local resettlement operations were effective and economical. However, voluntary agencies and their local affiliates generally had a lot of

freedom, in part because of the relative lack of government oversight. The authors of one government report on voluntary agencies observed that "the State Dept treats volags like small, friendly nations—treaties with them are not very specific, monitoring is limited, and there are few reprimands." They found that voluntary agencies received "only the broadest of instructions" and that "the whole process could benefit from more precise standards and more monitoring by the government."[87] The lack of monitoring was due in part to the federated organizational structures of the voluntary agencies.[88] In addition, voluntary agencies sometimes did not have any paid, full-time staff located near where refugees were resettled, which sometimes frustrated local government officials.[89] The administrative arrangements of resettlement, characterized by a complex bureaucracy and a dizzying chain of delegated responsibilities, presented opportunities for individuals involved in local operations to pursue their own objectives, which did not always coincide with the objectives and interests of other participants in the resettlement system.[90]

As was the case with international refugee relief and with national-level resettlement efforts, refugee assistance at the state and local levels was also an effort undertaken jointly by government and private voluntary agencies (see the table on the following page). Resettlement operations in Minnesota offer a useful illustration of how these institutions worked together. After Southeast Asian refugees began to arrive in 1975, Governor Wendell Anderson noted the absence of "common planning, information sharing, and problem solving among the involved parties."[91] To improve coordination among public and private agencies, he created the Governor's Indochinese Resettlement Task Force and the Governor's Indochinese Resettlement Office, which administered the Minnesota Indochinese Refugee Assistance Program. This collaborative approach continued after 1977, when the assistance program was transferred to the Minnesota Department of Public Welfare and renamed, first as the Indochinese Refugee Resettlement Office and then as the Minnesota Refugee Program Office, which was overseen by the Indochinese Advisory Council and the Minnesota State Refugee Advisory Council.[92] The Minnesota Refugee Program Office described its approach as "a consortium" that unites state and voluntary agencies in the provision of services. In this system, representatives from the voluntary agencies convened monthly with the state refugee coordinator to share information and resources and promote an orderly, efficient, and responsive resettlement process.[93] One of the decisions they made to maximize their impact was to assign each agency one area of refugee services in which to specialize. The International Institute of Minnesota (IIM) focused on English-language instruction, Catholic Charities focused on employment counseling and job training, and Lutheran Social Service focused on health and social adjustment services.[94] Such a plan streamlined the refugee assistance system and also improved the quality of their services. As Tom Kosel, who worked

National Voluntary Agencies with Local Affiliates and Religious Affiliations

Voluntary Agency	Religious Affiliation
American Council for Nationalities Service (ACNS) *Local MN affiliate of ACNS: International Institute of Minnesota*	Nonreligious
American Fund for Czechoslovak Refugees (AFCR)	Nonreligious
Buddhist Council for Refugee Rescue and Resettlement (BCRRR)	Religious—Buddhist
Church World Service (CWS)	Religious—Mainline Protestant, associated with the National Council of Churches
Hebrew Immigrant Aid Society (HIAS)	Religious—Jewish
International Rescue Committee (IRC)	Nonreligious
Idaho State Voluntary Agency (ISVA)	Nonreligious
Iowa Refugee Service Center (IRSC)	Nonreligious
Lutheran Immigration and Refugee Service (LIRS) *Local MN affiliate of LIRS: Lutheran Social Service*	Religious—Lutheran, associated with the Lutheran Council in the USA
Polish American Immigration and Refugee Committee (PAIRC)	Nonreligious
Rav Tov Committee to Aid New Immigrants (RAVTOV)	Religious—Jewish
Tolstoy Foundation (TF)	Nonreligious
United States Catholic Conference (USCC) *Local MN affiliate of USCC: Catholic Charities*	Religious—Catholic
World Relief (WR)	Religious—Evangelical Protestant, associated with the National Association of Evangelicals
Young Men Christian's Association	Religious—Christian

Source: Office of Refugee Resettlement.

with Catholic Charities, recalled, "There was just too much to be done, and you needed to start specializing."[95]

Reflecting the general pattern nationwide, the most active voluntary agencies in Minnesota were religious agencies. In 1976 only five voluntary agencies were involved in resettling the 4,300 Southeast Asian refugees in Minnesota: Catholic Charities, the local affiliate of the USCC; Lutheran Social Services, the local affiliate of the Lutheran Immigration and Refugee Service (LIRS); the IIM, the local affiliate of the ACNS; CWS, the humanitarian organization of the National Council of Churches; and the Christian and Missionary Alliance (CMA), an evangelical Protestant denomination that had sent missionaries to Laos in the middle of the twentieth century.[96] Two years later, World Relief, an agency affiliated with the National Association of Evangelicals, also began to resettle refugees in Minnesota. All of these agencies, with the exception of the IIM, were associated with Christian denominations or organizations. In general, other voluntary agencies that were active elsewhere in the United States—the Hebrew Immigrant Aid Society, the Tolstoy Foundation, and the IRC—maintained a relatively small presence in Minnesota during this period.

At the state and local level, religious organizations initiated a variety of community programs to assist refugees in their immediate and long-term adjustment to American life. These efforts were diverse in origin: some were public-private initiatives supported by government and voluntary agencies while others emerged from local churches. These programs often addressed the needs of different groups: children, elders, farmers, and seamstresses. What united all of these efforts, however, is the fact that they provided valuable services and support to refugees and filled the gap in social service provision at a time when local resources for refugee resettlement were often stretched thin.

One of the most important ways that religious groups supported refugees at the local level was through English instruction. One Catholic nun, Sister Rosemary Schuneman, started the Notre Dame ESL school, where she taught language skills as well as survival and job search skills.[97] Saint Mary's Catholic Church, which was home to the Southeast Asian Catholic community, also had an English language program.[98] And Christ Lutheran Church, in collaboration with the Southeast Asian Ministry and the Saint Paul Literacy Project, ran the Capitol Hill Refugee Project, which offered morning and evening English classes, along with childcare; its classes were filled to capacity.[99] These language programs became important when secondary migration to Minnesota swelled the Twin Cities Hmong population and budgetary constraints brought cuts to refugee programs. Especially when waitlists for English schools were long, the volunteer tutoring programs hosted by local churches served as a valuable resource for Hmong refugees who could not find a place to learn English elsewhere.[100]

Religious organizations also started a variety of innovative programs to help refugees find employment. A Dominican sister offered sewing classes for Hmong women seeking to develop job skills and to prepare themselves for the Minnesota winter.[101] Recognizing that Hmong people had a rich tradition of embroidery and needlework, the Southeast Asian Ministry helped create opportunities for Hmong women to market and sell their handicrafts.[102] Finally, religious groups supported community garden and agriculture programs designed to help refugees feed their families affordably. Some of the most ambitious projects, such as the Hiawatha Valley Farm Project initiated by CWS, aimed to help refugees turn their farming background into profitable careers in agriculture.[103]

Finally, recognizing that many Southeast Asian refugees suffered from poverty, religious groups ran charities that provided material goods and financial support. For example, Lutheran congregations supported and staffed the Southeast Asian Ministry's "Donation Room," which offered household goods and furniture to refugee families, and Catholic parishes continued to provide clothes, emergency housing, and other services to refugees.[104]

Though not obviously the most fruitful material for Hollywood humor, mention of this public-private, church-state approach to refugee resettlement found its way into the 2008 film *Gran Torino*. In one scene, Clint Eastwood, playing the cantankerous Walt Kowalski, interrogates a Hmong teenager, Sue, as he drives her to her home in Highland Park, Michigan. "I don't know how you ended up in the Midwest, with snow on the ground six months out of the year," he grumbles. After Sue corrects him for calling the Hmong "jungle people" ("Hill people!" she says), she decides his question deserves an answer after all. "Blame the Lutherans," she says. "They brought us over here."[105]

Hmong students at the Lao Family Community Center at the Young Men's Christian Association in Saint Paul. Photo by Michael Krieger. Courtesy of Minnesota Historical Society.

Father Hesburgh, Rabbi Mandelbaum, and Rev. Haines—the religious leaders who visited the White House to appeal to President Carter to increase aid for refugees—were not Lutheran, but they would have likely welcomed this blame. They and many other religious people concerned about the humanitarian crisis in Southeast Asia were eager to continue the long-standing tradition of church-state cooperation in refugee relief and resettlement because, in their view, it meant saving lives. Since the middle of the twentieth century, big international humanitarian crises have compelled national, state, and local governments to call for help and expand capacity by relying on nongovernment partners, especially religious organizations, to aid refugees at home and abroad. In the 1970s, when the United

States undertook the task of resettling one million Southeast Asian people displaced and traumatized by war, the government once again turned to private organizations, especially religious organizations, to handle a job that was deemed too big for the government to do alone.

Americans across the political, denominational, and theological spectrum have embraced this public-private, church-state resettlement system with relatively little criticism. This fact might come as a surprise to contemporary observers aware of recent public policy debates about Charitable Choice and government-funded "faith-based" initiatives, championed by President George W. Bush and other advocates of "compassionate conservatism." The discussion about these more contemporary measures might lead one to believe that the blurring of boundaries between church and state is a relatively new development in the United States and that the issue is characterized by a strong partisan divide. However, at least in the area of refugee resettlement, these public-private, church-state arrangements have existed for a long time, and politicians from both political parties have generally supported efforts to borrow capacity through partnerships with religious charities and churches. During the 1970s and 1980s, the decades when most Southeast Asian refugees were resettled, the few objections that did arise were voiced by individuals, rarely by institutions, and they never amounted to a serious reconsideration of a resettlement system that depends so heavily on religious groups.

Government officials have had little incentive to criticize this system because it meets its goal of resettling refugees in a way that uses minimal public funds. Indeed, voluntary agencies and religious organizations have shouldered most of the cost and performed most of the labor of aiding refugees. This was true in the 1970s, when Southeast Asian refugees were first resettled, and in the decades since, government dependence on religious groups has only grown. Government investment in refugee resettlement has declined in recent years, meaning private agencies, especially religious agencies, have been responsible for bearing more of the financial burden. A 2008 study conducted by LIRS found that the State Department funded only 39 percent of the actual cost of resettling a refugee while private giving covered the remaining 61 percent.[106] "Failing to adequately fund the costs associated with the system places a significant amount of stress on the resettlement agencies' ability to do their job effectively," argued Todd Scribner and Anastasia Brown of the United States Conference of Catholic Bishops. Such reduced funding, they said, "could in the long-term undermine the capacity of the system to continue functioning at a high level."[107] In these circumstances, voluntary agencies, especially religious groups, have picked up the slack and have continued to fill the yawning gap between the rising cost of resettlement and the declining availability of government resources. And yet despite the fact that private religious organizations provide most of the money and labor for refugee resettlement in the United States, the fate of refugees hoping to resettle in the United States ultimately depends on the federal government. The most striking illustration of this fact is the impact of President Donald Trump's decision to slash the number of refugees admitted for resettlement during his four years in office. Having no refugees to resettle, voluntary agencies were forced to close their local offices. By the start of 2021, both LIRS and World Relief had closed about a third of their local offices.[108]

However, this governing capacity has been bought at the cost of a new set of challenges, especially concerning matters of religious pluralism and religious freedom. In Southeast Asian refugee resettlement, the fact that this "shadow establishment" was accepted so readily did not mean it was free of conflict among the people who organized, administered, and received refugee aid. As we will see in later chapters, government, voluntary agencies, churches, individual volunteers, and refugees sounded the alarm about the perils of mixing religious, humanitarian, and government work. Their concerns centered on the fact that Christian voluntary agencies and sponsoring congregations were, at the end of the day, religious organizations with distinctly religious values and objectives. Most importantly, these organizations relied on the daily contributions of religious people, many of whom were unpaid volunteers who imbued seemingly secular tasks—housing, feeding, and tutoring refugees, for example—with deep religious meaning.

3

Ministering Resettlement

REFUGEE RESETTLEMENT AS CHRISTIAN

MINISTRY AND MISSION

The spring of 1975 found Kathleen Vellenga in low spirits. Before that point she had been happily raising her young children and channeling her energy into numerous community projects throughout Saint Paul, Minnesota. Everything came to a standstill, however, when a health problem forced her to undergo a major surgery. For a month after she recuperated in bed, and she grew restless and dissatisfied during her convalescence.

And then Saigon fell. In the quiet of her hospital room, she watched the humanitarian crisis unfold on her television. Before her were arresting images of American aircraft evacuating thousands of Vietnamese people who feared for their lives. Crowding onto helicopters were the lucky ones, who clutched the hands of crying children and the few possessions they were permitted carry. Left behind were throngs of refugees, thousands of them, many more than the helicopters could ferry to safety, and no less desperate and afraid. This scene of chaos—of crowds of people crushing one another to capture a seat on a helicopter—dramatically depicted the consequences of war and the magnitude of human misery suffered in its aftermath.

For Vellenga, witnessing the suffering of frantic people fleeing Vietnam was a profoundly moving and motivating experience. "I'm watching the TV in my room, and here [are] these people, you know, scrambling under the helicopters," she recalled. "I'm thinking, 'I have people coming in changing my sheets, giving me a drink of water, medicine, whatever I wanted. You know, I got totally out of my self-pity party and just said, 'When I get well, we're going to find a way that someone can stay here.'"

She kept her promise. A minister's daughter, she had long been active in her congregation, especially in projects that reflected her passion for social justice. She was also an enthusiastic and experienced leader who knew how to recruit volunteers, raise funds, and organize projects. In the months following her surgery, she did all of these things. Less than a year after her time in the hospital, she found herself awake in the early hours of February 17, 1976, braving the snowy Saint Paul streets to drive to the airport, where she and members of three local congregations welcomed one of the first Hmong refugee families to resettle in the Twin Cities.[1]

«««<>»»»

When government officials discussed refugee relief and resettlement efforts, they paid relatively little attention to the religious dimensions of their plan and their partners. They clearly had no qualms about working with religious people: they coordinated resettlement plans with religious voluntary agencies, they invited religious leaders to visit the White House and speak before Congress, and they appealed to religious communities to donate their time, talent, and treasure. In dealing with these institutions and individuals, however, government officials tended to ignore the fact that they were religious. Eager to find willing partners with whom to share the labor and cost of refugee resettlement, government officials treated religious voluntary agencies as simply one type of voluntary agency, congregational sponsorship as simply one form of group sponsorship, and people like Kathleen Vellenga as simply one of many civic-minded, good-hearted Americans. But for many church volunteers, involvement in refugee resettlement was more than an effort to support a government program—it was a religious practice animated by Christian ideals. Though some volunteers described their work as a ministry and others called it a mission, for almost everybody involved, the effort to aid and resettle refugees was an act of Christian love that mobilized a global corps of volunteers, whose sustained service on the front lines of the relief and resettlement effort helped to make the government's refugee program possible.

Across the country, there were thousands of other Christian volunteers who supported refugee resettlement efforts, often by working with their congregations to sponsor refugees.[2] In the complex system of congregational sponsorship, the national voluntary agencies (for example, Lutheran Immigration and Refugee Service, or LIRS) worked with local resettlement agencies ("local affiliates" such as Lutheran Social Service), which in turn depended on congregations to do much of the day-to-day work of refugee resettlement. These congregations promised to fulfill the "moral commitment" of assisting refugees in their first few weeks in the United States. However, congregational sponsorship was more than a mere moral commitment. It also involved significant material commitment, as resettling a refugee family cost far more than the per capita grant that the federal government provided. Congregational sponsors allowed the federal government to run a resettlement program for a fraction of the actual cost, and the government effort to resettle over a million Southeast Asian refugees was possible largely because of the manpower, money, and material resources donated by churches and their volunteers.

These congregational sponsors pursued resettlement work not as government work, but as religious work. To be sure, they understood and practiced this religious work in different ways, a reflection of their diverse cultural backgrounds, theological frameworks, and personal experiences. Some Christians pursued refugee resettlement as a ministry of Christian charity, an act of radical hospitality, a demonstration of familial care, and an expression of public penance and peacemaking. Others approached resettlement as a Christian mission and set out to share the gospel and save souls. Most people embraced a combination of these ideas and more.

The common thread through all of these different approaches, however, is that refugee resettlement was fundamentally religious work best understood as a form of "lived religion."[3] Hearing the stories of individuals doing the on-the-ground work of resettlement recovers an overlooked aspect of their labor and of the broader system of refugee resettlement in the United States. On the surface, the Catholic and Protestant resettlement agencies differed little from their nonreligious counterparts, and many of the things that the religious resettlement agencies did—helping refugees find jobs and homes, for example, and teaching refugees English—appear to have been conducted in nonreligious ways. However, a close look at congregational sponsorship reveals how heavily the American refugee program ran on the contributions of religious people, whose involvement in resettlement work served both God and government.

"A Congregation Offers a Diversity of Resources"

In the summer of 1975, a few months after the fall of Saigon, representatives of the leading voluntary agencies gathered in Washington, DC, for a series of congressional hearings about the progress of the refugee resettlement program. Although they had some encouraging developments to share, they also spoke frankly about difficulties, one of which was the problem of individual sponsorships. John McCarthy of the United States Catholic Conference (USCC) shared that sponsoring large Southeast Asian refugee families was too much of a responsibility for individual sponsors to handle.[4] Similarly, August Bernthal of LIRS testified that though offers of individual sponsorship were usually made in good faith, these efforts failed when people who did not understand the full responsibility of sponsorship were "unable to provide for all the long-term needs of the refugees." In some cases, individual sponsors did not even bear good intentions, with their sponsorship offers amounting "to little more than requests for indentured servants, bedmates, and cheap labor," said Bernthal.[5] By July 1975, LIRS officials noted that individual sponsorship threatened to become "a serious problem area."[6]

For these reasons, both government and voluntary agency officials promoted group sponsorship as the "more successful" mode of resettling refugees.[7] Many types of community groups—monastic communities, community service organizations, and college campus fellowships—organized efforts to aid refugees.[8] In Minnesota, even a local nursing home offered to support resettlement efforts. Residents at the Oak Terrace Nursing Home proposed that one of its vacant buildings "be made available as a Christian Connection Center" that would serve as "a temporary resettlement center" for Southeast Asian refugees.[9]

However, voluntary agency officials offered special praise for congregational sponsorship, a system in which voluntary agencies enlisted local churches and temples to provide critical support for refugees throughout the first few weeks after their arrival. The terms of sponsorship agreements changed over time and varied across agencies, but most voluntary agencies emphasized that sponsorship was at once a "moral commitment" and a practical obligation to provide for the material needs of newly arrived refugees. This sponsorship agreement from Church World Service (CWS) illustrates some of the core responsibilities of sponsorship:

> [Name of Congregation or Sponsoring Unit] hereby agree to assist a refugee family with their resettlement in the United States. In agreeing to assist the family, the congregation assures CWS that it will help them become self-supporting in the shortest possible time after their arrival in the community and will assist them in the following ways:
>
> 1. Meet the family at the airport upon arrival.
> 2. Arrange for temporary housing.
> 3. Assist with food, clothing, housewares, basic furniture, etc.
> 4. Assist in finding employment for the breadwinner.
> 5. Help the refugee and his family become oriented in the community.
> 6. Assist in enrolling in English classes.[10]

Although congregational sponsorship typically focused on meeting refugees' needs during their initial few weeks in the United States, the involvement of congregations in resettlement efforts changed as circumstances and needs evolved. For example, in the 1970s, congregations served as the sole sponsors of many of the first Southeast Asian refugees, but later, these refugees began to sponsor their own relatives, and resettlement efforts shifted to family reunification. In this later phase of Southeast Asian refugee resettlement in the 1980s, congregations sometimes served as cosponsors for local ethnic mutual aid associations and for refugee families that lacked the financial resources to support relatives on their own. Finally, beyond sponsorship, congregations supported the efforts of voluntary agencies to provide "follow-up services" and long-term programming for resettled refugees.[11] In sum, congregations functioned as extensions of the voluntary agencies in the same way that voluntary agencies functioned as extensions of the government. They helped voluntary agencies expand their capacity, stretch their resources, and widen the scope of their services. The reality was that, though experienced and established, voluntary agencies did not have the funds and staff at the local level to provide all the support that refugees needed. "The resettlement staff could not be responsible for every single bit of work to be done," said Tom Kosel.[12]

Voluntary agencies also worked closely with congregations because of the institutional context in which voluntary agencies operated. The most prominent voluntary agencies were religious agencies with ties to either major denominations or ecumenical coalitions. These denominations and coalitions offered the voluntary agencies a preexisting national network of congregations that were potential sponsors. Not surprisingly, Protestant voluntary agencies—LIRS, CWS, and World Relief—were most likely to rely on the congregational sponsorship model of resettlement, but the USCC used this approach, too.[13] In Minnesota, where Christian voluntary agencies predominated, congregational sponsorship was common, especially in the first decade of Southeast Asian refugee resettlement. In the 1970s and early 1980s, dozens of Protestant, Catholic, and Jewish congregations were involved in refugee sponsorship in the Twin Cities alone. A survey of the *Catholic Bulletin*, the newspaper for the Archdiocese of Saint Paul and Minneapolis, indicates that forty Catholic parishes sponsored Southeast Asian refugee families between 1975 and 1984, mostly in suburbs and small towns.[14] Although the involvement of congregations was due in part to the prominence of religious voluntary agencies in Minnesota, even non-religious voluntary agencies like the International Institute of Minnesota (IIM) enlisted churches to help with sponsorships, as they did with the Dayton Avenue Presbyterian Church (DAPC).

Congregations provided voluntary agencies with a variety of important resources. The first was crucial manpower for the labor-intensive work of resettlement. LIRS described "the labors of love, the common sense and the dedication of thousands of Lutherans" as "the most important single resource of the resettlement program."[15] John McCarthy of the USCC shared similar enthusiasm for "the parish adopting a family technique." As he explained to Congress, congregational sponsorship meant that "instead of having one family sponsor [a refugee], they have 1600."[16] In Minnesota, congregational sponsorship projects drew on the contributions of scores, even hundreds, of church volunteers. At Guardian Angels parish, sixty-five families were involved in resettlement; at the Catholic Church of Saint Rita, about a hundred families actively participated in the sponsorship project; and a joint sponsorship project of Immaculate Heart of Mary Catholic Church and Saint Joseph Catholic Church involved 290 people.[17]

Congregations also provided unparalleled financial support. Though the federal government granted voluntary agencies $500 per refugee, the true cost of resettling a refugee was much higher. Voluntary agencies did not have the financial resources to shoulder these expenses on their own, but congregations could help make up the difference. To illustrate this point, in 1976 LIRS submitted a report to Congress about a sponsorship project at Bethlehem Lutheran Church in Minneapolis. Taking account of housing, utilities, home furnishings, clothing, professional support, and more, LIRS found that it actually cost Bethlehem Lutheran Church $5,601 to resettle one Vietnamese refugee family—far more than what the government allocated through its grant.[18] Church sponsors offered such generous assistance that those refugees who were not sponsored by congregations sometimes complained. A letter from an IIM caseworker to a Hmong refugee who asked for more than what was offered to him reveals that both refugees and voluntary agencies knew that church sponsorship offered the best access to material resources. "In a way we resemble poor parents," the caseworker wrote. "We cannot give you as many things as a church-parish can when they sponsor a family. . . . As sponsoring 'parents' we wish we could do more for you and your family."[19]

Congregational sponsors were able to give so generously in part because the churches that resettled refugees tended to be relatively affluent. Helen Fein, a sociologist who studied congregational sponsorship in 1979 and 1980, found that sponsoring churches were likely to be white, nonethnic, mainline Protestant churches located in economically prosperous communities. The individual laypeople who led church sponsorship efforts also tended to be white, native-born, and college-educated members of the professional class.[20]

Congregational sponsorship also connected refugees with rich social networks that proved valuable in addressing a wide range of needs. The contacts that congregation members offered increased the odds that refugees could find employment, medical care, tutoring, and more. According to Ingrid Walter, director of LIRS, the involvement of so many different people allowed congregations to attend to the diverse needs of refugees:

> It is our conviction that a congregation offers a diversity of resources that equip it well to assist the refugee [to] build a new life in this country and to help him become self-sufficient. Some members of the congregation will be best at meeting the immediate physical needs, providing temporary housing or assisting him find employment. Others in the congregation will be best able to provide personal guidance in the many complicated facets of everyday life in the United States. Others will be best at providing the close emotional and spiritual support that will help the refugee become part of the community and give him a sense of being "at home" in a new land, while at the same time showing understanding for the refugee's culture.[21]

As Walter explained, when a large, diverse community undertakes a sponsorship project, "individuals within a congregation can become involved in the Christian ministry of resettlement in varied, yet personal ways."[22]

Another advantage of congregational sponsorship was that it was a particularly resilient form of sponsorship. Not only were church sponsorships less likely to break down than individual sponsorships, but churches were able to assist refugee families for a longer period of time and were a renewable resource in the ongoing work of resettlement. In one 1976 LIRS report, a regional consultant praised "the enduring capacity of our congregational sponsors," who are "sticking with it, continuing to minister to new kinds of needs."[23] Indeed, Minnesota congregations often chose to stick with refugee work for many years and in new ways as needs evolved. Congregations that first mobilized to help Vietnamese refugees after the fall of Saigon sponsored refugees from other countries when the opportunity arose. Trinity Lutheran Church of Wanamingo, for example, sponsored six refugee families—first a Vietnamese family in the 1970s and then Cambodian families in the early 1980s.[24] Other churches, like Messiah Lutheran Church, served as cosponsors to help refugees reunify with their families.[25] Congregations also sometimes pivoted to providing long-term support for refugees. When the sponsorship committee at the Catholic Church of Saint Rita realized that the family they had sponsored had transportation difficulties, they began to offer English classes in their parish for seventeen refugee adults.[26]

Finally, at the local level, congregations performed another important function that national resettlement leaders did not mention in their official reports or congressional testimonies: they helped refugees deal with local hostility and served as a buffer between them and the racist and xenophobic sentiment of the broader community. Congregations were well aware that refugee resettlement was not a popular undertaking and were sometimes on the receiving end of hostility. The sponsorship committee at Saint Odilia Catholic Church, for instance, received an angry letter about how their resettlement work was causing "race-mixing."[27] When public attacks on refugees occurred, religious people offered refugees some of the staunchest support. For example, when CWS's proposal to create the Hiawatha Valley Farm Cooperative in Hugo, Minnesota, prompted local opposition, local clergy offered the most vocal and vehement defense of Hmong refugees. It was, in fact, a local Episcopal priest named Rev. Joseph Minnis who owned the farm and planned to sell portions of it to CWS to support the project. Speaking before a town board meeting, Minnis referenced Biblical teachings in his call for the community to welcome the Hmong. "Let me ask, what does our Lord's great commandments mean?" he told the crowd. "Love thy neighbor as thyself. Does it only mean that we have to consider those that look like us, speak like us and live like we do?"[28]

To be sure, sponsorship could sometimes be a difficult experience. Resettlement planners constantly worried about "sponsorship breakdowns," which were difficult resettlement situations that forced voluntary agencies to find a new resettlement sponsor or placement.[29] Tensions certainly arose in sponsorship relationships. However, by 1976 the Health, Education, and Welfare Task Force found that sponsorship breakdowns were rather rare, and when troubles occurred, they were "handled by the voluntary agencies at the local level."[30] Similarly, Helen Fein found that all of the congregational sponsors in her study fulfilled their obligation to provide for the immediate needs of refugees, sometimes overcoming conflict in order to do so.[31]

Ultimately, local congregations provided such valuable contributions to the resettlement effort that the Christian voluntary agencies considered churches a fundamental component of the resettlement system. LIRS even built its resettlement structure around congregational engagement. "The congregation (or individual sponsor), as it continues its resettlement ministry in cooperation with DIRS [the Department of Immigration and Refugee Services], will be the primary working unit in the resettlement process," the agency said. According to the Lutheran plan, the national offices and local affiliates of LIRS existed primarily to "support congregations, sponsors and refugees."[32]

How exactly did congregational sponsorship work? To answer this question, it is instructive to return to Kathleen Vellenga, the young mother in Saint Paul who decided in her hospital room that she needed to help refugees find a safe home in America. The members of her congregation were initially skeptical of the project. "When I went to my church, they said, 'We're a little mission church. We can't take on someone from some other country! You're crazy,'" she recalled. But Vellenga found two other churches in the area— Macalester-Plymouth Church and House of Hope Church—that agreed to pursue a joint sponsorship project.[33] At the same time, she solicited congregation members to raise funds for the "DMP [Dayton Macalester-Plymouth] Sponsorship Fund," submitted a request for financial aid from the presbytery, and made arrangements for the prospective refugee family to be housed in Liberty Plaza, an affordable housing development in Saint Paul.[34] Other sponsorship committee volunteers prepared the townhouse and gathered donations of furniture and clothing from the congregation. Vellenga shared her excitement in the church newsletter. "THE CONTRIBUTIONS HAVE BEEN WONDERFUL!!!" she wrote in December 1975.[35]

The churches expected that they would sponsor a Vietnamese family, but plans changed when Vellenga contacted the International Institute of Minnesota (IIM). The agency was preparing for the new Lao resettlement program, which started in 1976, and the DAPC learned that it would be resettling the Vangs, a family of eleven from Laos. "The Vang family have been living in a refugee camp in Thailand since they had to flee Laos, and will be coming directly from there to us here in Saint Paul," Vellenga informed the congregation. "The family consists of 11 persons: the head of the house and his wife, their two babies; his mother; two adult brothers; and four school age brothers and sisters."[36] Beyond this information, she knew little else, and only when the Vang family arrived in February 1976 did she first hear the word "Hmong." The only thing she knew was that "they can't stay where they belong, they have to leave." As she confessed later, "I knew nothing about Hmong; I knew nothing about the Secret War."

Finally the family arrived, though not as either the IIM or Vellenga had expected. "They did not stop in California, as later groups did," Vellenga said. "They came straight from the camp, on the plane, to Minnesota. It's ten below zero." Because of this direct flight, which crossed the International Date Line, the sponsors were confused about the travel dates, and the Vang family arrived a day earlier than expected. "So we not only didn't know who they were, which was the most important thing—we didn't even know when they were arriving!" Vellenga recalled. Somehow, a member of the Vang family managed to contact Olga Zoltai, who worked at the IIM, and Zoltai then awakened Vellenga with an urgent telephone call at 6:30 in the morning. "They're here already!" Vellenga recalled Zoltai saying. A caravan of cars filled with church volunteers and agency staff made its way to the airport, where they found the Vang family in the middle of the deserted terminal. "They were huddled together so tight, I thought that if they tried to move, the whole thing would fall apart," Vellenga said. "They just looked so frightened."

The next few weeks saw the full force of a spirited community effort. "We worked with people from both churches in finding jobs," Vellenga said. Meanwhile, "we got the kids in school," and Vellenga worked with a church member who had been an English teacher to "go over and tutor the women." Due to the abundance of volunteers and the absence of adult English classes during this period, "we were trying to teach English ourselves!" Vellenga recalled with a chuckle.[37] Other church volunteers made time to bring the Vang family on "rides, shopping trips, [and] doctor visits," and "a dietician from Mac-Plymouth Church not only provided a well-researched supply of groceries the Vangs needed for their basic stock, but . . . endured the monthly hassles with the food stamp office."[38] In time, the congregations assisted the Vang family in filing the necessary paperwork for relatives to join them in the United States. Four months later, another Vang brother arrived. "It was such a big deal, the reunification," Vellenga said. "It was on the news that night—in part because we had a member of our church who was a newscaster."[39] Updates in the church newsletter reveal that the Vang family ultimately did well in America. After six months, Vellenga reported that the adult men had found stable jobs at the Minnesota State Data Processing Center and the Gold Medal Beverage Company. "Their adjustment to a totally different culture and climate has been amazing and we all marvel at their adaptability," Vellenga wrote.[40]

Vellenga described resettlement not only as a collective effort but also as a private voluntary effort with no government support. "Vangs are very appreciative of all the hands of friendship and the financial aid," she reported to the congregation in March 1976. "They were surprised that all the money comes from people in the churches and none from the government."[41] Later, she added, "It is difficult for them to understand that after all they risked and lost for the USA during the war that it is the church not the government that provides sponsorship for them now."[42]

In truth, the US government did contribute to the resettlement of the Vangs and other refugees. Each voluntary agency received a per capita grant to defray the costs of resettlement, a sum that certainly paled in comparison to the actual cost of resettling refugees, but it was at least something. It is possible that Vellenga viewed sponsorship as a church project because the IIM did not pass on the government grant money to sponsoring congregations. (Voluntary agencies were free to disburse the funds to congregations, local affiliates, or individual refugees as each best saw fit. Some voluntary agencies did, but others did not.[43]) Whatever the case may be, Vellenga's description of sponsorship is notable because it obscures the fact that congregations, as extensions of voluntary agencies that held contracts with the government, were built into the bureaucratic apparatus of refugee resettlement. More importantly, Vellenga's words not only show how sponsors thought resettlement worked—they also show what sponsors thought resettlement meant. For them, refugee sponsorship was not a government project but a church project that offered a powerful expression of Christian benevolence.

"As You Do to the Least of These, You Do It unto Me"

The Christian benevolence that animated refugee sponsorship was multifaceted and complex, and church volunteers committed their time and talent to refugee work for diverse reasons. However, despite their different backgrounds and interests, they often shared the view that refugee resettlement expressed deeply held Christian commitments to live by the Golden Rule and other Biblical teachings. Listening to the firsthand accounts of individuals involved with congregational sponsorship reveals that refugee ministry was a religious practice, one that expressed the idea that being a good Christian required people to *do*, not simply believe.

The voluntary agencies themselves promoted refugee resettlement as a form of religious practice. In particular, Christian voluntary agencies frequently described refugee resettlement in terms of the spiritual service of ministry. One LIRS brochure called resettlement a "ministry" that was "face to face."[44] CWS used similar language. "For Christians, refugee resettlement provides a unique chance to participate in the healing ministry Christ calls us to be a part of," read one CWS pamphlet.[45]

Stories shared by congregational sponsors active in the Twin Cities reflected this emphasis on the spiritual work of caring for refugees. Take, for example, Mary Mergenthal and Joanne Karvonen, two longtime members of the Refugee Core Committee at Saint Anthony Park Lutheran Church in Saint Paul, a congregation that resettled thirty-five refugee families from fifteen countries over a span of three decades.[46] Mergenthal and Karvonen were, in certain ways, very different. Mergenthal was a self-described "church activist" who, after joining the congregation in 1970, immersed herself in church life. Before getting involved in refugee resettlement, she served in the Sunday School, the music ministry, and church governance. When a seminary professor who had a "real heart for refugees and for social concerns" initiated a sponsorship project at the church, Mergenthal volunteered to be one of the original members of the refugee committee. For her, refugee work grew out of her enthusiasm for church work.[47] Karvonen, in contrast, was not even a member of the congregation when she started volunteering with Saint Anthony's refugee committee. For her, involvement in the church developed out of her enthusiasm for resettlement. "One of the reasons that we did join [the congregation] was their interest in refugees," Karvonen said, "and I started helping a little bit with refugee issues here before we became members because it was something that I was very interested in."[48]

What Mergenthal and Karvonen had in common is that they both imbued resettlement work with religious meaning and considered it an act of Christian charity and love. Mergenthal, like many Christians involved in refugee resettlement, explained her motivations in terms of the teachings of Matthew 25. Quoting the fortieth verse of this chapter—"As you do to the least of these, you do it unto me"—Mergenthal explained that as she considered whether to participate in sponsorship efforts, "It seemed to be no question in my mind but that we should help."[49] For her part, Karvonen echoed the obligation to provide help to people in need and also called attention to Biblical teachings. When asked why she chose to get involved in refugee work, Karvonen explained that the main reason was her commitment to "following the tenet of 'Love thy neighbor as thyself' and following the example of Jesus Christ in working with the poor and working with children and working with the downtrodden."[50] The reasons shared by Mergenthal and Karvonen reflected the values emphasized by the Christian voluntary agencies. As CWS explained in one brochure, congregations were "avenues of God's love to refugees," and sponsorship was an act of Christian love not only for the hungry and the homeless but for Jesus himself. "Jesus, Who was Himself a refugee, said that by helping refugees we are really helping Him," the brochure read.[51]

Karvonen also described refugee resettlement in another way: as an act of Christian hospitality to people who needed a safe place to live. "It just seems, you know, so obvious to us that this is what we must do, that here are these people that have no home," she said. "They have nothing, and in most cases it's through no fault of their own, and so, of course, as Christians, we would help them and help them in more than just materialistic ways. We would truly try to make them feel welcome and worthwhile in our society."[52] In a period when Americans did not broadly welcome Southeast Asian refugees, her commitment "to show hospitality to strangers" was unpopular—and audacious.[53]

Embracing resettlement work as a ministry of "welcoming the stranger" was one shared by other Christian resettlement volunteers. For some, the responsibility to welcome others felt particularly urgent, not simply because of global crises but because of local transformations. As the refugee population in the Twin Cities grew, churches and their members witnessed their neighborhoods change, and they felt compelled to respond. Dianne Anderson, for example, had grown up on the East Side of Saint Paul in the Dayton's Bluff neighborhood, where she was a member of First Lutheran Church. As Anderson explained, First Lutheran had resisted calls to move to the suburbs in the mid-1960s and was proud to be "an inner city church" that was dedicated to "serving and being a welcoming place for our neighbors and those in need." When Hmong refugees began moving into homes previously inhabited by Swedish, Norwegian, and German immigrants, the congregation wondered how it should meet the needs of their new neighbors. "Where does First Church go?" Anderson recalled the members of the church asking each other amid these transformations. "We are in this neighborhood. We are seeing changes in this neighborhood, and what does God want us to do in this place?" Because "welcoming our neighbors" was such an important value to her, Anderson chose to volunteer her time with Southeast Asian Ministry, a project of the Evangelical Lutheran Church of America Synod of Saint Paul, through which she helped to start a program to support Hmong elders. Her volunteer work with the Southeast Asian Ministry and the church's efforts to help its Hmong neighbors reflected a commitment to respond to the changing needs of a changing community. "I think, as scary and fearful as we could be of this, we still want to do it," she said. "It is where we belong and what we should be doing."[54]

Some Christian volunteers saw refugees not as their neighbors but as their brothers and sisters or sons and daughters, and they pursued refugee resettlement as an act of familial care. This approach to resettlement emphasized a warm relationship between refugee sponsors and refugees, one defined by bonds of intimacy, affection, and responsibility. One refugee sponsor, Bernice Herron, wrote an essay titled "The Adoption of the Thai Family," in which she described how she considered the Vietnamese woman she had sponsored to be her "daughter." In turn, Lisalan Thai, the Vietnamese woman, called Bernice Herron "mother."[55] Leaders and lay members of other congregations also spoke of welcoming refugees into their congregational "family," and resettlement coordinators sometimes referred to refugees as being "adopted."[56]

Although some church sponsors treated refugees as members of their own families, others expressed concern that paternalistic sponsorship relationships could demean refugees. "First of all, congregations who sponsor refugees soon become aware that these uprooted people are more than just characters in pathetic horror stories,"

Karvonen said. "They are not babies or pets to be coddled and shown off in their native garb."[57] Conscious of the temptation by some church sponsors to treat refugees as "pets," she and the other members of the Saint Anthony Park Refugee Core Committee laid down a few basic principles for how they would approach resettlement. "One of those was that we had a real concern about respecting the wishes and needs of the family," said Mary Mergenthal. The church intended to offer as much support and encouragement as possible, but also the privacy, space, and independence necessary for refugees to truly thrive.[58]

Finally, the particular context of the Vietnam War also shaped how Christians understood the religious work of refugee resettlement. For some, sponsoring Southeast Asian refugees was an opportunity for Americans to perform an act of public penance after years of sinfully waging war. "It may sound improbable at first that sponsoring a refugee will earn you God's forgiveness," said Archbishop Joseph-Aurèle Plourde of the Roman Catholic Archdiocese of Ottawa. "But we do have some sins to be forgiven as a nation. We ought to help the refugees now so we'll have the forgiveness of God to help us through troubles we may have in the future."[59] In Minnesota, Christian volunteers spoke of their involvement in resettlement as arising from their commitment to serve as peacemakers. Karvonen had fervently opposed the war in Vietnam, and when the war came home to Saint Paul in the form of Southeast Asian refugees, she connected her resettlement work to her long-standing anti-war convictions. "I was horrified at the Vietnam War and the effect that that had on that country, and so getting involved with the refugee program here was one little thing that I could do, since my letters to the President or Congress hadn't done too much," she said. "Helping individuals directly was something that I wanted to do."[60]

Meaningful as it was, the work of resettlement was sometimes stressful. Reflecting on three decades of such intensive work, Karvonen acknowledged that many churches chose not to continue with sponsorship work. Lutheran congregational sponsorship was popular in the 1970s and 1980s, a time "when refugee resettlement was novel and even somewhat glamorous," she said. "But as the years went by and it became apparent that the number of refugees was growing rather than decreasing, the prospect of working with refugees forever was daunting and discouraging." Church sponsorship declined, and by the early twenty-first century, Karvonen observed that only a handful of congregations continued to resettle new refugee families. Part of this decline owed to "the intensity of work" in helping new refugees after they arrive.[61] But the cost was not simply in time or money. The anthropologist Catherine Besteman, in her study of Somali Bantu refugees in Maine, found that the community members who were deeply involved in helping refugees were "engaged in the sort of affective work that attempts to buffer the blows of racism, xenophobia, and neoliberal demands for economic independence, self-sufficiency, autonomy, and self-help," all while being expected to show "compassion, mutuality, and love for an inclusive vision of community." The emotional and spiritual responsibilities of resettlement were sometimes heavy to bear.[62] But for Christians who placed high value on loving their neighbors, serving the poor, and welcoming the stranger, this hard work was embraced as holy work, which made the sacrifices worthwhile.

"We Wanted Them to Be Saved"

Like Karvonen, Mergenthal, and Anderson, Pearl Jones also approached congregational sponsorship as a religious practice. However, she was motivated by a different Biblical commitment: the Great Commission, or the instruction that Christians "make disciples of all nations." Jones, a member of a Baptist congregation in a northern Twin Cities suburb, saw refugee resettlement as a form of mission in which the primary purpose was to share the gospel.

For Jones, working with Hmong refugees was a lifelong dream fulfilled. From the time she was a little girl attending Sunday School at her Southern Baptist church, Pearl Jones had hoped to become a foreign missionary. But in 1981, God appeared to deliver a missionary project directly to her, right where she lived in Minnesota. Out of the blue, a Hmong man called her church in search of a congregation to help him sponsor his cousin and her two daughters from Thailand. At the time, Pearl Jones was working as a church secretary, and she was the one who picked up the telephone. Though she had never met a Hmong person before, she was eager to help the man. "Let's go for it!" she urged the church pastor. In her heart, she felt that the situation was exactly the mission project that she believed God was calling her to do. Thirty years later, looking back on that fateful day, she declared, "I never thought that God would pick up a whole people and move them to our country so we could do missions with them."[63]

And missions is what she did. As Pearl Jones put it, "sharing the gospel with these people [was] of the uppermost." "We wanted them to be saved," she explained, because "God, He expects us to do right, to choose the right way, and to help others find the way." To achieve this end, she and other members of her church made regular contact with the refugees they sponsored, picking them up every week to participate in Sunday worship services, teaching them in Sunday School, and leading them in Bible studies. Although Jones and the other volunteers were enthusiastic, they found the work challenging. "We never did get them to understand what the Ten Commandments were that Moses received in the wilderness," she said, looking back on one particular Bible study group that she helped to organize. But their labors had an impact. "Fourteen people were saved out of that group, you know, just meeting in their homes," she said. Jones believed that the most important way to introduce refugees to Jesus was to "just love 'em!" as she said God had taught her to do. "I just remember what God impressed on my heart, that 'If you love these people, I'll give you every one of them,'" she said. "And that's what God did." In her view, abundant Christian love was the missions approach that Jesus had taken and the approach she aspired to emulate. "I think the Scripture's pretty replete in itself when you do what Jesus did," she said. "Jesus just loved them, he cared for them, and it worked out, and it sure worked out for us because God did a great work in the church through getting the Hmong saved."[64]

Not all Christian volunteers were like Jones and identified sharing their faith as the primary goal of their work, but they were nonetheless delighted when they learned that the refugees they assisted had become Christian. "I can remember bringing a Bible to the family, and then I thought afterwards, 'What was the point of that? They can't even the read the language,'" recalled Dorothy Knight, a Christian volunteer who worked with refugees in Saint Paul. Years later, one of the daughters of this family visited Saint Paul to attend a Christian conference. Now a grown woman and a devoted Christian, she set aside time to visit Knight. "She wanted to make very sure that she had a chance to see me," Knight said with a delighted chuckle, "and I thought, wasn't that nice! You don't know what seeds have sprouted and how they have sprouted, but, kind of like in teaching, you have to sow as generously as you can because you're not going to be around for the harvest."[65] Other congregational sponsors were similarly thrilled if the families they had resettled chose to join their church or showed interest in Christianity. A LIRS report from 1975, early in the Southeast Asian refugee resettlement effort, included several such stories from delighted sponsors. "Our family attends church regularly as they have chosen to do themselves," said one volunteer. "The family, especially through the head of the household, has embraced Christianity as an emerging way of life," reported another. A third church shared that the family it had sponsored had named their newborn son "Paul Luther" in honor of the church.[66]

The fact that LIRS highlighted these stories in its newsletter illuminates an important point: that voluntary agencies themselves acknowledged that one underlying objective of resettlement was not only to help refugees find a new home in the United States but also in Christ. Sometimes they even described the work of resettlement as a powerful form of Christian missionary outreach. World Relief described the "heartbeat" of its refugee work as finding "places for people whose lives will be changed by Jesus Christ."[67] Compared to its evangelical counterpart, LIRS placed less explicit emphasis on saving souls, but it also urged sponsors to remember the missionary dimensions of resettlement. "In the give and take of resettlement ministry, who knows but they may become inquisitive about the Lord who governs your life," wrote Rev. Fredrik Schiotz in a 1978 issue of the *LIRS Bulletin*. "The most welcoming missionary work [is] that which is done in response to curiosity and a creeping spiritual hunger."[68]

Almost all of the voluntary agencies prepared materials for Christian evangelism in the languages of the refugees and made them readily available to sponsors. World Relief, for example, noted that "even though the majority of the refugees from Southeast Asia are not Christians, they will probably welcome literature and/or tapes in their own language." The agency provided several pamphlets in Southeast Asian languages.[69] CWS offered copies of the Bible in Vietnamese, Khmer, and Lao.[70] LIRS addressed the issue of Christian education with particular care. The agency noted that 75 percent of

Vietnamese being resettled were Buddhist, 10 percent were Catholic, 5 percent were Protestant, and 10 percent were other religions, and that about 10,000 were above the age of 11, which LIRS considered the "primary market." LIRS concluded that "there is an immediate need to have material to introduce the Vietnamese to Christianity and facilitate close contact between Vietnamese and Americans." It committed $25,000 for the New Life project, which produced "Christian education materials" for Southeast Asian refugees resettled by Lutheran congregations. The creators of the New Life project designed the material for "encounter sessions," which they recommended happen on Sunday mornings, when there would be a high chance that Vietnamese will go to service with sponsoring families or friends. They were also careful to emphasize that the educational material should be used in an informational manner. "The material prepared should in no way give the wrong impression at this point—and that could happen by the tone being heavily evangelistic or compelling—but should be seen as a natural response to many requests that have come from both Vietnamese and their sponsors that they learn more about Christianity—and that could happen if the tone is informative and instructive," they wrote. In their view, such material "will answer the felt need most directly, and out of it will come positive responses."[71]

The overlap of resettlement work with missionary work reflected the priorities of the voluntary agencies but also the individuals and local congregations involved in refugee sponsorship. Refugee resettlement work often attracted individuals who had backgrounds in Christian missions.[72] Jones had trained to do missionary work since she was a young child, and before relocating to Minnesota she had worked with a missionary project in Chattanooga, Tennessee.[73] Sister Rosemary Schuneman, who ran an English school for refugees in Saint Paul, had served as a missionary teacher for women in Africa.[74] And Rev. Paul Tidemann, the pastor of Saint Paul Reformation Lutheran Church, served as a missionary in a wide range of settings, from urban Chicago to Guyana, before settling in Saint Paul and leading an actively integrationist congregation that sponsored several Hmong refugees.[75]

If refugee resettlement drew individuals committed to missionary work, it appealed to congregations that shared the same priorities. Churches that volunteered to sponsor refugees often had a congregational culture oriented toward global missions. Jones, for example, described her congregation as a "missions-minded church" and a community of true "soul-winners" who "want people to come to the Lord and to know the truth."[76] Similarly, Mergenthal explained that Saint Anthony Park Lutheran Church had a special enthusiasm for refugee resettlement work because of its "missionary sensitivity" and its proximity to Luther Seminary, which regularly brought overseas missionaries to the Saint Anthony Park neighborhood and congregation.[77] The missionary orientation of the congregation became clear when they learned of an opportunity to sponsor a Hmong family in 1978. Congregation members, especially those with missionary backgrounds, saw this opportunity as "mission on our doorstep" and offered generous financial contributions because, as Mergenthal put it, "they all took the call to make disciples of all nations incredibly seriously" and viewed refugee resettlement work as a "mission right here."[78]

In addition, refugee resettlement engaged congregations that were already involved in domestic missionary projects. At Saint Paul Reformation Lutheran Church, for example, congregation members understood their efforts to welcome and serve one Hmong family as similar to their urban missionary efforts a decade earlier. In the eyes of many congregation members, teaching English to a Southeast Asian refugee family was "parallel to the decision a decade before to do tutoring with Black children" in an urban Saint Paul neighborhood.[79] The DAPC, located in an area designated a "mission" by its presbytery, was also involved in urban missions and had received $40,000 to pursue innovative urban outreach projects in the early 1970s.[80]

There were sometimes direct connections between the foreign missionaries working in Asia and the individuals sponsoring and serving Southeast Asian refugees in the United States. Father Daniel Taillez, who had worked as a Catholic missionary among the Hmong in Laos for fifty-two years, moved to Saint Paul in 1981 and eventually established the national Hmong Catholic Center.[81] Even more direct was the experience of Helen and Malcolm Sawyer. After working as CMA missionaries with the Hmong in Laos and Thailand, they returned to the United States, where they were responsible for initiating the Hmong resettlement effort in Wheaton, Illinois.[82] Refugee resettlement was a moment when, as Malcolm Sawyer put it, "missions has come home."[83] In their case, the saying was literally true: Helen Sawyer noted that one Hmong boy who was in her Sunday School class when she served as a missionary in Laos later moved to Illinois and lived just a few blocks from her home.[84]

If Hmong refugees took the initiative to seek baptism, how did churches proceed? The experience of Paul Tidemann offers one example of how churches introduced Christianity to Hmong refugees. In 1982, as pastor of Saint Paul Reformation Lutheran Church, Tidemann helped sponsor thirty-one Hmong refugees, all of whom were baptized into the Lutheran church shortly after their arrival in Minnesota. When he became pastor of that church, there was already one Hmong family that was part of the congregation. "They [the Hmong couple, Sue Lee and Mee Lo] came to me and said, 'We would like to invite some of our family who are in camps in Thailand to come here, but we need a sponsor body, a sponsoring agency,'" Tidemann recalled. The congregation discussed the matter and agreed to help the family resettle their relatives. Throughout the process, Lutheran Social Service was not very involved with the day-to-day work of resettlement—"We did that ourselves," Tidemann said—nor did it recruit the church. "This was something that we initiated ourselves" because of the Hmong congregants' request, he explained.[85]

When the family head, who was the husband of the first couple, requested that all thirty-one members of the group be baptized, Tidemann was cautious. "Most of them did not speak much English," he recalled. "They certainly were not Christian." Nonetheless, he said, "they just all showed up on a Sunday morning in the congregation." He was reluctant to deny the family the opportunity to fully participate in Sunday worship services. While other pastors might have felt uncomfortable about having unbaptized people receive Holy Communion, Tidemann believed that excluding the extended family from the ritual would send the wrong message. "My feeling was, these are people who are coming into an alien culture," he said, "and for me to do something that appeared to reject them in any way in terms of how they could participate, I felt would be injurious to their whole resettlement into a new culture and was not appropriate. So if they wanted to come to receive Holy Communion, I would not restrict that."

Understanding that Hmong people were coming from a very different religious and spiritual background, Tidemann tried his best to explain Christianity to the Hmong families and to find similarities between Christianity and traditional Hmong beliefs and practices. "We had to figure out how we were going to help them understand what it means to be Christian, what a worship service is about, all those kinds of things," he said. He believed that the family had come into contact with Christians previously, in either Laos or in Thailand, but to be sure that the family members understood what baptism and what Christianity meant, he visited each of the homes of the six nuclear families. The goal of these visits was not simply to teach the Hmong refugees about Christianity but to have conversations that would help him learn more about Hmong people and their life in Laos.

In these visits, Tidemann drew parallels between Christianity and the Hmong way. "Was there anything in their cultural background that was religious in some way, that had some relationship to that which is spiritual?" he asked them. That would be like Christianity. "Did they have any experiences with something like an initiation rite?" he asked. That was like baptism. "Did they have meals together? Did they have certain times in their family life where they celebrated birthdays or special occasions or anything like that?" That was like Holy Communion. Moreover, he explained his own role, as pastor, to be similar to the role of shamans in Hmong culture. Tidemann recalled that, throughout the process, "they were welcomed and included as part of the community, included in the Christian community, at Saint Paul Reformation," and, in keeping with the common argument in favor of congregational sponsorship, "the congregation became kind of their base community in this new culture." The church offered "a larger extended family."

All thirty-one Hmong refugees were baptized on May 16, 1982, in a service televised by a local news station. On that spring Sunday, Tidemann gathered together the new Hmong members of his congregation, along with their multiracial baptismal sponsors, and delivered a sermon on the importance of Christian friendship. He candidly acknowledged the differences that existed in the world and in their own church community and the possibility of faith in God to bridge these differences. "We are White people, originally coming out of Europe[,] and Black people, whose roots are in Africa," he preached. "Now, we welcome what we might call Brown people, who are very recent arrivals from the Hmong tribes of Laos—all of these people plus old people, middle-aged, young, single and married people, gay and straight people—all come here as friends in Christ . . . in Christ we work together and we become friends."[86]

In retelling this story, Tidemann acknowledged that a leader in the family had made the decision that the group should be baptized; he himself was not sure how some members of the family truly felt about baptism. "You have to understand that they were functioning on command of their patriarch, so they would be very polite and say in whatever way they could that they understood what I was talking about and were very glad to be part of a church," he said. Moreover, he understood the complex dynamics of baptizing people who had been generously helped by the church. He believed, however, that the Hmong family was naturally open to Christianity because the church had shown such genuine hospitality. "Their response was welcoming because they felt they were being welcomed," he said.[87]

From doing home visits to teaching about Christian beliefs, Tidemann's work with the Hmong at Saint Paul Reformation Lutheran bore some similarities to what Jones did at her Baptist church, but there were also some critical differences. First, Tidemann did not see resettlement as a soul-saving mission, as Jones did. Moreover, Tidemann, an experienced missionary, had a different approach to Christian missions that reflected broader changes in how some Christians were thinking about missionary work in the latter half of the twentieth century. By the 1960s and 1970s liberal Christians across denominations grappled with ideas about pluralism and multiculturalism and the practical reality of interreligious relations. Rejecting the assimilative and imperialist impulse of previous generations of Christian missionaries, they reimagined missionary work as cultivating relationships and pursuing "Christian presence," rather than simply winning converts and saving souls. By the 1970s and 1980s, even evangelicals were exploring the possibility of a missions approach involving "dialogue" with non-Christians.[88] Jones and Tidemann thus represented two different strains in Christian missions in the late twentieth century. On the one hand, liberal mainline Protestants and Catholics undertook missionary work, humanitarian work, and resettlement work with a focus on addressing social concerns rather than winning converts. On the other hand, evangelicals like Jones continued to prioritize saving souls over social change. In her study of congregational sponsorship, Fein observed this difference. "Although church federations and church-based Volags of both types [mainline Protestant and conservative evangelical Protestant] have endorsed and organized sponsorships and both justify it in similar terms as a religious imperative, the evangelicals also view it as a means toward the salvation of souls," she wrote.[89] Similarly, a 1981 study of voluntary agencies found that refugees did not complain about proselytism often. However, when such problems did arise, they were primarily associated with World Relief, the resettlement agency affiliated with the National Association of Evangelicals, despite the fact that proselytism is officially forbidden by national policy.[90]

Refugee resettlement, as an enterprise that united elements of both international and home missions, reflected these new developments in missionary work. For example, Schuneman, the Catholic sister who ran the English school in Saint Paul, strived to recognize and respect the issues and structures of the people to whom she ministered. "One of the things we say is when we go to a culture, it's sacred space," she said, as she reflected on the constitution of her religious order, the School Sisters of Notre Dame. She added, "We do not impose our culture on them or our traditions." This value was critical to how she assisted immigrants and refugees in adjusting to life in the United States. Her goal was to "help them here in Saint Paul to integrate their culture into the American culture," but not to "push down anything that they tell me is a part of their culture." This commitment arose from the belief that each person in her classroom is "sacred" and that "we belong to the same human family no matter where we go."[91] Other Christian volunteers articulated a similar belief in the idea that all people are part of "the same human family." Dorothy Knight saw all humans as part of God's creation, and she spoke of God's bigness and of the call to love across boundaries of religious and cultural difference. "I believe that God created the world—not just the people in one congregation in one particular place," she said. "If you're in the world, then you're part of creation. . . . I think we know so little about the love of God, that to differentiate who God loves and who God doesn't love, and what you should do at a certain time and what you should not do is so culturally oriented."[92]

In keeping with this vision for missionary work, resettlement volunteers endeavored to witness to their Christian faith through their loving presence and through their acts of care and service. "I am not teaching any Catholic doctrine," Schuneman emphasized. "Anything I teach about being a Christian is just who I am there."[93] Anderson held a similar philosophy. "[At First Lutheran Church] we tend to be kind of 'live by our actions and not our words' kind of a thing, where they'll know we're Christian by what we do, what's in our hearts," she said. Her commitment to this form of Christian witness moved her to share a story that, as she retold it, caused her to well up with emotion. One of the women participating in the Hmong elder program had explained to Anderson that the people at First Lutheran showered her with a warmth and kindness that she had never before encountered. "She didn't know what love really was until she met Christians in the United States," Anderson recalled the woman telling her. "And I think that's a wonderful statement for the religious community to hold onto."[94]

"The Church Helped Us in Everything"

Looking back on their first years in America, Hmong refugees recalled the central involvement of Christian religious communities in their resettlement. In fact, in telling of their migration to the United States, many Hmong refugees saw resettlement not as a government project but as a church effort. "I believe, I totally believe, that people who came to the United States here were just not sponsored individually by another relative," said True Xiong. "I believe that they were sponsored though churches . . . they're the ones who are responsible."[95] Hmong refugees often could not remember the denominations or names of the churches that had sponsored them—but they were certain that their sponsor had been a Christian church. Neng Xiong, for example, could only identify her sponsor as "the church near the plaza near [Interstate] 94 and Western."[96]

Even though churches loomed large in the collective memory of Hmong refugees looking back on their resettlement in the United

States, some Hmong refugees were not necessarily aware of what churches were. "I don't think we even realized that church was church," recalled Yia Lee with a laugh. Yia Lee, a Hmong woman in Saint Paul, had been a child when she and her family arrived in Minnesota and were sponsored by a church in Roseville. "It didn't even register" that her sponsors were Christian, she said. "It was just nice people helping people!"[97] Yia Lee's memory of her sponsors— as "nice people helping people"—reveals an important theme in Hmong resettlement stories that accords with how churches remembered their sponsorship experience: refugee resettlement produced many close relationships between refugees and Christian church volunteers. When asked what the most important help that Trinity Lutheran Church offered his family, Yong Kay Moua said, "I think that the friendship is number one." He was grateful for the outpouring of love shown by the congregation through home visits, phone calls, and warm conversations, all of which made the transition to the United States easier. The church, he said, brought "the friendship, the confidence, and the closeness to the community."[98]

When asked to describe their experience with church sponsorship, Hmong refugees often spoke warmly of their church sponsors. "We were so lucky!" said Rev. Timothy Vang. "The church helped us in everything." Sponsored by a Catholic church in Green Bay, Wisconsin, he recalled how one couple took charge of the resettlement effort and gave generously of their time and money as they helped the Vang family enroll in school, find jobs, and make friends. "That sponsor was very helpful to us!" he said. "I feel bad for the other families that did not have good sponsors like us."[99] Similarly, Yong Kay Moua expressed appreciation for the organized, comprehensive help he received from his sponsoring church, Trinity Lutheran Church in Eau Claire, Wisconsin. He had a job waiting for him immediately upon his arrival because one of the church members had a connection at a local company, and the church also made preparations for educating his wife and children. "Each week, one couple come to take us to do one thing," he said. "So, in order for us to go to school at that time, they already lined up babysitter for us, and some couple take morning, some couple take afternoon. And everything kind of laid down and had a plan for helping us at that time." Hundreds of people at the church offered friendship, he said.[100] Similarly, Fong

Her, a Hmong man who was resettled in Saint Paul, recalled the generosity of the church that assisted his family:

> When we got to Saint Paul, it was May the 9th, 1980. It was still cold that year. We don't have any coats, they passed us coats for that spring. A church sponsored us—it's a church it's not a family—that meant they had more funds to receive us at that time. We had a house ready to move in when we got here. We had food in the refrigerator. We had a lot of food. We never experienced that and then also, we had people—brother-in-law, aunt and uncle they were already here—so when we got to Saint Paul it was a lot easier for us kids and for the adults also because a lot of people that we knew were already here. It was a church that sponsored us, not a family[;] that meant we had everything ready when we got here.[101]

Hmong refugees frequently expressed gratitude for the churches' kindness and remembered their sponsors with great fondness. Love was a common element in Hmong memories. "My sponsor took very good care of us," said Bee Yang, adding, "They loved us very much."[102] Yong Kay Moua likened the care of his sponsoring church as similar to the love given by parents "raising a little baby from the beginning."[103] Sponsors were so close to the refugees that they sometimes participated in special, even intimate, occasions. Neng Vang, a Hmong woman resettled in Saint Paul, recalled that when she went into labor with her second child, her sponsor, Bob, accompanied her to the hospital to deliver the baby. Another volunteer family brought Christmas presents for her children every year.[104]

The closeness of these relationships, while often characterized by love and joy, could also be quite complicated. Tzianeng Vang, who arrived in Missouri as a teenager, recalled the close relationship he shared with the pastor of the church that sponsored him. "He was so proud of me," he said. "Every day I improved, I acquired a new word and would talk to him. . . . I became probably the son that he wanted because he only had two daughters." The pastor regularly brought the boy to two congregations that he led—"I'm his experiment" to show off, explained Tzianeng Vang—and once the pastor even brought him to a big church in a neighboring city for a special Thanksgiving service at which he had been invited to preach. There, at the center of this enormous church with balconies that resembled a grand theater, the pastor praised the boy's progress before the crowd of people and said that "he's so proud that, within a week [after] we arrived, this many English words I already acquired," said Tzianeng Vang. The attention in such a prestigious setting filled him with "awe." Later, the close relationship was one reason why it was difficult for the family to leave Missouri to reunite with relatives elsewhere. The pastor "didn't want us to leave him that soon, or maybe ever," Tzianeng Vang said, "and by leaving, he probably felt like we have—we did not live up to what our responsibilities as a sponsored family should have been to that [church and] to him, personally." It was for this reason that Tzianeng Vang and the pastor "got disconnected."[105]

Tzianeng's experience of getting "disconnected" raises a critical point: because many Hmong families like Tzianeng Vang's hoped to reunite with their relatives as soon as possible, sponsorship relationships were sometimes brief and not very close at all. For example, Rev. Cher Moua, a Hmong pastor in the Twin Cities, was sponsored by a Lutheran congregation in Washington, DC. However, he and his family had only a brief relationship with their church sponsor because, after only one week, his older brother made contact with a cousin and uncle in Pittsburgh, and Cher and family boarded a bus bound for Pennsylvania.[106]

Moreover, relationships with sponsors were not always warm and familial. Some sponsors, in Timothy Vang's opinion, were even "very cruel" to Hmong refugees by not giving them enough food to eat or bringing the children to school.[107] Sua Vu Yang, a Hmong woman in Minnesota, recalled her first days living in the home of her sponsors, who fed her family bread. Used to eating rice, she and her family could not stomach American food. "We thought we had made a mistake to come to this country because we had brought our children to a place like this," she said. "I could not eat and every time I looked at the food, my tears dropped immediately and I thought I would starve to death."[108]

Conflict, often rooted in cultural misunderstanding, caused some refugees to leave their sponsors. Yia Lee recounted an incident in which she and her siblings ate a bunch of bananas that were not intended for them. Her angry church sponsor, with whom her family was living, "made some kind of physical gesture that my dad didn't feel comfortable with," she said. Her father, in response, made preparations to leave the sponsor's house immediately. As Yia Lee recalled,

> In the middle of the night, that same night, my dad and my brothers, sisters, they were all packed, in the middle of the front yard. . . . And then the sponsor's husband, he called my uncle and said, "Tell them it's the middle of the night! They have to stay until morning." So they went back in. They stayed for one more night and morning and then my sister went and picked them up.[109]

Yia Lee's family had chosen to resettle as refugees in the United States because they believed that it was no longer safe for them to live in Laos and Thailand. In this instance, when it was an American church sponsor who made them feel unwelcome and unsafe, the family used a familiar strategy, which was to pack up and flee—even at night, if necessary. Moreover, the actions of Yia Lee's father reveal something more profound about the agency of Southeast Asian refugees: that despite the devastation of war and persecution and forced migration, refugees insisted on being more than victims. The decisions to pack the family's bags and leave the sponsor's house were, to borrow Yen Le Espiritu's words, "moments of action as refugees search for and insist on their right to more."[110]

«««◇»»»

The congregational sponsorship project organized by Kathleen Vellenga made possible the successful resettlement of thousands of refugees all across the country, but this strategy of resettlement later waned in popularity during the 1980s. Why congregational sponsorship declined is unclear. "Compassion fatigue" is one explanation, but the decline could have owed to structural changes, such as the shift to a case management system in which voluntary agencies offer more centralized services.[111] To be sure, some agencies, especially CWS and LIRS, still rely on congregations, though not as much as they have in the past.[112] Southeast Asian refugees, at least, relied less on congregations by the 1980s. As Southeast Asian refugees became more established in the United States, the link between Southeast Asian refugees and church sponsorship diminished as refugee families achieved enough economic stability to petition for, sponsor, and support relatives on their own.[113]

Though the congregations' role in Southeast Asian refugee resettlement waned and they often lost contact with the refugees sponsored, church volunteers recalled their experiences with congregational sponsorship with great fondness. In sharing their stories, Christian sponsors did not emphasize how they changed refugees' lives, but how refugees changed their lives. Dorothy Knight said that she learned as much from the refugees as they learned from her. She described her connection with refugees as "mutual," declaring that refugees had taught her that "if it isn't mutual, it isn't anything." In particular, she expressed gratitude for the Hmong families who had given her the gift of modeling the true meaning of "generosity, acceptance, enthusiasm, [and] excitement."[114]

To be honest, enthusiasm and excitement were not often in short supply among Christian resettlement volunteers. The people involved in congregational sponsorship were deeply committed to refugee resettlement as a fulfilling form of service and a ministry of Christian compassion. This deep commitment was the system's most distinctive asset. Nearly four decades after the fall of Saigon, long past the era when Southeast Asian refugees dominated the evening news, Joanne Karvonen and Mary Mergenthal continued to contribute to the Refugee Core Committee, Pearl Jones continued to maintain close friendships with the Hmong women who attended her sewing classes and Bible studies, and Sister Rosemary Schuneman continued to teach English, despite battles with cancer. For all of these women, the work of welcoming refugees reached far beyond finding jobs and homes and preventing welfare dependency, which were the primary issues that concerned government officials in charge of planning resettlement. For people like Karvonen, Mergenthal, Jones, and Schuneman, resettlement was a ministry imbued with moral meaning, a labor of heartfelt hospitality, and an expression of their lifelong commitment to putting their faith into action. Refugee resettlement, put simply, was lived religion.

Refugee resettlement was a responsibility handed down to churches by government, but church volunteers also saw refugee resettlement as a responsibility handed down to them by God. In this work, easy distinctions between religious and nonreligious work were difficult, even impossible. Church volunteers straddled the boundary between public and private, and church and state, in almost everything that they did. They practiced their religion not simply by sharing Bibles and participating in worship services but through serving the poor, feeding the hungry, clothing the naked, offering shelter to the war-weary—and implementing the public-private resettlement program of the state.

But while the religious character of resettlement work gave congregational sponsorship its dynamism, it also created its dilemmas. The overlap of church and state and the religiousness of church refugee ministries would raise concerns about the new requirements of serving an increasingly multireligious refugee population.

4

Pluralizing Resettlement

CHRISTIAN ENCOUNTERS WITH
THE HMONG WAY

When the members of Macalester-Plymouth Church agreed to sponsor a refugee family with the Dayton Avenue Presbyterian and House of Hope churches, they prepared for what they expected would be a Vietnamese family. They raised funds, gathered housewares, collected coats, and arranged for an apartment. Only later did officials at the International Institute of Minnesota inform them that they had been assigned a Lao family. Then, just days before the family was due to arrive, they learned more surprising news. The refugee family they would be sponsoring was not Vietnamese and not Lao, but Hmong.

The church volunteers scrambled to learn what they could about this group of people. One member of the sponsorship committee, Paula Nessa, was responsible for finding food for the refugee family. She had little knowledge of who the Hmong were, where they had come from, and, most pertinent to her assignment, what they might want to eat. Conscientious about her work and committed to feeding the family well, she visited the local library to look up "Hmong" in the encyclopedia, which unfortunately had little guidance to offer. Uncertain where else to turn, she visited several local Chinese restaurants in town to see if any of the people who worked there happened to know about Hmong people and Hmong food preferences.[1]

Nessa's experience was not uncommon. Nearly everybody involved in the early stages of Hmong refugee resettlement asked the same question: who are the Hmong? Several church volunteers confessed to knowing next to nothing about them, in part because Hmong people are an ethnic group without a state of their own. "I had never heard of Hmong people until shortly before we got the first family here," said Joanne Karvonen. "That was not a word that I was even familiar with, and I traveled quite a bit! But I did not know. I had heard of Laos, of course, but I hadn't heard about the Hmong tribes."[2] Some Americans did not even know there was a difference between Hmong and Vietnamese people. "I mean, because it was the Vietnam War, most people thought that everyone that was coming was Vietnamese, and it took a while for people to understand that the Hmong are not Vietnamese, and that was a stumbling block for a lot of people," said Tom Kosel, who worked with a refugee employment program at Catholic Charities. He recalled how people wondered, "What is this H-mong stuff?"[3]

Even members of Congress were unfamiliar with Hmong people. During a 1977 hearing about refugee admissions, Representative Hamilton Fish interrupted Richard Holbrooke, assistant secretary of state for East Asian and Pacific Affairs, during a report on Hmong refugees in Thailand.

"H-M-O-N-G is pronounced how?" asked Fish.

"Wong," responded Ambassador Charles Whitehouse, Ambassador to Thailand.

"Forget the H. Okay," said Fish.[4]

In truth, Whitehouse was incorrect; "Hmong" is not pronounced "Wong" at all. American officials planning for Hmong resettlement knew very little about the people they intended to help—and they could not even get past the name. The H sound that Fish declared he could simply "forget" is an important sound that cannot just be dropped. Fish's response encapsulates the encounter between Hmong refugees and American resettlement workers: whether it was with language or religion, many people in the United States struggled to make sense of different letters or rituals, and if these were not commensurate to their own letters or rituals, they sometimes responded by simply ignoring them and pretending they do not exist.

To their credit, many church sponsors readily recognized their lack of knowledge about Hmong people and earnestly tried to learn more. "We had to hustle around and learn what we could about

Hmong people," said Mary Mergenthal.[5] Church sponsors' desire to learn more about the Hmong arose in part from their practical responsibility to help refugees and also their curiosity about different cultures. The latter is perhaps what made refugee sponsorship "glamorous" in the early years of Hmong resettlement.[6]

But if the foreignness of Southeast Asian refugees provoked curiosity, it also generated concern. In 1964, a refugee affairs expert at the World Council of Churches observed, "We are now faced with the problem of refugees who are by and large nonwhite and by and large non-Christian . . . and it remains to be seen how we will react."[7] A little over a decade later, in the immediate days after the fall of Saigon, Pastor Tomas Meeks at Christ Lutheran Church in Saint Paul shared a similar worry about the impending arrival of Southeast Asian refugees. "Many problems will arise because of the new influx of people to America," he said. Meeks confessed that the arrival of "new people coming from different cultures and backgrounds" made him apprehensive about a resettlement project undertaken by a nation and a community already burdened by racial, ethnic, and religious strife. "What we will have is a new minority group in America," Meeks wrote. "How will these new immigrants be accepted?"[8]

«««‹›»»»

For most of their history, American voluntary agencies had not had to deal with the question of how they would react to a nonwhite and non-Christian refugee population. The agencies had typically served their own religious kind, or at least religious groups with which they were somewhat familiar.[9] But circumstances changed in the 1970s as new groups of refugees were in need of help. Ingrid Walter, former director of the Lutheran Immigration and Refugee Service (LIRS), recalled this period as a moment when Lutheran churches first intentionally sponsored refugees who were not Lutheran. "It was a group of refugees rather than Lutheran refugees," she said.[10] Other cultural developments created new conditions for resettlement work. Religious pluralism—both the social reality of religious diversity and the prescriptive ideal for managing it—reconfigured the terrain on which Christian voluntary agencies and congregations operated. In these new circumstances, the churches that agreed to sponsor Southeast Asian refugees were signing up for a resettlement project unprecedented in scope and unparalleled in its religious and cultural complexity.

Government, voluntary agencies, and sponsoring churches involved in Southeast Asian refugee resettlement strived to adapt to these new circumstances of religious diversity.[11] Voluntary agencies and church sponsors made sincere efforts to respect refugees' religions and to put ideals of religious pluralism into practice. Church sponsors demonstrated that they were genuinely interested in learning more about the refugees they sponsored and developing a deeper understanding of Hmong spiritual beliefs and practices.

However, three main problems undermined this pluralistic vision of resettlement. The first was that American resettlement workers simply did not have a good understanding of the Hmong way. Voluntary agencies and church sponsors had relatively little information about Hmong beliefs and practices, and the information that was available drew heavily from accounts by Christian missionaries who had worked in Laos several decades earlier. The missionary-based guides framed Hmong beliefs and rituals as primitive superstition or evil demon worship, and sometimes as both. Efforts by government to identify and describe Hmong beliefs and practices were also conceptually flawed and rooted in a Protestant-centric concept of religion that was incommensurate with traditional Hmong beliefs and practices.

The second problem was intricately tied to the first: that efforts to respect the religions of refugees was only possible when church sponsors recognized that refugees had a religion in the first place. Recognizing and respecting the religions of refugees was partly a matter of knowledge and familiarity. However, Hmong traditions posed a more fundamental problem in that they utterly confounded Americans' definition of religion, to the degree that Hmong beliefs and practices were often not legible as a religion. This confusion would have practical consequences for both Hmong refugees and the Christians who resettled them.

The third problem had roots in the "shadow establishment" structure of American refugee resettlement.[12] At the local level, the religious complications inherent in the church-state system of resettlement were most salient, largely because government and voluntary agencies relied so heavily on Christian churches, which were unequivocally religious institutions. This dependence on congregations undercut the goal of pursuing refugee resettlement as a religiously pluralistic enterprise. As discussed earlier, congregations sometimes undertook sponsorship with open missionary purposes. But even the resettlement activities that appeared to involve little religion at all—job placement support and English instruction, for example—were undertaken by institutions and individuals that were firmly rooted in a Christian worldview and culture. Christian assumptions about how to live, work, play, and pray shaped how resettlement workers interacted with refugees and guided their integration into American life.[13]

Voluntary agencies attempted to guide congregations in how to navigate the blurry boundary between church and state and how to understand and respect the beliefs and practices of Southeast Asian refugees. On both fronts, however, the guidance was ambiguous, confusing, and limited. At the heart of the problem was the question of what counts as religion, a matter that affected both sides of the resettlement encounter. On the one hand, there was uncertainty about which aspects of Christian resettlement work were religious, and on the other hand, there was uncertainty about which aspects of Hmong life were religious.

Ultimately, putting religious pluralism into practice was difficult to do, especially in the context of the American refugee resettlement system. Capitalizing on the enthusiastic volunteer efforts of congregations allowed government and voluntary agencies to expand the scope of their resettlement services and aid refugees at a fraction of the cost. At the same time, delegating work to churches, especially with little oversight, created new problems. It compromised efforts by voluntary agencies to respect religious differences, a commitment that was especially complicated to honor when working with the Hmong, a group that resettlement sponsors struggled to understand. Good intentions notwithstanding, neither the state nor its Christian partners could fully enact its own benevolence.

"Be Careful to Respect Their Religion and Their Religious Practices"

When Pastor Meeks at Christ Lutheran Church in Saint Paul worried about resettling "new people coming from different cultures and backgrounds," his concerns reflected a widespread unease about ongoing transformations in American life. Hmong refugees arrived for resettlement just as a series of midcentury immigration reforms were changing the ethnic and racial demographics of the United States. The most notable of these reforms was the Hart-Celler Act of 1965, which ended the discriminatory national origins quota system and contributed to increased ethnic and racial diversity in the American population.[14]

These immigration reforms also transformed American religious life, especially due to the arrival of new immigrants from Asia.[15] To be sure, the United States was home to some Asian Americans before 1965, and they had thriving religious communities.[16] But the increase in Asian immigration in the last three decades of the twentieth century directly contributed to the substantial growth of the Buddhist, Hindu, Muslim, and Sikh populations in the United States.[17] These new immigrants and the new religious diversity that they brought changed the American religious landscape and transformed many aspects of American public life, from schools to the military.[18] They also changed the racial and cultural makeup of American churches, facilitating what has been called "the de-Europeanization of American Christianity."[19]

As the United States became an increasingly multicultural and multireligious society, the ideal of religious pluralism gained currency. The term "pluralism" is in fact a couple centuries old, dating back to the eighteenth-century Anglican practice of holding two offices simultaneously. By the early twentieth century, however, American thinkers like Horace Kallen were using the term to refer not simply to ideas and practices in church but in society more broadly. As Kallen argued in 1915, the United States should not be a melting pot that assimilates immigrants and melts away their differences, but a symphony in which "each ethnic group is the natural instrument, its spirit and culture are its theme and melody, and the harmony and dissonances and discords of them all make the symphony of civilization." In other words, Kallen believed that diverse cultural and religious groups could live in harmony and together create a thing of great beauty—American civilization.[20]

Kallen's vision of America was particularly appealing later in the twentieth century. The embrace of pluralism was in part linked to the reality that as the American population became more religiously diverse, learning to get along with a Buddhist classmate or a Muslim coworker became both easier and more necessary.[21] But the embrace of pluralism also reflected the emphasis on national unity during World War II and the Cold War era. Americans celebrated the United States as a "tri-faith" nation of Protestants, Catholics, and Jews.[22] The global fight against Communism was an important context for how people thought about American religious diversity. Religious diversity was a social reality that needed to be managed carefully, and it was also used as powerful evidence of American exceptionalism.[23] A commitment to religious pluralism and religious freedom offered the United States the opportunity to differentiate itself from the Communist countries from which so many Cold War refugees had fled.

These Cold War refugees included Southeast Asian refugees, whom government officials recognized at the outset as posing some new religious problems. At one congressional hearing in 1975, officials from the Interagency Task Force shared several concerns about how religion disrupted the resettlement process. First, they hesitated to assign non-Christian refugees to Christian church sponsors. "It was very hard to ask a parish to be responsible for somebody of another faith or no faith at all," said Frank Wisner, a member of the Task Force. The needs of church sponsors were not the only consideration; there were also the needs of refugees, who sometimes refused to be sponsored by an agency or congregation that was not of their own religion. At the same congressional hearing, Julia Taft, also of the Task Force, noted that refugees' concerns about religion had produced an imbalance of caseloads among the voluntary agencies. Refugees were free to register with the voluntary agency of their own choosing, and because many Vietnamese refugees were Catholic, the United States Catholic Conference (USCC) ended up with three-quarters of Vietnamese refugees. Vietnamese refugees wished to be resettled by fellow Catholics and, as Taft explained, were "reluctant to be processed by a religious group of another denomination."[24]

At the state level, too, government resettlement planners acknowledged the need to handle religious differences delicately. In general, religious matters were of secondary concern to government officials, who tended to discuss religion only when it related to an employment, education, or health issue. For example, the Minnesota State Refugee Advisory Council (MSRAC) received a report about troubles at a local hospital, where refugee workers had been asked to do tasks that conflicted with their religious and cultural beliefs. "Two previous Indochinese women were hired for housekeeping and seemed to be doing well but then quit," the report read. "The problem was that they were occasionally required to clean in rooms with dead bodies. This violated some cultural and/or religious views of theirs, was very traumatic for them, and they quit."[25] Concern about refugee mental health also led the Health Task Force of the MSRAC to recommend better service coordination with "indigenous religious groups."[26] As these examples indicate, religious accommodation was not necessarily the primary concern of government and voluntary agencies, but they paid attention when beliefs and practices affected refugees' health or employability.

Unsurprisingly, voluntary agencies, especially the religious ones, discussed religion more often. Voluntary agency staff knew that they were expected to respect and accommodate the religious diversity of their refugee clientele and to refrain from proselytizing. Tom Kosel recalled how the new circumstances changed the resettlement work of Catholic and Lutheran agencies in Minnesota:

> Because you're receiving public funds and other sources of funding outside of your own religious community . . . there are certainly restrictions and so on in terms of promoting your own religion or requiring people to participate in services of your own religion. Those kinds of restrictions have to be followed. At Catholic Charities, you come in for services; you don't have to start the day praying or something. Some other agencies that provide services require their participants to be part of religious ceremonies or services. That's not something done at Catholic Charities or Lutheran Social Service, to my knowledge. It could be an optional thing in some circumstances, but, by and large, the promoting of a particular religious belief isn't done.[27]

The actions Kosel described reflected the instructions he and others received from the national leadership of the voluntary agencies and denominations. For example, according to the guidelines that the National Council of Churches gave to Church World Service (CWS) and its affiliated social service agencies, religious charities receiving public funds were required to ensure "religious liberty for all persons and groups." The National Council of Churches argued that the "establishment of religion, insofar as it entails governmental support, promotion, preference or control of churches or religion, is damaging both to prophetic Christian faith and to religious liberty.[28]

If the professionalized staff of the voluntary agencies were careful to avoid "the promoting of a particular religious belief," it was even more important that the sponsoring congregations did so, too, because the volunteers of these churches had the closest relationships with refugees and the most direct encounter with religious difference. As it turned out, though, ensuring that congregational sponsors respected religious differences and refrained from proselytizing proved difficult, for several reasons. For one, the driving force behind congregational sponsorship was its corps of volunteers, who often did not have the same experience as the paid staff of the professionalized voluntary agencies. Accountability was also a challenge, as congregations were one step removed from direct government oversight. Voluntary agencies were not always well positioned to monitor congregations, either. In some areas, the voluntary agencies did not have local offices to support and oversee sponsorships, and church sponsors had a tremendous amount of freedom.[29] "When a volag is getting in contact with a particular congregation there, there is supposed to be some good orientation process," said Kosel, "and you go in to have meetings with the parish leadership, and you explain the ins and outs of proper resettlement. To my knowledge, that's what's done, but that doesn't mean that there wouldn't still be individuals in congregations that either don't get that message or don't follow that message very closely. So you're dealing with individuals here that you can't always be on top of [in] all situations."[30] Working with a congregation's priest or pastor was one important strategy the voluntary agencies used. However, as LIRS discovered through a study of resettlement efforts in Iowa, lay people were often "more personally involved than the pastor" in sponsorship work.[31] The church volunteers involved in congregational sponsorship were generous and energetic, but also potentially difficult to manage.

Even more important, refugee sponsorship involved a fundamentally unequal relationship, and refugees' material dependence on sponsors created complex and often uncomfortable dynamics. One volunteer with a refugee agency acknowledged this power differential in an interview with the *Minneapolis Star Tribune*: "A lot of people say they feel obligated [and think] 'They do a lot of good things for us. In return, what should we do for them? What makes them happy?'"

According to this volunteer, in these circumstances, refugees faced significant religious pressures. "[Pretend that] you don't understand a word of English," the volunteer said. "You don't know what's going on in church. Do you think we enjoy that?"[32] Congregational sponsors also acknowledged that the circumstances of dependency caused refugees to avoid disagreeing with or disappointing their sponsors. As one Lutheran sponsor observed, "The refugees are very thankful and appreciative of what is being done for them. They want to please and be agreeable. . . . They want to please and are often reluctant to say anything they feel 'might cause trouble.'"[33]

Complicating matters further, congregational sponsors desired to actively shape the lives of refugees, often according to what the sponsors believed was best. The paternalistic and familial language that resettlement volunteers used to describe sponsorship reveals their desire for close bonds with the refugees, but also the subordinate role that they sometimes expected the refugees to assume. Kosel recalled how some sponsors treated Hmong refugees as if they were children "just because they were physically small and they didn't know how to speak English."[34] Similarly, Kathleen Vellenga criticized a "big brother" approach to sponsorship. "If you're coming in there [saying], 'I'm going to be your big sister, big brother,' it's not going to work," she cautioned. "Most little sisters and little brothers think their big brothers and sisters are too bossy."[35] For all these reasons, congregations, as sources of valuable help, could wield tremendous influence on refugees, including in the area of religious belief and practice.

Kosel was especially indignant about abuses of power that he witnessed during his time working in resettlement. He recalled one instance when a Vietnamese family in rural Minnesota experienced what he considered inappropriate religious coercion:

> One of the churches was, in effect, trying to "convert" the people to their religion, and they would actually pick them up, eight o'clock in the morning on Sunday, drive them over to their church, and have them attend their services, and then take them back home, and then, of course, being very practicing Catholics, they [the Vietnamese family] would then come to the Catholic church. And I didn't hear about that, or I wasn't aware of that, until quite a long time into it. But it was one of those things that has to be carefully watched when you're dealing with congregations and refugees—that there's a re-

spect for refugees' current religious beliefs. And we aren't here to change their beliefs; we're just here to help them.

Ensuring "respect for refugees' current religious beliefs" proved difficult when so much of the work of resettlement was done by congregations and church volunteers, who sometimes had openly evangelistic aims that conflicted with the pluralistic approach to resettlement generally favored by the voluntary agencies. This problem is not surprising, especially since many congregations saw their work as a form of Christian ministry, not as the delegated work of the state.

Religious voluntary agencies, which mediated between government and congregations, thus found themselves in a delicate situation: they needed to cultivate enthusiasm for religious service and also manage the religiousness of that service. Their effort to reconcile these two goals is evident in the sponsorship manuals and educational pamphlets that the voluntary agencies created to prepare congregations to serve as sponsors. The materials that they created reveal how voluntary agencies attempted to instruct congregations not only in the best practices of resettlement but also in the proper expression of religion and the appropriate responses to religious difference. While no doubt well intentioned, the guidance that the voluntary agencies provided in these sponsorship manuals was sometimes as confusing as it was clarifying.

For one, voluntary agencies declared almost uniformly that they expected congregations to respect the religious beliefs of the refugees. "Great care should be taken to refrain from showing disdain or disrespect for the refugees' religious beliefs and convictions," advised World Relief.[36] Similarly, the USCC urged sponsors to "Be careful to respect their religion and their religious practices."[37] And LIRS acknowledged that "it is natural for you to want to share with the refugees what is important to you and what you believe is beneficial" but emphasized that "respecting [refugees] as human beings means respecting their beliefs as well."[38]

The rationale for accommodating religious difference was that failure to do so undermined the overall resettlement effort. As explained in a CWS sponsorship manual, religion is "a fundamental part of one's identity," and the agency cautioned against "rushed or pressured religious changes or 'conversions,'" which the organization considered to be "disastrous both psychologically and emotionally for refugees." In making this argument, CWS emphasized the suffering experienced by refugees and explained that religious unsettlement complicated other aspects of well-being. "Religious beliefs and traditions may be one of the elements of their heritage that refugees have not lost in their flight," CWS stated. "Abruptly relinquishing these beliefs adds one more loss to their already overflowing burden of losses and grief and thus further complicates their adjustment, mental health and ultimate integration."[39]

At the same time, voluntary agencies acknowledged that sponsors felt a Christian commitment to share the gospel. "The willingness of the churches to reach out in sponsorship to refugees is based upon their religious beliefs and values," said CWS in the manual. "It is inevitable, therefore, that sooner or later various questions arise that are related to 'sharing faith' and the responses of the refugee in these matters. The desire to share our Christian heritage and faith is an important part of the church."[40] The key, then, was for the voluntary agencies to instruct the sponsoring churches in the proper ways of "sharing the faith" with refugees. As Rev. Jack O'Donnell explained in a 1977 memo to others in the Lutheran resettlement network,

> Some clear theological guidelines need to be offered sponsoring churches so that they can deal with the tension that is inevitable between accepting and respecting the non-Christian convictions of the refugee, and our un-qualified mandate to "make disciples of all nations." Close to that subject, some guidelines are needed relative to avoiding what, amongst the Indochinese, we recognize as "rice Christians." Surely there will be a counterpart of that in any group of refugees who come to us in the hope of gaining political and social freedom and with inaccurate perceptions of what life is like in the US. Most of the refugees wish to express their gratitude to their sponsors. But, joining the sponsoring church is not an appropriate expression of that appreciation.[41]

Voluntary agencies wanted to strike a balance between respecting the religious beliefs of refugees and respecting sponsors' desire and duty to share their Christian faith. To that end, voluntary agencies used the sponsorship manuals to give church sponsors practical guidance in distinguishing between appropriate and inappropriate means of Christian witness. For example, they encouraged congregations to invite refugees to worship services and other church events for the sake of facilitating bonds of friendship, which they considered essential for refugees' spiritual and emotional well-being. As the resettlement manual for World Relief put it, "Sponsors should feel free to invite their refugees to go to church with them" because one of the basic tasks of resettlement was "inclusion in spiritual experiences through church and church-related activities."[42] Similarly, LIRS advised that refugees should be "welcome to participate in church activities and services."[43] According to one LIRS sponsorship manual, refugees benefited from congregations that warmly offered "the fellowship of loving persons who are willing to share themselves with others." Even if the family is not Christian, LIRS stated, the refugee family "will appreciate being related to a family of persons who are concerned about them." LIRS emphasized the importance of offering a choice, since it is difficult to discern refugees' wishes. "Invitations to church activities may, in fact, be welcome," read the manual. "One refugee, for example, asked his sponsor if he could bring a friend with him to church. The sponsor assured him he could. 'Good!' the refugee said, explaining, 'He was not sponsored by Lutherans, and I did not know if it was all right.'"[44]

At the same time, the voluntary agencies urged sponsors to be careful that they are not coercive or aggressive when they invited refugees to participate in church activities. World Relief, for example, advised that "refugees must not be coerced or placed under obligation to accept" invitations to attend church.[45] The voluntary agencies also encouraged congregations to separate religious and nonreligious activities. For example, LIRS suggested that congregations "keep religious instruction and English-as-a-Second-Language training distinct." Although "teaching the Christian faith and English at the same time may seem to be a good idea," the manual cautioned that "to overemphasize religious instruction at the expense of language training is also unfair."[46] (In practice, many congregations did combine religious and language instruction, especially those churches that were not working with voluntary agencies as sponsors but offering programs to the community on their own. Saint Paul's Evangelical Lutheran Church in Minneapolis, for example, hosted a tutoring program called "Teaching Language and Christ," which served many Hmong refugees.[47])

Finally, voluntary agencies used the sponsorship manuals to clarify the goals of refugee resettlement. "The purpose of sponsorship is not to gain new members or convert refugees to Christianity or to Lutheranism," advised LIRS.[48] Religious leaders and voluntary agency officials urged churches and volunteers not to take advantage of the dependent relationship of sponsorship. "Jesus never bribed anybody to do anything," declared one interfaith leader in an interview with the *Atlanta Journal-Constitution*.[49] Ellen Erickson, director of the refugee resettlement programs at the Lutheran Social Service of Minnesota, echoed the same sentiment in an interview with the *Minneapolis Star Tribune*. "What's important is to offer the friendship and support," she said. "What you need to caution them [churches] is that there's not a price tag on your help."[50]

Because they recognized that many Southeast Asian refugees came from cultures and religions that were unfamiliar to congregational sponsors, the voluntary agencies also created a series of cultural guides about Southeast Asian refugees in order to educate churches and volunteers about the people they were resettling. These guides aimed to instruct sponsors about who the Hmong were, what the Hmong believed, and what precisely the "Hmong religion" was that resettlement volunteers were expected to respect. Most significantly, these guides translated Hmong beliefs and practices into a tradition that American sponsors could recognize and accommodate.

Although the goal of the cultural orientation literature was to promote understanding of Hmong refugees, the cultural guides produced misunderstanding. To create the guides, the voluntary agencies drew on the accounts of overseas missionaries who interpreted Hmong traditions through an evangelical Protestant lens. These manuals ultimately reproduced the perception of the Hmong way as an unstable and primitive set of rituals rooted in superstition and irrational fear. The missionaries of the Sawyers' and Andrianoffs' era thus continued to wield influence, this time through the cultural orientation guides that informed how American Christians understood the beliefs and practices of Hmong refugees several decades later.

The cultural orientation guide produced by LIRS offers a case in point. The guide, titled *The Hmong: Their History and Culture,* borrowed material from the National Indochinese Clearinghouse, part of the Center for Applied Linguistics. The guide included a "traditional/historical" article describing the people, culture, beliefs, and folktales of Northern Laos, the region from which many Hmong refugees originated. This article also happened to be the second chapter of the master's thesis of a University of Minnesota graduate student named G. Linwood Barney. Barney was not only an academic anthropologist but a devoted Christian and Missionary Alliance (CMA) missionary who, like Ted and Ruth Andrianoff, had worked at the missionary post in Xieng Khouang, Laos, in the 1950s. As explained in the LIRS guide, "The article has deliberately been left un-updated, to give you an unhampered picture of the life that the older Hmong refugees remember."[51] Given the context in which the information was gathered, the portrait was far from a neutral, "unhampered picture" of Hmong life and would have been better described as a portrait of a CMA missionary anthropologist's encounter with Hmong beliefs and rituals in Laos at midcentury. It is unclear why the creators of the guide chose to turn to Barney as the authority on Hmong beliefs and practices rather than a Hmong person, since Hmong experts were available. The other half of the guide focused on recent Hmong history in Laos and was written by Yang See Koumarn, a Hmong refugee resettled in the United States.

Barney made no prescriptions for burning home altars as the Sawyers and Andrianoffs did, but his particular perspective as an evangelical Protestant missionary in the 1950s shaped his discussion of Hmong beliefs and practices in important ways. To his credit, his description of Hmong rituals was more detailed than that of his peers. Noting that the Hmong were "animistic" and believed in many "*tlan* or spirits" living in the natural world, he described funeral and healing rituals and the significance of the shaman in curing the sick, negotiating with spirits, and interpreting events that portend the future. In identifying the supernatural beings as spirits—and not as "demons" or "devils"—he wrote a primer on Hmong traditions that was generally free of many of the damning statements characteristic of the accounts of his contemporaries, the Sawyers and the Andrianoffs.

Barney's article, however, reproduced the notion that the Hmong way is a set of primitive beliefs and practices that do not amount to a rightful religion. Throughout his description of Hmong rituals, for instance, Barney maintained a tone of suspicion that conveyed his dismissive attitude toward Hmong traditions, even if he did believe that the evil spirits posed harm. He wrote, for example, that Hmong "history contains certain ancestral heroes who are supposed to have taken on pseudo-spirit qualities." In describing the gongs and rattles that shamans use in communicating with the spirit world, Barney used the word "sacred," but he always placed the term in scare quotes. He emphasized that Hmong beliefs and practices were primitive and unstable, noting that "beliefs among the Hmong are vague and inconsistent concerning life after death and the spirit realm." Finally, his decision to use the word "fetish" to describe Hmong home alters and ritual objects reflected his assessment that Hmong beliefs and practices do not amount to a true religion, a judgment similar to that of the Sawyers and the Andrianoffs. Like other CMA missionaries, Barney hesitated to describe Hmong traditions as a "religion," only once describing Hmong beliefs as "religious."[52]

CWS produced its own cultural orientation materials that contained similar Protestant-centric interpretations of Hmong traditions. As with the LIRS cultural orientation guide, the pamphlets created by CWS were detailed and descriptive. One pamphlet, *Religion of the Refugees,* focused specifically on refugees and their religions and included a section that was dedicated to "animism," which CWS defined as "a belief in spirits, including the spirits of dead people as well as those that have no human origin."[53] The authors of the pamphlet explained that "all religious beliefs that are not a part of the world's major faiths are often lumped under animism" and that "even where some of the major faiths are the official religions of the land, the beliefs of the common people are essentially animistic." Such was the case of the Hmong, whose native beliefs and rituals include many of the elements outlined by the CWS pamphlet: belief in a "creator spirit," numerous nature-based spirits, "deified ancestors," and "spirits of the dead," only some of whom are benevolent.

Most striking about *Religion of the Refugees* was its judgment of animists as opportunistic, self-serving, and amoral—even immoral. In contrast to Christians, who were supposed to lead lives of virtue in order to honor God, animists, according to the authors of the pamphlet, "are far more anxious to placate the evil spirits that may do them harm than to honor the good spirits who might help them." Moreover, "rather than seeing themselves as passive victims of the spirit world, animists believe they can use spirit forces for their own benefit" through rituals, sacrifices, offerings, fetishes, and incantations. The pamphlet offered a cynical view of practitioners of the Hmong way and argued that "animists are essentially non-ethical." As the authors wrote, "They believe religious practices are only for getting the best advantage in the power struggle of the spirit world. The animist might turn for religious guidance to the most immoral man of the village, a medicine man whose reputation for antisocial acts may include everything from rape to murder. What matters for the animist is that this person knows the secrets of spiritual power." The pamphlet's suggestion that Hmong people value "the secrets of spiritual power" so much that they would tolerate rapists and murderers was not simply a condemnation of "the religion of the refugees"—it was a condemnation of Hmong refugees themselves.

At the end of the pamphlet, the authors underscored what they saw as the critical differences between animism and Christianity: the former's emphasis on power and agency and the latter's emphasis on grace. "It should be pointed out here that it is a big step from animism to Christianity," they wrote. "It is a step from the basic mistrust of an irresponsible spirit world, that has to be persuaded to do good, all the way to confidence in an eternal loving God." The authors of the pamphlet also wrote that Hmong people might take an instrumental approach to religious conversion. "Animists in the United States may be very happy to be called Christian in order to recap whatever benefits that action might bring without really understanding what Christianity is all about," they noted. "For animists, whatever worship brings the most benefits is the proper worship." The pamphlet, in other words, emphasized that Hmong people take a transactional approach to religious life.[54]

Another CWS pamphlet claimed that Hmong—and Southeast Asian people more generally—are less rational than Americans. In *A Guide to Two Cultures*, CWS aimed to instruct congregational sponsors in the fundamental cultural differences between American and Indochinese people, often doing so with a series of essentialist "us versus them" cultural oppositions intended to foster smooth social interactions. "Rapport is 'a thing of the spirit'; you may sometimes break his rules of social conduct—and he yours—and still become friends," read the guide's introduction. "But at least learn some rules even if, at first, you don't understand the traditions or the religious basis behind them." Among the most important differences that this pamphlet highlighted was Americans' emphasis on thinking and Indochinese people's emphasis on feeling. "REASONS vs. SENTIMENT," the authors stated, was "a basic difference in the American and Indochinese approach to life; this personal approach of the Indochinese cannot be emphasized enough."[55]

Though it is not clear how congregational sponsors read and interpreted these cultural orientation guides, it is at least clear that many congregational sponsors wanted—and desperately needed—information about the cultures and religions of the refugees they were resettling. For example, when Saint Anthony Park Lutheran Church sponsored a Muslim family from Somalia, a member of the Refugee Core Committee attended a seminar about Islam hosted by Augsburg College and reported back to the group about what she had learned.[56] Members of the sponsorship committee regularly shared informative books and magazine articles, planned educational events for the whole congregation, and attended workshops hosted by other community groups active in resettlement efforts. In the Twin Cities, which drew a particularly large population of Southeast Asia refugees, the desire for resources about the Hmong was especially strong. Almost a decade and a half after the first Hmong refugee family arrived in the United States, churches were still hosting cultural orientation events for the congregation and the broader community. First Lutheran Church, for example, sponsored a "Seminar on SE Asian Refugees" to help Saint Paul residents learn about their Hmong, Laotian, Vietnamese, and Cambodian neighbors. "We'll talk about why these people are making new lives in this country and what specific obstacles they have to overcome," the sponsors of the event explained in the church bulletin. "Open your minds and hearts. With knowledge comes understanding."[57] These educational efforts articulated sponsors' sincere intention to serve Hmong refugees with compassion and sensitivity. However, undermining this aspiration was the fact that the educational material about Hmong refugees made available by the voluntary agencies came from people whose cultural assumptions and religious worldviews profoundly constrained their understanding of Hmong people and Hmong beliefs and practices.

"Sit Down and Learn from the People Themselves"

Learning through pamphlets was one way that Christian resettlement workers gained knowledge about pluralistic resettlement; learning through experience was another. And before Southeast Asian refugees began to arrive in large numbers, there had been another group of non-Christian Asian people that the Christian agencies had resettled: Ugandan Asian refugees. Amid growing Indophobic sentiment that held that people of Asian descent were parasites on Ugandan society, Idi Amin, the president and military dictator of Uganda, expelled all noncitizen Asians from Uganda in August 1972.[58] Most of the forcibly removed Ugandan Asians went to the United Kingdom, though some were resettled in the United States, which authorized the admission of 1,500 Ugandan Asians between 1972 and 1973. Classified as "parolees" rather than refugees, Ugandan Asians had access to few resources from the government, and the five voluntary agencies that participated in the program shouldered the responsibility and sought help from the broader community.[59]

In certain ways, this resettlement project resembled subsequent efforts to resettle Southeast Asian refugees. Like Southeast Asian refugees, Ugandan Asian refugees were a non-European, nonwhite, and religiously diverse group, with Muslims, Hindus, Sikhs, and Christians among them. Also like Southeast Asian refugees, Ugandan Asian refugees were resettled by predominantly Christian voluntary agencies that worked with local churches to prepare for the refugees' arrival. In Minnesota, a dozen Lutheran churches and colleges welcomed twenty families—all together, eighty-two refugees from Uganda. As would happen with Southeast Asian refugees, the voluntary agencies and churches scrambled to get ready for the refugees' arrival. "We called it Operation Hectic," Rev. Einar Oberg of Gustavus Adolphus Lutheran Church in northeast Minneapolis told the *New York Times*. Because preparations moved very quickly and because there were so many refugees to house, most Ugandan Asian families lived with the Lutheran church members who sponsored them.[60]

Because most Ugandan Asian refugees were Hindu or Muslim, voluntary agency officials in charge of planning for Southeast Asian refugee looked to their experience with Ugandan Asians for guidance on how to practice pluralism in refugee resettlement. On this matter, they paid special attention to the writing of Nizar Motani, a Ugandan Asian refugee and Bowdoin history professor. Motani, who authored a report titled *The Brown Diaspora*, was curious about how Ugandan Asian refugees, as religious minorities, fared in a Christian resettlement system. "On the whole, the LIRS felt confident that it had performed the task splendidly. . . . But why were some Muslim and Hindu 'Ugaindians' regularly attending their sponsors' churches?" Motani wrote. "Were any of these recently uprooted and vulnerable people being taken advantage of? And what indeed was the religious impact of resettlement by a Christian voluntary agency upon the predominantly Hindu and Muslim refugees?"[61] The answer this question, he interviewed Ugandan refugees resettled at several sites throughout the United States.

Motani discovered some instances in which refugees were "taken advantage of." For example, Motani told of "a pastor inquiring of his single male Ugandan ward if he wished to become a worshipping member of the church" and of "two other families [who] were unsuccessfully pressured, unknown to their pastors, by individual members of the congregation to accept Christ as their Saviour." Moreover, he observed that cultural and religious differences between the sponsors and the refugees sometimes caused serious problems. "For example, a strictly vegetarian Brahmin was given work in a poultry processing plant," Motani wrote. "The resultant psychological and emotional strain, compounded by his family's separation from him because of the expulsion, could not be disguised. The concerned American sponsors naturally suggested psychiatric help which further aggravated the situation. This suggestion about visiting a psychiatrist was tantamount to declaring the Brahmin gentleman, in his mind, mentally ill!" As this situation made clear, Christian sponsors did not understand Hindu needs, and their understanding of what constituted a good job—a seemingly secular matter—in fact reflected their Christian assumptions and worldviews.[62]

Overall, however, Motani praised the good intentions and good practices of LIRS, the voluntary agency that was the focus of his study. While he acknowledged that the Hindu, Muslim, and Sikh refugees had valid reasons to be "very apprehensive about being resettled by Christian congregations," Motani wrote that refugees' worries "were largely laid to rest by the Lutheran congregations' fairly meticulous adherence to LIRS instructions on this matter." In his view, "LIRS rightly tried to alleviate any anxieties the Ugandans might have about their religious fate in America."[63]

Motani's positive assessment of how LIRS resettled Ugandan refugees may owe in part to the distinctive characteristics of Ugandan refugees, who were often urban and well-educated professionals. Because many Ugandan refugees spoke English, communication between refugees and sponsors was relatively easy, and Ugandan refugees were well equipped to advocate for themselves, especially about religious matters. Finally, Muslim, Hindu, and Sikh Ugandan refugees benefited from having recognizable religions. Even if their Christian sponsors were sometimes clumsy in their efforts at accommodation and understanding, those sponsors saw Islam and Hinduism as legitimate religions and made efforts to support refugees' religious observances. One Presbyterian pastor, whose church resettled an Ismaili Muslim family, described these pluralistic practices in an interview with the *Washington Post*. "We have made every effort to see that they pursue their own religious preference including taking them to a mosque in Washington on Sunday," he said. A church volunteer added, "Their religion doesn't allow them to eat pork, and we are careful to respect that when various church members invite the family for dinner." In these and other cases, church sponsors appeared to make a genuine effort to understand and respect the worship and eating practices of Muslim refugees. Their efforts were certainly not perfect; the holy day for Muslims is Friday, for example, and not Sunday, a difference that the Presbyterian pastor perhaps did not know. However, Christian sponsors at least knew that the refugee family they resettled had a different religion, and the congregation tried to adjust their resettlement efforts accordingly.[64]

Adapting resettlement efforts to meet the spiritual and ritual needs of Hmong refugees proved much more difficult, however, and church sponsors who were assigned Hmong families found themselves in an unusually challenging situation. They were called to respect refugees' religions but were given limited and often biased information about those religions. Some sponsors even appear to have been operating with incomplete or inaccurate information about the religious backgrounds of the Hmong. For example, in one update she sent to the members of her congregation, Kathleen Vellenga wrote that "because most Hmong are Christian they are objects for retaliation by the Communists and for this reason many had to flee."[65] In truth, most Hmong refugees did not identify as Christian. In this instance and in many others, congregations' attempts to respect the religious beliefs of the refugees they sponsored were fundamentally undermined by a lack of understanding about what those religious differences involved. In these circumstances, they drew on the resources available to them—what they knew from sponsorship manuals and from personal experiences dealing with Hmong people and other non-European, non-Christian groups. And, as with so many other aspects of refugee resettlement, they pursued the strategy of trial and error and experimented with different approaches to putting pluralism into practice.

Some congregational sponsors considered religion to be a private matter and made efforts to separate religion from resettlement work entirely. Elaine Kirk, a volunteer with the sponsorship committee at Macalester-Plymouth Church, believed that it was fundamentally inappropriate to discuss the issue of religion with the refugees her church sponsored. Even after cultivating a friendship with one refugee family for over a decade, she said that she never once asked them about their religion.[66] Paj Ntaub Lis, a Hmong woman who arrived in the United States as a child, described the couple that sponsored her family as taking a similar stance. The sponsoring couple visited her family frequently, treated them kindly, and was a steadfast source of support and encouragement. However, the couple never once raised the issue of religious beliefs and practices throughout the two decades that they knew her family.[67]

If some congregational sponsors believed that the safest way to handle religious difference was to avoid mention of it altogether, other congregations took a more interventionist approach to accommodation and made efforts to ensure that refugees could maintain their religious traditions. Many sponsoring congregations helped refugees find churches and temples to join, believing that church membership offered a valuable form of community support that is essential for newly arrived refugees to adjust and succeed in America. For example, at Saint Anthony Park Lutheran Church, volunteers with the Refugee Core Committee went to great lengths to find congregations for the Christian Hmong families they sponsored and regularly drove them to services at local Hmong churches.[68]

Holidays, especially Christmas, provided special opportunities to engage in dialogue and explore the similarities and differences in religious beliefs, practices, and traditions. Sponsors were eager to meet with Hmong refugees and "interview" them about how they celebrated Christmas in Laos.[69] At the same time, sponsors wanted to include refugees in holiday celebrations and introduce them to what they considered enjoyable American traditions. In December 1975, for example, the Catholic Archdiocese invited 700 Southeast Asian refugees to a Christmas party involving carol singing, Kris Kringle, and a traditional turkey dinner. As the resettlement coordinator for Catholic Charities explained to the *Catholic Bulletin*, the goal was "to show them how we do things and make them a part of it." Though many Southeast Asian refugees were Catholic, there were many non-Christian Southeast Asian refugees, and sponsors took care to explain Christmas to them and draw connections to refugees' religions and cultures. For example, the parishioners at Saint Odilia Catholic Church tried to explain the meaning of Christmas to the Vietnamese Buddhist family they had resettled. "We've told the family that Christmas gives us hope for growth in our lives and that's an idea that's important in Buddhism too," said the parish's sponsorship coordinator, Brother Jim Brigl.[70]

Congregational sponsors knew that Vietnamese and Cambodian refugees were often Buddhist and that Ugandan Asian refugees were often Muslim; these groups were members of world religions that were known to Christian resettlement workers, even if they did not have previous experience in directly interacting with these religious communities. However, sponsors of Hmong refugees had greater difficulty because Hmong people did not have an institutionalized religion that was recognizable to their Christian sponsors. In numerous ways, Hmong traditions did not fit the Protestant template for religion. Unlike the traditions of Muslim or Buddhist refugees, Hmong beliefs and practices are not centered in a mosque or a temple. They are not rooted in a sacred text or known by an official name. Hmong people do not even have a direct translation for the word "religion" in their native language.

For Americans eager to respect religious difference, of course, this situation put sponsors in a quandary: how does one accommodate religion when it is not even clear that Hmong traditions are a religion? The evidence suggests that there were sincere efforts to accommodate Hmong traditions when Americans viewed Hmong beliefs and practices as a religion. Biloine Young, in her profile of the Center for International Health in Saint Paul, described how a Hmong woman suffering a severe brain injury requested that her craniotomy be postponed so that she could seek the help of a shaman. According to Young, the neurosurgeon assigned to her case was "a deeply religious man" whose own faith opened his heart to the need of interreligious understanding. "The neurosurgeon respected and understood their position of faith," Young wrote. Rather than force the woman to have a procedure that she believed would harm her body and her spirit, the neurosurgeon encouraged the woman's family to bring her home for the shaman's ceremony and to return to the hospital if they decided that they would like to proceed with the surgery. The family brought the woman home for the shaman's ritual, which restored her spiritual health, and then agreed to have the woman undergo a craniotomy shortly after. Ultimately, it was the surgeon's understanding of the woman's convictions as religious—and his own belief in the importance of honoring religious commitments—that proved critical for a harmonious resolution to this situation.[71]

The pluralistic encounter between the Hmong woman and her neurosurgeon went more smoothly than some of the person-to-person efforts made by congregational sponsors and pastors. Because Hmong beliefs and practices were so foreign to them, Christian re-settlement workers struggled in their efforts to comprehend and classify Hmong beliefs and practices and used what they did know to make sense of the Hmong way. Some church sponsors, particularly those coming from an evangelical Protestant background, considered Hmong traditions to be a form of devil worship, just as the Sawyers and Andrianoffs had decades earlier. Pearl Jones, for example, described how she feared for the souls of the Hmong refugees, whose rituals, she believed, centered on "evil spirits." "They worshipped them in the jungle," she said, and they "go out and take food to them and all this stuff." Her understanding of Hmong beliefs and practices sometimes elided Hmong traditions and other Asian religions. At one point, for example, she described how the Hmong "were worshipping Buddha back in Thailand." Like Linwood Barney, she described Hmong beliefs and practices as "demonic things that they had to put up with."[72]

In contrast, Catholic and mainline Protestant church sponsors took a more liberal stance. Rather than viewing the Hmong way as a form of devil worship or spirit bondage, they considered it a spiritual tradition that merited respect and understanding. Applying the same anthropological lens used by their missionary counterparts overseas, these Catholic and mainline Protestant church sponsors viewed Hmong traditions through the lens of other world religions and cultures, especially those of Native Americans. In Minnesota, church sponsors were often familiar with the Dakota and Anishinaabe peoples who first populated the upper Midwest, and they drew parallels between Hmong and Native American rituals. "If you take a look at some of the Native American practices, they can seem pretty similar to some of the Hmong practices," said Tom Kosel. In his view, these similarities "helped people to understand the Hmong culture a little bit more."[73] Similarly, Dorothy Knight took note of resemblances in beliefs and practices and shared historical experiences. She regarded both Hmong and Native American people as highly adaptable, as they were used to "being on the run." Hmong people's ability to survive, especially in the face of encroachments by imperialistic outsiders, was "not too different from what Native Americans experienced when the settlers came into their territory in the United States," she said.[74]

Rev. Paul Tidemann, the Lutheran pastor whose church sponsored and baptized thirty-one Hmong refugees in 1982, also drew parallels between the Hmong and the Native American and Guyanese communities he had previously served. His "transcultural ministry" at Saint Paul Reformation Lutheran Church was guided by inclusivist theological principles—"There are many, many expressions of the oneness of God's creation," he preached on the Sunday he baptized the Hmong families—and also by his direct, practical experience.[75] Before coming to Saint Paul Reformation, Tidemann had ministered to the local Native American community at Holy Trinity Church in Minneapolis and had served as a missionary in Guyana. His missionary experiences at home and abroad made an indelible impression on him, as they exposed him to a rich array of spiritual traditions that used rituals to contend with the presence of active, and sometimes malevolent, spirits. In Guyana, for example, he ministered to African-descended Guyanese who practiced obeah, and in Chicago's South Side, he worked with an Episcopalian priest who planned

an exorcism to heal congregation members who suffered myste-
rious, persistent sickness. Due to this practical education in the mission field, Tidemann possessed "a basic understanding of how other
cultures function" and a greater comfort in dealing with beliefs and
practices that contrasted sharply with his own American Lutheranism. As a result, Tidemann explained that he did not find himself
"totally lost" in ministering to the Hmong church members, whom
he aimed to understand in light of their preexisting religious and
cultural framework. Familiar with communities that believed that
bodily and spiritual afflictions were bound up in one another, he
was cognizant of any "stuff up on the wall"—a home altar, for
instance—that indicated spiritual practices, and he understood that
struggles with sickness "may have something to do with what's going
on in the back of their minds with regard to prior cultural or religious experience." In remaining sensitive to both spiritual and physical wellness, he saw similarities between his work and that of a
Hmong shaman. "When I'm working with Hmong people, and the
shamans are working with Hmong people, they're dealing with some
parallel sorts of things, in some ways," he said.

Tidemann's awareness of the needs and perspectives of non-
Christian people allowed for an appreciation of the significance of
shamanism in Hmong life and a greater willingness to accommodate its rituals. In particular, he appeared more willing to honor
Hmong church members' requests to practice rituals that other Lutheran pastors condemned. As far as he knew, none of the Hmong
families he had known at Saint Paul Reformation Lutheran Church
visited shamans, but, reflecting on how he might have responded had
such a situation occurred, he responded that he "would be okay"
with his church members conducting shamanistic rituals, as long as
these practices were not "causing them pain, difficulty of any sort."
"If the advice that they are getting from a shaman, or the religious
expression that they are engaged in with the shaman, is helpful for
them, all well and good," he said.

Broadly speaking, he did not see Lutheranism and the Hmong
way as mutually exclusive, and in his work with Hmong Lutherans,
he affirmed the value of traditional Hmong culture, beliefs, and
practices. "I think we need to help people acknowledge aspects of
their spirituality which might be helpful, and other aspects of their
spirituality which might be harmful, and that goes for Christianity

as well as any other religion," he said. He believed that one of the most important ways that he could help Hmong refugees was "to affirm who they basically are as human beings out of the culture from which they come." Moreover, he emphasized that "to become a Christian does not mean that you throw everything out the door with regard to the cultural and spiritual experience that you have had."[76] Significantly, Tidemann described Hmong rituals as "cultural and spiritual experiences" and not religious experiences, and he did not say whether he viewed the rituals of shamanism as part of a distinctive Hmong religion. His decision to describe Hmong shamanism as an aspect of Hmong culture made space for the possibility that Hmong shamanism could be compatible with Christianity, which, in his view, can and should affirm cultural diversity.

Most church sponsors, even if they were interested in missionary work, did not have the same experience with obeah in Guyana to inform how they approached Hmong traditions. Rather, they became aware of the practice and significance of Hmong beliefs and practices primarily through their direct relationships with Hmong people and the face-to-face ministry of resettlement. Herein lay both the greatest strength and the greatest weakness of the congregational sponsorship model: if close encounters with religious difference increased the odds that misunderstandings and conflicts would occur, so, too, did close encounters improve understanding of the Hmong way and increase the likelihood that misunderstandings and conflicts could be avoided. In Tom Kosel's view, sponsorship manuals helped, but they needed to be supplemented by real experience:

The other, most important way is to be able to sit down and learn from the people themselves, what their practices are and why they do things the way they do. You learn by being part of it and being with the people. And one of the advantages of the host family situation is that you do get people together and they do have a chance to talk about what things . . . in their lives are done differently in one culture or another. You can't just sit from the outside and throw a blanket over it and say, "This is the way we do it." You have to be with people and talk it over and try to understand it by talking it through.

Like Tidemann, Kosel called Hmong rituals "practices" and framed them as a part of Hmong culture, effectively rendering

Hmong rituals as secular cultural traditions that did not conflict with Catholic religious beliefs and practices. As was the case with Tidemann, Kosel's understanding of Hmong rituals as culture, rather than as religion, may have made it easier for him to spend time with Hmong people and try to understand and accept them. Because of refugee resettlement, he argued, "People learned that there's more than one way of looking at things, and, like I've said before, it broadened people's horizons. They understood why they would do things this way rather than that way, and it helped people to be a little more accepting of other ways of living."[77] In his view, this willingness to engage in open, generous, sincere dialogue with others was an important responsibility of refugee sponsorship, which was most successful if sponsors were able to get to know refugees and meet them on their terms.

In addition to the direct human encounter between people of different beliefs and practices, a shift toward being "more accepting of other ways of living" arose from the notion that Hmong people were part of God's creation and that the Hmong way was a legitimate expression of God's sacred reality. Rejecting life in a Christian "enclave," Dorothy Knight, like many other church volunteers, participated in traditional Hmong rituals when she was invited to do so. Some Hmong shamans she knew—refugees whom she had assisted and later considered dear friends—invited her to attend important ceremonies, such as the "birthing ceremony" for a newborn baby. The ritual was new to her, and fascinating. "A chicken was killed in the kitchen, as part of the traditional celebration," she recounted. "Lots of food and lots of different flavors for me, and it was a wonderful thing to be included in the celebrating because everybody was very happy." Knight also appreciated being included in Hmong funeral ceremonies, which she found "very moving." It was educational for her to witness the practice of Hmong rituals, and, beyond that, she found that the experience of participating in these ceremonies strengthened bonds of friendship and elevated her appreciation of their common humanity. "The main issues of life are very similar, and the emotions can vary a great deal, but there's a lot of similarity," she said, adding that "It's very special to be included in what's important to them."[78] Christian resettlement volunteers not only participated in Hmong rituals when they were invited to do so, but sometimes even incorporated Hmong practices into their daily lives as a gesture of respect. For example, Father Robert Wellisch, a Catholic priest serving the Twin Cities, was known to wear strings, which were tied around his wrist as a blessing during a Hmong *khi tes* ceremony. Doing so demonstrated his connection to the Hmong community to whom he ministered.[79]

However, if sponsors found ways to understand the Hmong beliefs and practices, they did not necessarily do anything with this information. Refugee resettlement, no doubt, was a demanding, time-consuming ministry. Refugees had abundant immediate needs and sometimes arrived with only a few hours of notice. Church sponsors had their hands full, leaving little time to do extensive research on the cultural and religious backgrounds of the families they resettled. "Through reading, through talking, through sometimes referring to counselors, appropriate counselors, we've tried to address the cultural differences and tried to learn what we need to know to deal with these people as human beings," said Joanne Karvonen. However, she added, "There isn't always time to learn about the culture in depth and to really say all the things that you think you should say to these people because you're so busy setting up a bed and finding blankets and getting them winter jackets and those things. It's really easy to let those materialistic concerns take over, which they have to, to a certain extent."[80] Ultimately, in a government resettlement program that emphasized economic independence, finding a job mattered far more than finding a lost and wandering soul. Moreover, in the Christian ministry of refugee care, helping Hmong refugees to locate a shaman or secure a chicken for a ritual sacrifice was often not a priority. In the eyes of some resettlement workers, doing so might actually have been a sin.

«««◇»»»

The World Council of Churches official was perhaps right to express concern about how well the United States would handle "the problem of refugees who are by and large nonwhite and by and large non-Christian."[81] The arrival of a multicultural, multireligious refugee population did indeed introduce new complications to the American system of refugee resettlement. The Christian voluntary agencies had historically served fellow Christians from Europe, and the arrival of Ugandan Asian and Southeast Asian refugees in the 1970s forced significant changes in how they operated and handled the matter of religion in refugee resettlement. As LIRS saw it, the highest priority in resettlement was no longer "spiritual and pastoral care," as it had been with Lutheran refugees from Europe. The new Asian refugee population required revising their understanding of the role of religion in resettlement, which LIRS recategorized as "'the fruits of the gospel' or 'signs of faith.'"[82] Importantly, Christians not only changed how they thought about resettlement, but also how they practiced resettlement, at the level of both the voluntary agencies and the sponsoring congregations.

The public-private system of resettlement did not set them up for success in achieving their pluralistic vision, however. Sponsoring churches and their volunteers had a lot of responsibility but also a lot of freedom. To be sure, it is not clear that congregational sponsors violated the rules set forth in the resettlement manuals, but it is not clear that they abided by them, either. With limited oversight, local congregations were able to interpret the rules as they best saw fit, and even if sponsoring congregations made honest efforts to respect the beliefs and practices of refugees, as voluntary agency and government officials urged them to do, it was not easy to do so. Putting abstract concepts of pluralism into practice in the day-to-day work of resettlement was new and sometimes difficult, especially for Christian sponsors who resettled refugees with beliefs and practices that were so unfamiliar and foreign that they were invisible.

In the end, the advice to meet refugees on their terms was perhaps impossible to achieve. In the process of resettlement, the state had an extraordinary amount of power over refugees' lives. Nothing was ever done on Hmong terms, and this was particularly true when it came to the matter of religion, the contested category through which resettlement workers hoped to find some sort of shared experience. Because Hmong traditions were so incommensurable with how most Americans defined religion, it was hard to find common terms on which to meet. The difficulty of actualizing ideals of pluralism exposed a fundamental problem of American religious pluralism in the first place: the forcing of a particular understanding of religion on other groups and the willingness to accommodate only some types of difference but not others.

The religious challenge of resettlement work is rendered even more clearly when seen from the perspective of Hmong refugees, whose transformations in belief, practice, and identity we turn to next. The experience of Hmong people showed that efforts to make resettlement a respectful and pluralistic enterprise, while successful in the eyes of resettlement workers, were not necessarily respectful and pluralistic in the eyes of the Hmong refugees these efforts intended to serve.

II

RELIGIOUS CHANGE

5

Disrupting the Old Way

THE IMPACT OF REFUGEE POLICY

ON HMONG RITUAL LIFE

Paja Thao's arrival in the United States in February 1984 marked the end of a long and painful journey. In 1975 the war had forced him to flee his village, and for fifteen days he trekked through the jungle to seek safety in Thailand. He spent eight years as a refugee at Nam Yao camp. Finally, nearly a decade after his escape from Laos, Paja Thao resettled in America, where, instead of living high in the mountains, he lived on the eighth floor of an apartment building in the Uptown neighborhood of Chicago.

Paja Thao was one of the fortunate ones. Though he had survived the war and resettled in the United States, many of his relatives remained in Laos and Thailand, where their fates were unknown to him. He had not had any contact with his oldest son since last seeing him in Laos. Two of his daughters remained in Ban Vinai camp with his grandchildren. Countless other members of his clan and community were also left behind in Asia.

The United States was supposed to be a safe haven for victims of war and persecution, and in many ways it was. But for Hmong people like Paja Thao, resettlement in America also brought a new and unexpected problem: spiritual harm, due to an inability to practice the Hmong rituals that had long kept them well. Paja Thao, a shaman, found himself an ocean apart from the people he needed to conduct traditional Hmong rituals. In the United States he no longer had the guidance of elders who offered important ritual knowledge, nor could he draw on the assistance of kin who played an essential part in Hmong healing, funeral, and wedding ceremonies. For those who practiced the Hmong way, these were not insignificant barriers; the failure to conduct rituals correctly could cause spirits to inflict physical harm on humans.

In this chant, sung six months after his arrival in Chicago, Paja Thao expressed the deep frustration he felt as a shaman called to practice traditional Hmong rituals in almost impossible circumstances:

> Now there is only my family
> I, all alone, am not sure how to follow this way
>
> Also, the Bull Spirit
> And the Pig Spirit
> I never feed these spirits as well
>
> But I can remember a little bit
> The rhyme and way the words fit together
> So I can remember some of the way
>
> How to feed these spirits
> Maybe if I try to do it
> Maybe I can do it
>
> But all the elders say
> If you have never done before
> You cannot do it the right way
>
> So it is with the Bull Spirit
> And the Pig Spirit
>
> Maybe I cannot do it
> Because I am all alone[1]

Paja Thao was not only unsure about following the Hmong way—he was also unsure about life in America. As Eric Tang put it, Southeast Asian refugees like Paja Thao were deeply "unsettled" by being resettled.[2] From their very first days in the United States, Hmong refugees found resettlement to be riddled with contradiction. On the one hand, the United States promised to be a place of peace and refuge, with Americans presenting themselves as benevolent providers—a narrative that obscured the role of the United States in causing the war and refugees' forced migration in the first place.[3] On the other hand, Southeast Asian refugees struggled as the experiences of migration and resettlement set in motion profound, and often painful, transformations in their economic, social, and cultural lives.

While most public attention has focused on the economic and social dislocation of Hmong refugees, forced migration and resettlement also changed Hmong beliefs and practices. Like other migrants, the Hmong turned to their traditions as a source of strength amid the tumultuous experience of migration. They strived to preserve the Hmong way, which, for some, became even more important in the American context. In this regard, their experiences had much in common with those of other migrants who came to the United States many decades earlier. Writing about the importance of religion for "the uprooted" European immigrants in the nineteenth and twentieth centuries, the immigration historian Oscar Handlin observed that "a man holds dear what little is left. When much is lost, there is no risking the remainder."[4]

Holding dear to what is left and sustaining their ritual traditions in the United States was not easy, though. At first glance, American refugee policies appeared to have nothing to do with religion. However, listening to Hmong stories reveals that refugee resettlement disrupted the practice of the Hmong way and threw Hmong ritual life into disarray. Resettlement policies separated Hmong refugees from ritual experts, elders, and family members whose participation was necessary for the proper practice of traditional rituals. In addition, those policies placed Hmong refugees in urban settings where it was difficult to find the space and material needed to practice ceremonies rooted in their historically rural culture. Finally, the government resettlement program delegated significant responsibilities to religious voluntary agencies and local congregations. Hmong refugees found themselves in close relationships with Christian resettlement workers and worried that practicing their traditional rituals would imperil their relationships with the very people on whom they depended for housing and other essential needs.

Nao Thao, like many other Hmong refugees, had looked forward to living in "a country that has the most freedom."[5] The Americans who planned and administered the refugee resettlement program expressed their commitment to freedom, too. But the truth is that

Hmong refugees often found their ritual lives constrained by the forces of war, migration, and government resettlement policies. Yaw Yang, a Hmong refugee in Minnesota, described the predicament thusly: "America is where freedom is, but I don't feel free at all."[6]

"We Think We Got Lost"

When Hmong refugees fled Laos for Thailand, their most obvious need—survival—propelled them forward in their search for safety. But once they found themselves in the refugee camps, their lives were in limbo, and their next steps became less clear. As they considered their next move, so much remained unknown: the perils of returning to Laos, the prospects of reuniting with family members left behind, and the possibilities for their future lives should they resettle in the United States, Australia, or Canada. Yong Kay Moua described the months of hoping for a sponsor, conferring with family members, and wondering about the future as "just like gambling," while Nao Thao recalled that she felt like she was "walking in the dark" and "living in a dream."[7] "We did not know whether or not we will be able to go back or to go somewhere else," recalled Cziasarh Neng Yang. "We had no information, and we had no plan. The number one thing is to be alive and to be healthy and just to live."[8]

In these uncertain circumstances, some Hmong refugees stayed in the Thai refugee camps for only a few months, but many others languished there for years. They remained in the camps for a variety of reasons. Some were unwilling to accept offers of resettlement in a third country until their family was fully reunited or until they were certain that the political conditions in Laos foreclosed the option of returning home. The availability of sponsorship overseas also affected the length of stay in the refugee camps. Finally, Hmong refugees expressed a wide variety of fears about life in the United States. A Hmong American delegation sent to Thailand found that Hmong refugees had withdrawn their applications for resettlement because, among other things, they were afraid that "there will be no way for them to survive economically," that their children would "grow up and become criminals," and that "their wives will abandon them and their children will not respect them." There were also worries about the continuation of Hmong ritual life. "Older and elderly Hmong ex-military were concerned that they would not receive proper burial in the United States according to Hmong culture and tradition," the delegation reported. "For example, a Hmong man expressed fear that when he dies, his body will just be thrown into the river. Others said that they did not want an autopsy performed after death."[9]

Even those who believed that a return to Laos would endanger their lives did not necessarily embrace the opportunity to resettle in the United States, in part because they often knew little about life in America. Rumors circulated that cannibals, wife thieves, and malevolent supernatural beings called *dab* and *nyab* terrorized newly arrived Hmong.[10] "If they hear one little rumor somewhere, then it's like breaking news in [Thailand], so that's why some people don't want to come," recalled Sarah Fang, who spent her childhood in the refugee camps. To be sure, years of working with the US military and residing in refugee camps had exposed Hmong people to American people and some aspects of American life. Refugees also underwent cultural orientation programs before they arrived in the United States.[11] Finally, throughout the course of the resettlement decades, Hmong refugees who migrated to the United States often sent letters and cassette tapes with recorded messages to family members back in Thailand to assuage their fears and inform them about the realities of American life. Nevertheless, Hmong refugees, especially the ones who first left the refugee camps in the 1970s, remained uncertain about what lay in store for them on the other side of the Pacific.

Nao Thao's family arrived in the United States after spending five years in the refugee camps in Thailand. They were hopeful about a future in the United States, and when she and her family finally arrived in Wisconsin in November 1987, they were trembling with excitement—until they peered out the window and their eyes fell upon the forlorn landscape of Eau Claire in late fall. Seeing the bare branches of the trees and the bleak buildings along the street, they wondered if they had arrived in "a ghost town." They later sent tearful messages recorded on cassette tapes to relatives in the refugee camps and warned them not to come to the United States. "Don't look forward," Nao Thao and her family said. "We think we got lost."[12]

Southeast Asian refugees arriving at Hamilton Air Force Base, ca. 1980.
Courtesy of Mitchell I. Bonner.

The idea that Hmong refugees were "lost" in America was common in media portrayals. Among the several Southeast Asian groups resettled in the United States during this period, the Hmong had the reputation as the most exotic and adrift in American society. "No other newcomers to the United States suffered greater culture shock than these primitive tribesmen who suddenly crash-landed in a society light years away from their own," the Associated Press reported in 1984. The Hmong journey to the United States was "an odyssey through time as well as through miles, from thatched roofs to skyscrapers, from pre-literacy to computers, from the Stone Age to the Space Age."[13]

Journalists were not the only ones who offered sensational depictions of Hmong refugees as hopelessly primitive; so, too, did government officials. John Finck, a Hmong specialist for the Rhode Island Office of Refugee Resettlement, said that because the Hmong were "emerging from the mists of time," he was not sure they would be able to survive in the United States. "Whether they make it or not is anybody's guess," he told the Wall Street Journal.[14] That opinion was shared by resettlement officials in Minnesota. "Of all the Indochinese refugees, these [the Hmong] are the most difficult to resettle," said Diane Ahrens, a Ramsey County commissioner, in an interview with the *Christian Science Monitor*. "They have many assets, but they're used to very primitive living, and the catch-up job is enormous."[15]

In many ways, it was true that Hmong refugees experienced a difficult transition to life in the United States. The 1984 Hmong Resettlement Study, prepared by the University of Minnesota's Center for Urban and Regional Affairs, illustrated the multiple hardships faced by Hmong refugees in the Twin Cities. Few Hmong refugees spoke English, which was the most common problem identified by Hmong household heads in the survey. Hmong refugees also struggled to find employment. According to one measure, only 15 percent of adult Hmong were employed at the time the study was undertaken. Those who were unemployed were unable to work for a variety of reasons: family responsibilities, old age, and health problems, including war injuries. Those who were employed often labored in minimum-wage positions in food service, cleaning and maintenance, and factory assembly—jobs that did not provide sufficient income for supporting large Hmong families. Finally, those who were searching for employment struggled to find jobs in part because they had little, if any, formal education. Of the adult Hmong in the Twin Cities, 74 percent had received no formal education in Laos, and the percentage was even higher—89 percent—for Hmong women. As a result of all of these circumstances, Hmong refugees struggled with poverty, and many relied on public assistance. Sixty-eight percent of Hmong in the Twin Cities received financial support from Aid to Families with Dependent Children (AFDC), and 16 percent received General Assistance funds. In 1982, 90 percent of the Asian families in public housing in Saint Paul were Hmong.[16]

Hmong refugees were clearly frustrated with the difficulty of their economic struggles. Relying on the government for food and housing was a situation that Hmong refugees had not expected. "We ask that the American people be patient with us. They may ask why we are coming, why should we be on welfare," said Xang Vang, a teacher in Saint Paul, in an interview with the *St. Paul Dispatch*. "When we came, we never dreamed there was such a thing as welfare."[17] His plea for patience was a response to an additional cruelty of life in the United States: the public scrutiny and racist hostility from the anti-refugee public. Hmong refugees such as Yer Moua expressed frustration at the contradictions in how Americans treated Hmong people. Recalling a painful confrontation with a man at a local welfare office, she explained how the resentment directed toward her and other refugees was ignorant, hypocritical, and unfair:

> [The main at the welfare office] told me that how come you did not go to work and why are you just keep coming to us to ask for money. . . . But he did not know how much struggling we had been through. He did not know how lucky we are to stay alive so we could come to this country. Maybe he would still say all those things about us. The only reason we are having this problem is because of the Americans who came to our country and caused all these problems. That is the reason why we came to this country, but he does not know about that and all he sees is that we are here to use his money and take his country and his home. . . . They really hate the people who are on welfare like us. For those who went to work to support their own families then the Americans said that now they are taking away our jobs.

In Yer Moua's view, Americans had put Hmong people in an impossible position. The United States had drawn Hmong people into a war, then told Hmong people to be thankful to be in America when the war was lost. The portrayal of refugee resettlement as an American act of benevolent rescue belied the fact that Southeast Asian refugees' forced migration owed first to American acts of war making.[18] Moreover, American policies put tremendous pressure on Hmong people to become economically self-sufficient but did not necessarily give Hmong and other Southeast Asian refugees adequate support or time to do so. Refugees sometimes found themselves in isolated rural communities, while others found themselves resettled in neighborhoods characterized by racial segregation, concentrated poverty, unsafe housing, and high levels of crime.[19] Finally, Yer Moua's story reveals the contradictory criticisms that characterized the Hmong as both a threat and a burden. As she pointed out, Americans complained that Hmong people were not working, then complained that Hmong people were stealing Americans' jobs. "It seems like we do not have any peace at all," she said.[20]

However, there was more to Hmong uprooting than the economic matters that preoccupied government and voluntary agency officials.

There was also the trauma that Hmong refugees endured as a result of their experience during war, their flight to Thailand, and their resettlement in the United States. Mental health problems were common, and the psychological, social, and spiritual distress of Hmong refugees was poignantly illustrated by the case of the Yang family, who had been resettled by a group of churches in Iowa. Isolated and in extreme despair, the entire family—the two parents and their four children—had attempted to hang themselves in their basement. One of the parents had a change of heart at the last moment and cut the nooses of the other family members, but not in time to save their eight-year-old son. This event, detailed in a story published in the *New Yorker,* drew national attention to the multiple resettlement struggles of Southeast Asian refugees.[21]

The case files of Hmong refugees resettled by the International Institute of Minnesota (IIM) reveal other stories of human suffering and vulnerability that express far more than the Hmong Resettlement Study statistics. In these case files are handwritten notes from IIM caseworkers who visited the homes of Hmong refugee families in the Twin Cities. Many of the notes in the case files describe situations of urgent poverty. In one family's file, the caseworker noted that "the family received less money [from AFDC] but the rent went up. No food to feed the children." The IIM case worker made a home visit and found that the family did not have any food in the refrigerator except for some juice.[22] The case files also reveal that the Hmong refugee population suffered not only from poverty but from the anguish of loss they had experienced during the war. One English teacher made the following observations about one of her Hmong students:

> [She] daydreams constantly. . . . [She] learns quickly if I can get her attention. This is extremely difficult. . . . She tries very hard and when she pays attention, she does fine. But she loses interest quickly and doesn't concentrate. She has mentioned that she lost her entire family. They were shot by the Vietnamese. . . . [She] seems motivated and her learning pace depends directly on her attention span. She day-dreams a lot and this slows her down in both English and Math. She can count and add small numbers. She should stay in low level.[23]

It was not only the loss of loved ones that was the source of grief for Hmong refugees but also the loss of status and control as they struggled to make a new life in a new country. "[He] is systematic in his study and he is well-respected," one English teacher said of an older male student. "Recently he has been distracted which I believe is due to a sudden loss of respect in an environment in which he cannot solve the problems of his people." Another teacher observed that the stress of working and caring for family made going to English classes nearly impossible for some refugees. One teacher noted that her student "gets up at 5:00 a.m., has several children, drinks a can of pop for breakfast and can hardly keep her eyes open in class. Consequently, hasn't learned much beyond 'I don't know.'"[24]

Stories shared by refugees themselves reveal how a multitude of losses—of friends and family, of country and culture, of dignity and freedom—coalesced to make resettlement an experience of deep heartache for Hmong people in the United States. Yaw Yang explained,

> In America we were like aliens. We suffered a lot of pain coming to America, and also the thought of knowing that none of my family members nor I could speak, read, write, or understand the language and culture we were exposed to. For the last twelve years, I personally suffered the painful feeling of loss—the lost feeling of belonging and the lost feeling of not knowing much about America. Just like an infant, starting to know how to talk, eat, ask for food and water.[25]

In the context of these struggles, some Hmong refugees regretted their decision to come to the United States. "It has been very hard for me," said Boua Xa Moua, a Hmong man in California. "Like I said, if I would have had a choice, I would have remained back in Laos. Or if I could, I would like to go back now. It's much nicer and peaceful back home. Here everything feels too lonely. Everything is too much. I always find myself lost in this world."[26]

The public scrutiny of Hmong refugees as a "lost" people dwelled not only on unemployment figures and mental health difficulties but also on cultural and religious differences. Media narratives that depicted Hmong people as exceptionally unsuited to American life often did so by highlighting the foreignness of Hmong beliefs and practices. These stories harked back to racialized debates about non-Christian Asian migrants in previous eras. From the "heathen" Chinese to the "hindoo" Indians, religious difference has long been central to the construction of racial difference and an issue that has buttressed arguments for Asian exclusion.[27] A similar theme emerged in the 1970s and 1980s, when news stories pointed to Hmong beliefs and rituals to emphasize Hmong people's foreignness. In particular, sensational portrayals of Hmong struggles often mentioned Sudden Unexplained Nocturnal Death Syndrome (SUNDS). Described as "the curse of the Hmong," SUNDS was a medical condition that claimed the lives of young, otherwise healthy Hmong males for reasons that remain unknown. News media reported that Hmong men had been "frightened to death by nightmares" or simply killed by "the stress of resettlement in a strange new culture."[28]

"You Have Nobody to Give You the Proper Way"

Even if many Americans saw Hmong beliefs and practices as strange and foreign, many Hmong refugees nevertheless hoped to continue their traditional rituals in the United States. These rituals were important for many reasons: they ensured harmonious relations with the spirit world, they brought comfort and support during the painful experience of resettlement, and they affirmed their identity as Hmong people. However, Hmong refugees found it difficult to follow the Hmong way in the United States, in no small part because of American refugee resettlement policies.

To begin, the policy of dispersal separated Hmong families and communities. Hmong refugees often found themselves isolated in small towns, far from relatives or other Hmong people. Cher Vang and his immediate family, sponsored by a Lutheran church, first lived in rural Wisconsin in a town called Loganville, which had a population of a couple hundred people. "We came to a small town and we felt kind of lonely," he said. "We say to our sponsors, 'We cannot stay here, because there's just five of us in the family.'"[29] Similarly, Khu Thao, a Hmong woman in Minnesota, recalled how she was first resettled in Iowa because a sponsor was available there. "We didn't know anyone in Iowa," she said.[30]

The scatter policy had important negative consequences for Hmong ritual life because it deprived Hmong refugees of kin who played essential roles in traditional rituals. For Hmong people, celebrating major life events—funerals and weddings, for example—requires the involvement of many clan and community members, who help perform ritual songs, cook ritual food, and prepare ritual spaces. Being separated from extended family thus imposed a significant hardship on Hmong people intending to practice Hmong traditions. Yong Kay Moua, for example, recalled that the separation of his family members—and the uncertainty of whether they would be able to reunite with them ever again—caused his family to question the feasibility of maintaining their traditional rituals in the United States. "We wish to do [these rituals], but in our tradition, you just cannot do on your own," he said. "You can do many steps, even in your home, because when you have [some] worry, concern, you can pray for your ancestor, your tradition. But if we end up having a wedding, having someone pass away, we need a lot of people to help." For Yong Kay Moua, the people to whom he would normally turn for help with these rituals were located not just across the country but around the world: he and his wife and children were sponsored by Trinity Lutheran Church in Eau Claire, Wisconsin; his uncle, the leader of the extended family, was resettled in Providence, Rhode Island; and still other relatives were sent to California or remained in the refugee camps in Thailand. "At that time [before the Refugee Act of 1980], we don't know that the rest of the people will be able to come," he recalled.

Some Hmong refugees chose to relocate to be near relatives, but relocation did not happen overnight, nor was it always possible. "Even for yourself, if you would like to go to where your family lives, or your relatives, you cannot find jobs there," said Yong Kay Moua.[31] Moving away from the site of initial resettlement meant leaving not only jobs but the furnished homes, educational opportunities, and financial support offered by church sponsors and voluntary agencies, which typically did not assist refugees who chose to relocate to a new city or state.[32] Thus, despite the fact that Hmong refugees resisted dispersal and strove to reconstitute their families and communities in the United States, doing so was not easy and sometimes required time to plan and save money. By the time families were finally able to relocate and reunite, the scatter policy and sponsorship system had often already left a mark on Hmong beliefs and practices.

The preference system under which refugees gained admission into the United States was another dimension of American refugee resettlement policies that disrupted Hmong ritual life. Southeast Asian refugee resettlement categories were based on both the long-standing principle that the United States should reward its Cold War allies and the emerging commitment to human rights and humanitarianism.[33] In general, Hmong individuals who had served in the military and had been employed by the US government during the war received highest priority, as they were considered "high risk." Most of these first arrivals were young people who were former members of the clandestine army that supported the CIA during the war.[34] But the younger people who were favored by American preference categories also happened to be a subset of the Hmong population that had comparatively little knowledge of traditional Hmong rituals.

The people who were typically the lowest priority and who were left behind in the refugee camps in Thailand were the elders—the people who were the Hmong community's spiritual and cultural leaders and the revered authorities on the proper practice of traditional rituals.[35] Having had less direct involvement with the war, these elders fell under a different preference category, and their arrival in the United States was delayed until much later, when their children were able to sponsor them. Jacque Lemoine, an anthropologist and expert on Hmong shamanism, noted that shamans were far less common in the United States in the early 1980s, in part because shamans were more reluctant to leave Asia, but also because,

A Hmong shaman in Frogtown, Saint Paul. Courtesy of Wing Young Huie.

as he put it, shamans "were excluded from the resettlement list as useless religious practitioners."[36]

In the initial years of resettlement, young Hmong refugees thus found themselves spiritually adrift in the United States, where they had little knowledge or guidance on how to conduct traditional ceremonies. "Back in Laos and in Thailand, we always depend on . . . the elders who know how to do this ritual," said Cziasarh Neng Yang. "Now, when you are alone in a foreign land, and you have nobody to give you the proper way how to conduct the ritual or the tradition, you just don't know . . . what to do or how to do it."[37]

Young people had some experience with traditional practices, but their knowledge was often limited. "Of course when my parents held ceremonies with shamans or had soul calling ceremonies (hu plig) I helped, but I was only there as an observer," said Bo Thao, a Hmong woman in Minnesota. "If I were to fully practice animism today I don't think I could do it. I don't know enough."[38] Kim Yang expressed a similar concern about her lack of knowledge about Hmong ritual traditions. "If someone in your household passes away, we will not know what to do," she said.[39] For many young Hmong people, decades of instability due to war, forced migration, and refugee camp life had denied them the tutelage of elders and the opportunity to participate in community ritual life, which was the foundation of a traditional education in the Hmong way.

Young Hmong people were reluctant to undertake traditional rituals with which they had insufficient knowledge and experience. If they made an error, it could have severe consequences for the Hmong residing in both the seen and the unseen worlds. "If [young people] don't spend time learning the old ways exactly, they may call the wrong spirit," said Wang Kao Her, a Hmong man in Minnesota. "They must follow 'the rules' exactly step by step. When something is done wrong, the bad spirit may punish or curse a family for many generations. This worries people."[40] Many Hmong refugees, alone in the United States without elders to guide them, thus found themselves in a spiritual quandary: they could choose not to perform traditional rituals, a decision that would provoke the ire of spirits, or they could attempt to do the rituals with the high likelihood that they would make a mistake—and still anger the spirits.

Resettlement policies shaped Hmong religious life in yet a third way: by relocating Hmong refugees to cities. If Hmong refugees had been able to choose where they would live in the United States, many might have opted to reestablish themselves in settings similar to what they had known in Laos: rural areas with mild climates, where large Hmong families could live on farms with enough room to raise crops and livestock. In fact, some Hmong refugees left the site of their initial resettlement and moved to California's Central Valley specifically to resume their lives as farmers.[41] As a matter of policy, however, resettlement officials sent Hmong refugees to places where sponsors and resources were available to support them—which was often cities, all across the country.

In an urban environment, Hmong refugees found it difficult to conduct the elaborate rituals so closely tied to their rural lives in Laos. For one, the material resources for traditional Hmong rituals were in short supply. Animals such as cows and pigs were costly for cash-strapped refugees, and because Hmong rituals are so deeply rooted in the specific environment of Southeast Asia, the plants of sacred significance were simply not available in the United States. Paja Thao, the shaman in Chicago, complained about the lack of appropriate altar wood, which needed to be harvested in a particular way:

> Long ago they said
> From all the kinds of trees
> You must choose only two
> All the others are not for this
>
> You just choose the chestnut
> And the spirit tree
> When you go to cut
>
> You must pick two straight trees
> The same size
> Side by side
> You cut one
> And you leave one
>
> You must cut the tree
> So that it falls towards the sunset
> Then it is good
>
> But here we do not have
> So I must do the custom imperfectly

Hmong females in traditional costume, Frogtown, Saint Paul, in 1993.
Courtesy of Wing Young Huie.

Paja Thao expressed a willingness to improvise. He worried, however, about the serious consequences that could arise if their creative
solutions displeased the spirits.[42]

Many Hmong rituals were traditionally conducted outside, but
open outdoor space was another resource in short supply in cities.
Moving rituals to indoor spaces such as garages, apartment buildings, and funeral homes sometimes gave rise to tensions with neighbors and at times violated city regulations. Even the weather posed
a problem. Wang Kao Her noted that Minnesota's frigid winters
made it difficult to practice rituals that were common in Laos. "It
is easier to call a spirit through an open door in a warm climate!"
he said.[43]

Hmong rituals sometimes clashed with local regulations on farm
animals, which were necessary for a variety of ceremonies that
Hmong people had traditionally conducted in their homes. Nao
Khue Yang and his wife Sarah Fang laughingly recalled how, in the
early years, they had snuck pigs and chickens into the basements of
their apartment buildings. The strictest shamans demanded live pigs,
which were sacrificed at the site of the ritual. Hmong people went
to great lengths to fulfill these requirements. They traveled to dis-

tant farms, transported livestock in the back of borrowed cars and trucks, chased down the occasional pig that managed to break free and run loose on highways and city streets, and surreptitiously sacrificed live animals in basements and garages, sometimes without the knowledge of the landlord.[44]

Many Hmong refugees, especially those who considered themselves progressive and modern, did not always feel comfortable with these clandestine efforts. Nao Thao described how her husband and father-in-law argued about sneaking a pig into their house:

> I remember my father-in-law, one time, he said that he wanted to have . . . a ritual in the home, so he asked my husband to go buy the pig in the farm. And he said, "No, I'm not going to. It's not legal." And my husband and his dad kind of argued on that, so my father-in-law got kind of a little upset, and so he stopped asking my husband. He went on asking the second brother to go get a pig from the farm. So he bought the pig from the farm and brought it to the home. And my husband [said], "Just to let you know, the police might come, if the neighborhood [hears]. The police might come, so my suggestion [is] you should put it in the garage." And my father[-in-law] said, "But this is for the spirit! We need it for the ritual! We need the pig in the home!" So he [was just] quiet. He didn't say anything. So they brought the pig in. . . . After they did the ritual through, the first part, then they took the pig to the garage and butchered [it in] the garage. And my husband felt very uncomfortable. . . . He didn't say much because he was the son and the dad was the one . . . who had the power.[45]

Nao Thao and her husband were both young people who aspired to be respectable, rule-abiding Americans. At the same time, however, they were operating in a traditional family hierarchy that placed high value on honoring the wishes of elders and maintaining harmonious relations with family members and spirits.

Hmong refugees hoped to be on good terms with their American neighbors, and concerns about offending American customs and tastes made some Hmong refugees nervous about practicing rituals in their own homes. Smoke from burning incense and paper money alarmed the neighbors, whose 911 calls caused fire fighters to pay unexpected visits to Hmong homes where families were conducting rituals.[46] Hmong ceremonies, which involved hand bells and drums and singing, were also loud. "The early '80s wasn't easy because of the drumming, the chanting, and the noise, and it bothered the neighbor," said Nao Thao. Fortunately for her family, their first home was a second-floor apartment located directly above an office. "During the daytime, the people kind of worked in the office," she explained. "But at the nighttime, they were all gone. So we didn't have issues for doing the chanting, the shaman ritual, in the evening."[47] Most Hmong refugees, however, had to deal with neighbors' disapproval at one point or another. They learned to head off these complaints by explaining the importance of rituals to their neighbors and by notifying them of any upcoming ceremonies.[48] Over time, both Hmong refugees and their neighbors learned to develop a sense of humor about their cultural differences. "We have some issue with the butcher shop in Hugo, [Minnesota,] where the neighbors complain that the Hmong who butcher the pig over there makes the neighbor[hood] smell bad," said Cziasarh Neng Yang. "One of my American friends responded to the complaint with the joke, "'But to God, it smells good!'"[49]

In certain situations, however, it was not only difficult but also dangerous to carry out Hmong ceremonies in secret. Healing rituals were hard to conduct in American hospitals, where regulations about the presence of live animals, incense, and shamans were considerably stricter. "The old beliefs and traditions call for sacrifices, and the sacrifice must be done close to the sick person," said Wang Kao Her.

> For example, if a pig is to be sacrificed, a rope tied to the pig is held by the hand of the sick person. . . . Also, burning incense and special "gold paper money" must be done by the shaman in front of the altar inside the house. These things can't be done in hospitals or American homes. It would disturb those who are not Hmong and also, with oxygen in the hospital room, it is not allowed.[50]

Practicing Hmong funeral traditions was particularly challenging in an American context. Traditionally, funerals lasted between three and ten days, during which time drummers, ritual chanters, and qeej (a mouth organ of bamboo reed pipes often used in Hmong rituals) players assisted the soul in its journey to its spiritual home, while family members gathered and feasted around the clock. American funeral homes, open for only eight hours each day, did not readily accommodate these crowded, noisy ceremonies, and conducting funerals in these circumstances was very stressful for Hmong people.

Family members charged with the task of conducting rituals that led the spirit of the dead to the ancestors did not want to rush the proceedings, for fear that skipping a step or making a mistake would result in the spirit of the dead returning to trouble the living.[51]

If Hmong people found it difficult to find the appropriate human and material resources to conduct their rituals, it was even more difficult to practice their rituals when Christian churches served as their resettlement sponsors. Voluntary agencies expected congregations to respect and accommodate religious and cultural differences. However, some Hmong refugees felt that it was still inappropriate for them to maintain their traditions if Christians had sponsored them, and they found it difficult to speak honestly and openly about their desire to practice their rituals.

For one, language barriers hindered communication, and the delicate issue of Hmong traditions was simply not discussed. According to Houa Vue Moua, the silence on the issue was mutual. "One, they [the church sponsors] never happened to ask," she said. "Two, we never happened to share. It [was] just ignoring or pretending that nothing exists."[52] Receiving such generous help caused some Hmong refugees to feel uncomfortable about talking about, much less pursuing, beliefs and practices that were clearly different and possibly offensive to their sponsors.

This discomfort and silence about religion characterized refugee-sponsor relationships even if the differences were relatively small. Rev. Timothy Vang and his family were committed Christians when they arrived in the United States. A member of the Christian and Missionary Alliance (CMA) Church, he had begun to preach even as an adolescent in Laos and Thailand. When he was resettled in the United States, a Catholic parish in Wisconsin sponsored him and brought him to Mass every Sunday, almost immediately—"the next week after we arrived," he said. He and his family continued to attend Catholic Mass for two years before he finally confessed to his sponsor that they were not, in fact, Catholic, but devout members of the CMA Church. "Our sponsor was very gracious," he recalled. "She said, 'No problem!'" She encouraged them to attend a church from their own denomination on Sundays. When asked why it took so long for him to talk about this issue, Vang said with a laugh, "In fact, I don't remember that the sponsors ever asked anything about that."[53] For Vang, attending a church service of a different denomination was not necessarily a problem. Shong Yer Yang agreed. Though he is Protestant, he attended Mass when his Catholic sponsors brought him. "No, we never really thought about saying anything like that [about their religious differences] because it was the same Bible, it was just different ways of doing things in the church," he said.[54]

Sometimes, Hmong refugees discussed the religious differences they had with their sponsors. Rev. Pa Mang Her, a Hmong Baptist minister, recalled a conversation that he had with the Presbyterian pastor of the church that sponsored him. "I saw him baptizing babies, sprinkling them with water, and he smoked cigars," he said. He was curious and also critical of Presbyterian practices. "I sat down with him and told him that I disagreed with him and I knew that he loved me very much," he said. "I could not accept how he baptized the babies by sprinkling water. I just can't do that. I won't." Her explained to the pastor that he did not believe that baptism was either salvation or symbolic. "So he told me that I was a Baptist and sent me to a Baptist church," Her said. "He and I are still very good friends after that."[55] Her's experience—which was characterized by honest interfaith dialogue, mutual respect, and genuine friendship—was a model of how Christian sponsors aspired to practice religious pluralism in their resettlement work. But silence appears to have been a more common response to religious and cultural difference. As many Hmong refugees recalled, sponsors never asked Hmong refugees if they were Christian or what their religious preferences were, even if sponsors brought them to church. Some Hmong refugees recalled that their sponsors did not discuss religion at all.

Hmong refugees who practiced the Hmong way were sometimes frustrated by congregational sponsors who brought them to church without asking about their religious preferences. Tzianeng Vang's experience with his Methodist sponsors in Missouri was one such case. When asked if he told his sponsors that he and his family practiced traditional Hmong rituals, he replied, "No, because we were never asked." He continued:

It's typical, I guess. When you are only one family, you already received so much help from them. I guess they just kind of took the liberty of thinking, "Okay, I think they probably like what they have,

so we're just going to continue to impose or help the best we can."
So, nobody never asked . . . and even if they did, we would not have
understood what they said anyway. Nobody actually sat down and
said, we sponsored you but we still want you to have the religion,
religious freedom of choosing whether you will remain animist—
Hmong animist—or you want to convert to Christianity based on
the Methodist philosophy.

Tzianeng Vang's experience involved precisely what many sponsoring
churches explicitly hoped to avoid: refugees adopting Christianity
and attending church because they felt obligated or pressured to do
so by sponsoring congregations. His story suggests that even if
church volunteers had good intentions and followed the given guidelines, the people whom they served may have interpreted their actions and intentions differently.[56]

Even when they were equipped with excellent English skills,
Hmong refugees often struggled to speak clearly about what they
believed and practiced. Paj Ntaub Lis recalled how, as a child, she
functioned easily as "the communicator" between her family and
her sponsors, but she stumbled when it came to discussing the beliefs and practices of her family. Either because the family that sponsored them was "upper-class" or because they were Christian, she
found it difficult to talk openly about Hmong traditions, and it took
"a long time to be okay with talking" about Hmong rituals and beliefs. Part of the problem was that she lacked the vocabulary to do
so, since there is no easy word for "religion" in Hmong, and the
Hmong way did not translate easily into the Christian-centric vocabulary of religion. "It took us a long time before I was able to find
the correct words in English to tell them what we believed in," she
said. The sponsoring family, for their part, also seemed to be reluctant to discuss the issue of religion in the first place. "They never
asked us what we believed in," she said. Only later, as an adult, did
Paj Ntaub Lis speak about her family's ritual life with her sponsors,
who remained close family friends. She had been called to become
a shaman, and she wanted to share her journey with her Lutheran
sponsors.[57]

Some refugees found that their sponsors were aware of Hmong
traditions and supportive of those who desired to practice them.
"The Americans knew about our ways and they found places for us
to buy animals for our religious ceremonies," said Xai Thao, a

Hmong woman in Minnesota. "Overall, the Americans were very considerate. They would not allow us to perform our religious ceremonies in the house but we were provided with a place to perform them."[58] Xai Thao's experience, however, appears to have been unique. More sponsors were like Houa Vue Moua's church sponsors, who did not offer a space for rituals and, in general, did not discuss the issue of Hmong beliefs and practices at all. Committed to respecting religious differences, many Catholic and mainline Protestant churches encouraged the Southeast Asian refugees they sponsored to continue to practice their religious and cultural traditions. However, refugees who practiced the Hmong way did not have an institutionalized tradition that was as readily recognized as a religion. As a result, they faced greater challenges in securing respect, support, and accommodation compared to the Buddhist Lao, Cambodian, and Vietnamese refugees who were resettled during the same period.

Initially, Hmong refugees did not appear to consider their traditional beliefs and practices to be something that might be protected by law. For Cziasarh Neng Yang, the realization that he was free to follow the Hmong way in the United States came when he learned about Roger Williams and Anne Hutchinson, two early religious dissenters in seventeenth-century America. Looking back, he emphasized how little Hmong people understood their freedoms when they first arrived. "We did not know the Constitution," he said. "We did not know that there's an amendment that allows people to believe what they believe and do what they do. We did not know that."[59]

"What Do We Have in Our Culture if We Don't Have Shamanism?"

The separation from family, the absence of ritual experts, the relocation to new geographic settings, and the complications of being sponsored by Christian churches: together, these forces created a crisis for Hmong people in their early years in the United States. Although resettling in a new country had held the promise of greater security and freedom, Hmong people found themselves deeply unsettled by life in America, where they lived with even less spiritual security and religious freedom. They struggled with the reality that it was difficult, and sometimes even impossible, to practice the rituals that had long sustained their spiritual and bodily well-being, and they worried about the future of their souls, as well as the fate of their Hmong beliefs, practices, and cultural identity.

For many Hmong people, the ritual crisis set in motion by American refugee resettlement policies was not a theoretical or abstract concern but a matter that could result in real, immediate, physical suffering. Hmong people worried, for example, about how they could cure an ailment and remain healthy if they could not call a soul home during a *hu plig* ceremony or ask a shaman to recapture a wayward soul during the *ua neeb*. The uncertainty about having access to a shaman and conducting traditional rituals was enough to convince some people to abandon traditional Hmong shamanism altogether. For example, Ong Vang Xiong, a Hmong woman living in the Twin Cities, ultimately made the decision to "believe in the new religion" for this reason. "I came to this country," she said. "It was very hard to find a shaman, so it was very, very hard for me. That is why I went to believe in the new religion, so I do not have any more hard times."[60]

Even if Hmong people had access to a shaman in the United States, they were often constrained by other practical limitations. The particular demands of a shaman's work—for example, the need for a permanent house where a shaman's spirits can reside—made practicing Hmong shamanism a challenge, especially in the context of the poverty and housing instability that so many refugees experienced in their first years in America. Nhia Yer Yang, a Hmong shaman in the Twin Cities, was "really happy" about all of the help he had received from Americans, but his lack of permanent housing was one reason why he struggled to continue traditional rituals. He pleaded for more help from the government and pointed out the spiritual consequences of his lack of permanent housing. "I hope the government would understand where this puts me as a shaman," he said. "It makes it really hard. I don't have a home. . . . It is most difficult for me, I cannot adapt to this, the house is not my own. I cannot continue the traditional spiritual [traditions], to be 'in touch.' It is really hard, but hopefully in the future I can have my own home." As he explained, the problem was not merely that he did not have a home to call his own, but that his shaman's spirit needed to move with him every time he moved, and the lack of a permanent home created not only housing instability but also spiritual instability. "If I have to move and I'm in touch with the spirit and it lives in that home, I have to ask the spirit to leave," he said. "Hopefully, one day I will have a steady place and won't have to move around so much."[61]

Amid these challenges, Hmong people nevertheless found creative ways to continue shamanism, often relying on transpacific social networks to do so. The anthropologist Dwight Conquergood observed that Hmong refugees in Ban Vinai camp actively participated in the ritual lives of Hmong people resettled abroad and thus played a vital role in sustaining Hmong traditions. He recalled how one family conducted a ceremony that involved relatives in both California and Thailand:

> Xiong Houa's neighbors, two partitions down from his room, had received money from relatives in the United States to buy a huge pig and perform a proxy ceremony for the grandfather now resettled in California. They explained the patient's symptoms and failure to find satisfaction with Western health practitioners on the tape cassette that accompanied the money. Because it was more difficult to perform these rituals in the United States than in Ban Vinai, and also because they wanted the Ban Vinai relatives to share in the healing ceremony and feast, they were arranging this "long-distance" cure. The shaman in Ban Vinai, Thailand, would perform for the patient in California.

Conquergood discovered that this Hmong family was not the only family whose rituals spanned the globe; other families participated in transnational rituals, too. "I first became aware of the practice when I attended healing rituals where no patient was visibly present," he said. "In response to my question, 'Where's the patient?' the officiants would reply, 'In Iowa,' or 'Paris,' or 'St. Paul.'" As he explained, Hmong people conducted these rituals in this fashion because, on both sides of the Pacific, Hmong refugees faced challenges to their rituals, but also had different resources to offer:

> The Hmong in the West have greater access to cash but more difficulty in carrying out these elaborate rituals. There is no lack of shamans and appropriate contexts in Ban Vinai, but money to purchase the sacrificial animals and accessories is hard to come by. The Hmong on both sides of the world benefit from this cooperative arrangement.

The Hmong resettled in Western countries are able to maintain their traditions and meaningful connections with their relatives left behind. The resident Hmong in Ban Vinai profit from the protein supplement to their diet that comes from the sacrificed animals. Moreover, they are deeply satisfied knowing that they are performing an important spiritual service for the Hmong in the diaspora. They become, in effect, stewards of the sacred practices of their people.

In other words, even if Hmong people in the West had the money to conduct rituals, they no longer had the shamans or the proper settings for shamans. They depended, in the end, on relatives in Asia to be the "stewards of the sacred practices of their people."[62]

Like sickness, death was another occasion when Hmong refugees acutely felt the ritual crisis produced by resettlement. For reasons similar to practicing shamanism—the separation from family, the absence of resources and ritual experts, the change in geographic setting—conducting a traditional Hmong funeral was extremely challenging during the early years of resettlement. As Joua Tsu Thao argued, funeral rituals done "in the old way" were "the most difficult ceremonies that anyone can do in the United States."[63] Hmong funerals were difficult to conduct in the early years partly because they can be lengthy, complex, and often expensive.

Because Hmong people have traditionally believed that funeral rituals ensure the safe passage of the soul into the afterlife, the stakes were also high. Funeral practices can vary among different clans and subclans, but in general the purpose of a Hmong funeral is to help the soul of the dead retrace the steps it had taken on earth, return to its homeland, reunite with the ancestors, and eventually be reincarnated. Like the arduous journey undertaken by the soul, traditional funerals are lengthy and demanding events that require a large number of family members to conduct rituals day and night over the course of three days. During this time, relatives prepare and feast on ritually sacrificed animals and present the deceased with a variety of other items—a crossbow for hunting, a rooster for guidance, a sum of money—with the goal of making the journey and the afterlife as safe and as comfortable as possible. Throughout the funeral, musicians sing funeral chants and play "the death song" on the *qeej*.[64] According to Chai Lee, a professional *qeej* musician and teacher, the *qeej* aids the journeying soul by "communicating" and "talking to the deceased all the time," giving directions for the

A Hmong man playing the *qeej* in Frogtown, Saint Paul, in 1994. Courtesy of Wing Young Huie.

journey and protecting the soul from malevolent spirits and monsters.[65] Hmong people traditionally conduct these elaborate funeral rituals with great care because they believe that if the funeral service is not completed properly, the consequences are significant: the spirit of the deceased will never rejoin the ancestors and will never be reincarnated, but instead forced to wander or endure other forms of punishment. They may also haunt and trouble living relatives, who face the possibility of spiritual or physical affliction that could possibly last for generations.[66]

Conducting a traditional Hmong funeral properly was very difficult during the early days of resettlement, though. To begin, Hmong people in the United States did not have the ritual experts or the extended family necessary for the elaborate ceremonies. As Keith Vang explained, funerals are a "family gathering," and for very practical reasons: a large number of people who are knowledgeable and experienced in Hmong funeral traditions are needed to conduct the elaborate, labor-intensive rituals.[67] "In the old tradition, you have to have helping hands," said Yia Lee. "You can't kill a pig yourself, cook and feed a family, a whole house full of people, yourself."[68] But in the absence of clan, community, and other critical resources, holding a traditional Hmong funeral was impossible for Hmong refugees, especially in the early years of resettlement. The inability to provide a proper funeral was a source of great grief for Hmong people, who often had no family with them, either because they had died during the war or remained in the refugee camps in Thailand. "I was very sad when my husband passed away because there were no relatives left to conduct his funeral and we were very poor," said Khu Thao.[69]

Finding an appropriate space for the funeral presented another problem. American funeral homes, designed to accommodate funerals that lasted no more than a few hours, did not meet the needs of Hmong people: they needed a facility that they could use for twenty-four hours a day, three days in a row. "We were limited so much," said Nao Khue Yang. "We knew that from this time to this time, we did what we could, and then if it was time to close, we would stop and then resume again the next morning because we didn't have a choice." Aside from the limitation on hours, American funeral homes did not readily accommodate traditions involved with a proper Hmong burial. For example, the burning of paper money, which ensured that the soul of the deceased would enjoy wealth in the afterlife, at times caused concern among non-Hmong neighbors, who alerted the fire department when they saw smoke and fire. Because funeral rituals involve many people who work together over a long period of time, Hmong people have typically hosted important meals at the funeral site. However, American funeral homes have generally not allowed eating and drinking. "We had to cook at home, then we had to pick up the people at funeral home, drive them to the home, eat, send them back to the funeral home," said Nao Khue Yang. "And so it was very stressful."[70]

For all of these reasons, Hmong people in the early years of resettlement faced a painful situation. Traditional Hmong funerals were nearly impossible to conduct properly in the United States. However, doing a traditional funeral was, for many Hmong people, one of the most important obligations to their family. What was at stake was not simply the maintenance of a sacred cultural tradition but the fate of the soul of the deceased as well as the physical and spiritual well-being of the living. Soua Sue Lee, a funeral expert in Minnesota, recalled how the inability to do traditional funerals the proper way worried Hmong people, who were deeply troubled by the spiritual harm that an improper or incomplete funeral might inflict on the family. "It scared everyone here," he said. He even felt the need to explain the circumstances to the souls of the deceased. "We have to tell who passed away that this is not our country, this is not our home, this is not our town," he said.

Determined to complete the funerals but burdened by the lack of material resources, space, and ritual expertise, Hmong people in the United States improvised and conducted funeral ceremonies as best as they were able. As with healing rituals, they sometimes relied on the expertise of relatives who remained in the Thai refugee camps. For example, after a Hmong family buried a relative in the United States, they gathered some of the dirt from the cemetery where the deceased person had been interred and sent the soil by mail to family members in Thailand. There, relatives finished the funeral and conducted the rituals that their Hmong American relatives had not been able to do. As Soua Sue Lee explained, "We just do the simple [rituals] and send everything back to the refugee camp."

Handling ritual animals during funerals and other ceremonies was another thorny issue, and on this matter, Hmong people were especially inventive. In Laos, Hmong people typically conducted funerals outdoors, where it was easy to present a whole, living cow to the deceased and to slaughter the animal near the body. In the 1970s and 1980s, Hmong people resettled in the United States attempted to continue this tradition, but American funeral homes generally did not welcome livestock indoors or allow their slaughter next to the casket. But Hmong people found a solution to this prohibition: they transported the live cow in a trailer, which they parked as close to the casket as possible. Relatives then used a piece of string to connect the live animal with the body of the deceased in order to communicate to the deceased that the animal was offered for him. Soua Sue Lee's daughter remembered this practice vividly. "I saw the trailer with the actual living cow in the back of the trailer," she said. "Because the funeral home was really big, there's a door that's pretty close to where the casket's at, and I would see a string going from the cow to the deceased person's hand."[71]

If resettlement in the United States caused a ritual crisis, it also gave rise to a spiritual crisis. For some Hmong people, the inability to conduct traditional rituals coincided with the erosion of faith in traditional spirits and beliefs that had long been a source of stability, strength, and hope. Overwhelmed by the challenges that they faced in the United States, many Hmong people felt dispirited—literally. In the eyes of some older Hmong people, America was a foreign country with foreign spirits that competed for the loyalty of Hmong people and led the younger, more vulnerable generation astray. Reflecting on interviews he had conducted with several Hmong refugees in California, Ghia Xiong observed that Hmong elders "were lost in this enormous American jungle" and felt a profound sense of "despair." "As wise and determined as many of them were, they could not see their way to the light," he said. "The older people watch helplessly and hopelessly as the 'strange spirits' from the American jungle cast a spell on their children who do not want to learn about their ancient and rich culture, who do not want to listen to their elders, who go to gangs or take other strange paths for their direction." In many ways, Ghia Xiong called attention to the schisms that often separate the first generation of migrants from their children, who are born and raised in the United States and are thus more acculturated into American society. But what makes his observations notable is that the Hmong people he had interviewed offered a distinctly spiritual explanation for the changes that they witnessed. "The elders feel powerless because no matter how hard they try to warn their children of dangers, strange spirits seem to have come over the children," he said. "Not even with the help of the shaman spirit can the elders understand where the souls of their children have gone or why they follow alien spirits."

While Hmong elders were demoralized by witnessing their children abandon their traditional beliefs and practices, Ghia Xiong observed that American-born Hmong often did not see any evidence that the spirits of their elders did anything for them. "To many of the young ones, She-Yee [Siv Yis], the shaman spirit their parents call on to guide them, does not have power," he said. "Their own She-Yee is the spirit they have met in the American jungle. To these young people, it is that new spirit that will guide them like She-Yee's spirit guided their parents from Laos and Thailand. It is only the new spirit, they say, that will help them survive the American jungle."[72] Shoua Vang made a similar observation with his own children. While he hoped that his children will "advance in this society," he worried that "their traditional beliefs will never be strong," in part because Hmong people have increased access to tools that give them more control over their fates. "In Laos, we performed many ceremonies to pray for successful crops," he said. "Even here, we can't control nature. But we have [a] better chance for success because of chemicals and technology. This alters traditional Hmong beliefs. The children become much more materialistic and don't pray as much."[73]

The loss of traditional rituals and traditional spirits signaled something even more ominous: the loss of Hmong culture and identity altogether. While resettlement in the United States may have saved their lives, many Hmong people worried that it came at the cost of the beliefs and practices that, in their view, defined who they are as Hmong people. "What do we have in our culture if we don't have shamanism?" asked Shone Yang, a Hmong man committed to practicing Hmong shamanism. "It is our tradition, our religion, our medicine—and maybe it will soon be gone." Chronicling the history of missionaries in Asia, he noted that Hmong people had faced challenges to their beliefs and practices before. "People have been trying to make us lose our shaman beliefs for a long time," he said. But the new circumstances in the United States made him particularly worried. He predicted that in a decade, Hmong people "won't be practicing the shaman religion anymore."

It was thus out of the determination to hold onto their Hmong identity and culture that many Hmong people remained steadfast in continuing the traditions of the Hmong way, despite the challenges. They believed that Hmong rituals not only ensured prosperity and peaceable relations with the spirit world but also affirmed and authenticated their identity and culture, which risked being lost in "the American jungle." For Shone Yang, practicing shamanism was an important cultural obligation because it told the world who he was and where he belonged. "To me, culture is like an ID card," Shone Yang said. "You have to have an ID. If someone asks you, 'What is your culture,' you have to have something to show them." Although he had been raised partly in the United States, he was not one of the young people whom elders criticized for abandoning the Hmong way. He insisted on continuing its traditions. "So even though I have been here since I was in my teenage years, everything about our Hmong culture is still very important to me," he said. "Shamanism is very, very important." To explain its importance to Hmong people, he drew parallels between Hmong commitment to shamanism and American commitment to Christianity. "For us, it's like your prayer," he said. "You go to your church and you pray; we talk and we ask our ancestors to guide us and to protect us from evil spirits and bad lucks."[74]

Practicing the Hmong way in the United States often seemed an impossible task, but many people remained determined to sustain the beliefs and rituals that kept them connected with their homeland, their ancestors, and their history—even if they were uncertain how or if they would be able to continue these traditions for long in a new American context. "Even if our traditional religion is hard to follow, we must keep true to it," said Sia Ly Thao, a Hmong woman in Minnesota.[75] At stake was preserving who they were as Hmong people because, as Mai Neng Moua explained, "for Hmong people, these rituals and traditions were synonymous with their identity."[76] After losing their homes and their loved ones during a decade of brutal war, Hmong refugees resettled in the United States resolved to hold fast to what they had left: their identity as Hmong people, and with that, their traditional beliefs and practices. Mai Lee, a Hmong woman, expressed this sentiment simply. "We are Hmong," she said. "Remember that we are Hmong. Remember and do not become Christians, and follow the Hmong traditions."[77]

«««‹›»»»

Refugee resettlement policies unsettled the practice and preservation of the Hmong way and changed the trajectory of Hmong spiritual and religious life. In a country that "allows people to believe what they believe and do what they do," as Cziasarh Neng Yang put it, Hmong refugees were not always free to practice their chosen rituals and determine the destinies of their own souls. Over time, Hmong Americans relocated to be closer to family, established ethnic institutions, and found creative ways to maintain the practice of their traditions. During the tumultuous first years in the United States, however, refugee resettlement policies imposed significant barriers to the Hmong way. The government and voluntary agency officials who planned resettlement do not appear to have realized that these policies impeded the practice of traditional Hmong rituals. Part of the problem was that they were focused on an idea of religion that was defined by Protestant norms, which hold that religion is individual, private, and focused on belief and personal conscience. In contrast, the Hmong way is collective, public, focused on practice, and, for many observers, not obviously a religion. Pluralism is premised on the idea that people could—and should—respect one another across lines of religious and cultural difference. But for the Hmong, who did not have an obvious religion in the eyes of their Christian sponsors, the difference may have been too great for this vision to be realized.

In these circumstances, Hmong people felt a combination of both despair and determination, helplessness and hope. Paja Thao expressed these feelings in one of his chants:

> I still believe Hmong religion
> In my country Laos none of my cousins changed to Christians
> But now all my cousins come to America
> And all of them change to Christians
>
> Now only my son and I
> Hold to Hmong religion
> But I am not sure how much longer
> Before my son changes to Christian
>
> As for me, I will never be Christian
> Because my father and mother gave birth to me
> I am not the only one
> There are many from every clan
> Who still believe Hmong religion
>
> I shall never forget my own culture
> I am a Hmong
> My father and mother gave me a birth
> I shall call to feed their spirits.[78]

Although many people, like Paja Thao, "still believe Hmong religion," the reality was that refugee resettlement introduced significant disruptions and ritual uncertainties. In part because of this new sense of spiritual vulnerability, many Hmong refugees in the United States chose to adopt Christianity. But what, precisely, did it mean for Hmong people like Paja Thao's cousins to "change to Christians"?

6

Following the New Way

REFUGEE POLICY AND HMONG
ADOPTION OF CHRISTIANITY

Kia Vue and her family arrived in Oklahoma in the middle of the night, and there was nobody to meet them at the airport. Waiting in a strange building in a foreign land and all alone, she and her family were frightened. They thought back to the rumors about America that they had heard in Thailand—warnings of "monsters who would eat people," for example—and her father wondered if they had fallen into that world. To their relief, a man arrived from the Catholic parish that sponsored them and he took the family to the church, where they spent the rest of the night.

Kia Vue and her family were thankful that they had not, in fact, landed in a horrific realm of monsters. Still, their new home was strange, and their new lives upsetting. The tiny town in Oklahoma where they were resettled was isolated, two hours away from Oklahoma City, and there were no other Hmong people for miles around. "I was very lonely at that time," she said. "Every time we saw a city bus run by, we thought, oh my gosh, they're probably bringing our people here! But we don't see anybody." She and her family felt abandoned. "It was almost like we landed in jail," she said. "That's how we felt in Oklahoma."

Fortunately, the priest and the volunteers from their sponsoring parish visited regularly and were "very nice." "They had helped us in many ways," she recalled. "When it came to Halloween time, they took us around to get candies, they come and teach us at home, and taught mom and dad, and sometimes they bring teachers from the church to come and teach us about the Bible, and on Sundays, too."

Learning about the Bible was something new for Kia Vue, and being resettled by a Catholic parish was her first experience encountering any type of Christianity. She attended Mass with her sponsors and admitted that she found the experience bewildering. "They just speak, and we just listen," she said with a laugh. But she ended up deciding to join the church anyway. When asked why she chose to become Christian, she emphasized her gratitude. "After the church helped us, we decided—the whole family decided—to be baptized," she said. There were other reasons, too. She explained that she adopted Christianity because she also believed that starting her life over in the United States required major changes, and she aspired to be American. "We had become part of the people," she said.

In truth, she and her family hoped to practice the Hmong way. But in Oklahoma, the absence of Hmong ritual experts who could help with traditional ceremonies posed a significant problem. The family considered it prudent to turn to Catholicism as an alternative. "We decided that there were no Hmong around, so it's not going to be helpful for us to continue our practices," she said. They could not do the traditional rituals because "at that time, there wasn't a lot of people, and the people who knew it [the rituals], there wasn't a lot of them there." She also found that the Catholic Church was a reasonable home for her, though. Compared to other Christian denominations, it was more accommodating of Hmong practices. "I like the Catholic Church more because they're not so strict," she said. "I didn't hear anything as far as restricting us from practicing."

Later in life, she left Oklahoma for Wisconsin and then Minnesota, where she lived among more Hmong people and had more access to ritual experts. In these new circumstances, she resumed practicing traditional Hmong rituals, which she was never willing to abandon because its rituals had proven useful to maintaining her health. "This has helped us," she said, "and so that's why we continue to do this." She observed that other Hmong refugees made the same decision to return to practicing traditional rituals when they had the opportunity to do so. She drew a clear connection between the change in circumstances and the change in religious practices: "We thought we were going to be part of the American family," she said, "and so because we don't see any Hmong family around . . . that's why we decided to [convert]," she said. "But later we saw lots and lots and lots of Hmong people, and so many of the Hmong people who were converted went back to the old ways."

For Kia Vue, returning to the old ways did not require abandoning the new ways she had learned in Oklahoma. She continued to practice Christianity, though by 2012 she was a member of a Protestant congregation. Throughout her life, she made many religious migrations, adopting a variety of religious practices along the way. To maintain her spiritual and bodily well-being, she drew from Catholicism, evangelical Protestantism, Hmong shamanism, and Western medicine. "A mixture—it works better," she said.[1]

«««‹›»»»

As Kia Vue's story shows, American refugee resettlement policies made it more difficult for Hmong refugees to practice their traditional rituals. However, resettlement policies shaped Hmong religious life in yet another way: by creating close and dependent relationships between Hmong refugees and Christian churches. By entrusting resettlement work to Christian voluntary agencies and congregations, the government initiated influential encounters between Hmong refugees and Christian church sponsors and set the stage for Hmong people to adopt Christianity. Put simply, refugee resettlement policies undermined the traditional Hmong way at the same time that they helped introduce Hmong refugees to "the new way," Christianity. The decision by Hmong refugees to convert to Christianity was thus not simply the result of individual spiritual awakening, as conversion is often framed, or a desire to become Americans. Their conversion was also the product of the state, its resettlement policies, and the relationships that it fostered.

However, the state-centered explanation for the Hmong adoption of Christianity is just part of the story, one that covers only those events that unfolded in what Hmong people referred to as the "seen world." A more nuanced interpretation of religious change must consider Hmong people's relationship with the unseen spirit world, which, in traditional Hmong belief, exerts enormous power over daily life. Many Hmong refugees made the decision to adopt Christianity in the context of resettlement policies that deprived them of the human or material resources necessary for traditional Hmong ritual life. Finding themselves in a troubling ritual void, they turned to Christianity as an additional, alternative means of ensuring good health and peaceful relations with the spirit world. When conditions changed, so, too, did the Hmong. Always adapting and responding to the shifting circumstances of their lives, they crossed and recrossed religious borders, moving back and forth between the Hmong way and Christianity as their spiritual needs demanded. Hmong people were thus not only refugee migrants but also religious migrants. For people like Kia Vue, Christian conversion was one of many religious changes that Hmong people pursued throughout an entire lifetime of seeking spiritual security and bodily well-being amid the tumult of war, dislocation, and resettlement. Shari Rabin, writing of Jewish immigrants, described religion as "a mobile assemblage of resources for living," and so it was for the Hmong, who drew on a wide array of spiritual and religious resources often with a single purpose in mind: survival.[2]

Hmong religious change was far more complex than the simple story of refugees shepherded, willingly or not, into the fold of their sponsors' churches. Resettlement policies produced contact, but also combination—the exchange of religious ideas and practices that generated religious innovation, borrowing, and, in some cases, conversion, which Hmong people pursued in accordance with their traditional spiritual worldview. "Conversion" for many Hmong refugees was not binary, and the embrace of Christian beliefs and practices did not preclude continuing the Hmong way. Hmong refugees often continued to pray to their ancestors, conduct soul-calling ceremonies, or visit shamans when they were sick, even as they identified as devout and observant Christians. Moreover, Hmong converts often incorporated Christian beliefs and practices into their preexisting spiritual lives, and they believed that Christianity offered access to rituals and spiritual entities that would help them to maintain harmonious relations with the spirits. Throughout this process, Hmong refugees were pragmatic, flexible, and eclectic in their willingness to experiment with different religions and rituals, even as their spiritual framework remained fundamentally the same. The story of Hmong religious change is thus not simply one of conversion, but of synthesis—an example of what Catherine Albanese described as "combination" and what Linford Fisher, in his study of Native American religious life, described as a type of "religious engagement" that was "practical and provisional" and characterized by "dynamism and inherent instability."[3] As he argued, most non-Christian people have approached religious change "more in terms of testing, sampling, and appending to existing customs and practices, rather than conceiving of religious change in terms of a wholesale renunciation of one set of ideas in favor of another."[4] Similarly, for the Hmong, conversion was an additive process that involved acquiring new ways of managing spirits and navigating the complex relationship between the seen and unseen worlds.

"The Americans Took Us to Church, so We Went"

Looking back at their first days in the United States, Hmong refugees recalled that church sponsors made earnest efforts to share Christianity with them from the very beginning. For example, Neng Vang described how shortly after she arrived in Saint Paul in 1989, a church volunteer, whom she only knew by the name of "sister," visited the family's home to talk to them about Christianity. "She gave her a Bible that was written in Hmong, a big one," recalled Paj Ntaub Lis, Neng Vang's daughter. "She was telling my mom and them to go to church." Neng Vang accepted the Bible and told "sister" that she would read through the material and that she needed some time to make a decision about going to church.[5]

In the stories Hmong people told of their experiences of going to church with their sponsors, the precise intentions of the resettlement volunteers are sometimes difficult to discern. Missionary purposes—what Pearl Jones described as a desire "to introduce them to Jesus" to ensure that they are "saved"—may have motivated some sponsors to bring refugees to church every Sunday. The "sister" who visited Neng Vang and gave her a Bible clearly had this objective. However, sponsors may have brought Hmong refugees to Sunday services with no missionary objectives whatsoever. For example, they may have intended to introduce them to a support network, help them find new friends, and include them in the life of the community, as voluntary agencies had encouraged sponsors to do. Perhaps sponsors

Yong Vang Yang and family on their first day in Saint Paul. Courtesy of Minnesota Historical Society.

brought Hmong refugees to church in order to raise awareness of refugee issues and increase financial support from the congregation, as the Refugee Core Committee at Saint Anthony Park Lutheran Church did.

However, these nuances were often lost on the refugees whom they sponsored. Because of the language barrier, Hmong refugees said that they understood little of what the sponsors told them. All of the guidance that the voluntary agencies shared in their sponsorship manuals—that refugees were not required to attend church, that the church's help was freely given with no expectation of conversion, and that refugees were free to practice their own religion if they chose to do so—was difficult to communicate when, as Tzianeng Vang said, the only means of talking to one another was through "hand gestures" and "charade games."[6]

Hmong refugees recounted how their sponsors sometimes simply showed up at their homes, picked them up, and brought them to church without asking about their preferences. "When we came, we found out that it was a Catholic church that had sponsored us, and they, the sponsors, started taking us to church," recalled Soua Lo, a Hmong woman in Saint Paul. Some people who wanted to continue the Hmong way, like Yia Lee and her family, felt free to stop attending church. "[The sponsors] took us to church a couple times," she said, "but it was just not us, so we decided that we didn't go anymore."[7] But many others did not consider church attendance a choice and felt beholden to the church sponsors on whom they depended. Another Hmong woman in Minnesota, Mai Vang Thao, recalled that she first attended church only because the church that had sponsored her made her go. "When we arrived in this country, the Americans took us to church, so we went," she said. She did not know if she had the option not to attend, and she spent seven or eight years going to church. In truth, she did not want to attend at all. She described herself as committed to "traditional beliefs" and admitted that she "did not like Christianity" and "did not like to go to church."[8] Tzianeng Vang similarly felt that resettlement placed his family in a religiously coercive situation. "With the churches that sponsored us, we didn't have a choice," he said. "They sponsored us, so we came every Sunday." Later he added that the pastor "would just come and put us in his car and took us to church."[9]

Attending church for the first time was sometimes a bewildering experience. Soua Lo and her family had no prior experience with Catholicism before coming to the United States, but her Catholic sponsors brought her to Mass on Sunday. There, they watched and mimicked what the parishioners around them did: they held the Bible, they knelt on the hassocks, and they took Holy Communion. "They led us, and we just follow[ed]," she said. "We just didn't even know what we were doing."[10] Differences in language were just as important as differences in ritual and belief. Neng Xiong was a practicing Catholic, and she looked forward to attending Mass when she was resettled in Minnesota. "I was excited about going," she said. "So, you know, seven o'clock every weekend, I would be up and ready to go." However, Mass at the cathedral in Saint Paul was all in English. "I really don't understand what's going on, and I don't understand what's being communicated," she said. "So, when they stand, I stand; when they sit, I sit; when they go, I go; I just follow them."[11]

Many Hmong refugees eventually chose to go beyond following the movements of their neighboring parishioners and opted to follow "the new way" and adopt Christianity. In the stories they tell of their religious change, they often attributed their decision to the fact that Christian churches had sponsored them. Bo Thao's conversion story is a typical one. "When we first came, we were sponsored by the churches, so when we arrived here, my parents went to church," she said. Her mother and father "were even baptized."[12] Their narrative of religious migration was intertwined with their refugee migration, as well as the government resettlement policies that directed it. However, the forces that shaped Hmong people's decision to adopt Christianity were more complicated.

To begin, some Hmong people viewed adopting Christianity as a necessary step in becoming American. Perhaps because of their contact with missionaries in Laos and in Thailand, where the association between Christianity and Western culture was strong, they arrived in the United States believing that conversion to Christianity would help them fit into their new communities. Kim Yang's perspective on Christianity illustrates this viewpoint. "I believe that we need to change, because we are living in a new country that has lots of changes, so we need to change too," she said.[13] Rev. William Siong, a Hmong Lutheran pastor, observed that for Hmong people and other refugees, the desire to belong in the new society was strong. "At first, when you came here, you want to be like the white people," he said.[14] And Keith Vang, the son and brother of a shaman, explained the decision to go to church in the simplest terms: "When we came, we wanted to fit in."[15]

Others linked their conversion to Christianity with receiving material assistance from voluntary agencies and sponsoring congregations. Drawing on language often used to describe Christian converts in Asia, Mai Neng Moua directly related her family's religious choices to the help they received from churches. "My family converted to Christianity when we came to Pittsburgh in 1981," she said. "At first, Niam [mother] was a typical 'rice-bowl' Christian. The 'rice' came in the form of furniture and clothes, English as a Second Language classes for the adults, and Sunday school for the kids."[16] In this instance, Christian conversation was a means of securing a variety of essential resources.

In addition, Hmong refugees sometimes considered the adoption of Christianity to be an act of respect, loyalty, and obligation to the churches that had helped refugee families so generously. Some Hmong refugees who were sponsored by congregations participated in Christian churches in the belief that participating in churches was a proper demonstration of loyalty and reciprocity. Soua Lo, who was resettled in Pittsburgh, was a member of the Christian and Missionary Alliance (CMA) Church when she arrived in the United States, but she felt required to attend Mass at the Catholic parish that had sponsored her. "From January until April, we were there in Pittsburgh, and we went to a Catholic church because we felt like we had to, because we were sponsored by a Catholic church, and so we felt obligated to go," she said. She saw her participation in the Catholic Church as one of many instances in which resettlement required Hmong people to make changes that they did not necessarily welcome. Like paying taxes or stopping at red lights, going to church was simply something new that she thought they were expected to do in America. "We knew that it was different from what we believed, and that it's different from what we are used to in Laos, but we just know we had to do something in ways that we just didn't know," she said.[17]

A feeling of obligation may have been one reason why Rev. Bea Vue-Benson's mother became a Lutheran. She recalled how her mother, who had been raised in a family with a few relatives who had been "very faithful Christians," was married to a shaman who continued to practice the Hmong way. "I actually grew up in a very shamanistic family," she said. When her mother and sisters arrived in Wisconsin, having been sponsored by Trinity Lutheran Church in Eau Claire, her mother chose to be baptized into the Lutheran church soon after they arrived. Trinity Lutheran had been very generous with the family, which she believed shaped her mother's decision. "Financially they [the church] played a very big role," she said, "and socially and spiritually played a very integral role in our family." She explained that she did not fully know the reasons why her mother chose to have the family baptized. "But I'm guessing . . . maybe she felt obligated to be a part of the community that had sponsored us," she said.

If her mother felt obligated, Vue-Benson had reasons for adopting Christianity that were different. The central themes in her conversion narrative were not obligation but gratitude, awe, and admiration.

Adopting Christianity, for her, was the product of a warm encounter with Christian kindness and charity:

> My story about becoming a Christian—and I have lots of wonderful Christian friends who continue to encourage me and remind me why I'm a Christian—and it's because of the way our church loved us, even as they didn't know who we were, and even as we didn't deserve and didn't earn—we didn't earn this love from Trinity. We didn't. I mean, that's the story of the Christian Gospel. It's grace, and the Lutheran tradition is the story of grace, unearned love, unmerited love. And I do believe that the Gospel proclaims that grace and unmerited love, unearned love and unearned forgiveness. And I think about the Prodigal story, the son returning home after [he] wasted his resources and having, you know, betrayed his dad, and being received with so much love and forgiveness.

In her view, the kindness that Trinity Lutheran Church offered her family introduced her to concepts of God's grace. "I didn't earn—our family did not earn—their love and support," she said. "They gave it out of their understanding of God's commandment to love their neighbor." The congregation's example inspired her. Active in the life of the church throughout her youth, she attended a Lutheran college and then Luther Seminary, where she would train to become the first Hmong woman ordained a Lutheran minister. Her aspirations for life would come to reflect what she had learned through the generosity and hospitality she witnessed when Trinity Lutheran Church sponsored her family. "I want to live my life and give to people," she said, "and not think about if they've earned it or not."[18]

As these conversion narratives reveal, Hmong refugees adopted Christianity in the context of resettlement for a great variety of reasons. Some people felt a bond of gratitude and obligation while others believed that attending church was the American way. Still others became Christian because they were impressed by the kindness and compassion shown to them by their church sponsors. Ultimately, though, these diverse stories were all consequences of a common force: the government resettlement policies that helped put Hmong refugees into contact with Christianity in the first place.

"There's No Shamans I Could Go Pursue, so I Just Thought I'd Go to Church"

Government refugee resettlement policies contributed to the shift to Christianity in yet another crucial way: by disrupting the practice of traditional Hmong rituals. Contending with the scarcity of ritual experts and community members, young Hmong refugees who arrived in the United States in the early years of resettlement found themselves unable to conduct the traditional Hmong ceremonies that maintained good relations with the spirits. Looking for alternatives, they turned to the most obvious one, which was the Christianity of the churches that had sponsored them.

In explaining why they decided to convert to Christianity, many Hmong people emphasized their concerns about the future of the Hmong way. Some Hmong refugees worried about sustaining their ritual traditions and considered adopting Christianity even before they set foot on American soil. Rev. Pa Mang Her, a Hmong Christian pastor, recalled that in 1976 he warned other Hmong refugees coming to the United States that continuing Hmong traditions would be impossible. "At that time we told them to be believers [in Christianity] because there was no other way they could worship their spirits anymore," he said.[19]

At least in the short term, Her was correct: Hmong refugees in the first few years of resettlement found it difficult, even impossible, to continue the Hmong way, and it was due to their spiritual precariousness that they chose to adopt Christianity. Cziasarh Neng Yang, for example, explained that he decided to become a baptized Catholic because he believed that traditional Hmong rituals were not a viable option. "We do not know whether or not we will be able to conduct our traditional ritual," he said. He and his brothers began to look for a "way out," and, as he recalled, "that was when my brother and my brother-in-law were, you know, encouraging us . . . to associate with the Catholic Church." Thirty-five years later, as he looked back on that period of his life, he emphasized that "during that time, our life was not stable."

This instability owed in part to the absence of Hmong ritual experts, and Hmong people turned to Christian clergy as replacement ritual experts. "When you don't have a shaman to come and cure your family or conduct the ritual in your household, then you are hopeless," said Cziasarh Neng Yang. "You need something to lean on, so the Catholic priest, the church, were the one who [we] rely on, and they come and pray for you, and they serve as the substitute for the shaman."[20]

The absence of family members also caused Hmong people to turn to Christianity as a substitute for the Hmong way. Yong Kay Moua, for example, was sponsored by a church in Wisconsin, where he had no family nearby. Not long after his arrival, he telephoned his relatives who had also been sent elsewhere in the United States, and upon the urging of a family leader in Providence, Rhode Island, they made the collective decision to discontinue Hmong traditions. In their view, the circumstances of family separation made Hmong rituals unfeasible and necessitated their conversion to Christianity. "[The family leader] mentioned to us that now, since we came to America, each of us live distant to each other, so we need to change to Christian," he said. Like Cziasarh Neng Yang, Yong Kay Moua spoke of his family's decision in terms of instability. When he first resettled in the United States, he decided that the situation required him to commit to either the Hmong way or the new way of Christianity. His family, he said, had "one foot on each different boat," and the situation felt spiritually hazardous. "You have to decide which way, which boat that you would like to stand in," he explained. It was better "just [to] make only one way."[21]

The religious decisions of early-arriving refugees like Cziasarh Neng Yang and Yong Kay Moua often had a strong influence on the choices of Hmong refugees who resettled in the same community later. In the Pennsylvania town where Tzianeng Vang reunited with his extended family, most of the people in the Hmong refugee community, including his relatives, already practiced Christianity. He and his parents became Southern Baptists because they realized that it was simply too difficult to continue traditional Hmong rituals alone. "In Pennsylvania, all your peers go to church, your relatives go to church, not many people find it plausible [and], you know, pleasing to continue the animist way," he said. "So everybody goes to church, so you just go."[22]

As his story suggests, even if they had hoped to continue Hmong traditions, those who lived in a predominantly Christian Hmong community found it necessary to adopt Christianity, too, given the scarcity of relatives, shamans, and community members with traditional ritual expertise. One Hmong woman, Mao Yang, felt she had no choice but to go to church. "She did not want to go," her daughter-in-law explained. "She was still waiting to get connected with the relative who was already here, so that she could go continue her old practices." However, she was sponsored by a Baptist church that encouraged her to adopt Christianity, and she was resettled in a small town where the few other Hmong people were Baptists who were uncompromising in their repudiation of traditional rituals. In these circumstances, Mao Yang believed that joining the Baptist church was her only option. Practicing traditional Hmong rituals was impossible to do on her own, and in that small town, she said, "There was just no Hmong people who did it!" She was especially worried about what would happen if she or a family member fell ill. "Who am going to go get?" she said. "There's no shamans I could go pursue, so I just thought I'd go to church."[23]

The story of the Lee and Vang families offers another illustration of how the absence of other practitioners of the Hmong way influenced their religious choices. When she and her family first arrived in Minnesota in 1989, Neng Vang and her husband needed to set up a household altar called a *dab xwm kab*. Typically located in a place of prominence in the main room of a family home, this altar honors the household deity that ensures fortune and prosperity. For traditional Hmong families like the Vangs, the altar is an important place for making offerings of food and paper money to honor household and ancestral spirits. The alter and its associated rituals not only ensure prosperity and good harvests but also help protect the family home from malevolent spirits.[24]

Neng Vang and her family had one major problem, though: they did not know how to properly set up the *dab xwm kab*. Without a *dab xwm kab*, the Vang family felt spiritually vulnerable, and so they began to look for a substitute spiritual guardian for their house. At one point, a member of one of the Lutheran congregations that had sponsored the family gave them a crucifix, which the family hung on the living room wall. Neng Vang and her husband hoped that by putting the crucifix in their house, Jesus would offer her family spiritual protection and the Christian God would prevent any evil spirits from harming her family. Paj Ntaub Lis explained, "Because Hmong people, we believe that whether you have Buddha or whatever, you have something to protect your home, and I think Jesus Christ served us well in the few probably days that it was up, you know, as protection of the home." After a couple years, however, Neng Vang encountered a frightening apparition that appeared in the middle of the night and impressed upon her that she and the family had made a grave error. Paj Ntaub Lis described the incident, which she and her mother interpreted as a warning from the spirits:

> So my mother woke up the one night, and she saw the cross shaking on the wall. She was up—I mean, she wasn't sleeping. She woke up, and so she saw it shaking on the wall and that scared her. . . . And so she felt that maybe because we have our own beliefs in ancestors, that she felt that, "Ooh, they're probably not happy." So then she thinks she might have made a mistake. And that's why she saw it—they felt she made a mistake. And that's why she threw it out.

The next afternoon, upon coming home from school, Paj Ntaub Lis discovered that her mother had discarded both the crucifix and the Bible given to her by the missionaries. And soon after, aware of the spiritual urgency of the situation, family members found an elder to assist in setting up a *dab xwm kab* in their living room. After that point, Paj Ntaub Lis said, there were "no more crosses in the home."[25]

Christian Hmong pastors observed this trend. Joua Tsu Thao, who had been one of the earliest Hmong refugees to arrive in Minnesota and who later pastored a Hmong Baptist congregation in Roseville, observed that many of the people who came to the United States in the first years of resettlement adopted Christianity because they did not have enough knowledge and expertise in the proper practice of Hmong rituals. "Most of the young people who came here on the first or second category, which is most of the people who worked directly to the United States, we don't know how to worship the old way, and most of the people became Christian," he said.[26] Rev. Timothy Vang, reflecting on his experience as a Hmong pastor with the CMA Church, came to the same conclusion:

> Those who came earlier were those educated people such as doctors, nurses, government officials, and top military leaders, who had no experience or who had not learned how to do those kinds of chores of shamanism and spiritism. So when they arrived in America, they would say, "Oh, we don't know what to do anymore. If a person is

sick—what do you do? If the person dies, how do you do the funeral for them?" So, those who came earlier, they said, "Oh we have to go to church. That's it. Go to church. If the sponsor asks, just go to the sponsor's church." As a result, many of them were converted during those first three years when they arrived here, knowing that it would be difficult for them to practice animism, so they accepted Christianity.[27]

Even Hmong shamans observed this shift. Paja Thao, the Hmong shaman in Chicago, chanted about the religious changes he witnessed among his own kin. The paucity of ritual knowledge caused his clansmen to convert to Christianity, and, with all his relatives following the new way, he questioned his ability to carry on Hmong traditions on his own:

> Now some of my clansmen come to America
> None of them knows how to feed these spirits
> They do not know these spirits
> All my clansmen change to Christians
> Now there is only my family
> I, all alone, am not sure how to follow this way.[28]

When Hmong people chose to "go to the sponsor's church" and "change to Christians," what precisely did this decision mean? To answer this question, it is necessary to take a close look at how Hmong people understood and experienced conversion. When doing so, we must remember two aspects of Hmong belief and practice: first, that Hmong people have historically seen religion as centered on practice rather than on belief, and second, that they have been open to adding new practices and incorporating them into their pre-existing repertoire of rituals and beliefs.[29] Both of these approaches to religious and spiritual life shaped their experiences of conversion, which were varied and complex and which did not necessarily involve the abandonment of old ways. At the same time, while Hmong people hoped that following the new way would bring stability to their lives and offer a "way out" of their ritual crisis, adopting Christianity introduced new complications to their spiritual lives.

For some Hmong people, Christianity was truly a new way that involved a sharp break from the past. The CMA Church, the denomination that today boasts the greatest number of Hmong members, has forbidden many practices associated with the traditional Hmong way. For example, Timothy Vang, the pastor at a Hmong CMA congregation in Maplewood, Minnesota, explained that he saw traditional Hmong rituals as practices of demon worship that true Hmong Christians should abandon: "So most of the things that the Hmong people do really are non-Christian. 80 to 90 percent of what they claim to be culture, it's not pure culture—it always relates to demons. That is why a Hmong who becomes Christian has to forsake many of the traditional Hmong customs. He either has to separate himself, or if he goes back to them, anything that he participates [in] will involve demons."[30] Seeing the Hmong way as a form of slavery rooted in "the fear of demons or torture from demons," Vang considered Hmong people to be "like prisoners in Satan's prison," held "captive in that kind of belief and fear."[31] In addition, he considered Hmong beliefs and practices to be "a very primitive form of religion" and animism, more generally, to be "the most primitive form of religious practice on earth." In contrast, he said, "Christianity is the most scientific, reasonable belief system in any religion."[32] Cher Moua, a Hmong pastor at an evangelical church in Saint Paul, offered a slightly different approach to the question of whether the Hmong way was compatible with Christianity, but he arrived at the same conclusion: there is no place for the practice of certain traditional Hmong rituals in the lives of faithful Hmong Christians. "The Bible clearly says we need to be careful for us to discern what is physical, what is spiritual," he said. "Anything that is associated with spiritual conflict, we need to understand, we need to discern, we need to advise people against participating."[33]

Like their pastors, lay Hmong Christians in evangelical Protestant denominations often shared the belief that Christianity was incompatible with the Hmong way. Tzianeng Vang, who spent much of his adulthood as a member of the CMA Church, likened conversion to Christianity to a "sworn-in citizenship process" in which "there's no if and but" about leaving the Hmong way behind.[34] Devout Hmong Christians such as True Xiong described practitioners of traditional Hmong rituals to be "enslaved" to demons.[35] Similarly, Bee Yang saw the Hmong way as a morally repugnant set of rituals that had brought only suffering to her life. "The thought of going back is not even as big as a hair strand," she declared. She believed that practicing shamanism and conducting a soul-calling ceremony were wicked practices "because the Bible said so" and also because God had told her so. "The Spirit of God speaks to my heart, that it is a sin," she said. "Enough is enough," she said, "and I'm just really sick and tired of it, and I just don't want to have anything to do with it anymore." She later added, for emphasis, "If you force me to go back, I would rather die."[36]

The compatibility of traditional Hmong rituals with Christianity has been the focus of intense controversy among Hmong Christians. Importantly, many of the religious rifts that Hmong people discussed focused less on heretical belief and more on the sinfulness or spiritual error of specific practices. Hmong Christians debated whether they should participate in major rituals, such as a soul-calling ritual or shaman's healing ceremony. In addition, they weighed questions about smaller decisions that pastors like Timothy Vang still considered the work of "demons": whether to eat ritually sacrificed meat at a funeral, for example, or to have *khi tes* strings tied around their wrists at New Year celebrations. Especially since Hmong people have started to equate their traditional household rituals to the Western idea of religion, participation in any ritual act, whether Christian or Hmong, has articulated their commitment and loyalty to a greater degree than self-applied labels and proclamations of belief and faith.[37]

Hmong Christians were not the only ones who saw incompatibility and conflict—so, too, did Hmong people who practiced the old way. Some Hmong families believed that Christian and traditional Hmong ways simply could not be reconciled. As Mai Neng Moua explained, "Animist Hmong believe it is a violation of religious practices for people of different religious rituals to live in the same house."[38] But for many Hmong families, the most pressing issue was not which beliefs and rituals were right or wrong or whether they could coexist in the same space. Of greater concern was the future spiritual direction of the individual as well as the entire family. For example, You a Vang Yang, a Hmong man in Minnesota, expressed concern that in the afterlife, the soul could be confused and "caught in the middle," unable to find a final resting place with either the Hmong ancestors or in the Christian heaven.[39] Moreover, because kin are essential to the practice of traditional Hmong rituals, the decision to adopt Christianity directly affected the ritual lives of other family members. As a result, religious change often produced significant family conflict. "My children want to be 'Christianity,' but I still want to believe the spirit," said Yang Cha Ying, a Hmong man in Minneapolis. "There is a lot of controversy about this. I am worried day and night. For me, I want my children to do the same thing as I do, but they never do. They adapt the American culture." Although the conflict about religion was for him real and unresolved, he had already made some accommodations. "We have learned to celebrate Christmas, because our children like it," he said. "So we have adapted to it. We have a tree and presents for our children."[40] It was a small accommodation, but part of a larger, more painful issue: Hmong families sometimes found themselves torn apart when one member of the family became Christian.

In the eyes of many Hmong Christians, particularly evangelical Protestants, conversion to Christianity necessitated a separation from all aspects of the Hmong way, especially life-cycle rituals that involved significant family participation. According to Cher Moua, leaving the Hmong way often meant that new Christians also "leave brothers, sisters, parents, [and] children behind." This "spiritual separation" produced "a hostile relationship for a period of time."[41] The possibility of family separation especially angered parents who expected their sons to conduct important rituals on their behalf. When William Siong converted to Christianity, his father, who was still living in Asia, announced that he had "betrayed" the family and sent his son cassette tapes with furious messages. "He said that 'If I know that you're going to convert to Christianity, your mom and I would not raise you up in the first place!'" Siong recalled. Only a teenager at the time, he described the event as being "very, very painful." "Many nights that I was crying," he said, "and didn't know [what] the future will be like because my father no longer wants me to be his son . . . because of the religion thing."[42]

These bitter family schisms over "the religion thing" were a matter of such controversy and concern that it was the subject of *The Garden of the Souls*, an original play that the Pom Siab Hmoob Theatre in Saint Paul staged in 1995. Developed by a group of ten writers through nine months of conversations with Hmong elders and community members, the play focused on one Hmong American family struggling with this religious split.[43] The family's father, who identified as "traditional," constantly argued with the mother, who was

Christian, about the religious direction of the family. Animal- and food-centered rituals were the center of particularly heated argument. At one point, the mother acted like a midcentury CMA missionary in Laos: she cut off her child's wrist strings, which Hmong people wear to protect their spirits. "There," she said. "You are free. You are not a prisoner of the spirits. You don't have to call to them, and you don't have to satisfy them with sacrifices." She later announced, "You don't need *ua neng* or *ua dab*," referring to two important Hmong healing rituals. But later in the play, the matter of the *ua neng* arose again, and it was clear that her husband cherished this ritual as central to uniting the traditional Hmong family. "The church is not a place for my family," he said to his wife. "Jesus Christ won't let your relatives come over to your house to eat with you. They won't touch your food, like you put poison in it. They won't take your hospitality. They treat you like you have disease. They won't even talk to you. All because of Jesus Christ. *Ua neng* brings the family together. I never thought I would see my family torn apart like this."[44]

"We Feel Like Becoming Christian Is Like I-PASS to Go to Heaven"

The narrative of families and communities "torn part" by a clash between old and new ways is powerful and pervasive, but it obscures an important reality: for many Hmong Christians, adopting Christianity did not involve such a radical break from the past, and even describing their change as "conversion" can be controversial. In recounting their personal religious histories, many Hmong people used the language of "convert," but Cher Moua, an evangelical Protestant pastor who himself had become a Christian as a young man, vehemently rejected the term. "I hate the word 'converted'!" he said.[45] There were many reasons why he may have disliked the language of conversion. For example, it emphasizes the changes that broke up families and highlights change rather than continued commitment to Hmong family, identity, values, and culture.

More than anything, describing Hmong Christianity in terms of conversion fails to capture the fact that the religious change experienced by Hmong refugees was not binary. Hmong refugees often adopted Christianity selectively, according to their own needs and interpretation. In a classic case of what religion scholar Lamin Sanneh described as "indigenous appropriation," they incorporated Christianity into their preexisting beliefs, practices, and world-views.[46] Moreover, for many Hmong Christians, practicing Christianity did not necessarily preclude practicing traditional Hmong rituals. Seeing religion as additive, rather than exclusive, Hmong people chose to merge past and present and straddle religious boundaries that were more ambiguous and unstable than the teachings of religious hardliners suggested. Ultimately, being Christian and being "traditional" often involved overlapping, rather than discrete, religious beliefs, practices, and identities.[47] According to Lu Vang and Phua Xiong, a medical doctor, "Converted Christians take new concepts or ideas and incorporate them into their old ways while doing away with some parts of animist traditions." Because of the long-standing integration of ideas about spirits, rituals, and bodily well-being, they said, "many Hmong find it difficult to completely give up their traditional ways of doing things and fully adopt American Christian ways."[48]

The degree to which Hmong Christians participated in traditional Hmong rituals depended on the particular denomination of Christianity they pursued. In general, Hmong people who were part of Catholic and mainline Protestant churches have been more comfortable with practicing traditional Hmong rituals alongside Christianity. This tendency is owed in part to Catholic and mainline Protestant teachings and leadership, which have viewed many traditional Hmong practices as secular, nonreligious expressions of Hmong culture, rather than as religion.[49] As Daniel Taillez, a Catholic priest who ministered to the Hmong community for over half a century, put it, "We respect any cultural customs that are not contrary to the Gospel."[50] And, in practice, the range of practices that fell under the category of "cultural customs" was often broad enough to include eating ritually sacrificed meat and participating in soul-calling ceremonies.

This interpretation allowed Catholics and mainline Protestants to see Hmong rituals as compatible with Christian beliefs and had important practical implications for the ritual lives of Hmong Catholics and mainline Protestants. For example, Father Chue Ying Vang, the first Hmong American Catholic priest, embraced traditional ceremonies. During his ordination, he included Hmong rituals such as the presentation of eggs, which is a sign of good luck, and the tying of wrist strings, or a *khi tes* ceremony, which, according to traditional Hmong belief, prevents the release of spirits but in this context was seen as another emblem of good luck.[51] "I try to help my parishioners to be more open to older traditions," he told a local newspaper.[52] Similarly, lay Hmong Catholics often made space for Hmong rituals such as the *hu plig* and *khi tes,* which they understood as blessings, prayers, and rituals that held social and cultural— rather than religious—meaning.[53] Some saw the continuation of these rituals as a reflection of not only Hmong commitments but Christian commitments. Yang Dao, a devout Catholic, considered the decision to honor Hmong traditions to be an expression of a truer, more tolerant Christian faith. In an interview with the *St. Paul Pioneer Press,* he described a funeral where he had witnessed a traditional *qeej* player and a Protestant minister cooperate in a shared ceremony. "Now, that is an honest pastor who understands the teachings of Christ," Yang Dao said. "He is building a more human world."[54]

Even Hmong people who were members of more conservative churches found it difficult to turn their back on the old way completely, largely because of family relationships. Pastors in denominations such as the CMA warned their church members against backsliding, called on Hmong Christians to abstain from participating in traditional rituals, and criticized the Catholic and mainline Protestant approach for indulging what they deemed to be demonic practices. ("If someone did the sort of thing Chue Ying Vang did at the [Hmong Christian] Alliance, people would be rolling in the grave," said Lee Pao Xiong, a local Hmong leader, in an interview with the *Twin Cities Reader.*[55]) In practice, however, enduring family bonds often meant that Hmong Christians did not completely abandon traditional rituals. Mai Neng Moua, for example, recalled that the pastor at her Southern Baptist church repeatedly taught congregants not to mix old and new ways because, as he put it, "You cannot serve two masters." But Mai Neng Moua's family chose to participate in traditional Hmong ceremonies anyway. "Niam [mother] has always told me that we may have gotten rid of the animist spirits, but we did not get rid of our families," she explained. When a shaman performed a *ua neeb* or *hu plig* for a family member or when a relative had a traditional Hmong funeral, Mai Neng and her devoutly Baptist family still attended, participated in the feast, and helped to prepare the food and clean up afterward. Participation in these big family events reflected Mai Neng Moua's broad-minded religious upbringing. She grew up attending Sunday School and singing Christian hymns, and she also read about traditional Hmong practices and observed the shamans' rituals simply because she thought "they were important to know."[56]

In truth, for many Hmong people, conversion to Christianity involved as much continuity as it did change—a fact revealed, for instance, in the role of congregations in the lives of Hmong Christian converts. As is often the case for migrants, Christian churches provided Hmong refugees a source of stability amid the immense social, cultural, economic, and political dislocations of refugee resettlement. Yia Lee, for example, emphasized the emotional and spiritual support she gained from being part of a congregation, and she praised her church for being a community of "very supporting people" who were "very loving and caring."[57]

Christian churches provided not only comfort and care to Hmong Christians but also a source of ritual support that was traditionally provided by kin. In this regard, Christian churches—Hmong-led churches in particular—were not simply institutions of the "new way" but were, as Chia Youyee Vang put it, "a nexus of their negotiation between the old and the new."[58] Churches fulfilled the Hmong need for a network of ritual and spirit support. If Hmong people turned to Christian rituals as a substitute for rituals that they were no longer able to practice, Hmong people turned to Christian churches as a substitute for a family separated by war, refugee migration, and resettlement policies. As Mai Neng Moua observed, the network offered by her mother's Southern Baptist congregation provided familiar forms of support. "The church became her 'clan,' taking care of all the things the clan did—weddings, funerals, visiting the sick in the hospital, settling disputes, and comforting the lonely," she said. "The only differences were that many clans belonged to one church, and the church was bound by the blood of Christ, not family."[59]

Adopting Christianity was also a way to maintain ties to the Hmong ethnic community. Hmong Christian churches, much like other immigrant churches in the United States, served as important community institutions that reinforced Hmong identity, built ethnic cohesion, and provided mutual assistance.[60] Many Hmong Christians preferred to join Hmong congregations, such as Timothy Vang's church, or participate in dedicated Hmong-language services and ethnic ministries supported by the major Christian denominations. Hmong Christians cherished these church programs as opportunities to befriend other Hmong people and participate in the broader Hmong community. Mao Yang recalled that even if she was unenthusiastic about Christianity as a religion, she regularly attended church services at the Hmong Baptist church in her small town because church participation provided the only opportunity for her to connect with other Hmong people. If she did not go to church on Sundays, she said, she would not have been able to see Hmong people at all, a possibility that deeply saddened her.[61]

If churches, as institutions, functioned as sites for maintaining Hmong clan and community ties, Christianity, as a religion, offered alternative practices to maintain spiritual harmony and to operate within a preexisting Hmong cosmological framework. Christianity was "the new way," but in reality, Hmong Christians were quick to find parallels between Christianity and the Hmong way. In her study of Hmong Mennonites in Ontario, Canada, Daphne Winland observed that Christian notions of sacrifice appealed to Hmong people for whom ritual oblations had been a traditional way of showing respect to ancestors and other spiritual entities. She also observed that Hmong Mennonites understood Jesus as a liberator, one who saved them not only from the bondage of sin but also from the bondage of evil spirits known as *tlan*.[62]

Hmong Christians also found similarities in religious symbols and ritual practices. Houa Vue Moua, for example, explained that the Christmas wreath resembled the bamboo ring that Hmong people traditionally made during the New Year; that Easter eggs reminded her of the eggs that Hmong people typically understood as symbols of peace, benevolent spirits, and good health; that the Christian cross was similar to a design Hmong women traditionally sew into their embroidery and a gesture that Hmong people made when they desired protection from evil spirits during a journey; and that Thanksgiving corresponded to Hmong New Year, a celebration of the harvest. Even the chants of the *hu plig*, the traditional Hmong soul-calling ceremony, were "like a hymn in the Bible." All of these similarities,

Houa Vue Moua said, made her feel "comfortable" in Christianity, but also at home in the traditional Hmong way.

Houa Vue Moua did not consider her participation in a *hu plig* to be at odds with her Lutheran faith, a position that reveals another important continuity amid Hmong religious transformations: ritual practices often remained the same. Unlike Bee Yang, who stated that she preferred dying over practicing Hmong rituals, Houa Vue Moua was open to participating in traditional ceremonies and continued to practice the Hmong way even as she identified as a devout Christian, held Christian beliefs, and participated actively in a Christian church. "I don't see anything wrong," Houa Vue Moua said.[63] Her stance, which is a common one, is obscured by the culture-clash narrative of Hmong conversion from "primitive" Hmong animism to "new" Christianity, as well as by dramatic stories of family schisms over religious differences. In reality, most Hmong Christians have straddled religious boundaries, a fact that is especially clear when one considers Hmong American ritual practices. Anne Fadiman, for example, noted the hybridity of Hmong religious life when she was writing her book about Hmong Americans in Merced, California. As she recounted, "Animal sacrifices are common, even among Christian converts, a fact I first learned when May Ying Xiong told me that she would be unavailable to interpret one weekend because her family was sacrificing a cow to safeguard her niece during an upcoming open-heart operation. When I said, 'I didn't know your family was so religious,' she replied, 'Oh yes, we're Mormon.'"[64]

This interaction illuminates two key aspects of Hmong American spirituality. First, there is Fadiman's use of the term "religious," which May Ying Xiong understood as a description of her family's identity as Mormon, though not as a term related to the family's practice of traditional Hmong rituals, which she may have considered to be a form of (nonreligious) culture. As in so many cases, Fadiman and May Ying Xiong do not appear to have the same understanding of what "religious" means. In addition, the exchange illustrates the additive nature of Hmong American spiritual life. May Ying Xiong and her family pursued lives that made space for both Mormonism and the Hmong way, and ritual practices offered Hmong people particularly rich opportunities to express their dual commitments to both Christianity and Hmong traditions. Similarly, MayKao Hang, a Hmong woman in Minnesota, spent half her life raised in a Christian household and half in a traditional one, and her practices reflected her commitment to the two ways. "You can say I do both," she said.[65]

Hmong Christians often turned to traditional rituals at major life events such as birth, serious illness, or death. Bea Vue-Benson, for example, recalled how her mother chose to be baptized into the Lutheran church shortly after she was resettled in Wisconsin and was a committed Christian throughout the remainder of her life. However, as she neared the time of her death, she requested a traditional Hmong funeral rather than a Christian burial. "In fact, my mother passed away and explicitly—explicitly—asked that she be buried in the traditional Hmong animistic way," she recalled. In keeping with the request, Vue-Benson and her family organized a Hmong funeral in which they burned paper money and invited "Hmong traditional ritual experts" who played the *qeej* and performed "the chanting to guide her spirit back to the ancestral world." Lasting seventy-two hours, the funeral was no small investment, but Vue-Benson respected her mother's decision and understood why the funeral was so important to her. "Because my father was a shaman," she said, her mother "didn't think that she could be reunited with him if she were buried the Christian way." In addition, "she wanted to be reunited with my ancestors, who were not Christians, so we honored her wish." That Vue-Benson's mother found peace and security in familiar Hmong traditions at a time in her life when she felt that she needed them most—when her soul was ready to be reunited with her ancestors—was testimony to her enduring commitment to the Hmong way, even though she was also a devout Christian.[66]

Vue-Benson's support of her mother's decision shows how Catholics and mainline Protestants embraced a relatively accommodating stance on Hmong rituals. She, along with other Hmong Lutherans, emphasized the need to "be respectful of Hmong folks who are not Christian" and refused to "separate" herself from others. As an ordained Lutheran minister who also had many relatives who were not Christian, Vue-Benson did not consider her participation in traditional rituals to be a sin but rather an expression of her commitment to inclusive and loving relationships with her family and community. "I want to be respectful," she said, "and I'm not one of those Hmong Christians who feel very strongly that I can't participate in a meal

where a . . . Hmong shamanistic or traditional ritual has been performed, like a spirit-calling ritual or a meal where a shaman has
been called to perform a healing ceremony. I don't exclude myself
from those [rituals and] from my participation in those ceremonies
because I really do believe in a God that's bigger than rules and
rituals."

Foundational to Vue-Benson's view on this matter was her belief
that Christianity and the Hmong way are not mutually exclusive but
different ways of honoring God and participating in God's creation. "Ultimately, I do believe in a God that's much bigger than what
we make God to be," she said, "and that God can accept, and that God
is really okay with me participating in a Hmong traditional shamanistic ritual, and that I'm not going to be condemned to hell if I participate in it." Her understanding of God as "bigger than any religion"
and as accepting and inclusive was why she chose to carry out her
mother's request to have a "traditional shamanistic funeral." She
believed that her mother would be "still accepted by God." On this
point, she found inspiration in Romans 8:38–39, in which Paul wrote,
"For I am persuaded that neither death nor life nor angels nor empires
nor armies nor things present nor things to come nor height nor
depth nor anything else created shall be able to separate me from the

Men playing the *qeej* at a Hmong funeral, Frogtown, Saint Paul, in 1994.
Courtesy of Wing Young Huie.

love of God, which is in Jesus Christ our Lord." Vue-Benson loved this passage and took its message "very seriously." In her view, the passage shows that "nothing, not even shamanism, can separate me from the love of God, or anyone else from the love of God."[67]

While Vue-Benson emphasized God's bigness, other people found different idioms to express a similar theology. Vue-Benson's sister, Houa Vue Moua, used the modern metaphor of electronic highway fare payment systems. "We feel like becoming Christian is like I-PASS to go to heaven," she explained. "[If] you were to ask me, between Christian and non-Christian, what is the difference, I would say [it is] exactly just like the highway I-94 or I-90—that you pay iPass or pay token." The Hmong way, she said, required that "you stop and make a long line," but Christianity was like having an automated pass—"like we're already registered to God"—that allowed Christians to drive straight to paradise.[68] However, on the matter of whether one holds an I-PASS or pays by token, she believed that God and the ultimate destination of mankind—heaven—remained the same. This description of Christianity and the Hmong way as different routes to the same God sounded similar chords of pluralistic harmony expressed by some of their Christian church sponsors. In addition, Houa Vue Moua's interpretation of religious change through the metaphor of the I-PASS reveals another aspect of the additive, adaptable, and inventive character of Hmong religious life: how Hmong people incorporated Christianity into their preexisting cosmological framework and interpreted its theology through analogies to American life—in this case, modern American highways and electronic toll systems.

Ultimately, what Houa Vue Moua's story shows is that even when Hmong refugees adopted Christian beliefs, practices, and identities, their understanding of the seen and unseen worlds often remained fundamentally the same.[69] Mai Neng Moua recalled how her devoutly Christian mother behaved similarly and continued to move through the world guided by a traditional Hmong spiritual framework. Even after she joined a Southern Baptist church, her mother would still take time to acknowledge the spirits around her and talk to the souls that she worried had gone astray:

Although Niam [mother] has been a Christian since we came to the United States, I could still remember her calling, "Let's go! Let's go home. Let's not stay here," at the end of the church picnic at Battle Creek Park in Saint Paul. My brother and I were standing right next to her, ready to get in the car. In retrospect, I realize that she was not talking to us. She was talking to our multiple souls who may have wandered off somewhere. She was calling them, telling them not to stay at the park. She was telling them to come home with us. Just like the time she spent four days in the hospital. When we were getting ready to go home, she said, "Let's go home. Do not stay here." She was calling her souls to go home with her and not get stuck at the hospital.

Mai Neng Moua's mother did not see these actions as at odds with her Christian beliefs and practices, which were layered on top of enduring Hmong beliefs about how the spirit world works. As Mai Neng Moua explained, "the 'traditional' animist worldview is the base to which Hmong people refer."[70]

"Which One Can Protect My Family? Who Can Best Serve Me?"

This traditional "base" informed not only how Hmong Christians understood the spirit world, but also how they actively used rituals to maintain good relations with the spirit world. Eager to ensure their spiritual and bodily well-being, Hmong people in the United States drew on an eclectic array of practices, which became more numerous and varied as they encountered different forms of Christianity. As they tried out different rituals, they looked for indications of their efficacy. This approach to rituals was not new. Back in Laos, Hmong people had long approached other religions, including the Christianity of foreign missionaries, with the expectation that rituals would demonstrate their efficaciousness. The same was true in the United States. Hmong Christians looked for empirical evidence—manifested in an improvement in health, in particular—that their rituals solved their problems. Signs of a religion's power and efficacy gave Hmong people reason to adopt new practices.[71]

In an American context, Christianity appealed to Hmong people for the same reasons it had in Laos: because it provided a set of tools to facilitate harmonious relations with the spirits, whose disfavor caused a variety of calamities, especially sickness. Conversion to Christianity ultimately gave Hmong people a new way to solve spiritual problems. Lu Vang and Phua Xiong noted that Hmong people refer to Christian conversion as *lawb dab,* which translates as "be rid of the spirits." "Not everyone who converts to Christianity believes in Jesus or knows what Christianity really is," they explained. "Some Hmong do away with the spirits but do not believe in God or Jesus (*lawb dab xwb tsis ntseeg*). When most people throw away the spirits, however, they believe they are hiding their souls away from the spirits that can cause illness."[72] In other words, they might convert to Christianity as a means of getting "rid of" or evading harmful spiritual entities, not necessarily as a way of drawing closer to Jesus.

This approach to Christianity was familiar to Hmong people—it had shaped their religious choices in Laos and Thailand—but it mattered more in the context of resettlement. In the United States, Hmong contact with Christianity increased significantly at the very same time that Hmong people experienced heightened social, cultural, and spiritual dislocation and unprecedented barriers to using traditional tools to address their suffering. As ever, Hmong people remained pragmatic in their commitment to health and well-being and open-minded in their consideration of different ritual options. They turned to Christianity as a means of actively coping with suffering when traditional Hmong rituals were neither effective nor available as a way to solve an array of spiritual problems, including sickness.

Two main spiritual problems motivated Hmong people to adopt Christianity. First, some Hmong people believed that Christianity would offer a solution to a spiritual curse. Pa Mang Her recalled how one clan adopted Christianity because of a "curse." Many members of the clan had suffered from a variety of afflictions, including opium addiction, poverty, early death, and infertility. "The Hers were really scared," he recalled, "so when they heard that if you became a believer that you'd be okay, they started to believe and God helped them and they escaped the curse." Later, as a pastor in America, he encountered other Hmong people who turned to Christianity when they believed that malevolent spirits were tormenting them. A member of his Minneapolis congregation "was possessed by a spirit" and eventually converted to Christianity to rid himself of the troubling spirit. Her said that he visited to pray with the man, and the next day "the spirit left him alone," which they considered to be a "sign from God."[73]

Health problems were the most common explanation that Hmong people gave when describing their decision to convert to Christianity. Hmong conversion narratives often centered on experiences of sickness and healing. Believing that sickness was not simply a bodily problem, but a spiritual problem related to the loss of a soul, Hmong people traditionally turned to shamans to mediate relations with the spirit world and ensure a return to bodily and spiritual health. For Hmong people, Christianity was an appealing alternative to shamanism when there were no Hmong shamans available to help or when traditional Hmong rituals had proven ineffective. "Many sick Hmong men and women convert to Christianity as a last option or hope for recovery after unsuccessful results with traditional Hmong therapies, such as shaman, soul-calling, or magic healing (*khawv koob*)," said Lu Vang and Phua Xiong. "If they cannot reunite their souls with their sick bodies or appease the spirits that have brought them harm, they may try to sever their relationship with the spirits as a last chance for survival. Converting to Christianity or other religions may help sick people regain their health because they believe it breaks the bonds between their souls and the spirits."[74]

As was the case in Laos, Hmong conversion narratives centered on freedom from sickness and malevolent spirits. Reflecting on her Christian friends and family members and their decisions to attend church, Neng Vang observed that most people adopted Christianity "because people get sick, and they're looking for other ways" to be "healed."[75] Yia Lee shared how her family's story illustrates this phenomenon. She explained that her mother-in-law's sickness was the reason she and her husband became Christian. "She was so sick, and we did everything we could," she said. "The doctor couldn't find any help for her. . . . We did everything that we know how, [and it] didn't work." But her mother-in-law had a sibling who was a pastor, whom she believed could help her get well. "He came, and that's how we became Christian," she recalled. "That's how we converted." Yia Lee added that it was challenging to practice traditional Hmong healing rituals because they involved animal sacrifice, sometimes inside the house, and that it was frustrating to depend on a shaman to conduct healing rituals. In contrast, Christianity offered a more direct approach for requesting divine intervention in times of illness. "I know that I can talk to God straight," she said, "and God will heal me, or I can tell God what I feel."[76]

Similarly, Mary Her believed that becoming Christian would help her solve the multiple health problems that had plagued her and her family. After she resettled in the United States, she began to go to church, where she prayed for healing—and soon, she said, her "eyes started healing." "The mercy of God is very strong," she said. "He's very powerful, so going to church helps me, gives me the energy, and helps me overcome all my sickness because I've been a very sick person all my life." She believed that had she become Christian earlier in her life, her entire family would have survived. "It's because I didn't know God earlier," she said, "and that's the reason my children died."[77]

In their search for rituals that could solve their spiritual and bodily afflictions, Hmong people sometimes experimented with a variety of approaches before settling on the practices that had shown themselves to be the most efficacious. True Xiong said that since her childhood, a "bad spirit" had followed her, even after she left Laos and resettled in the United States. She became a Catholic and, later, a member of an Assemblies of God church to "have freedom away from the bad spirit." Her parents, who had been shamans in Laos, had not been able to help her, nor were the Catholic priests able to rid her of the demon. Only later, when she became a born-again Christian and a member of the Assemblies of God church did she believe that she had access to "that power to help me, to release me away from that bad spirit." She was adamant that Christianity offered a unique power that allowed her to overcome her lifetime of spiritual and bodily suffering. At the same time, she understood why many of her relatives continued to practice traditional Hmong rituals—none of them were ever as sick as she. "It doesn't matter because for them who are not sick, they're not going to go seek it, and so it's okay," she said. True Xiong, unlike her relatives, identified herself as a "person who needs medical attention." For her, needing "medical attention" first meant needing the services of a shaman, and when she found that a shaman could not solve her problem, needing "medical attention" meant seeking the services of a Christian pastor instead. True Xiong was eager to experiment, observe, and compare the efficacy of different solutions to her illness, and she was wholly pragmatic in her search for the best practices that would heal her spiritual and bodily afflictions and restore her to full health. In trying an eclectic array of healing approaches and evaluating their outcomes, True Xiong was practicing her own version of evidence-based medicine—what one might describe as evidence-based religion.[78]

The opposite happened as well: Hmong people evaluated the effectiveness of traditional Hmong rituals, and if they produced demonstrable benefit, then they chose to continue or even return to the Hmong way. For example, See Lee, a Hmong woman in Minnesota, said that her "religion is still the old tradition," and she gave a practical reason for continuing Hmong rituals. She explained that the Hmong way had helped her overcome her infertility:

> I didn't have any children. I thought I would not have any babies. Due to my religious belief, my husband asked a spiritual doctor to pray to our ancestors as well as cleanse my body and soul. After several of these spiritual rituals, I was able to conceived and have children. I prayed and prayed! The Spiritual doctor called my ancestors and asked for children, then I had one child then four more children. I could not conceive after my fifth child. We asked the Spiritual doctors again. After several visit to my husband, I conceived and had three more children later.[79]

Nao Thao, the shaman, also believed that since she became a shaman, her "family has become more healthy." She admitted that her family could have become healthier for reasons beyond her work as a shaman—better medical care in the United States, for example— and that it is difficult to know precisely why things happen the way that they do. However, she saw a clear relationship between ritual practices and personal health and well-being and continued to believe in the interdependence of the seen world and unseen world.[80]

In a similar vein, some Hmong people decided to abandon Christianity when their personal experience indicated that Christian rituals were less powerful and effective in dealing with spirit-related health problems. Mao Yang, for example, left the church when she felt that it was no longer benefiting her life. The Hmong Baptists, she recalled, had told her that if she called on God and prayed about everything that worried her, then God would answer. However, when she became sick, her prayers to God brought no response, nor did Christianity help her when her children and her mother died. Frustrated, she returned to practicing the Hmong way later in life and said that "nothing's gone bad" since. She believed that one's religion depended on what worked for that particular individual. For her, the decision to return to the Hmong way was the obvious choice because Hmong rituals provided a better solution to her problems. She believed that the ancestors listened more attentively to her and offered a more effective and efficient response to her spiritual and health problems than Christianity did.[81]

For Hmong people, becoming Christian was not simply an experience of inner personal transformation, as is typical in many narratives of Christian conversion, but an active decision to find new ways to manage old spirits and solve real-world problems that affect daily life. Reflecting this willingness to try different approaches to solving spiritual dilemmas, Hmong people pursued a ritual life that was additive and adaptable, characterized by bricolage and borrowing. If for much of their history Hmong people turned to shamans to enter the spiritual world and negotiate with spiritual entities, their encounter with Christianity when they resettled in the United States opened up new possibilities. And if praying to a Christian God or singing Christian hymns appeared to help in their dealings with the spirit world, then these new religious practices were, in the minds of many Hmong people, worth adopting.

At the heart of this understanding of conversion is a particularly practical and open-minded understanding of religion and ritual life. Stories of Hmong religious change illustrate that many Hmong people considered religion to be, as Paj Ntaub Lis put it, "a resource" that they evaluated carefully and comparatively. "Which one can protect my family?" she said. "Who can best serve me?"[82] These were the questions that Hmong people asked themselves as they weighed their religious options and debated which way would allow them to live and survive. Nhia Long, a shaman in the Twin Cities, put it this way: "Whatever is good, join. If it's church that helps you, join. No matter what religion it is, you have to be open minded. There must be only one beginning for all of us. We all must die, so we're all trying to find a way that makes us feel good about life."[83]

As the reasoning of Nhia Long and Paj Ntaub Lis reveals, the religious lives of Hmong people reflected their resourcefulness and their responsiveness to changing circumstances. Amid the upheaval of war and their forced migration from Laos to Thailand and then to the United States, Hmong people were also frequent spiritual migrants who crossed and recrossed religious borders throughout their lives, traveling between Christianity and the Hmong way as conditions evolved. Hmong people, having a flexible understanding of religious belonging, sometimes changed religious affiliation multiple times, and the adoption of Christianity upon resettlement in the United States was sometimes one of many spiritual and religious changes that a Hmong individual could pursue within the span of a lifetime. As Nhia Long put it, Hmong people were "open minded"— open to adding new rituals to their spiritual repertoire, open to different religious communities, and open to experiencing multiple religious conversions—because they wanted to "feel good about life." More fundamentally, they wanted to survive.

Hmong people made these decisions as individuals, but also in the context of kin and clan, and changing family circumstances often shaped religious choices. For one, parents influenced their children's religious choices. "At one point, I was thinking about converting to the Lutheran faith and talked to my parents about it, and they were not supportive, so I've decided not to at this time, and since then I just haven't thought about it again," said Pacyinz Lyfoung, a Hmong woman in Minnesota.[84] Timothy Vang observed that prospective members of his church postponed the decision to convert to Christianity out of respect for the wishes of their parents: "They would say, 'Well, we still practice animism because our parents are still alive, but when they are gone, we have to go to church. We are tired of doing these things, and we would like to change.'"[85]

Marriage relationships and gender roles also encouraged women to adopt Christianity or to practice the Hmong way. "Before I married my husband, I was not a Christian," said Kim Yang, "but after I married my husband, I am a Christian." Kia Vue and Mao Yang also converted to Christianity because of their spouses, although some women admitted that they were not entirely comfortable with the change.[86] Marriage also encouraged religious change in the other direction. For example, Bao Vang, a Hmong woman in Minnesota, explained, "Before I got married, we went to church and believed in God, but I married my husband, and they still practice the traditional religion." She followed suit.[87] Women often aligned their religious identities with those of their spouses, a decision encouraged by the Hmong tradition of women joining their husbands' family after marriage and by the Christian teaching that wives should submit to their husbands, considered the spiritual head of the family. "Whatever religion my husband is, that's what I am, as a girl," said Yia Lee. "So whatever he decides, that's where you go."[88] However, some women, facing religious differences within their own marriages, chose to pursue both Christianity and the Hmong way. "Now that I am married to my husband, and he is a Lutheran, so I've changed, I have to practice Christianity," said MayKao Hang, "but . . . I believe in the traditional religion as well as the new religion."[89]

The loss of a spouse also shaped religious choices. Hmong widows sometimes adopted Christianity because, after losing their husbands in the war, they did not have male relatives to conduct important rituals. According to Hmong tradition, when a woman marries, she enters the spiritual world of her husband's family, and male relatives carry out rituals that ensure that in the afterlife, her soul can find a place to rest among the ancestral spirits of her husband's family. However, if the husband dies and there is no son to conduct the rituals, widows find themselves in what Mai Neng Moua described as a "void," and they face the possibility that they will "wander in the land of darkness with no ancestors to return to" in the afterlife. Converting to Christianity, however, offers the option of "bypassing the animist rituals" because, "as a Christian, she doesn't need anyone to send her spirit to God the Father."[90]

In addition to family obligations, community responsibilities shaped religious decisions. Keith Vang's father, a shaman, became a Lutheran after being sponsored by a Lutheran church in Michigan. A series of spiritual troubles also led him to believe that he should no longer practice the Hmong way. However, word circulated among the Hmong refugees resettled in his town that he was a shaman, and a sense of duty compelled him to return to practicing Hmong rituals. As he recalled, "When more Hmong people came to Lansing, and they knew that he was a shaman back in the days, they came and begged and begged him." His father, wearing the large cross given to him by the Lutheran church, informed the visitors that he was now Christian and no longer practicing as a shaman. One visitor, who "doesn't know anything about being a Christian," continued to plead for help. "My father was always a kind person," said

Keith Vang, "[and] he decided, 'Well, maybe one time will be okay. But maybe just this once.'" He performed the ritual but "felt the shaman spirit wasn't with him anymore," which caused him to say, "okay, maybe this is becoming something that I can't just hide behind the church anymore." In his home he built an altar, which is essential for shamans to communicate with spirits, and he continued to be a practicing Lutheran. As Keith Vang recalled, "when we had Bible study they would cover the altar."

Trouble arose when his obligations to the Hmong community conflicted with his commitment to his new Christian community. Keith Vang's father later approached the pastor, who may not have been familiar with Hmong shamanism, to ask if he sanctioned the practice of Hmong traditional rituals. The pastor asked, "Are you doing something to harm someone, or is it something good?" The shaman replied that the rituals were, indeed, good. "And the pastor, without realizing what my father was doing, said, 'It's okay. If it's good, it's okay,'" said Keith Vang. But afterward, when the pastor learned more about Hmong shamanism, he announced that he disapproved of the ceremonies. "And then they took my parents to church and they talked to them about taking down the altar and really just being Christians, sticking to the word of God," Keith Vang recalled. "And during this time there were a lot of Hmong people in Lansing already. A lot of people had a lot of expectations of my father and he decided with the pastor. . . . I felt he was pressured into taking down the altar."

Believing that his father was happy about the decision, Keith Vang assisted in dismantling the altar, only to realize later that doing so was what Hmong people considered a grave error. His sister-in-law informed him that the "the shaman spirit is going to attack" their father. His father, aware of the risks to his spirit and his health, was "scared to death" and "traumatized" and later "experienced a lot of sickness." Meanwhile, the Lutheran pastor offered little help in return. "We didn't have the support from the church," Keith Vang said. "They didn't come to pray for him."[91] Abandoned and alone, his family felt disappointed in the pastor and the church, as it failed to fulfill one of the most fundamental obligations for Hmong people: coming together as a community to help a family conduct rituals to assist a friend or family member in times of spiritual trouble and vulnerability. It was ultimately the church that had perhaps committed the graver sin.

«««<>»»»

American refugee policies had a powerful impact on Hmong ritual life. Rules governing refugee admission and resettlement undermined the practice of the Hmong way. At the same time, the public-private resettlement system set up close relationships between Hmong refugees and Christian churches and created the conditions for religious contact and change. Put simply, American refugee policies changed Hmong religious life by limiting one set of beliefs and practices, then facilitating access to another. To be clear, there is no evidence that policy makers in charge of planning for Southeast Asian refugee resettlement had any intention to use refugee policies as a tool to convert Hmong refugees to Christianity. Nonetheless, American policies had an undeniable impact on Hmong religious life, a fact that becomes quite clear when one compares Hmong experiences in the United States with Hmong experiences in Australia, where different resettlement policies produced different religious outcomes.

Yet this story is not a simple tale of religious assimilation. Hmong refugees like Kia Vue adopted Christianity on their own terms and in accordance with the understandings of religion and conversion that were particular to their traditional Hmong spiritual framework. Rather than a story of clash between the old and new ways, Hmong religious change is better understood as a story of synthesis. While some Hmong Christians completely foreswore traditional rituals, the reality is that many, if not most, Hmong people did not think that adopting Christianity required the wholesale abandonment of traditional Hmong beliefs and practices. Hmong Christians often practiced both Christianity and the Hmong way at the same time, and they sometimes switched between the two throughout the course of their lifetimes. Their straddling of religious boundaries illuminates central insights into Hmong religious logic: religion was something that they did in order to maintain harmonious relations with the spirit world, and conversion gave Hmong people a new set of practices—a new way—that helped them find spiritual well-being and security. Thus, conversion did not involve trading one set of practices for another. Rather, it was an act of widening the arsenal of practices from which Hmong people drew to cope with spiritual and bodily afflictions.

As William Siong explained, when Hmong people adopted Christianity in the United States, they did so as Hmong people. To illustrate this point, he recalled how a missionary visiting his church preached about the importance of affirming cultural heritage in developing faithful Christians. "No matter how long you put an alligator in the river," the missionary had said, "it will not pretend to be a crocodile." These words inspired Siong, and they became a central feature of the message he shared with his Hmong Lutheran congregation: "No matter how long we are in here, we are still Hmong; no matter how long we join, convert to Christianity, we are still Hmong."[92] For a man whose own conversion to Christianity had caused a painful rift with his father, these words—"we are still Hmong"—conveyed a powerful message. It expressed his conviction that becoming Christian did not require new converts to assimilate into white Christian America and turn their backs on their Hmong family, traditions, and identity. Rather, the declaration "we are still Hmong" emphasized the survival of Hmong community and culture, and it underscored that Hmong converts have been first and foremost Hmong people, who adopted and practiced Christianity on Hmong terms. Christianity was the new way, but it did not entirely supplant an older way centered on a distinctly Hmong spiritual worldview, ritual tradition, familial network, and self-imagination. In crossing the ocean and coming to America, many Hmong refugees became Christian. But like the alligators that crossed the river, they remained who they were. They were still Hmong.

7

Remaking the Hmong Way

THE CREATION OF A HMONG

AMERICAN RELIGION

Suspended in midair and dangling on an invisible thread was a golden airplane. Fashioned of gleaming foil paper, this three-dimensional model of a passenger jetliner hung at the center of the funeral home, ready to carry home the soul of a Hmong man who had recently passed away. The Hmong traditionally believe that when humans die, their souls must travel, retracing the course of their lives, revisiting every village they had once called home and returning to the piece of earth where their parents had buried the placenta that once nourished them in the womb. From there, they continue on to their final home with the ancestors. In the past, before the war, a horse would have sufficed for this voyage; in that era, there had been no oceans for the traveling soul to cross, no continents to traverse, no airplanes needed for the trip. But this man had traveled many miles in his life, as had thousands of other Hmong Americans who had migrated from the mountains of Southeast Asia and resettled in cities across the United States. On this breezy summer morning, several dozen family members gathered together in a spacious urban building, one of several Hmong funeral homes in the Twin Cities, to assist their relative's soul in his arduous final passage.

In many ways, these funeral rituals reinforced the connections between the past and the present, linking the Hmong in Minnesota
with their ancestors and their agrarian way of life in Laos. On one
wall hung a large banner bearing an image of a Hmong man sitting
astride a horse and traveling alongside a cow and a rooster amid a
verdant mountain landscape. In the carpeted space in front of the
banner, a ritual funeral singer chanted a *qhuab ke,* a "showing the
way" song. Another man beat a drum, while a third musician cir-
cled the room, playing the *qeej,* a mouth organ of bamboo reed pipes
often used in Hmong rituals. Relatives prepared the meat of several
cows that had been offered as sacrifice. At the front of the funeral
home lay the deceased man himself, a traditional Hmong crossbow
tucked under his arm and a stick of sweet, musky incense burning
at his elbow. Yet everywhere, there was evidence that honoring this
man meant acknowledging not only his Hmong origins but also his
life in America. Against the wall, in between ornamental flowers
formed of gold-foil paper money, relatives had arranged a series of
portraits, photographic evidence of an individual whose life straddled two worlds. In one portrait, he was dressed as a serious busi-
nessman, and in his suit, he posed proudly before a field of corn. In
another photograph, he wore traditional Hmong clothing and stood
smiling against the backdrop of a car-lined street, in a neighborhood
that could have been in any corner of the United States.

The funeral rituals reflected the fact that this man had not only
crossed cultures and continents but had traveled great distances in
an era when international mobility was highly regulated by governments. The careful arrangement of the man's body carried evidence
of the modern rules of migration: tucked under one of his hands lay
several documents, including a Social Security card and a passport.[1]
Family members understood the risks involved in attempting to cross
international borders without proper paperwork, and though they
did not know if a passport was necessary for spiritual travel, they
took no chances for this final and most important journey. Should
the traveling soul be turned back at the border of Laos or Thailand,
the consequences would be dire. Failing to fulfill the documentary
requirements of international migration and thus barred from retracing his life's journey and rejoining his ancestors, the man's spirit
would be trapped in a state of limbo and might trouble the family
members left behind.

A collection of papers slipped under his hand, a golden airplane suspended overhead: these small, loving acts of care by family members preparing a man for his last spiritual voyage offered rich evidence of how resettling in the United States—both the experience of forced migration and the policies directing it—had left an imprint on the ritual practices and religious imaginations of a Hmong community in diaspora.

«««‹›»»»

Although Hmong refugees initially experienced resettlement as a moment of profound unsettlement, a few critical changes occurred during the 1980s and 1990s that enabled Hmong people in the United States to revive their practice of the Hmong way and, like the journeying soul during a Hmong funeral, return to the spirits of their ancestors. First, families that had been separated by resettlement were reunited. Hmong refugees who had been scattered across the United States by the dispersal policy eventually relocated to live among relatives and in burgeoning Hmong ethnic enclaves. In addition, people who had arrived during the first wave of resettlement began to sponsor relatives remaining in the Thai refugee camps. Through these international and domestic migrations, Hmong people in the United States reunited their families, reconstructed their communities, and reconnected multiple generations—all of which made it more feasible to practice the Hmong way again.

At the same time, Hmong people who at first felt lost in "the American jungle" eventually found their bearings. Through secondary migration and continued resettlement, they formed vibrant communities, especially in the Upper Midwest and in the Central Valley of California. There, with a critical mass of Hmong Americans gathered in cities such as Sacramento and Saint Paul, they won notable success in politics. They created nonprofit organizations to educate the public about their history and advocate for their needs. They established businesses to serve their ethnic community and cultural institutions to promote and preserve their traditions. Finally, they achieved significant upward social mobility, attained higher levels of education, joined the professions, and entered the middle class, sometimes within the span of a single generation. If at one point they were viewed as a primitive "Stone Age people" unsuited to modern American life, Hmong people proved themselves a success story.

Importantly, Hmong refugees became Hmong Americans on their own terms. The process was not simple assimilation into American ways but selective and creative adaptation of Hmong ways. As Hmong people adjusted to life in the United States, so, too, did they adjust their beliefs and practices to an American setting. They refashioned and reinvented rituals. They created new institutions such as funeral homes, butcher shops, and cultural schools. They even formed new religious congregations for the sake of safeguarding centuries-old ceremonies. Shaping all of these changes was Hmong people's experience of being a displaced community in the United States. In all areas—economic, social, and political life, but also spiritual life—surviving and thriving in the United States required Hmong people to engage with the very aspects of American society that in many ways had also threatened the future of their ritual traditions. Significantly, Hmong Americans pursued these adaptations in conversation with the spirit world. In their view, the scope of these changes reached beyond the bounds of the "seen" earthly world and mirrored developments in the "unseen" spiritual realm.

One of the most significant changes that occurred in the forty years after their first resettlement in the United States was the effort by Hmong people to transform the Hmong way into a Hmong American religion in line with American laws, customs, and institutional expectations. To be sure, Hmong people were not the first group to undertake such a project. Hmong efforts to adapt their traditions to an American setting and create a distinctively Hmong American religion had much in common with how other minority groups have reconfigured their beliefs, practices, identities, and institutions to be legible as a religion in the eyes of both the American government and the American people. Claiming a religion has allowed these groups to resist conformity, secure rights and respect, and ensure the continuity of their community's rituals in the context of oppression and vulnerability.[2]

Creating a Hmong American religion involved two key developments. First, they described their beliefs and practices as a type of religion, in courts and in other contexts. In addition, they reconfigured their beliefs, practices, and institutions so that they were commensurable with the Protestant model of religion.[3] If in the begin-

ning they "did not know the Constitution," as Cziasarh Neng Yang
put it, they quickly learned about it and adapted to a country where
the First Amendment is sacred and where claiming a religion offers
important legal, political, and cultural advantages.[4] In particular,
they were aware that such claims typically are evaluated according
to Christian criteria. Because it is not centered on a common scripture, creed, clergy, or congregation, the Hmong way does not easily
conform to the Protestant template of religion, and in a country
where religious recognition often hinges on a tradition's commen-
surability to Christian standards, Hmong people were at a disad-
vantage. Therefore, when it was useful, Hmong Americans drew
parallels between the Hmong way and Christianity, and when they
created new institutions—churches and temples, for example—they
did so with an eye to the Protestant norms of religious belief and
practice that have currency in the United States.

The incongruity of Hmong traditions with Christianity in the end
provided Hmong people with valuable opportunities. They sometimes
found it useful to draw upon the construct of the secular—the category of nonreligion that itself is rooted in Protestant Christianity—
in order to describe their traditional beliefs and practices as a nonreligious form of "culture." In other words, they made use of the
uncertain status of their traditions and chose to define the Hmong
way as *both* "religion" and "culture," depending on the need at hand.
In reality, the Hmong way could never easily be sorted into the Western
categories of religion and secularity. However, by strategically claiming
and disclaiming religion, they deployed the flexible categories of religion and culture to preserve their traditions and to ensure accommodation of their beliefs and practices. By embracing their status
as betwixt and between, Hmong Americans found a way to make
a home.

"And So We Come Back to the Culture Again"

When Tzianeng Vang and his family first arrived in the United States
and resettled in Missouri, he recalled how his father at one point
requested a tape recorder. His father wanted to record cassette tape
messages to send to relatives, Tzianeng Vang explained, "to tell them
where we are and for them to come and rescue us." Unhappy about

living apart from other Hmong people, his father had one priority: "How can we get out of this place, you know, and be with people we can actually communicate [with] and [be] understood."[5]

Tzianeng Vang's father was not the only one who found it miserable to live apart from family and in areas of the country where there were few Hmong people. As with many other migrants, he and other Hmong people found it painful to be separated from loved ones, some of whom were resettled on the opposite American coast while others remained far away in the refugee camps in Thailand. They longed for the support of family and community, and they wanted to live among people who spoke the same language, ate the same foods, and practiced the same rituals. These desires, common among all migrants, were particularly intense for the Hmong, whose clan-based culture historically placed great significance on the involvement of family and extended relations in both everyday life and in important life-cycle events.

Thus, despite the fact that the government aimed to scatter Hmong refugees across the country and prevent the formation of "new ethnic communities," Hmong people desperate to reunite with family and clan did exactly what the government hoped they would not do: they created new ethnic communities. They did so in two ways. First, as soon as they were able, Hmong people helped their relatives resettle in the United States. Those who had arrived in the early years of Hmong resettlement—people who fell under a higher priority category because they had more direct ties to the US military and government— eventually began to sponsor their older relatives later in the 1980s and throughout the 1990s. Sometimes congregations even helped Hmong people bring over their relatives. For example, Cher Vang's church sponsors agreed to help his parents come over from Thailand.[6]

Hmong Americans also reconstituted their families and communities through secondary migration. Many Hmong people chose to abandon their site of initial resettlement to join kin who had been resettled elsewhere. In some cases, this secondary migration began almost immediately, with Hmong refugees relocating to new cities to reunite with family members within weeks, even days, after their arrival in the United States. Cziasarh Neng Yang, for instance, left Providence, Rhode Island, where he was first resettled, to reunite with his brother in Columbus, Ohio, only two weeks after his arrival.[7] For other Hmong people, the decision to leave their site of initial resettlement came later because it took time for relatives to reconnect with one another, to gain the stability to support another relative, and to gather the resources to move themselves. Khu Thao, for example, was initially resettled in Iowa, though she had relatives who lived in Minnesota. About a year after she first arrived, these relatives traveled to Iowa to retrieve her, much to her relief. "I was so happy to see them," she said. "I thought that I had lost contact with them all."[8]

Information circulating through their social networks also shaped their decisions. As they weighed the decision about when and where to move, Hmong people listened carefully to friends and relatives who shared news about opportunities in other parts of the country. In particular, they heard promising reports about California, where the mild climate offered a chance to return to a life of farming and where Vang Pao, the Hmong military leader, had resettled. By the early 1980s, nearly a decade after the first Hmong refugees arrived in the United States, two epicenters of Hmong American life had emerged: the Twin Cities and California's Central Valley.[9]

The reconstruction of clan and community, made possible through both secondary migration and ongoing refugee resettlement, was a turning point for Hmong ritual life in the United States. If separation from relatives and ritual experts had disrupted the practice of Hmong rituals during the early years of resettlement, reunification with relatives and ritual experts facilitated a return to the Hmong way. Increasingly throughout the 1980s, larger numbers and multiple generations of Hmong people were able to live together, as they had in Laos, and it became more feasible to conduct the traditional ceremonies that require the ritual expertise of elders and the helping hands of clan and community members. The increased presence of relatives, especially those more knowledgeable of and committed to Hmong traditions, encouraged the revival of traditional ritual practices. Mao Yang, for example, revived her practice of Hmong rituals when she moved to Fresno. In contrast to the small town in Illinois where she was first resettled, Fresno was home to more people who knew the Hmong way—in particular, recently arrived family members who preferred to practice traditional rituals rather than Christianity. "The new arrivals were fresh with the traditions, and they came and they had resources, too," she said. In Fresno, for example, she was able to live near a family member—a grandfather—who was a shaman.[10]

Hmong New Year at Highland Junior-Senior High, Saint Paul. Courtesy of Minnesota Historical Society.

Christian Hmong leaders recalled the late 1980s and 1990s as a period when Hmong people became less disposed to adopting Christianity and when those who had converted to Christianity in the early years of resettlement began to return to the Hmong way. During this time, "A lot of Christian turn[ed] back, go back to the old way of worship[ping] ancestors," said Joua Tsu Thao.[11] Rev. Timothy Vang made a similar observation. "Later on, when they were able to sponsor their relatives, and when the Hmong people come in bigger numbers, then there were shamans, and those who know how to do that kind of animistic rituals came in great number," he said. "Then, those who are interested in Christianity, the number reduced, significantly." In his view, people who followed the Hmong way felt "safe" during this period because, should a funeral or a wedding occur, "They have someone who knows how to deal with those things." During this period, he said, the increased presence of elders and ritual experts meant that "the receptive attitude toward Christianity begins to fade."[12]

The religious changes described by Timothy Vang and Joua Tsu Thao, both Hmong pastors, echoed stories shared by Hmong laypeople. Cziasarh Neng Yeng, for example, decided to return to the Hmong way when he was able to leave Ohio and join his parents, who had resettled in the Twin Cities. "We stayed Catholic, I think, until 1980, when we moved from Columbus to Minnesota to reunite with our parents and with the larger Hmong community," he explained. "And then we ceased to go to church . . . I think because we were able to reunite with our folks who can conduct our own rituals and traditions. And so we come back to the culture again."[13] MayKao Hang described a similar situation in her family. Her father had adopted Christianity after resettling in the United States, but he later stopped attending church. MayKao Hang recalled that he seemed suddenly "ashamed." As she recalled, "My dad said that it was because my grandpa had come, and because my grandpa did not approve of us practicing the new religion, and he wanted us to go back and practice our traditional religion."[14]

"The Spirit and the Human, We Are Pretty Much Living in Parallel"

For Hmong people like MayKao Hang to go back to the traditional Hmong beliefs and practices was easier said than done in the United States. The Hmong way is rooted in the physical landscape of the Southeast Asian highlands, where most Hmong people lived and farmed in rural communities. When Hmong refugees arrived in the United States, they found the flat terrain, endless concrete, and dense cities to be a starkly foreign setting, not only physically but also spiritually. The chants of Paja Thao offer a glimpse at how, even in the early years, Hmong spiritual beliefs and the ritual practices were already evolving in response to their new American environment. In his description of the process of "calling and feeding ancestors," Paja Thao noted that the spirits of the Lao wilderness were not the only spirits that needed to be acknowledged. The spirits of American institutions demanded recognition, too:

> And you call the wild jungle spirits of the village
> And the river spirits
> You call all the wild spirits to come and eat
> Then it is finished

Now you come to live in America
When you have a feast
You must call the spirit government of Chicago
    And the spirits of the mountains and hills
    And the spirits of the borders
You must call all of them
Whether you have a small meal or a big feast

You must call them to come to eat
And drive away the evil sickness
    To protect my family

In taking care to "call the spirit government of Chicago," Paja Thao was adapting to the imperatives of operating in a new spiritual landscape, which he understood to be populated by both new and old spiritual actors who made different demands of Hmong people.[15] His chants reveal how Hmong people were grappling with the possibility that engaging with the unseen world changed according to their geographic location in the seen world.

Over a quarter century after Paja Thao recorded his chant, a new generation of Hmong Americans have been at the forefront of change, doing so in response to what they discern as the evolving expectations of the spirits. Explaining that "times have changed," Nao Thao noted that a younger generation of Hmong Americans supported adjustments to Hmong ritual practice, including shifting away from animal sacrifice. She emphasized that it was the spirits, not the humans, who led the call for these changes. "This is how we have been told—what I personally [have] been told—by the spirit," she said. "That now, because we are in a modern country, and we are looking for the modern life, there's no need to butcher or sacrifice another life to heal another life. That is not part of our healing . . . we have to adjust to fit into the modern life." In Nao Thao's view, the unseen spiritual realm and the visible realm mirror one another. "The spirit and the human, we are pretty much living in parallel," she explained. "So [if] we change, the spirit world is changing, too."[16] The "parallel" between the seen and unseen worlds has been reflected not only in what Hmong American practitioners of traditional rituals are doing but in who is doing it. Groups such as "Next Wave Shamans" reveal that shamans in the Twin Cities include younger, American-born Hmong people, including women.[17]

Hmong Americans have also adjusted their rituals in response to the legal and cultural norms of a new American setting. For example, Hmong American shamans, aware that killing dogs is illegal in the United States, have begun to use stuffed toy dogs in lieu of live animals. The spirits, they said, are just as satisfied with this substitution.[18] Rituals involving animal sacrifice have not only become easier but also less common, particularly among second-generation Hmong Americans. "Younger people, they try to work on not butchering animals," said Nao Thao. "Burning the paper monies and the incense, that's pretty much [it] for now. You look at the elders, they still practice the old way of butchering animal[s] to offer to the spirit or something, but the younger try to shift from there." In her view, it was both the younger generation and the spirits that together had initiated the shift away from sacrificing animals for certain healing rituals.[19]

These changes in how Hmong people have used ritual animals reflect a broader trend: Hmong Americans have endeavored to make ceremonies simpler and easier to conduct. For one, funerals have become less expensive over the years. J. Kou Vang, the owner of a Hmong funeral home in Maplewood, Minnesota, estimated that in the mid-2000s, an average Hmong funeral cost around $27,000; since then, the cost of Hmong funerals has dropped by almost 50 percent. The younger generation, he explained, rejects excess. "The spirit of the deceased can't take twenty cows with them," he said. "It's too many!" Instead, animals at Hmong funerals are "more and more of a symbol than anything else." Ceremonies have also become shorter. Both J. Kou Vang and Chu Wu, the owner of Koob Moo Hmong funeral home in Saint Paul, noted that a decade ago, funerals began on Friday and ended on Monday, with rituals taking place around the clock over the full four-day period. Today, many funerals begin later, on Saturday, and no longer involve ceremonies throughout the night. In certain respects, funerals have become, in J. Kou Vang's view, "more elaborate" in presentation, with chair covers, attractive drapery, and decorative runners adorning the funeral parlor. At the same time, funerals have demanded less time and money.[20]

This younger generation of Hmong Americans has pushed for change boldly, sometimes with great urgency, and not necessarily waiting for the leadership of elders. "Hmong traditions, if you wait until everyone is on the same page about everything, that day will never come," said Mai Neng Moua. "The young people are already changing. The way to not have headaches is to stay ahead of the game. We need to change."[21]

"Standardize and Modernize Hmong Religion"

Beyond adjustments in the rituals themselves, the most important way that Hmong people have adapted the Hmong way to an American setting is through the establishment of their own cultural and religious institutions. In Laos, Hmong people practiced their ceremonies in their own homes and passed on ritual knowledge to younger generations through oral tradition and direct family participation. However, the challenges that Hmong refugees experienced in the 1970s and 1980s made clear that continuing Hmong rituals in the United States required a new approach. The development of a large urban Hmong population in the Twin Cities in the 1980s and 1990s helped make it possible for Hmong Americans to create and sustain a variety of institutions to ensure that the Hmong community will have the ritual expertise and the human and material resources to conduct traditional ceremonies on their own terms and for generations to come.

The broader effort to institutionalize the Hmong way has given rise to a variety of organizations. Hmong funeral homes now offer flexible hours and spacious settings that accommodate traditional Hmong funerals. Hmong businesses now sell animals and ritual objects necessary for Hmong ceremonies. Educational organizations such as the Hmong Cultural Center (HCC) now provide the community with opportunities to receive formal instruction in playing the *qeej* and conducting funeral and household rituals. Medical centers now provide programs that support the practice of Hmong shamanism. Finally, new religious congregations now offer Hmong Americans a formal setting where they can practice the Hmong way. While these efforts represent a radical departure from how Hmong people have practiced their rituals in the past, the effort to institutionalize Hmong beliefs and practices and to shift rituals away from private spaces and into public settings is rooted in a simple goal: the preservation of Hmong traditions. Put simply, Hmong Americans created new ways to follow the old way.

FUNERAL HOMES

The creation of Hmong funeral homes such as Legacy Funeral Home in Maplewood, Minnesota, and Koob Moo in Saint Paul has been one of the most important developments in the practice of Hmong rituals. Soua Sue Lee, an expert on Hmong funerals, estimated that around 80 percent of the Hmong American population in the Twin Cities want to hold traditional Hmong funerals.[22] The problem was that they did not have a place to host these funerals. According to Chu Wu, as recently as 2000, Hmong families were "struggling to find a funeral home that will provide the type of service that will meet the different cultural needs." He added that the great majority of Twin Cities funeral homes "had their own culture and religious practice" and "were not open or were not welcome to especially the Hmong and other culture group[s]."[23] The establishment of Hmong funeral homes allowed Hmong Americans to maintain many of their traditions by relocating funeral rituals from individual homes to spacious, professionally managed, government-regulated indoor settings.

Reflecting the transition that the broader Hmong American community experienced throughout the past three decades, the individuals who established these Hmong funeral homes were part of an emerging professional class—second- or 1.5-generation Hmong Americans who were well educated and driven by a deep commitment to use their skills and connections to serve their ethnic community. When asked how they became funeral home directors, both Chu Wu and J. Kou Vang admitted that they had never expected to enter the funeral home business. "We started the funeral home kind of by mistake," said J. Kou Vang, who runs Legacy Funeral Home. "I've always known that there's a need for a funeral home because at that time, we had two Hmong funeral homes in the Twin Cities and the backup was, oh, eight to ten weeks." With such an urgent need for a third Hmong funeral home in the region, he did not feel that he could responsibly say no when a group of elders and local leaders approached him for help. In his view, getting involved in the business proposal was "the right thing to do for the community." Fifteen years and four funeral chapels later, J. Kou Vang's business was thriving. Nevertheless, he still insisted that the funeral business was not for him. "I have no desire doing that," he said. "I don't want to be in the funeral home business! I never wanted it."[24] If a sense of responsibility to the Hmong community kept J. Kou Vang at Legacy Funeral Home, a similar commitment shaped Chu Wu's work at Koob Moo Funeral Home. However, Chu Wu's sense of duty extended not only to other Hmong Americans in the Twin Cities but also to the spirits who "called" him to work in the funeral home. "I just realized that I guess I've been chosen . . . so I told the spirit, well, I'll accept it!" he said with a laugh. "Whether you punish me or not, I can't go anywhere."

Committed to meeting the specific ritual needs of Hmong Americans, Chu Wu and J. Kou Vang paid attention to details that other funeral home owners might not consider. For example, when designing Koob Moo, Chu Wu insisted that the layout of the space respect the Hmong belief that the door should face east or west and the body of the deceased should be placed in either the east or north corner of the building.[25] And because many Hmong people object to being buried in caskets that contain metal parts, J. Kou Vang started a casket-making plant in Laos to build special metal-free, pine caskets for his customers. At the same time, Chu Wu and J. Kou Vang have served as cultural intermediaries, communicating with the local government to ensure that the funeral homes abide by local health and safety ordinances. Knowing that burning paper money is an important practice at Hmong funerals, for example, J. Kou Vang worked with the city fire department to secure proper permits and develop safe burners that satisfy the fire department's safety recommendations.[26] When helping Hmong families plan a funeral, both Chu Wu and J. Kou Vang have also taken care to explain the safety regulations about cooking food and drinking alcohol. "There are a couple of regulations—you know, city ordinances and state health laws that, yes, funeral homes have to comply with and the family have to comply with," said Chu Wu. "And so the funeral home, when we do arrangements, [the] family come[s] in and either my funeral director or I have to explain it to the family so that they understand: these are some of the regulations in the city codes that they have to follow."[27] In this way, the funeral home owners have helped smooth relations and meet the mutual needs of Hmong families and the local government. "You know, [we're] just trying to work with the system so that we can understand what the laws are, what the ordinances are, what is the intent of those ordinances, how do we meet the spirit of the ordinance, and still provide culturally sensitive opportunities for our people," said J. Kou Vang.[28]

BUTCHER SHOPS

Hmong Americans have established other institutions to sustain and support the practice of Hmong rituals. One early challenge faced by refugees in both Thailand and the United States centered on access to live animals necessary for traditional rituals. Today, special Hmong butcher shops sell pigs, chickens, and cows used for funerals and other ceremonies. (One of the Hmong American meat markets in the Twin Cities is called Long Cheng, after the Laotian military base in Xiang Khouang province where many Hmong soldiers were based during the war.[29]) Like Hmong funeral homes, these butcher shops have become essential community institutions and have made the practice of Hmong traditions much more convenient, at least compared to life in Saint Paul in the 1980s. "[Since] 1990 to now, we've got everything," Soua Sue Lee said. "[It is now] more easy because we have our own funeral home, and also we have a farm, we have our own cow, we have our own pig. . . . We can do everything now."

Funeral rituals adapted alongside these new Hmong butcher shops. Hmong Americans eventually found the old method of using a trailer to bring a live cow to the funeral home to be too onerous, so they developed an easier and more efficient method. First, Hmong families purchased a slaughtered cow at a special butcher shop, where Hmong butchers familiar with the funeral rituals removed the nose and tail of the cow. The families brought those parts of the cow to the funeral home, where they used a string to connect the cow parts with the body of the deceased. Relatives then burned joss paper and thanked the sacrificed cow for accompanying the spirit of the deceased on the journey to the ancestors.[30]

CULTURAL EDUCATION

In addition to funeral homes and butcher shops, Hmong Americans in the Twin Cities created educational institutions to preserve and formalize the transmission of ritual knowledge and cultivate new generations of ritual experts. In the 1970s and 1980s, the absence of ritual experts such as shamans and *qeej* players made it difficult for Hmong refugees to conduct rituals properly. To address the deficit in ritual knowledge and the need for skilled and experienced practitioners, Hmong Americans in the Twin Cities eventually established the HCC, which centralized and institutionalized Hmong ritual education. Founded in 1992, the HCC's original mission was "to ensure the Spiritual, Social, Emotional, Cultural, Moral philosophy, Traditions and Value of Hmong." From the very beginning, the HCC endeavored "to increase Hmong language and cultural literacy," and offering classes on playing the *qeej* and Hmong wedding and funeral songs was one of its first projects.[31] The center expanded its community education programs over time to include instruction in household rituals, marriage ceremonies, Hmong embroidery, and more.

An early *qeej* class at the Hmong Cultural Center in Saint Paul. Courtesy of Hmong Cultural Center.

Providing Hmong ritual education in a formal setting marked an important shift. Soua Sue Lee, who started teaching at the HCC in 1998, explained that "in Laos, we have no classrooms" because most people farmed, and ritual knowledge was passed down orally. But the United States is different from Laos, he said, and "the Hmong Culture Center, a lot of people need [it]." One of his classes has focused on home rituals, such as making offerings to ancestors and maintaining the *xwm kab* altar. He has also trained dozens of people through his funeral rituals course, which requires learning and practicing funeral chants for at least three hours every Sunday for two full years. The course requires a tremendous amount of learning by rote, and to graduate, students must be able to recite every song from memory. "Everything should be in here," he said, with a gesture toward his head.[32]

One of the HCC's most popular cultural education programs teaches the community to play the *qeej*. Chai Lee, a young man raised in the Twin Cities, began studying the *qeej* at the HCC as a child and went to the center's after-school classes with other American-born Hmong children throughout his youth. Following years of study, he became a *qeej* teacher at the HCC. Chai Lee first came to the HCC with a firm commitment to maintaining Hmong culture. He had learned about Hmong manners, rituals, and language from his family, which he described as a "really Hmong traditional family." "We have a lot of relatives in Saint Paul, so on the weekend, there was always some sort of get-together or some sort of shaman ritual that we would do," he said. In his free time, if he was not playing with his brothers in the yard, he was "inside learning something Hmong." But if he already had a well-developed appreciation of Hmong traditions through his family, the HCC played an important part in helping Chai Lee and a new generation of Hmong Americans deepen their engagement in Hmong ritual arts.

The HCC's *qeej* courses have not only preserved a distinctive Hmong musical tradition but also supplied the Twin Cities region with a steady supply of young ritual experts who can play the *qeej* at funerals and other ceremonies. As a result of the HCC's *qeej* program, Chai Lee believed that "there's definitely enough" *qeej* players to meet Hmong ritual needs in the Twin Cities.[33] The HCC received praise from other Hmong Americans, who have observed that the center's *qeej* classes and other cultural education projects have had a positive impact on Hmong ritual life in the Twin Cities. "I would say it's much easier [to practice traditional Hmong rituals in the United States] because they have cultural classes where people can learn how to play the *qeej*," Cziasarh Neng Yang said. "They have cultural classes to teach our younger generation how to perform a soul-calling tradition or to be a *mej koob* [a Hmong marriage negotiator]. You can learn how to become the *txiv xaiv*, the one who prays or sings during the funeral for the family. So it becomes easier."[34]

Aside from the HCC, there have been other efforts to help younger generations develop ritual knowledge. Shoua Vang, for example, was involved in a cooperative farm in a rural area of Minnesota. Because Hmong people historically conducted rituals outdoors and in rural settings, he saw an opportunity to combine farming with cultural education. "On our farm, we set up a cultural center for Hmong to have the chance to carry on and learn our traditional ceremonies," he said. "In Hmong society, youngsters learn by watching older people and repeating their words. Hmong come to our center from Wisconsin, Iowa, California, even from France, because they

A New Year blessing with a shaman at the Hmong Cultural Center in Saint Paul. Courtesy of Hmong Cultural Center.

live in cities and have no place in the countryside. They perform ancestral remembrances, and other ceremonies for good fortune or thanksgiving."[35]

ANIMIST CHURCHES

Hmong Americans also established religious congregations, where people can conduct Hmong rituals in church-like institutions that have 501(c)(3) status. Hmong ritual life has historically been located in family homes rather than in formal religious settings. However, Hmong Americans have pursued new forms of organization that reflect the legal context of the United States as well as the social and cultural influence of their Christian neighbors. In some cases, Hmong people's personal experiences as former members of Christian churches also shape these institutions. One example of these new religious organizations is Poj Koob Yawm Ntxwv (PKYN), founded in 2008 by Vaj Lis Thum, who built a base of followers in California, Wisconsin, and Minnesota.[36] According to Tzianeng Vang, a member of PKYN, the group aimed to turn traditional Hmong beliefs and practices into "something more close to religion" and resembled "an organized institution like a temple or church."[37]

Tzianeng Vang's journey to PKYN was in many ways intertwined with his journey to the United States, and his embrace of the movement originated in both his desire to honor Hmong traditions and his dissatisfaction with Christianity. Tzianeng Vang was raised in a family that practiced the Hmong way until they became Southern Baptists shortly after their resettlement in the United States. He remained a devout Southern Baptist for many years. However, he experienced an awakening in 2009, when he traveled to Thailand and visited the Mekong River, where many Hmong refugees had suffered and died as they attempted to make the dangerous crossing from Laos into Thailand. Walking on the riverbank and meditating on the significance of this sacred site, he had a revelation about the limitations of his Southern Baptist faith and the significance of Hmong ritual traditions:

> Somehow all the mighty rivers in the world doesn't offer me the same mystique or the spirituality as the Mekong River because the simple fact is that Mekong River represented life and death for me because

I swam across the river, and I also had a lot of relatives that perished in that river. So the first time I set foot on it, I just couldn't help my-self—I just [was] overcome with this emotion that I was just bawling. Tears dropped for thirty minutes. And I would not say that my Christianity, [my] faith did not rescue me there, then, but I kept thinking, I'm a Christian now, but if I was not a Christian, I wish there's a way that I could do a *hu plig*, you know? I would feel so good. . . . So I just thought, it would be so cleansing and so spiritual for me if I could do something like that, but I couldn't.

At that moment, something "clicked" inside Tzianeng Vang. The Hmong way, not Christianity, "is the spirituality that I need to follow," he realized, and he decided he needed to return to his an-cestors' traditions.

This realization had been long in the making. By the time he took his trip to Thailand in 2009, he had already become frustrated with his life as a Southern Baptist, which he felt had erased an essential part of himself. "The Bible and Christianity has very little or nothing about my own creation, you know?" he explained. "So that's be-come a constant battle with me." Small things troubled him, such as the narrow language of Christian prayer. "You were never taught to use your Hmong words to substitute for 'amen,'" he said sadly. At the same time, Tzianeng Vang yearned for something "tangible" that could connect him to his history and his ancestors. After his walk along the Mekong, he wanted a "peaceful Hmong faith-based group," an "institution we belong to, so I could have [and] still main-tain that spirituality." He found that in PKYN.

According to its brochure, PKYN stated that its mission is "to preserve, sustain, [and] teach the rich heritage, religion and origin of Hmong culture and to promote Hmong Principle of Life." It pur-sued this mission through both safeguarding and "modernizing" Hmong culture, and it situated the organization in the broader his-tory of Hmong ritual adaptation. According to the brochure, Hmong traditions are "altered based on the cleverness of the individual and the environment in which one lives," and there have been times when "the knowledge was lost, forgotten, altered, or need an upgrade to fit the new era." PKYN, in keeping with the Hmong tradition of adapting and doing an "upgrade" to new times and new places, arose in response to the needs of younger generations of Hmong Americans who faced the challenge of conducting their rituals in a new and often inhospitable setting. "Coming to industrial countries like the USA, shamans and prophets are slowly losing grounds due to economical life changing situations, public health issues, local, state, federal rules and regulations and the interest of the younger generations," the brochure explained. PKYN thus aimed to ensure that Hmong rituals are "carefully recorded" and "evaluated to implement in today's world." The hope of the founders was that PKYN's efforts would help young and modern Hmong people sustain the rituals that connect their past, present, and future. "Ultimately, one will understand PKYN pledges to standardize and modernize Hmong religion, culture, ceremonial rites, and principle foundation [sic] and yet preserves each element in its original form," read the brochure.[38]

PKYN not only aimed to "modernize" Hmong traditions but did so in a way that hewed closely to a Protestant model of religion. First, it created a standard scripture, which it called "The Book of Origin." This scripture reflected the recent development of a written Hmong language and the desire by Hmong people to modernize their traditions by recording Hmong beliefs and practices in writing. It was also a direct response to the fact that many young Hmong people lacked ritual knowledge. According to the brochure, the Book of Origin "explains many key features the younger generations do not quite get[,] the answers to why things were always done this way." The Book of Origin, described as "the footprint toward harmony," in many ways contained elements similar to those found in the Bible: origin stories, narratives of historical events, detailed descriptions of rituals, and disquisitions of core principles. The decision by PKYN to center its efforts on the creation of a sacred text reflected the Protestant-dominated American context from which this movement emerged. And yet the Book of Origin was also distinctively Hmong, as illustrated by its discussion of "the Hmong journey through times of success and hardships" and its descriptions of ceremonies for "the Hmong New Year" and "Naming a New Born Child."[39]

PKYN'S effort to establish official houses of worship was another way that the movement aligned with Protestant norms of religion. The effort to relocate Hmong rituals to a common, formal "temple" marked a significant departure from historical practice. "Hmong has always practiced rituals in their own homes as family affairs," the brochure explained. "There was not any place of worship to provide hopes, teach the principle foundation, and practice cultural rites." PKYN aimed to "take out all of the spirituality out of the home" and shift it to "an organized, unified standard facility where everybody could go—you know, like a temple, Buddhist temple, or a mosque or a church." Not merely a site for conducting rituals, the PKYN temple also served as a center for reviving the spirituality of individuals and the broader Hmong community. As the brochure put it, the temple was "a sacred location where all members gather to ask for spiritual rejuvenation" and "a place of belonging, hope and support, and eye opening to be reborn on becoming a good citizen."[40]

The Temple of Hmongism is another, better-known movement that aims to institutionalize Hmong beliefs and rituals as a religious community. Like PKYN, the Temple of Hmongism has endeavored to preserve Hmong traditions in new American form and shift Hmong practices from the home to a common central worship site. In addition to these goals, it has sought to modify Hmong rituals so they are easier and more affordable. The Temple of Hmongism identifies its "primary purposes" as follows:

> (1) to revise and simplify the traditional Hmong religion into the so-called Hmongism, (2) to centralize Hmongism out of the houses into the Temple of Hmongism where its members can worship and perform spiritual and religious rituals, (3) to reduce the cost of Hmong religious rituals, especially funeral expenses, (4) to recruit people to become members of Hmongism in order to save our people from religious and financial burdens, and (5) to provide the best and most cost effective services to its good standing members regarding their spiritual and religious needs.

As these objectives reveal, the Temple of Hmongism reflects the broader trend in Hmong life toward streamlined rituals that fit the practical needs and expectations of Hmong American families. "We believe that our traditionally lengthy, repetitive, at times controversial, and very costly rituals have not produced any obvious rewards or blessings but burdens for the living family members, and thus they should be revised and simplified to cut down time and cost, and that this reform shall be handled by scholars, practitioners, and well informed individuals," the founders stated. Pointing specifically to the high costs of funerals, they declared that "Hmongism in its simplified form, offering more effective services at much lower cost, will lead us forward, individually or collectively, toward a more financially prosperous and independent future."[41]

Like PKYN, the Temple of Hmongism explicitly described its movement as a "religion," one that in many ways fits the Christian template of religion. For example, the Temple of Hmongism has a clergy. According to its bylaws, the Temple of Hmong, which is based in Saint Paul, is committed to "train its own priests, or *txiv plig* or *txiv coj dab,* and only those men or women properly trained in Hmongism may perform marriage, shamanism, spiritual and religious rituals for its members within the intended guidelines of Hmongism." In addition, it shifted the traditional Hmong focus on ritual practice to religious faith—again, a reflection of the influence of Protestantism. The bylaws included, for example, a "statement of faith," which not only emphasized a central religious doctrine but also described Hmongism as the "national" religion that Hmong people have practiced for millennia. The statement of faith in the bylaws included the following "basic beliefs," meant "to establish a doctrinal foundation for those choosing to affiliate with the Temple of Hmongism":

1. We believe in the inspiration and teaching of Hmongism and that Hmongism is a religion that has been practiced by the Hmong for thousands of years;
2. We believe that being Hmong also means that we have our own religion that offers its own uniqueness of Hmong;
3. We believe that all Hmong, regardless of clans, dialects and regions, have a common, national religion of Hmongism, and that those practices that are different from clan to clan or within a clan are not national religions but cultural or local practices that should or can be confined within the families or clan.

If the founders of the Temple of Hmongism insisted that Hmongism is the religion of Hmong people going back thousands of years, they also insisted that this ancient religion required adaptation in order to survive in the twenty-first century. "We believe that the centralization of Hmongism where members have a place to worship and hold their religious rituals is the best idea to preserve and practice

A Hmong man carrying a blood-stained crucifix and marching from the Minnesota State Capitol to downtown Minneapolis to raise awareness of Hmong persecution in Laos. Courtesy of Wing Young Huie.

Hmongism in today's modern world, and that it has nothing religiously wrong against it," the founders declared. Later in the statement of faith they framed their movement as necessary to ensure that the next generation of Hmong Americans will continue to follow the Hmong way. "We believe that the reform of Hmongism will prevent young, educated Hmong from converting to other religions or become non-religious completely," they said.[42]

HOSPITAL-BASED SHAMANISM PROGRAMS

Finally, in instances when Hmong people have not been able to establish their own independent institutions, Hmong Americans have advocated for mainstream institutions to accommodate their beliefs and practices. Hospitals, for example, have established formal programs to include and support Hmong shamans, who care for patients alongside doctors and nurses trained in Western medicine.

These programs emerged because, despite initial fears among Hmong refugees that their healing traditions would die out, Hmong shamanism thrived in the United States. One study published in

2002 found that three-quarters of the Hmong Americans surveyed practiced shamanism, usually in addition to Western medicine. Moreover, every single one of the shamans included in the survey practiced a combination of shamanism and Western medicine. While practitioners of Hmong shamanism initially worried that Western medicine posed an existential threat to their tradition, researchers found that Hmong people typically saw shamanism and Western medicine as complementary: they sought the services of a shaman when they experienced what they believed to be "spiritual illnesses"— stress, for example, or night fright and unhappiness—and they turned to physicians when they suffered an obviously physical problem, like a broken bone or hypertension. "We believe the traditional religion and the medical treatment," one survey participant said. "If we cannot fully depend on the medical support, we reach out to the traditional healing. Both treatments are good for us. We can depend on either one. They are there to save us."[43]

Hmong shamans did not see their work as mutually exclusive with Western medicine, and the same was true for many Western health-care providers, who began to make greater efforts to accommodate Hmong shamanism in the 1980s and 1990s. This development owed in part to increased interest in medical anthropology, cross-cultural healing, and Eastern and alternative medicine.[44] In addition, American health-care providers learned through their own direct experience that they needed to be more attentive to the beliefs and ritual needs of their Hmong patients. Most importantly, changes in attitudes and policies were the result of efforts by Hmong Americans themselves, who worked to improve public awareness of Hmong beliefs and practices. All of these developments transformed the climate for Hmong Americans who wanted to continue shamanism.

In the Twin Cities, both hospitals and individual health-care providers found ways to accommodate and support Hmong practitioners of shamanism. By 1989, University Hospital was allowing shamans to burn incense and conduct rituals in hospital rooms, and Saint Paul's Children's Hospital had launched a Hmong awareness program.[45] Health-care providers sometimes made a special effort to support the ritual needs of their individual patients. For example, one Hmong woman believed that one of her twelve spirits had been lost when she had received treatment at Saint Paul Ramsey Medical Center's psychiatric clinic. Neal Holtan, a physician who had studied

Sudden Unexplained Nocturnal Death Syndrome and was familiar with Hmong beliefs and practices, cleared out the clinic to allow a shaman to conduct a ritual to retrieve the lost spirit.[46] Hmong Americans appreciated this shift toward greater respect and accommodation. Shoua Vang observed that openness to Hmong practices increased as understanding of shamanism improved. "We are fortunate that in the Twin Cities there are Americans at local universities who are familiar with Hmong culture," he said. "For instance, in Saint Paul, when Hmong people are ill they see both American doctors and traditional healers. The two styles of medicine have become integrated. At local hospitals, American doctors recognize our need for both. Sometimes they allow us to bring herbs or do our ceremonies in their facilities."[47]

Even as American hospitals demonstrated a greater willingness to understand and accommodate Hmong shamanism, Hmong shamanism still continued to confound Western categories of religion, culture, and medicine. The Hmong shaman program at Mercy Medical Center in Merced, California, offers a useful case in point. In 2009, Mercy Medical Center created the first program in the nation to offer formal licenses for Hmong shamans, who were approved by the hospital to conduct nine traditional healing rituals. On the one hand, the shamans at Mercy Medical Center are like chaplains. They have unrestricted access to patients, as do clergy members, and their work is treated and regulated as a form of prayer. The shaman program was thus an act of religious equality. At the same time, both Hmong people and hospital staff treated shamans as healers whose rituals could have an observable impact on the Hmong patients they served. Staff members at Mercy Medical Center recounted incidents during which Hmong shamans performed ceremonies that produced miraculous improvement in Hmong patients' health. These events made a "big impression," said Jim McDiarmid, a psychologist and residency program director, in an interview with the *New York Times*.[48]

However Hmong shamans were understood, the shaman program at Mercy Medical Center illustrates the great distance that the Hmong way has traveled to become an accepted fixture on the American religious landscape. In truth, it was perhaps pragmatism, not legal requirement or pluralistic ideals, that most powerfully compelled Americans to accommodate Hmong shamanism. Nevertheless, the presence of Hmong shamans in hospitals symbolized both the survival of Hmong traditions and their acceptance by American society. By the twenty-first century, Hmong Americans no longer practiced their traditional rituals in secret, fearing they were bothering their neighbors. Instead, they were conducting their ceremonies in public, claiming their place in America with pride.

"Religious, Cultural, or Some Mix of Both"

As spiritual healers who blur the boundary between clergy and doctor, the shamans at Mercy Medical Center occupy a curious status and are the latest chapter in debates that have accompanied the Hmong throughout their lives in Laos, Thailand, and the United States. What is "Hmong religion"? Do Hmong beliefs and practices constitute a religion? If so, which aspects? Or are Hmong rituals better understood as culture, as many Hmong people have described them? To be sure, Hmong people disagree on the precise distinctions between religion and culture. As has been noted earlier, the category of religion, which is rooted in Protestant Christianity, is a nonnative concept that does not align with how Hmong people have historically understood and practiced their spiritual and ritual lives, and for many Hmong Americans, being forced to organize Hmong beliefs and practices into separate spheres of religion and culture has been frustrating. For instance, when asked if playing the *qeej* is a cultural or religious activity, Chai Lee responded that playing the *qeej* is "definitely cultural" because in the United States, "it has become sort of like an art form." However, as soon as he said that, he immediately qualified his answer. "It has to do with spirits, so maybe it would be spirituality, too," he said. When he considered the word "religion," the matter became even more complicated:

> But religiously, it's become kind of weird because I have friends that are Christian, and they're still Hmong, and they still do Hmong culture because they still eat Hmong food, and they still have these Hmong clothes and stuff like that. But then I see *qeej* as Hmong culture, too. . . . When they [the Hmong Christians] do the funerals or the weddings and stuff like that, they do it differently now, and they don't do [it] the same way that the Hmong—like how traditional Hmong people would do it. . . . And then it kind of makes it seem like the *qeej* is kind of religious. It's like religion, [a] religious thing now, too.

After contemplating the fact that his own *qeej* teacher is a devout Christian, Chai Lee sighed, worn out by the absurdity of trying to sort Hmong practices into these categories. "Yeah," he said. "It's complicated."[49] Lee Pao Xiong agreed that the matter of what counts as religious and nonreligious is a thorny one. "We need to figure this stuff out," he told the *Twin Cities Reader*. "And it will take the entire Hmong religious community coming together to look at what's cultural and what's religious. Because for all of us, that issue is very confusing."[50]

The question of whether playing the *qeej* is religious or cultural may be impossible to answer, and it might not be useful to apply either label to an ethnic community that traditionally has not organized its life according to these social categories. Nevertheless, whether Hmong ritual traditions constitute a religion is still a question that matters. Hmong Americans reside in a nation that confers important legal protections and social and cultural privileges to people who can claim a rightful religion. In these circumstances, Hmong Americans do not appear to be set up for success: for them to claim (or not claim) that their beliefs and practices constitute a religion reveals that throughout American history, Protestant Christianity has fundamentally shaped how individuals and institutions have defined "religion," a category that does not easily accommodate the Hmong way at all.

However, Hmong Americans arrived in the United States at a moment of important transformations in First Amendment jurisprudence. In the second half of the twentieth century, the legal landscape began to change with a pair of US Supreme Court decisions—*Cantwell* in 1940 and *Everson* in 1947—that held that the due process clause of the Fourteenth Amendment incorporated key aspects of the First Amendment. In these rulings, the Supreme Court determined that the Free Exercise Clause and the Disestablishment Clause of the First Amendment constrained the actions of not only the federal government but also state and municipal governments.[51] As a result, the second half of the twentieth century saw the Court take a more active role in settling religious freedom and disestablishment debates at all levels of American society.[52] In addition, the period after World War II saw an uptick in legal challenges by non-Christian people seeking First Amendment protection and accommodation. In the 1970s—the decade when Asian migration surged and accelerated the religious diversification of American society—Free Exercise cases, including those involving adherents of minority religions, increased substantially. The claimants in these Free Exercise cases succeeded at higher rates than before, winning 37 percent of their claims, which was about three times as many as they had won in the decade after World War II. Most importantly, these legal victories, along with the broader context of an increasingly multireligious society, had a profound impact on how the courts understood religion, which they gradually interpreted in a way that was more expansive and inclusive of nontheistic traditions and Asian religions. To be sure, Protestant-centric ideas of religion still wielded significant power in the courts, which continued to privilege religion that is individual, private, and belief-centered. Nonetheless, this period brought increased opportunities for religious minorities to secure religious recognition in the courts.[53]

Hmong Americans made use of these legal opportunities, and they also found surprising possibility in the incommensurability of their traditional beliefs and practices. A juxtaposition of two legal cases—*Yang v. Sturner* and *State v. Tenerelli*—illuminates the fundamental challenge of defining religion in an American setting characterized by both a Protestant majority and unprecedented religious pluralism. Just as important, these two cases shed light on the benefits that can arise when people do not fit easily into one category or another. The Hmong Americans at the center of these cases shrewdly used the ambiguous definition of "Hmong religion" and the fluid categories of multiculturalism and pluralism to their advantage, describing Hmong rituals and beliefs as "religion" and other times as "culture" to ensure their accommodation and protected status. *Yang v. Sturner* and *State v. Tenerelli* illustrate the curious fact that both claiming and disclaiming religion can be in the best interest of a particular group. More broadly, an analysis of how particular communities like the Hmong have encountered, interpreted, and deployed the First Amendment underscores the creativity and agency of minority communities, the cultural and historical specificity of the meaning of religion, the possibilities and limitations of religion as a category, and the capacity of liberal societies to fulfill their commitment to religious tolerance and freedom.[54]

Yang v. Sturner is one instance in which Hmong Americans persuasively argued that their traditional beliefs are religious beliefs meriting the protection of the First Amendment. One night in 1987, a twenty-three-year-old Rhode Island Hmong man named Neng Yang was sleeping when he suffered a seizure that caused him to lose consciousness. Neng Yang was rushed by ambulance to Rhode Island Hospital, where he passed away three days later, on December 24. The hospital staff, unable to explain why Neng Yang had died, contacted the office of the state medical examiner. On December 25, without informing or securing the permission of the Yang family, William Sturner, the chief medical examiner, conducted an autopsy on the body.

You Vang Yang and Ia Kue Yang, Neng Yang's parents, were horrified to learn of the autopsy and argued that the state's autopsy statutes "violate their first amendment right to exercise their religion freely." According to court documents, the Yang family "adhere to the religious beliefs of the Hmongs, one of which prohibits any mutilation of the body, including autopsies or the removal of organs during an autopsy." Such an autopsy disrupted the spirit's journey after death, causing consequences not only for Neng Yang's spirit but for the rest of the living family. As the Yang family explained to the court, "the spirit of Neng [their son] would not be free, therefore his spirit will come back and take another person in his family."

Throughout the case, Judge Raymond Pettine was moved by the intense expression of the family's convictions, which he considered to be sincere religious belief. "I have seldom, in twenty-four years on the bench, seen such a sincere instance of emotion displayed," he said. "I could not help but also notice the reaction of the large number of Hmongs who had gathered to witness the hearing. Their silent tears shed in the still courtroom as they heard the Yangs' testimony provided stark support for the depth of the Yangs' grief." The "tearful outburst in the courtroom during the hearing" caused the judge to believe that the Yangs' beliefs were "deeply-held."

The beliefs that brought the Yang family to court were accepted as not only sincere but also religious. The defendant, William Sturner, did not call into question "the sincerity of the Yangs' religious beliefs" or "claim that the Hmongs' prohibition of autopsies is not a basic tenet of their religion." In his defense, he argued that having

REMAKING THE HMONG WAY 271

encountered several unexplained deaths in the Southeast Asian refugee population in Rhode Island, he believed that an autopsy was necessary to determine if "an infectious agent capable of spreading an epidemic within the state" had been the cause of Neng Yang's death. However, not once did he challenge the idea that the Yang family's beliefs were religious in nature.

Ultimately, the court ruled that Sturner had violated the Yang family's religious beliefs as protected by the First Amendment, on the grounds that there was no evidence that such unexplained deaths posed harm to the broader population of Rhode Island. According to the decision, there was no "'compelling state interest' in performing autopsies to overcome the Yangs' religious beliefs." Moreover, the judge decided that "it is reasonable to believe that when a medical examiner receives the body of a person who might be a Hmong, he should realize that an autopsy would violate the religious beliefs of the descendant's next of kin." The court later withdrew the decision, upon considering the outcome of *Employment Division v. Smith,* which was decided a few months after *Yang v. Sturner.*[55] Nonetheless, the idea that Hmong beliefs about spirits were valid religious beliefs was never questioned.[56] Just like Czisarah Neng Yang, You Vang Yang and Ia Kue Yang understood that it was powerful to "know the Constitution," and they insisted that their Hmong traditions amount to a legitimate religion and that they have a First Amendment right to believe and practice this religion.

The Yang family's legal strategy of claiming religion was not the only way Hmong Americans have used the law to secure accommodations and protections—they have also done the opposite and have successfully argued that Hmong beliefs and practices do not constitute a religion. Such was the case in 1999 in *State v. Tenerelli,* in which the Minnesota State Supreme Court ruled that the stabber of a Hmong man could be required, as restitution, to cover the costs of a *hu plig,* the Hmong soul-calling ceremony. In contrast to *Yang v. Sturner,* in which Hmong Americans claimed that their traditions amounted to a religion in order to gain restitution for an autopsy that conflicted with their beliefs, in *State v. Tenerelli,* Hmong Americans disclaimed religion to secure accommodation for their rituals.

On July 15, 1996, Txawj Xiong was driving home from a picnic in Saint Paul with his son, Meng, and his wife, Joua Vang, when he encountered two men, Anthony Tenerelli and Jeremy Wade Benton. Tenerelli and Benton, who had been arguing before Xiong arrived at the intersection, approached Xiong's car, and Xiong, fearing for his safety, opened the trunk of his car, which contained a Hmong carving knife. Details of what happened next remain unclear, but a violent confrontation ensued, during which Xiong was hit, kicked, and stabbed in the back twice with the Hmong carving knife. A jury convicted Tenerelli of second- and fifth-degree assault. The Ramsey County District Court required that Tenerelli serve time in prison and, as restitution, assume responsibility for the expenses associated with a *hu plig* ceremony for Txawj Xiong.

Tenerelli appealed, arguing that the *hu plig* is a religious ceremony and that the requirement that he cover its costs violated the Establishment Clause. By 1999, the case had made its way to the Minnesota State Supreme Court, where the discussion focused on the nature of the *hu plig*—its practices and significance, both for the Hmong community and for Txawj Xiong in particular. The burden lay on Tenerelli to prove that Txawj Xiong's *hu plig* was a religious ceremony and that the Establishment Clause was thus implicated.

To answer the question of whether the *hu plig* was a religious ceremony, the court relied on the expertise of two Hmong Americans familiar with the *hu plig* and its cultural context. In preparing the victim impact report, a probation official with the department of corrections contacted William Yang of the Hmong American Partnership, a Hmong community organization based in Saint Paul. In this report, which was filed with the trial court, William Yang described the *hu plig* as a ceremony "to restore the soul of a victim, normally a person who has been physically or emotionally traumatized." He added that there was a "deeply-held belief, particularly among elders of the Hmong community, that without the restoration ceremony the person will become sick and eventually die."

To support his case, Tenerelli turned to another cultural expert, a Hmong American man named Neng Xiong, who had been born in Laos and had lived in the United States for thirteen years. Educated in American schools and trained in sociology, cultural anthropology, and law, Neng Xiong hailed from "a traditional Hmong family" and was also the son of a shaman. Neng Xiong concurred with

William Yang's description of the *hu plig* and added that "90% of the Hmong people living in the United States over the age of 40 who have not converted to Christianity still believe in the traditional Hmong practices and ceremonies." However, when questioned if the *hu plig* is "partially a religious ceremony" during the trial court, Neng Xiong declined to characterize it as such. "It is difficult to say because in the tradition itself, my understanding is that, from my cultural anthropology studies, that a religion has to be a form of belief that is institutionalized," he said. "But at the same time [for] the Hmong also, this is a kind of a form of belief from thousands of years ago and the thing has never been institutionalized yet." In other words, Neng Xiong did not say definitively that the *hu plig* was or was not a religious ceremony, only that Hmong traditions had not yet become "institutionalized," meaning that the status of this Hmong ceremony, both in the eyes of Txawj Xiong and the broader Hmong community, remained uncertain.

Tenerelli made one further effort to bolster his case that the *hu plig* is a religious ceremony: he argued that shamans are religious authorities. In the victim impact statement submitted to the court, Txawj Xiong had said that a shaman would conduct the *hu plig*. The use of a shaman, argued Tenerelli, was further evidence that the *hu plig* is a religious ceremony because shamans do fundamentally religious work.

Aside from the question of whether the *hu plig* is a religious ritual, another related debate emerged during the case: was the *hu plig* that Txawj Xiong proposed commensurate with his suffering? The expenses of the *hu plig* planned by Txawj Xiong were submitted to the trial court and itemized as follows:

$15.00—Replacement T-shirt
$894.46—Automobile repair
$380.00—Suit for *Hu Plig* ceremony
$20.00—Shirt for *Hu Plig* ceremony
$540.00—Cow for sacrifice for *Hu Plig* ceremony
$90.00—Pig for sacrifice for *Hu Plig* ceremony
$10.00—Two chickens for sacrifice for *Hu Plig* ceremony
$155.15—Roast pig for *Hu Plig* ceremony
$200.00—Shoua woman to conduct *Hu Plig* ceremony

During his testimony, Neng Xiong contested the scale of the proposed *hu plig*. According to Neng Xiong, the number of animals sacrificed for a *hu plig* depends on the severity of the injury. After consulting with three Hmong elders, Neng Xiong testified that sacrificing four animals was suitable for a "major" injury, but that Txawj Xiong's injuries were only "medium." For this reason, he suggested that they disallow restitution for the cost of the two chickens, on the grounds that the cow and pig would be enough to satisfy the spiritual requirements and that the two chickens would be "excessive."

In the end, the Minnesota Supreme Court upheld the lower courts' decision to require that Tenerelli cover the costs of the *hu plig* as restitution. Writing for the majority, Chief Justice Kathleen Blatz wrote that Neng Xiong's testimony failed to provide enough evidence that Txawj Xiong's *hu plig* was indeed a religious ceremony. Furthermore, the court found that shamans could be religious authorities but were not exclusively so. "While a shaman can be thought of as a religious leader, the record indicates that shamans also serve other functions in the Hmong community," Blatz wrote. Blatz also pointed out that "even some of the Hmong people who have converted to Christianity continue to engage in these traditional ceremonies." Finally, the court agreed with the lower courts' decision to adjust the expenses of the *hu plig* downward and disallow the restitution of the two chickens, as well as the suit and shirt.

Two justices chose to write separate opinions that revealed the complexity of the task of determining whether the *hu plig* is a religious ceremony. Justice Paul Anderson agreed with the majority and chose to write a special concurrence. "We simply do not have in the record the information necessary to prudently conclude that Txawj Xiong's *Hu Plig* was or was not a religious practice," Anderson wrote. "What is or what is not a religious practice is a difficult question to answer and the search for an answer has in many cases led to contradictory and arbitrary results when court-prescribed tests for religious practices have been applied. Such tests are indeterminate in nature and subject to variations in the general level of scrutiny employed." Anderson referred to *United States v. Ballard,* which stated the court must determine if "beliefs are sincerely held and whether objectively the claimed belief occupies the same place in the life of the objector as an orthodox belief in God holds in the life of one clearly qualified for exemption."[57] Anderson then applied this reasoning as he considered Txawj Xiong's beliefs about the *hu plig*:

> The key to our analysis of whether Txawj Xiong's Hu Plig is or is not a religious ceremony turns on the fact that it appears there are different levels at which the Hu Plig ceremony is conducted. The record indicates that, depending upon the belief of the beneficiary, the Hu Plig in some circumstances may be a cultural and social ceremony and, in others, may be a religious practice. Thus, at least in part, the question of whether the Hu Plig is religious appears to depend on the nature of the beliefs of the individual for whom the ceremony is conducted. The victim impact statement indicates that Txawj Xiong "went through a Hmong traditional healing ceremony," but there is no evidence on the record of Txawj Xiong's beliefs and no clarifying information on his beliefs or his purpose in having the Hu Plig. Neng Xiong conceded that it was difficult for him to say whether the Hu Plig was a religious practice, but according to his anthropological studies, he understood that a belief must be institutionalized to be religious and that the Hu Plig is not institutionalized. While there is much on this record that leads me to believe that under certain circumstances a Hu Plig may be in whole or in part religious, it is unclear whether Txawj Xiong's beliefs concerning his Hu Plig are religious, cultural, or some mix of both.

In Anderson's view, Tenerelli failed to prove that Txawj Xiong himself understood and pursued his *hu plig* as a religious ceremony. "Tenerelli's argument may contain some merit for, in certain circumstances and to certain individuals, the Hu Plig may be a religious ceremony," he wrote. "Nevertheless, Tenerelli has failed to demonstrate that Txawj Xiong's Hu Plig was conducted at a 'level' such that it must be viewed as a religious practice rather than at a level that does not meet the constitutional standard for a religious practice." Finally, Anderson wrote that had the *hu plig* been deemed a religious ceremony, the court's determination that the sacrifice of the two chickens was excessive and would have neared an "excessive entanglement with religion."

Justice Anderson's opinion hinged on a Christian standard for what counts as religion. First, he emphasized "the nature of the beliefs of the individual for whom the ceremony is conducted," a reflection of the Protestant view that religion centers on individual belief rather than on collective practice. Even more, Anderson's

Christian-centric definition of religion informed his insistence that "a belief must be institutionalized to be religious." Hmong traditions, typically passed down through oral tradition and practiced in family homes rather than in churches and temples, did not conform to this template.

Justice James Gilbert offered the lone dissent, stating that the ordering of restitution for the *hu plig* ceremony "delved into significant religious and spiritual traditions," resulting in "excessive entanglement." The problem, Gilbert wrote, is that the lower courts had relied too heavily on the testimony of Neng Xiong, whose unwillingness to categorize the *hu plig* as a religious ceremony stemmed from the fact that Hmong traditions are not "institutionalized." Gilbert pointed to the objective test established by *United States v. Seeger*.[58] Gilbert then argued that there are other means of determining if a ceremony is religious:

> In *Seeger*, the United States Supreme Court recognized "the richness and variety of spiritual life in our country" and the diverse forms of expression these religions encompass. The Court stated that a belief is religious if it is a "sincere and meaningful [belief that] occupies a place in the life of its possessor parallel to that filled by the orthodox belief in God." Thus, to determine whether a belief is religious, a court must decide whether it is sincerely held and whether it is, objectively, religious.
>
> There is no dispute in this case regarding the sincerity of the victim's deeply held belief. There is, however, a dispute as to whether the Hu Plig healing or soul restoration ceremony is religious. This court now must determine the resolution of that dispute. The answer to the religious question is dependent on whether the ceremony "occupied a place in [the victim's] life parallel to that filled by the orthodox belief in God." In concluding that the Hu Plig ceremony is not religious, the trial court ignored the Seeger test, instead relying exclusively on an expert witness' statement that the ceremony had not been "institutionalized."
>
> Had the trial court used the appropriate test in determining whether the Hu Plig ceremony was religious, several undisputed facts would have led it to the conclusion that the ceremony was religious. According to the victim impact statement, which is not contradicted in the record, the Hu Plig ceremony is based on the belief that the "victim's soul is replaced by that of animals," and that without the restoration of the soul through the Hu Plig ceremony, the victim will

become sick and eventually die. Although specific practices differ among religions, many religions focus on the existence and restoration of the soul. Furthermore, the Hu Plig ceremony is performed by a shaman ("holy man") or shao woman ("holy woman"). It is undisputed in the record that these holy people are "religious leaders in the Hmong community." Thus, they are objectively as vital to the Hu Plig ceremony as other religious officials are in other religions. Thus, the appellant has met his burden of proof that the Hu Plig ceremony is, from an objective perspective, religious, regardless of the institutionalization of that ceremony.

State v. Tenerelli shows, first, that it remains difficult to argue in courts that Hmong rituals are religious. Hmong traditions were, and continue to be, relatively unfamiliar to most Americans and incongruent with Protestant definitions of religion. In addition, judges have generally valued claims that centered on belief and personal conscience rather than on ritual and practice.[59] Given these obstacles, Anthony Tenerelli faced an uphill battle in proving that a *hu plig* is, in fact, religious.

Moreover, this case demonstrates that disclaiming religion might have its own advantages. In thinking about how religious minorities endeavor to preserve their traditions in the United States, one might assume that it would always involve claiming religion and using the First Amendment to secure protection. That groups might find it advantageous to deny the label of religion challenges assumptions about how non-Christian groups might strive for accommodation. Further, *State v. Tenerelli* revealed how the noninstitutionalized character of the Hmong way offered a surprising—and ultimately useful—flexibility.

Yang v. Sturner and *State v. Tenerelli* reveal long-running debates about how to make sense of "Hmong religion" in a society and legal system historically shaped by Christian definitional criteria of "religion." As evident at other moments in Hmong history, the application of categories such as "religion" and "holy man" to describe Hmong beliefs and rituals have not always been accurate or helpful. However, as both *Yang v. Sturner* and *State v. Tenerelli* indicate, Hmong Americans have discovered opportunities in the incommensurability of their traditions with Protestant Christianity. Arriving in the United States without identifying with a church or a major world religion meant that it was difficult for Christian resettlement

sponsors to understand and accommodate Hmong beliefs and practices. However, when they were in a position to advocate for themselves, Hmong Americans found a way to dwell in the space between
"religion" and "culture," and the flexibility and uncertainty of their
position provided useful freedom to claim one category or another.
"Hmong religion," as always, was on the move.

«««◇»»»

If Hmong refugees found themselves spiritually lost in their first
years in the United States, they were not lost for long—they eventually made their own way. As Hmong people acclimated to their
new American environment, they adapted their beliefs and practices and created new institutions to ensure that their traditions
would endure and thrive. Educational organizations like the HCC
supported the preservation of Hmong traditions and the transmission of ritual knowledge to the next generation. They protected
their most valuable resource—ritual experts—and ensured that
the Hmong community would never again find themselves unable
to conduct a ceremony due to the lack of a shaman, a *qeej* player,
or a funeral singer. Hmong-owned funeral homes, butcher shops,
and congregations provided space and material resources, which
made it easier to conduct traditional rituals. Finally and perhaps
most importantly, Hmong Americans established their traditions
in an American context and presented their beliefs and practices as
a religion, which put them in a better position to advocate for rights,
recognition, resources, and respect in American courtrooms, hospitals, and more.

Less obviously, there have been drawbacks to institutionalizing
the Hmong way and conforming to American norms. For one, the
rich internal diversity and distinctions among clan traditions have
diminished.[60] Reflecting on the changes in Hmong funerals in the
past decade, J. Kou Vang observed that funerals have become more
"standardized" across clans and sub-clans, as an established class
of ritual experts has assumed primary responsibility for conducting
ceremonies for the entire Hmong community. "[There will be] one
Hmong way of doing things, regardless if you are a Vang, a Lee, a
Xiong, you know, a Yang," he predicted. "There's going to be one
way because the reality is, if you go to one of these Hmong funerals,

you see the same group of people doing it: the same group of sha-mans, the same group of *qeej* players."[61]

By institutionalizing their traditions, Hmong Americans have also run the risk of losing the useful opportunities found in re-taining their tradition's flexibility and ambiguity. As *Yang v. Sturner* reveals, describing their traditions as religion helped Hmong people to secure First Amendment recognition and protection. *State v. Tenerelli,* in contrast, shows that claiming religion was not always useful—indeed, it could be clearly disadvantageous. As these cases demonstrate, Hmong Americans have made good use of the flexible categories of religion and culture and the fluid boundaries of their traditions. This approach was one that developed over time. Especially in the early years of resettlement, the illegibility and uncertain status of the Hmong way created problems for Hmong people. However, Hmong Americans eventually learned to turn their tradition's un-certain status into an asset, one that would help keep their beliefs and practices alive and thriving, albeit in new, reinvented forms.

These complex maneuverings are perhaps not surprising, given the genius for adaptation required of a people who have a history of being on the move. Even in death, their souls must travel. At times, the migration has been welcome—a journey to heaven, perhaps, or an odyssey on a golden airplane to reunite with the ancestors. Other times, their movement has been forced and tragic, with war, pov-erty, and spiritual troubles precipitating their uprooting and flight. Wherever they have gone, so too have their ritual traditions gone, bearing the mark of these journeys and the interactions with people, spirits, and even governments they encountered along the way.

Conclusion

ALTERNATIVE ENDINGS

In recounting the spiritual odyssey of the Hmong people, Rev. Young Tao of the Hmong Christian Church of God did not end the story in America. At the 1991 Thanksgiving celebration, Tao described how God had delivered the Hmong from Laos to Thailand and from Thailand to the United States. He then spoke of a more wonderful place yet to come: heaven, the final resting place for a people who had long suffered as "strangers and exiles to the many countries of the earth." Now that Hmong people have made it safely to America, he said, the "Hmong are seeking the country to come that is heaven."[1]

But "how can the Hmong get into heaven?" Tao asked. He believed the answer was through Christianity, *kev cai tshiab,* the new way through which Hmong people could find a type of safety and security that is not possible on earth. He shared a powerful providential story of spiritual homecoming that resonated with the Hmong refugees in his church, and it went like this: After decades of colonial violence, war, and forced migration, Christianity had given Hmong people the way to come to America, and by giving Hmong people a way to heaven, Christianity now gave them the option of no longer having to live life on the run. Ultimately, Tao

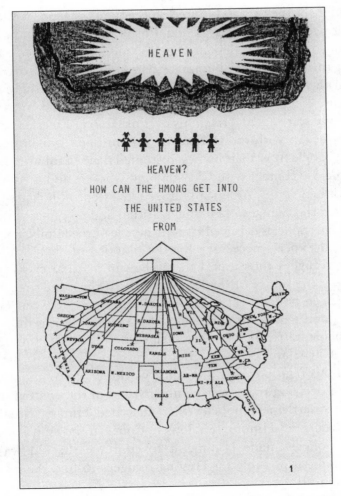

Illustration for the Hmong Christian Church of God 1991 Thanksgiving celebration. Courtesy of the family of Rev. Young Tao.

said, Christianity offered them what they had long sought as a people: a homeland where they could live in eternal peace and freedom.

Understanding how Hmong people made their way to these new homes—America, rather than Asia, and the Christian heaven rather than the place of Hmong ancestors—is the purpose of this book. There are of course many reasons why Hmong people made these particular journeys. Tao pointed to the hand of God, while other Hmong people spoke of a personal need for healing and spiritual stability or a collective desire to become modern Americans. But my goal in this book is to illuminate one important and overlooked force in the story of Hmong people's religious and refugee migrations: the US government, which produced profound transformations in the spiritual and religious lives of Hmong Americans. These changes began with the US-backed war in Laos, which uprooted Hmong people from their homes, disrupted their ritual lives, and put them in close contact with Christian aid workers and missionaries. In the United States, American refugee resettlement policies further intensified the changes in Hmong spiritual and religious life. American refugee policies deprived Hmong people of the family, resources, and ritual experts necessary for the practice of their traditions. Hmong refugees thus found themselves in a ritual crisis, uncertain about the future of the Hmong way. At the same time, American refugee policies set up close relationships between Hmong refugees and Christian churches. These churches not only sponsored their resettlement but also helped to introduce Hmong refugees to Christianity. Many Hmong refugees, eager to maintain harmonious relations with the spirit world, chose to adopt Christianity, a decision that must be understood in the context of government resettlement policies that unsettled Hmong ritual lives and restructured Hmong religious options. In the end, American refugee policies made it difficult to continue the old way and helped make it possible for Hmong refugees to find the new way of Christianity.

Hmong people in the United States had a wide range of opinions about these religious changes and the government's role in causing them. Some individuals, like the shaman Paja Thao, were distressed. "I will never be Christian," he said. "I shall never forget my own culture/I am a Hmong."[2] But others were thankful. It was a deep gratitude that compelled Tao to lead an annual Thanksgiving celebration, which was an opportunity to celebrate Hmong people's geographic migration to America and spiritual migration to Christianity. To Tao, it was clear who was responsible for Hmong people's rescue. "Thanks God, and the United States Government," he declared.[3]

"They Really Look After the People Coming to Australia"

The story could have ended differently. Religious changes were ultimately the product of human relationships that were, in turn, the product of American refugee policies. What would have happened if the US government had approached resettlement differently and had not created relationships between Christian resettlement workers and Hmong refugees in the first place? Not all Hmong refugees were resettled in the United States, and not all governments resettle refugees by relying on a "shadow establishment" of voluntary agencies and churches.

The experiences of Hmong refugees resettled in Australia underscore the religious impact of government resettlement policies and reveal a host of different possibilities and outcomes. Gary Yia Lee, who has played a leading role in researching and supporting Hmong refugees in Australia, found that Hmong Australians' experiences contrasted sharply with those of their American counterparts and that Australian refugee resettlement policies were in fact conducive to the practice of traditional Hmong rituals. "A lot of people who have gone to America have substituted or have replaced the Hmong cultural or religious traditions and practices by becoming Christian, so as not to be in spiritual limbo, so many of them have changed to being Christian in America," he said. "But in Australia, here, because there's a small number of Hmong being accepted to this country, very few have been converted."[4] In explaining what led Hmong Australians to follow a different path, he called attention to two central differences: Australia's resettlement system, which relied on government agencies rather than religious institutions, and Australia's emphasis on multiculturalism rather than assimilation.

In contrast to the public-private, church-state system in the United States, the Australian government did most of the work of resettling Southeast Asian refugees. "The Australian Government's refugee program does not depend entirely on church and community sponsorship," Gary Yia Lee observed. "Most of the Hmong were admitted under this official program which provides all necessary support services with minor assistance from voluntary agencies. They do not, therefore, come into early contacts with people who may influence

A toy dog sacrificed at a *tso plig* ceremony in Sydney, Australia, in 2015.
© Melissa May Borja.

them to doubt their traditional religion and to embrace a new one."[5]
By doing much of the resettlement work itself instead of relying on
churches to implement its policies, the Australian government created a situation in which Hmong refugees did not develop close,
dependent relationships with Christian churches and charitable
organizations. As a result, Gary Yia Lee said, "there hasn't been a lot
of systematic conversion of refugees by church groups in Australia."
This approach differed significantly from the American system,
where Hmong refugees "feel either obliged to become Christian or
to these church groups, or else they don't know where to go, they've
got no support, they don't know how to get help."[6]

Australia also had an explicit policy of promoting multiculturalism, which was another crucial difference with the United States.
An assimilation-oriented scatter policy made it difficult for Hmong
refugees in America to continue their traditional rituals. In contrast,
the 2,000 or so Hmong refugees who were resettled in Australia
found themselves in a country that made an open commitment to

affirming different religions and cultures. "The Australian Government actively supports the idea of a multicultural nation, as mentioned previously, and has made funds available to various groups to test out the concept, especially in the fields of culture, arts and education," Gary Yia Lee wrote. He noted that Hmong refugees arrived at an opportune moment—"when this experiment is only at its beginning stage"—and that refugees were "encouraged to carry on with their changing traditions while learning to adapt to the host community."[7] In Australia, this policy commitment to multiculturalism reached into the realm of religion. The Australian government made efforts to identify the religions of refugees and, under the aegis of a policy of multiculturalism, actively engaged in policies supporting religious pluralism.

Gary Yia Lee, who worked with the government to support Hmong refugee resettlement, made a point of emphasizing to his fellow Hmong Australians that this multiculturalism policy meant that they could and should practice their traditional rituals without "fear." As he explained,

> The government's policy of promoting multiculturalism has allowed us to pursue a lot of these cultural traditions and healing traditions, unlike in America [laugh], where's there no multiculturalism. And that's another reason why a lot of Hmong there have become Christian, you see. When the Hmong came here, I was working in the field of migration and settlement, and I know very well what the government policy is, so I kept saying to them, no fear. You know, just do what you believe, and do what you want to do, so long as you don't offend your neighbors, or something that would be against the law. But anything that you believe in and what you're comfortable with, then keep to it and do it. And so this is the reason why nearly 98% of the Hmong [in] . . . Australia here have remained pretty much traditional in their religious beliefs and carry on with their rituals.[8]

Gary Yia Lee's encouragement alone did not mean that Hmong refugees found it easy to continue their traditions in Australia. Practicing traditional Hmong rituals in Australia was initially very difficult for Hmong refugees for many of the same reasons that it was difficult in the United States. Hmong Australians frequently worried that their rituals would cause tensions with their neighbors. Kou Her, who lived in Cairns, Queensland, explained the challenges of living in urban settings and in such close proximity to non-Hmong

Australians. "In Laos we can kill the animal at home," he said. "Kill the chicken, pig, cow, goat, or sheep. [You] can kill at home, but this country we cannot. . . . We cannot burn anything at home, and we can't do anything too noisy at home, so in this country, they [do] not allow for that because the neighborhood don't like [it]."[9] Fay Chia Lee and Jor Vue, two Hmong men from Innisfail, said that even in rural settings, like where they lived in Queensland, it was difficult to have access to material resources that were necessary for rituals, such as chickens and pigs. They also described how their neighbors were unfamiliar with and suspicious of their activities. When their ceremonies were "too noisy," the neighbors believed that there was fighting and called the police.[10] Elizabeth Her emphasized this latter point, explaining that the challenges were not due simply to the lack of space or the noisiness of the rituals, but the different cultural context. "Living in a Western society country," she said, "it's a bit more difficult to do those activities because you've got neighbors around you."[11]

But the most important reason why Hmong refugees found it difficult to continue their traditions in Australia was the lack of other Hmong people, especially Hmong people with ritual expertise. Hmong Americans and Hmong Australians thus struggled with many of the same challenges. Kou Her said that part of the problem was the youth, who "don't know about the old culture."[12] Elizabeth Her pointed to another aspect: the absence of "elders who actually know what the ritual activities require." The lack of experts in Hmong traditions, she said, led to "a slow deterioration of those activities."[13] Pao Lee, a Hmong man in Sydney, complained that even though there were some ritual experts, there were "very few of them," and "not many people know to be a shaman."[14] Finally, Charles Saykao, a Hmong man who lived in Victoria, explained that the problem was not only that there were "few that can support us now" but also that Hmong people "live[d] scattered everywhere," making it difficult for Hmong Australians to have access to qeej players, shamans, and helpful kinsmen.[15] Gary Yia Lee agreed that the lack of ritual experts was an important problem. "In the first ten years, we used to have many younger families, so that religious rituals are something that only a few knew about," he said, "and the result is that, for the first ten years, we didn't have older people who could perform ceremonies, rituals, or shamanic healing."[16]

In response to this problem, Hmong Australians formed the Hmong Australia Society (HAS) in Melbourne in 1978. Charles Saykao recalled how the people who formed the organization shared the concern that the Hmong would "be the lost people in Australia" if they discontinued their ritual traditions. They determined that they needed to "bring more Hmong" and "build up community" so they could practice and preserve their rituals. In particular, they realized that the Hmong people whom they needed most were the people who knew how to conduct rituals like the *hu plig*. Unfortunately, these valuable ritual experts were still in the refugee camps in Thailand, where they remained because, as Charles Saykao put it, they "had no relationship with other country," "don't have brother or sister, daughters that go overseas," and were therefore "still stuck in the camp." The HAS therefore developed a proposal to present to the government to address this problem. "We want the governments here to help us to bring these people no matter [whether] they [are] related to us or not," Charles Saykao said.[17]

The HAS began with an organized effort to educate government officials about the ritual challenges Hmong people faced in Australia. In 1981 Ong Ly, president of the HAS, wrote to the Senate Standing Committee on Foreign Affairs and Defence and explained that one of their community's greatest challenges was "the religious needs of Hmong refugees in Australia arising from lack of persons with expert knowledge in the performance of religious teaching and ceremonies because most of those already here are young untrained in this area."[18] Similarly, in 1986, HAS representatives made a presentation to government officials from the Department of Immigration and Ethnic Affairs. The HAS spokespeople emphasized that the absence of elders put Hmong families in a precarious cultural position. "Without these elders, the Hmong could be headed to extinction," said Pao Saykao, one of the representatives. "We need all the help you can give." Pao Saykao pointed out that, unlike the United States, Australia had a policy of multiculturalism that justified government support for Hmong religious and cultural traditions. Representatives of the DIEA agreed that "the Hmong should have [been] given a special consideration because . . . their religion, traditions and background are different."[19]

Observations from researchers and community groups confirmed that Hmong Australians were experiencing a religious and cultural crisis like what was underway in the United States. The Ethnic Communities' Council of New South Wales, an association uniting 400 ethnic organizations in the state, submitted a report to the Senate Standing Committee on Foreign Affairs and Defence in which they argued that Hmong Australians were "spiritually lost and helpless because of the lack of religious guidance or the inability to practise their beliefs under the leadership of some expert persons."[20] Another government-commissioned assessment emphasized how the uncertain future of Hmong rituals contributed to a sense of vulnerability and dislocation. The authors of *Home from Home: Refugees in Tasmania,* a report produced for the Department of Immigration and Multicultural Affairs, noted that Hmong culture was "dependent upon the maintenance of Hmong medical and religious practices," which Hmong people hoped to incorporate into their new lives in Australia. "Probably the most important thing to me is to be allowed to practise religion freely without any restrictions," one Hmong refugee told the report authors. However, the report authors found that the difficulty of "securing the services of a Hmong shaman and being able to conduct appropriate religious practices" meant that "religious problems were cited as their [Hmong refugees'] single biggest problem."[21]

Community members and refugee advocates argued that these "religious problems," which were so central to refugees' ability to thrive in Australia, were issues that the Australian government could potentially solve. The Ethnic Communities' Council of New South Wales declared that "the Government or the Australian community should attempt to understand them and accept these practices as a part of the refugees' customs and culture." Even more, they argued that the government had a responsibility to go beyond simply tolerating the Hmong way. In their view, the government needed to take an active role in providing for the religious needs of Hmong and other non-Christian Southeast Asians:

> Many refugee groups do not have access to a place of worship or to persons well versed in their own religious beliefs and practice. This is particularly the case with those refugees who are not Christian. . . . The needs for spiritual leadership and facilities are most acutely felt among the Vietnamese Buddhist. . . . The Lao group in Sydney at least have some Thai monks to go to for worship and in times of need such as sickness or bereavement. There is a need for

the Government recognising the limitation set out in the Constitution to at least allow some spiritual leaders or monks to be admitted into Australia from the refugee camps overseas to serve the needs of the refugees here.[22]

To gain government support for the program to bring ritual experts from the refugee camps in Thailand, Hmong Australians made use of the policy of multiculturalism. The HAS worked with the Melbourne office of the Department of Immigration and Ethnic Affairs to develop a proposal for what became known as the Cultural Lobby Program. This program called for "a number of Hmong refugees to be considered for special resettlement on the basis of particular religious and cultural knowledge"—for example, shamans, qeej players, and other ritual experts—for the specific purpose of helping Hmong refugees in Australia practice their rituals and maintain their cultural traditions. Through this program, the Hmong community in Australia brought five ritual experts from the refugee camps in Thailand.[23]

A decade and a half after the creation of the Cultural Lobby Program, Hmong observers noted that the program had made a difference. "It's only since then that, in the last 15 years, that we've had enough ritual experts to serve the community," said Gary Yia Lee.[24] Hmong people were not alone in benefiting from these special migration programs. Under the same multiculturalism policy, the Australian government helped bring imams to support Muslim Australians in the practice of their religion. In both these efforts, the Australian government demonstrated a commitment to supporting migrants' practice of rituals that were understood as both cultural and religious. To be sure, the Cultural Lobby Program was a modest effort, and it did not solve all of Hmong Australians' ritual problems. Although the ritual experts brought over from the refugee camps served the immediate needs of community, they were less successful in contributing to the long-term maintenance of ritual knowledge in the Hmong Australian community.[25] Still, the program—and the Australian government's support of it—left a positive impression on Hmong Australians. Xao Lor, a Hmong man in New South Wales, recognized that the government had made the effort so that "Hmong can live better." He declared with appreciation, "They really look after the people coming to Australia to make them happy, to make the people happy."[26]

To be sure, some aspects of Hmong religious life changed in Australia for some of the same reasons they did in the United States. Hmong Australians expressed concern about passing on ritual knowledge to the Australian-born generations and worried about the future of Hmong rituals in Australia.[27] At the same time, some Hmong Australians adopted Christianity, especially with the arrival of Hmong American Christian missionaries, who are frequent visitors in Australia and Asia.[28] As in the United States, the adoption of Christianity only sometimes involved the abandonment of Hmong traditions. There was a similar degree of religious mixing among Hmong Australians. Vang Yee Chang, for example, attends church every Sunday but still practices traditional rituals. "I believe in Christian, but I also believe in the Hmong traditional cultures," he said. "It's not different . . . it's the same way."[29]

Overall, however, Hmong Australians experienced different religious outcomes. Australia had different resettlement policies, along with a smaller refugee population and a particularly democratic and responsive ethnic leadership. Because of these factors, Gary Yia Lee argued that "unlike some of those in the United States of America, the Hmong in Australia have never questioned the relevance of traditional beliefs to their new life."[30] The fact that fewer Hmong refugees became Christian in Australia illuminates a few key points about the importance of government policies in shaping Hmong religious life. First, the Australian government's policy of multiculturalism, in which Hmong rituals were considered an important aspect of "culture," created circumstances in which Hmong refugees felt free to continue their traditions. In addition, this policy created opportunities for Hmong refugees to advocate for their interests and for the Australian government to take positive action to help Hmong refugees continue the Hmong way. Most notably, practical support through the Cultural Lobby Program made it possible for Hmong Australians to continue traditional funeral ceremonies, healing rituals, and more.

Ultimately, Hmong experiences in Australia offer a useful counterpoint to Hmong experiences in the United States, where the decision by many Hmong people to adopt Christianity was not the natural consequence of living in a predominantly Christian nation but a decision facilitated by the US government's approach to resettlement. Comparing Hmong experiences in Australia and the

United States underscores how the prominent role of religious voluntary agencies and churches in resettlement shaped Hmong people's religious choices. At the same time, the incorporation of Protestant ethics and practices into purportedly secular spaces limited both Hmong religious choice and Americans' capacity to accommodate traditional Hmong beliefs and practices.

"Tell the Story of the 'Religious Freedom' in America"

When Australian government officials discussed the ritual needs of Hmong Australians, they described Hmong beliefs and practices as religious.[31] In contrast, the people who planned and implemented the resettlement program in the United States were less inclined to recognize Hmong traditions as religious. Recognizing a religion mattered. As we have seen, Christian voluntary agencies in the United States were aware of the increased religious diversity of refugees, and they urged church sponsors "to respect their religion and their religious practices," as the United States Catholic Conference put it.[32] But traditional Hmong beliefs and practices did not conform to a Protestant template of religion and were thus less legible as a religion. How would Hmong refugees have experienced resettlement if Americans had readily seen them as having a rightful religion in the first place?

A consideration of the resettlement experiences of other Southeast Asian refugees offers a useful comparison that suggests an alternative ending: that Hmong refugees in the United States might have been able to continue their traditional rituals more easily and with greater support if they had been viewed as having a religion. Lao, Cambodian, and Vietnamese refugees were resettled in the United States during the same period, under the same policies, by the same voluntary agencies, and often in the same communities and by the same sponsoring congregations. In addition, their resettlement was shaped by the same ideological commitments to religious pluralism, multiculturalism, human rights, and Cold War anticommunism. However, the Hmong differed from these other Southeast Asian groups in culture, language, geographic origin, and, most importantly, religion. As noted earlier, most Lao, Cambodian, and Vietnamese refugees were Buddhist, and some Vietnamese refugees were Catholic. But nearly all of them had something that Hmong refugees did not, which was a religion that government, voluntary agencies, and church sponsors could more readily identify and accommodate. Government officials, voluntary agencies, and church sponsors believed that the maintenance of refugees' religious and cultural traditions was a critical aspect of effective resettlement. For this reason, they actively assisted Buddhist refugees in the search for monks and temples that could support the continued practice of their religion. It is clear that Buddhist refugees benefited from these measures. Importantly, none of these measures were ones that government, voluntary agencies, and churches offered to Hmong refugees.

If the United States saw itself as a "tri-faith," Judeo-Christian nation during this period, the military chaplains saw Vietnamese refugees as a "tri-faith" people comprising "the three major VN religious groups"—Protestants, Catholics, and Buddhists. Accordingly, the military strived to provide religious support for each of these communities.[33] In refugee camps overseas, camp officials organized three types of religious services for Vietnamese refugees. "Mass for 10,000 people had been held by the Bishop of Guam; Protestant and Buddhist services were held regularly," noted one staff report.[34] In the four military-run resettlement camps where Vietnamese refugees stayed until they were matched with sponsors, the Task Force Staff Chaplain Office supported the Indochinese Refugee Religious Programs and organized Catholic, Protestant, and Buddhist services in the "Chapels of three major Vietnamese faiths."[35]

At Fort Chaffee, Task Force chaplains supported Vietnamese Buddhists in a variety of ways. Most significantly, they hired Rev. Thich Tinh Tu, a Buddhist priest, to serve as one of its contract clergy, just as they had Catholic and Protestant clergy. They also provided a range of support programs that addressed refugees' religious, cultural, and social needs. For example, they planned "religious meditation and vocational training activities" and "open house cultural art exhibits." There were also special events, such as the highly popular "Festival of the Full Moon," an event where refugee children were "fashioning very attractive lanterns out of empty beer cans and making a street dragon from paper/cloth."[36] The Buddhist chaplain at Fort Chaffee even provided support to Vietnamese refugees who lived beyond camp walls. A Buddhist couple in Houston requested the Vietnamese Buddhist priest from Fort Chaffee to conduct their marriage ceremony.[37]

Knowing that refugees would not live in the camps indefinitely, the chaplains at Fort Chaffee worked with a network of religious and community leaders to smooth refugees' transition to the outside world and to establish Buddhist communities for refugees beyond the camp. This network explored the possibility of supporting "an American-Vietnamese Buddhist congregation," perhaps with Tinh Tu serving a permanent post in Houston after the camp at Fort Chaffee closed.[38] The Vietnamese clergy at Fort Chaffee also provided lists of "available Churches and Pagodas" in the cities where the refugees were being resettled. They acknowledged that there are "not too many Buddhist Monks in America as yet," but they offered Vietnamese Buddhist refugees a note of encouragement. "There are already established Buddhist Temples and Churches or organizations who will help you even though they are not Vietnamese," they said. The Vietnamese Buddhist chaplaincy also offered to assist the refugees throughout their transition.[39]

All of these projects may have been rooted in a principled commitment to religious freedom, but there was a very practical reason for supporting Vietnamese religious communities and hiring Vietnamese Buddhist leaders: resettlement officials wanted to alleviate refugees' concerns and facilitate their movement out of the camps. Buddhist refugees were very concerned about being able to remain Buddhist if they were resettled by Christian churches in the United States. The Fort Chaffee chaplains observed that one of the primary concerns of Vietnamese refugees was "the fear of not being able to worship their chosen faith, and the fear of overbearing sponsors."[40] Counselors at Fort Chaffee found that, time and again, anxious refugees asked about "freedom of their religions while living with or being assisted by their sponsors."[41] Indeed, refugees' "fear of sponsors ultimately using pressure to convert refugees from their religious position to that of sponsors" was one reason why Vietnamese Buddhists did not embrace sponsorship and leave the camp as quickly as resettlement officials would have liked. The Task Force chaplains, especially the Vietnamese clergy, thus played a critical role in assuaging refugees' fears. Their objective was to "guide and counsel the refugees wherever and whenever is possible to build and sustain confidence among refugees involved." They played a critical part in "reducing Vietnamese fear of proselytizing" and "dispelling this common fear." The Task Force chaplains considered it their responsibility "to tell the story of the 'religious freedom' in America," especially since "Vietnamese people have a very high regard for their religious leaders."[42]

After they left the camps, refugees were in the care of the voluntary agencies and sponsoring congregations, which strived to meet the religious needs of Vietnamese Buddhists. The voluntary agencies produced cultural orientation materials to educate church sponsors about Vietnamese culture and religion. In addition, voluntary agencies and congregations organized efforts to connect Vietnamese refugees with local Buddhist leaders and organizations. For example, reporting on Vietnamese resettlement in a congressional hearing in 1975, the Lutheran Immigration and Refugee Service (LIRS) shared that "two congregations in Oregon have arranged for a Buddhist monk to visit their families." (LIRS noted that the interreligious interaction was a "great experience" for the church sponsors because it taught them that "there are more people in the world than 'blond Lutherans.'")[43] Cambodian Buddhist refugees also received religious support from the Christian churches that sponsored them.[44]

To be sure, sponsorship by Christian churches did cause some Vietnamese Buddhists to start attending Christian churches. For example, in a "cultural guidebook" it created for the public, the Minnesota Refugee Resettlement Office noted that "the lack of Buddhist pagodas in the United States is a problem for refugees" and that "a number of them have followed their American sponsors to church on Sunday." However, in the view of the guidebook's author, the refugees were comforted "by the fact that they have a religion to worship despite the discrepancies between Buddhism and Catholicism."[45] Similarly, the *Wall Street Journal* reported that the Church of the Brethren in Lancaster, Pennsylvania, had sponsored a Vietnamese Buddhist family and that the Buddhist family attended the local church. "They're Buddhist, but that doesn't make any difference to us," a congregation member told the reporter. "And it doesn't make any difference to them."[46] It is possible that it did not actually make any difference to the Vietnamese family and that they, like some Hmong refugees, were happy to participate in the worship services of their Christian sponsors, perhaps out of genuine interest or gratitude. Yet it is also possible that these Vietnamese Buddhist refugees felt coerced into attending church, were unhappy about doing so, and did not see Buddhism and Christianity as interchangeable religions in the same way that sponsors and government officials did. As in so many situations, we do not know because the news story and the guidebook focused on the perspective of the government and religious institutions in charge of resettlement, not on the perspective of refugees themselves.

When we do have the opportunity to hear refugees' voices, we can hear at least a little uncertainty about how they navigated American religious politics. The *New York Times* reported on the resettlement experiences of the Hoanh family, who was accidentally assigned two sponsors, a Jewish family and a Christian and Missionary Alliance group. The newspaper described how the three sons of the Buddhist Hoanh family had learned to bow their heads and conclude their mealtime grace with a pronouncement of "amen." This action caused lively debate between the Hoanhs' two sponsors, which the *Times* detailed:

> "What they need is a sense of self-sufficiency," Mr. Becker [the Jewish sponsor] said, "not passive surrender."
>
> The other sponsor is pleased.
>
> "We believe," said the woman [the Christian sponsor] at the center, "they are learning to love the Lord."
>
> Mr. Hoanh is confused.
>
> "There is so much I do not understand," he said.[47]

There was indeed much that Mr. Hoanh did not understand, and this is the most important point. One of the most bewildering religious tasks that Southeast Asian refugees faced in the United States was learning to move through a different type of multireligious society. Like their sponsors, they, too, had to learn to put religious pluralism into practice. And while there was much that they did not understand, it is worth considering what Mr. Hoanh and his two sponsors probably did understand. Mr. Hoanh knew that the practice of bowing heads and saying "amen" was meaningful to his Christian sponsors. Moreover, the Christian woman knew that the Hoanh family was Buddhist, and she was delighted by the small signs of missionary success. Finally, Mr. Becker, who described himself and his family as "the token Jews," knew that the Hoanhs were non-Christian religious minorities like himself. He probably knew that there were prohibitions on proselytizing, and he was perhaps uncomfortable with the Christian sponsors' eagerness to teach the Hoanh family about Christianity. What all three participants in this interaction had in common was that they each recognized, in their own ways, the reality of religious difference among them, and they engaged in their difference through the shared knowledge that each had a religion. Having a different religion meant that the Hoanh family still had uncomfortable experiences. However, it ultimately set them up for a different interaction than those experienced by Hmong refugees. One wonders how the Hoanhs' Christian and Jewish sponsors would have responded if the Hoanh family had been Hmong and seemingly religion-less, with a set of beliefs and rituals viewed as primitive or demonic, rather than a legitimate religion.

Like Mr. Hoanh, Hmong refugees found that there was so much they did not know or understand in America, but they at least knew this: they needed to survive, and in order to survive, they needed to adapt. Resettlement officials like John Finck were not sure if the Hmong could do it. "Whether they make it or not is anybody's guess," he told the *Wall Street Journal*.[48] But they adapted and survived, including in their spiritual lives. Eager to maintain the well-being of their bodies and souls, they continued to seek harmonious relations with the seen and unseen worlds. In the United States, it was not necessarily clear how they could do that at first. Over time, however, they drew on an ever-widening array of spiritual and religious resources, including the Christianity of their sponsors and the rituals of their ancestors, in order to create a new American way for themselves. Throughout this process, they were often on the move. As Young Tao described it, Hmong people have long been "strangers and exiles" who have a long history of migration marked by suffering and loss. But this long history of migration also involved adaptation, resilience, and survival.

A Hmong legend tells the story of Siv Yis, the father of all Hmong shamans, and his encounter with nine evil spirit brothers. The evil spirit brothers ambushed Siv Yis while he was walking home one evening and challenged him to a fight. The clever and courageous Siv Yis accepted. The oldest of the evil spirit brothers, believing that he could easily conquer the clever shaman, transformed into a raging wild water buffalo with ferocious horns and fangs. Siv Yis, however, transformed into a brutish beast, and the two struggled fiercely for some time, until the other eight evil spirits became water buffalo, intending to aid their older brother. Realizing that he could not defeat all nine alone, Siv Yis changed into a human being and sliced the spirits to pieces with his magic saber. But when he saw that the nine evil spirit brothers could easily pull themselves together again, Siv Yis turned into an airy wisp of cloud that drifted high into the refuge of the sky. The evil brothers, determined to catch Siv Yis, transformed into a mighty gust of wind that blew the cloud around, sending Siv Yis tumbling topsy-turvy toward the burning sun. So Siv Yis changed into a drop of water, hoping to plunge to the earth and disappear into the dew. And when one of the evil brothers turned into a treetop leaf to capture him, Siv Yis became a long-legged deer that trampled on the leaf and galloped swiftly away to the safety of the forest, leaving the evil spirit brothers behind, defeated in the dust.[49]

Like the famous shaman Siv Yis, Hmong refugees have survived several decades of war through flight and self-transformation. Resilient and responsive to changing circumstances, they have found that religious change—especially the adoption of Christianity and the transformation of traditional Hmong beliefs and practices—has achieved many aims, including the security of home and health and the vitality of families and communities. Yet these religious changes arose not only from Hmong people's will for survival; they have been due in equal measure to external circumstances to which Hmong people have creatively responded. Like Siv Yis, who transformed into a cloud wisp and a raindrop in response to the transformations of the evil spirit brothers, Hmong refugees have survived through self-reinvention and dynamic interaction with the changing world around them. For many Hmong people, to follow the new way has meant to become Christian, and yet that has not been the only way that Hmong people have changed in order to stay alive. There are, indeed, many ways.

Abbreviations

ACNS	American Council for Nationalities Service
AFDC	Aid to Families with Dependent Children
ARC	American Refugee Committee
BGC	Billy Graham Center
CCSDPT	Committee for the Coordination of Services to Displaced Persons in Thailand
CMA	Christian and Missionary Alliance
COWE	Consultation on World Evangelization
CWS	Church World Service
DAPC	Dayton Avenue Presbyterian Church
DIRS	Department of Immigration and Refugee Services
DPN	*Dayton Parish News*
ELCA	Evangelical Lutheran Church of America
ESL	English as a Second Language
HAS	Hmong Australia Society
HCC	Hmong Cultural Center
HOHP	Hmong Oral History Project, Minnesota Historical Society
HOHPCU	Hmong Oral History Project, Concordia University
HWATOHP	Hmong Women's Action Team Oral History Project
IHRC	Immigration History Research Center
IIM	International Institute of Minnesota
IRC	International Rescue Committee

JVA	Joint Voluntary Agency
LCUSA	Lutheran Council in the USA
LIRS	Lutheran Immigration and Refugee Service
LSA	Luther Seminary Archive
LVP	Lois Visscher Papers
MDPW	Minnesota Department of Public Welfare
MHS	Minnesota Historical Society
MSRAC	Minnesota State Refugee Advisory Council
PHS	Presbyterian Historical Society
PKYN	Poj Koob Yawm Ntxwv
RPO	Refugee Program Office
RSC	Refugee Studies Center
SUNDS	Sudden Unexplained Nocturnal Death Syndrome
UMN	University of Minnesota
UNHCR	United Nations High Commission on Refugees
USAHEC	US Army Heritage and Education Center
USCC	United States Catholic Conference

Notes

Introduction

1. Hmong Christian Church of God, Folder 27, Box 6, Refugee Studies Center (hereafter RSC), University of Minnesota (hereafter UMN) Records, General / Multiethnic Collection, IHRC2968, Immigration History Research Center (hereafter IHRC), UMN.
2. Abby Budiman, "Hmong in the U.S. Fact Sheet," *Pew Research Center's Social and Demographic Trends Project* (blog), accessed January 20, 2022, https://www.pewresearch.org/social-trends/fact-sheet/asian-americans -hmong-in-the-u-s/.
3. For an overview of Hmong life in Laos and Hmong beliefs, practices, and religious identities, see Gary Yia Lee and Nicholas Tapp, *Culture and Customs of the Hmong* (Santa Barbara, CA: Greenwood Press, 2010).
4. Boxes 21–24 and 51–52, Case Files, International Institute of Minnesota (hereafter IIM) Records, IHRC3257, IHRC, UMN.
5. Chia Youyee Vang, *Hmong America: Reconstructing Community in Diaspora* (Urbana: University of Illinois Press, 2010), 87.
6. "Our Story," Hmongdistrict.org, accessed January 20, 2022, https://www .hmongdistrict.org/our-story.
7. Vang, *Hmong America*, 87.
8. Linda A. Gerdner and Shoua V. Xiong, *Demystifying Hmong Shamanism: Practice and Use* (Golden, CO: Bauu Press, 2015); Doualy Xaykaothao, "To Be Both Midwestern and Hmong," *The Atlantic,* June 3, 2016, https://www.theatlantic.com/politics/archive/2016/06/wausau-wisconsin -southeast-asia-hmong/485291/.

9. Brian Bonner, "Religious Divide," *St. Paul Pioneer Press*, December 17, 1995.

10. David Schimke, "Devils and Shamans," *Twin Cities Reader*, August 21, 1996.

11. Ruth Hammond, "New Faith, Old Belief," *St. Paul Pioneer Press*, September 16, 1984.

12. Kari Lyderson, "Hmong Capital of U.S. Girds for New Influx," *Washington Post*, July 16, 2004.

13. Lao Family Community, Inc., University of Minnesota Center for Urban and Regional Affairs, and Northwest Regional Educational Lab, *The Hmong Resettlement Study, Volume I: Final Report* (Washington, DC: Office of Refugee Resettlement, 1985), 38–40.

14. Bruce Downing et al., *Hmong Resettlement Study Site Report: Minneapolis–St. Paul* (Minneapolis: Southeast Asian Studies Project, Center for Urban and Regional Affairs, University of Minnesota, 1984), 16–18.

15. State Plan for Refugees, FY 81, Program History Files, Records of the Refugee Program Office (hereafter RPO), Minnesota Department of Public Welfare (hereafter MDPW), Minnesota Historical Society (hereafter MHS).

16. Downing et al., *Hmong Resettlement Study Site Report*, 68.

17. Melissa Borja, "Speaking of Spirits: Oral History, Religious Change, and the Seen and Unseen Worlds of Hmong Americans," *Oral History Review* 44, no. 1 (2017): 1–18.

18. Yang Sao Xiong, Nengher N. Vang, and Chia Youyee Vang, "Charting New Paths for Critical Hmong American and Diaspora Studies," *Amerasia Journal* 44, no. 2 (August 1, 2018): xxii–xxiii.

19. Nancy Ammerman, *Studying Lived Religion* (New York: New York University Press, 2021); David Hall, ed., *Lived Religion in America: Toward a History of Practice* (Princeton, NJ: Princeton University Press, 1997).

20. E.g., Lois Ann Lorentzen et al., eds., *Religion at the Corner of Bliss and Nirvana: Politics, Identity, and Faith in New Migrant Communities* (Durham, NC: Duke University Press, 2009); Aihwa Ong, *Buddha Is Hiding: Refugees, Citizenship, the New America* (Berkeley: University of California Press, 2003).

21. E.g., Nancy Ammerman, "Golden Rule Christianity: Lived Religion in the American Mainstream," in Hall, *Lived Religion in America*, 196–216; Courtney Bender, *Heaven's Kitchen: Living Religion at God's Love We Deliver* (Chicago: University of Chicago Press, 2003).

22. Vincent Her, "Hmong Cosmology: Proposed Model, Preliminary Insights," *Hmong Studies Journal* 6 (2005): 1; Daphne Winland, "Christianity and Community: Conversion and Adaptation among Hmong Refugee Women," *Canadian Journal of Sociology* 19, no. 1 (Winter 1994): 24.

23. U.S. Department of State, "Reception and Placement," *United States Department of State* (blog), accessed January 20, 2022, https://www.state.gov/refugee-admissions/reception-and-placement/.

24. William Novak, "Public-Private Governance: A Historical Introduction," in *Government by Contract: Outsourcing and American Democracy*, ed. Jody Freeman and Martha Minow (Cambridge, MA: Harvard University Press, 2009), 23–40; Freeman and Minow, *Government by Contract*.

25. Brian Balogh, *The Associational State: American Governance in the Twentieth Century* (Philadelphia: University of Pennsylvania Press, 2015); Elisabeth Clemens, "Lineages of the Rube Goldberg State: Building and Blurring Public Programs, 1900–1940," in *Rethinking Political Institutions: The Art of the State*, ed. Ian Shapiro, Stephen Skowronek, and Daniel Galvin (New York: New York University Press, 2006), 380–443; Axel Schaefer, *Piety and Public Funding: Evangelicals and the State in Modern America* (Philadelphia: University of Pennsylvania Press, 2012); Brent Cebul and Lily Geismer, eds., *Shaped by the State: Toward a New Political History of the Twentieth Century* (Chicago: University of Chicago Press, 2019).

26. E.g., Dorothy M. Brown and Elizabeth McKeown, *The Poor Belong to Us: Catholic Charities and American Welfare* (Cambridge, MA: Harvard University Press, 1997); Maureen Fitzgerald, *Habits of Compassion: Irish Catholic Nuns and the Origins of New York's Welfare System, 1830–1920* (Urbana: University of Illinois Press, 2006); Alison Collis Greene, *No Depression in Heaven: The Great Depression, the New Deal, and the Transformation of Religion in the Delta* (New York: Oxford University Press, 2017); Schaefer, *Piety and Public Funding*; Beth S. Wenger, *New York Jews and the Great Depression: Uncertain Promise* (New Haven, CT: Yale University Press, 1996).

27. Elisabeth Clemens and Doug Guthrie, *Politics and Partnerships: The Role of Voluntary Agencies in America's Political Past and Present* (Chicago: University of Chicago Press, 2011); Schaefer, *Piety and Public Funding*.

28. E.g., Heather D. Curtis, *Holy Humanitarians: American Evangelicals and Global Aid* (Cambridge, MA: Harvard University Press, 2018); Sara Fieldston, *Raising the World: Child Welfare in the American Century* (Cambridge, MA: Harvard University Press, 2015); Britt Halvorson, *Conversionary Sites: Transforming Medical Aid and Global Christianity from Madagascar to Minnesota* (Chicago: University of Chicago Press, 2018); Hillary Kaell, *Christian Globalism at Home: Child Sponsorship in the United States* (Princeton, NJ: Princeton University Press, 2021); David King, *God's Internationalists: World Vision and the Age of Evangelical Humanitarianism* (Philadelphia: University of Pennsylvania Press, 2019); Arissa H. Oh, *To Save the Children of Korea: The Cold War Origins of International Adoption* (Stanford, CA: Stanford University Press, 2015).

29. Peter Beyer, "Deprivileging Religion in a Post-Westphalian State: Shadow Establishment, Organization, Spirituality and Freedom in Canada," in *Varieties of Religious Establishment*, ed. Winnifred Fallers Sullivan and Lori Beaman (London: Routledge, 2016), 75–91.

30. I developed this point in Melissa Borja, "The Government Alone Cannot Do the Total Job: The Possibilities and Perils of Religious Organizations in Public-Private Refugee Care," in *Shaped by the State: Toward a New Political History of the Twentieth Century*, ed. Brent Cebul, Lily Geismer, and Mason Williams (Chicago: University of Chicago Press, 2019), 261–288. See also Carl Bon Tempo, *Americans at the Gate: The United States and Refugees during the Cold War* (Princeton, NJ: Princeton University Press, 2008); Paul Bramadat, "Don't Ask, Don't Tell: Refugee Settlement and Religion in British Columbia," *Journal of the American Academy of Religion* 82, no. 4

(2014): 907–937; Anastasia Brown and Todd Scribner, "Unfulfilled Promises, Future Possibilities: The Refugee Resettlement System in the United States," *Journal on Migration and Human Security* 2, no. 2 (May 8, 2014): 101–120; Geoffrey Cameron, *Send Them Here: Religion, Politics, and Refugee Resettlement in North America* (Montreal: McGill–Queen's University Press, 2021); Gil Loescher and John Scanlan, *Calculated Kindness: Refugees and America's Half-Open Door, 1945 to the Present* (New York: Free Press, 1986); Laura Madokoro, *Elusive Refuge: Chinese Migrants in the Cold War* (Cambridge, MA: Harvard University Press, 2016); J. Bruce Nichols, *The Uneasy Alliance: Religion, Refugee Work, and U.S. Foreign Policy* (Oxford: Oxford University Press, 1988); Stephen R. Porter, *Benevolent Empire: U.S. Power, Humanitarianism, and the World's Dispossessed* (Philadelphia: University of Pennsylvania Press, 2016); Todd Scribner, "'Not Because They Are Catholic, but Because We Are Catholic': The Bishops' Engagement with the Migration Issue in Twentieth-Century America," *Catholic Historical Review* 101, no. 1 (Winter 2015): 74–99; Schaefer, *Piety and Public Funding;* Norman Zucker and Naomi Zucker, *The Guarded Gate: The Reality of American Refugee Policy* (San Diego, CA: Harcourt Brace Jovanovich, 1987).

31. David North, Lawrence Lewin, and Jennifer Wagner, *Kaleidoscope: The Resettlement of Refugees in the United States by the Voluntary Agencies* (Washington, DC: New TransCentury Foundation, 1982).

32. Helen Fein, *Congregational Sponsors of Indochinese Refugees in the United States, 1979–1981: Helping beyond Borders* (Rutherford, NJ: Fairleigh Dickinson University Press, 1987).

33. In thinking about the conjoined relationship of church and state, I am informed by Johnson, Klassen, and Sullivan's concept of "churchstateness." See Paul Christopher Johnson, Pamela E. Klassen, and Winnifred Fallers Sullivan, *Ekklesia: Three Inquiries in Church and State* (Chicago: University of Chicago Press, 2018).

34. In considering the religiousness of secular situations, I draw on notions of the Protestant secular. See Charles McCrary and Jeffrey Wheatley, "The Protestant Secular in the Study of American Religion: Reappraisal and Suggestions," *Religion* 47, no. 2 (April 3, 2017): 256–276.

35. E.g., Ram A. Cnaan, *The Invisible Caring Hand: American Congregations and the Provision of Welfare* (New York: New York University Press, 2002); E. J. Dionne and Ming Hsu Chen, eds., *Sacred Places, Civic Purposes: Should Government Help Faith-Based Charity?* (Washington, DC: Brookings Institution Press, 2001); Rebecca Sager, *Faith, Politics, and Power: The Politics of Faith-Based Initiatives* (New York: Oxford: Oxford University Press, 2012); Robert Wuthnow, *Saving America? Faith-Based Services and the Future of Civil Society* (Princeton, NJ: Princeton University Press, 2004).

36. Brown and McKeown, *The Poor Belong to Us;* Fitzgerald, *Habits of Compassion;* Wenger, *New York Jews and the Great Depression.*

37. The scholarship about religious pluralism in the United States is vast. For historical perspectives, see William Hutchison, *Religious Pluralism in America: The Contentious History of a Founding Ideal* (New Haven, CT:

Yale University Press, 2003); Martin E. Marty, "Pluralisms," *ANNALS of the American Academy of Political and Social Science* 612, no. 1 (2007): 13; David Mislin, *Saving Faith: Making Religious Pluralism an American Value at the Dawn of the Secular Age* (Ithaca, NY: Cornell University Press, 2015); and Nicholas Pruitt, *Open Hearts, Closed Doors: Immigration Reform and the Waning of Mainline Protestantism* (New York: New York University Press, 2021). For scholarship on religious pluralism in contemporary America, see Thomas Banchoff, ed., *Democracy and the New Religious Pluralism* (Oxford: Oxford University Press, 2007); Courtney Bender and Pamela Klassen, eds., *After Pluralism: Reimagining Religious Engagement* (New York: Columbia University Press, 2010); Charles L. Cohen and Ronald L. Numbers, eds., *Gods in America: Religious Pluralism in the United States* (New York: Oxford University Press, 2013); Diana Eck, *A New Religious America: How a "Christian Country" Has Now Become the World's Most Religiously Diverse Nation* (San Francisco: HarperSanFrancisco, 2001); Stephen Prothero, ed., *A Nation of Religions: The Politics of Pluralism in Multireligious America* (Chapel Hill: University of North Carolina Press, 2006); R. Stephen Warner, *A Church of Our Own: Disestablishment and Diversity in American Religion* (New Brunswick, NJ: Rutgers University Press, 2005); Robert Wuthnow, *America and the Challenges of Religious Diversity* (Princeton, NJ: Princeton University Press, 2005).

38. Bender and Klassen, *After Pluralism*, 2.

39. *Face to Face: The Ministry of Refugee Resettlement,* Lutheran Immigration and Refugee Service Assorted Publications, Lutheran Council in the USA (hereafter LCUSA), Department of Immigration and Refugee Services (hereafter DIRS), LCU 10/1, Archives of the Evangelical Lutheran Church of America (hereafter ELCA), Elk Grove Village, IL.

40. Scribner, "'Not Because They Are Catholic, but Because We Are Catholic.'"

41. Courtney Bender and Jennifer Snow, "From Alleged Buddhists to Unreasonable Hindus: First Amendment Jurisprudence after 1965," in Prothero, *A Nation of Religions*, 181–208; Sarah Barringer Gordon, *The Spirit of the Law: Religious Voices and the Constitution in Modern America* (Cambridge, MA: Belknap Press of Harvard University Press, 2010).

42. Stephanie Nawyn, "Faith, Ethnicity, and Culture in Refugee Resettlement," *American Behavioral Scientist* 49, no. 11 (July 1, 2006): 1509–1527; Bramadat, "Don't Ask, Don't Tell."

43. Shari Rabin, *Jews on the Frontier: Religion and Mobility in Nineteenth-Century America* (New York: New York University Press, 2017), 7.

44. For examples of scholarship about the relationship between religion, becoming American, and civic engagement, see Carolyn Chen, *Getting Saved in America: Taiwanese Immigration and Religious Experience* (Princeton, NJ: Princeton University Press, 2008); Fenggang Yang, *Chinese Christians in America: Conversion, Assimilation, and Adhesive Identities* (University Park: Pennsylvania State University Press, 1999); and Alyshia Galvez, *Guadalupe in New York: Devotion and the Struggle for Citizenship Rights among Mexican Immigrants* (New York: New York University Press, 2009).

45. E.g., Prema Kurien, *A Place at the Multicultural Table: The Development of an American Hinduism* (New Brunswick, NJ: Rutgers University Press, 2007).

46. Robert Orsi, *The Madonna of 115th Street: Faith and Community in Italian Harlem, 1880–1950*, 2nd ed. (New Haven, CT: Yale University Press, 2002), 150.

47. Thomas Tweed, *Crossing and Dwelling: A Theory of Religion* (Cambridge, MA: Harvard University Press, 2006).

48. Sucheng Chan, *Survivors: Cambodian Refugees in the United States* (Urbana: University of Illinois Press, 2004); David W. Haines, ed., *Refugees as Immigrants: Cambodians, Laotians, and Vietnamese in America* (Totowa, NJ: Rowman & Littlefield, 1989); Jeremy Hein, *Ethnic Origins: The Adaptation of Cambodian and Hmong Refugees in Four American Cities* (New York: Russell Sage Foundation, 2006); Vincent Her and Mary Louise Buley-Meissner, eds., *Hmong and American: From Refugees to Citizens* (Saint Paul: Minnesota Historical Society Press, 2012); Nazli Kibria, *Family Tightrope: The Changing Lives of Vietnamese Americans* (Princeton, NJ: Princeton University Press, 1995); Mark Edward Pfeifer, Monica Chiu, and Kou Yang, eds., *Diversity in Diaspora: Hmong Americans in the Twenty-First Century* (Honolulu: University of Hawaiʻi Press, 2013); Yang Sao Xiong, *Immigrant Agency: Hmong American Movements and the Politics of Racialized Representation* (New Brunswick, NJ: Rutgers University Press, 2022); Carolyn Wong, *Voting Together: Intergenerational Politics and Civic Engagement among Hmong Americans* (Stanford, CA: Stanford University Press, 2017).

49. E.g., Yen Le Espiritu, *Body Counts: The Vietnam War and Militarized Refugees* (Berkeley: University of California Press, 2014); Madokoro, *Elusive Refuge;* Mimi Thi Nguyen, *The Gift of Freedom: War, Debt, and Other Refugee Passages* (Durham, NC: Duke University Press, 2012); Eric Tang, *Unsettled: Cambodian Refugees in the New York City Hyperghetto* (Philadelphia: Temple University Press, 2015); Ma Vang, *History on the Run: Secrecy, Fugitivity, and Hmong Refugee Epistemologies* (Durham, NC: Duke University Press, 2021).

50. Vang, *History on the Run.*

51. For examples of historical immigration scholarship that explores how religion shapes attitudes in support of immigration exclusion, see Hidetaka Hirota, *Expelling the Poor: Atlantic Seaboard States and the Nineteenth-Century Origins of American Immigration Policy* (Oxford: Oxford University Press, 2017); Khyati Joshi, *White Christian Privilege: The Illusion of Religious Equality in America* (New York: New York University Press, 2020); and Beth Lew-Williams, *The Chinese Must Go: Violence, Exclusion, and the Making of the Alien in America* (Cambridge, MA: Harvard University Press, 2018). For examples of scholarship about how religion is a site of immigration advocacy for more inclusive policies, see Galvez, *Guadalupe in New York;* and Grace Yukich, *One Family under God: Immigration Politics and Progressive Religion in America* (New York: Oxford University Press, 2013).

52. E.g., Madeline Yuan-yin Hsu, *Dreaming of Gold, Dreaming of Home: Transnationalism and Migration between the United States and South China, 1882–1943* (Stanford, CA: Stanford University Press, 2000); Aihwa Ong, *Flexible Citizenship: The Cultural Logics of Transnationality* (Durham, NC: Duke University Press, 1999).

53. E.g., Orsi, *The Madonna of 115th Street.*

54. E.g., Eiichiro Azuma, *Between Two Empires: Race, History, and Transnationalism in Japanese America* (Oxford: Oxford University Press, 2005); Linda G. Basch, Nina Glick Schiller, and Cristina Szanton Blanc, *Nations Unbound: Transnational Projects, Postcolonial Predicaments, and Deterritorialized Nation-States* (Langhorne, PA: Gordon and Breach, 1994); Peggy Levitt, *The Transnational Villagers* (Berkeley: University of California Press, 2001); Ong, *Flexible Citizenship.*

55. Ong, *Flexible Citizenship.*

56. Catherine Albanese, "Exchanging Selves, Exchanging Souls: Contact, Combination, and American Religious History," in *Retelling U.S. Religious History,* ed. Thomas Tweed (Berkeley: University of California Press, 1997). I draw on scholarship on Native American religion to make sense of religious change in the context of threats to survival. See Linford Fisher, *The Indian Great Awakening: Religion and the Shaping of Native Cultures in Early America* (New York: Oxford University Press, 2014); Jennifer Graber, *The Gods of Indian Country: Religion and the Struggle for the American West* (New York: Oxford University Press, 2018).

57. Lee and Tapp, *Culture and Customs of the Hmong,* 38.

58. Anne Fadiman, *The Spirit Catches You and You Fall Down: A Hmong Child, Her American Doctors, and the Collision of Two Cultures* (New York: Farrar, Straus and Giroux, 1998).

59. Glenn Hendricks, Bruce Downing, and Amos Deinard, eds., *The Hmong in Transition* (New York: Center for Migration Studies and the Southeast Asian Refugee Studies Project of the University of Minnesota, 1986); Bruce Downing and Douglas Olney, eds., *The Hmong in the West: Observations and Reports: Papers of the 1981 Hmong Research Conference, University of Minnesota* (Minneapolis: Southeast Asian Refugee Studies Project, Center for Urban and Regional Affairs, University of Minnesota, 1982).

60. Christine Desan, "A Change of Faith for Hmong Refugees," *Cultural Survival Quarterly* 7 (1983): 45–48.

61. Her and Buley-Meissner, *Hmong and American;* Pfeifer, Chiu, and Yang, *Diversity in Diaspora;* Vang, *Hmong America.* For an overview of the scholarship on Hmong studies, see Xiong, Vang, and Vang, "Charting New Paths for Critical Hmong American and Diaspora Studies."

62. Siu-Woo Cheung, "Millenarianism, Christian Movements, and Ethnic Change among the Miao in Southwest China," in *Cultural Encounters on China's Ethnic Frontiers,* ed. Stevan Harrell (Seattle: University of Washington Press, 1997), 217–247; Alison Lewis, "The Western Protestant Missionaries and the Miao in Yunnan and Guizhou, Southwest China," in *Turbulent Times and Enduring Peoples: Mountain Minorities in the Southeast Asian Massif,* ed. Jean Michaud (Richmond, UK: Curzon, 2000), 79–98;

Tam T. T. Ngo, *The New Way: Protestantism and the Hmong in Vietnam* (Seattle: University of Washington Press, 2016); Nicholas Tapp, "The Impact of Missionary Christianity upon Marginalized Ethnic Minorities: The Case of the Hmong," *Journal of Southeast Asian Studies* 20, no. 1 (March 1989): 70–95; Vang, *Hmong America;* Winland, "Christianity and Community"; Daphne Winland, "Revisiting a Case Study of Hmong Refugees and Ontario Mennonites," *Journal of Mennonite History* 24 (2006): 169–176.

63. Not only is conversion undertaken for different reasons, but the idea of conversion has changed over time. See Lincoln A. Mullen, *The Chance of Salvation: A History of Conversion in America* (Cambridge, MA: Harvard University Press, 2017).

64. Xiong, Vang, and Vang, "Charting New Paths for Critical Hmong American and Diaspora Studies," xxi.

65. Jason Ananda Josephson, *The Invention of Religion in Japan* (Chicago: University of Chicago Press, 2012); Severin Fowles, *An Archaeology of Doings: Secularism and the Study of Pueblo Religion* (Santa Fe, NM: School for Advanced Research Press, 2013); Tomoko Masuzawa, *The Invention of World Religions: Or, How European Universalism Was Preserved in the Language of Pluralism* (Chicago: University of Chicago Press, 2005); Tisa Wenger, *We Have a Religion: The 1920s Pueblo Indian Dance Controversy and American Religious Freedom* (Chapel Hill: University of North Carolina Press, 2009).

66. Winnifred Fallers Sullivan, *The Impossibility of Religious Freedom* (Princeton, NJ: Princeton University Press, 2005), 8.

67. Bender and Snow, "From Alleged Buddhists to Unreasonable Hindus."

68. Gregory Johnson, *Sacred Claims: Repatriation and Living Tradition* (Charlottesville: University of Virginia Press, 2007); Michael David McNally, *Defend the Sacred: Native American Religious Freedom beyond the First Amendment* (Princeton, NJ: Princeton University Press, 2020); Wenger, *We Have a Religion.*

69. Russell Jeung, Seanan S. Fong, and Helen Jin Kim, *Family Sacrifices: The Worldviews and Ethics of Chinese Americans* (New York: Oxford University Press, 2019).

70. Jonathan Z. Smith, "Religion, Religions, Religious," in *Critical Terms for Religious Studies,* ed. Mark Taylor (Chicago: University of Chicago Press, 1998), 269–284.

71. Vincent K. Her, "Reframing Hmong Religion," *Amerasia Journal* 44, no. 2 (August 1, 2018): 31.

72. Nicholas Tapp, "Hmong Religion," *Asian Folklore Studies* 48, no. 1 (1989): 59–94; Timothy Dunnigan, "Processes of Identity Maintenance in Hmong Society," in Hendricks, Downing, and Deinard, *The Hmong in Transition,* 41–53; Her, "Hmong Cosmology"; George Scott, "The Lao Hmong Refugees in San Diego: Their Religious Transformation and Its Implications for Geertz's Thesis," *Ethnic Studies Report* 5, no. 2 (1987): 32–46; Winland, "Christianity and Community."

73. Jacque Lemoine, "Shamanism in the Context of Hmong Resettlement," in Hendricks, Downing, and Deinard, *The Hmong in Transition,* 346.

74. Her, "Hmong Cosmology"; Lee and Tapp, *Culture and Customs of the Hmong*, 23–45. Her has even proposed using the term "Siv Yigism." See Her, "Reframing Hmong Religion," 38.

75. Sullivan, *The Impossibility of Religious Freedom*, 1.

76. Her, "Reframing Hmong Religion," 32.

77. Nao Xiong and Yang Sao Xiong, "A Critique of Timothy Vang's Hmong Religious Conversion and Resistance Study," *Hmong Studies Journal* 9 (2008): 1–21.

1. The Origins of Religious Unsettlement

1. Boxes 21–24 and 51–52, Case Files, IIM Records, IHRC3257, IHRC, UMN.

2. Nao Thao, interview by the author, September 11, 2012, Saint Paul, MN.

3. Boxes 2124 and 5152, Case Files, IIM Records, IHRC3257, IHRC, UMN. Other scholars have discussed how encounters with bureaucracy forced people into foreign, Christian-centric religious categories that do not work. See Tisa Wenger, *We Have a Religion: The 1920s Pueblo Indian Dance Controversy and American Religious Freedom* (Chapel Hill: University of North Carolina Press, 2009).

4. David Chidester, *Savage Systems: Colonialism and Comparative Religion in Southern Africa* (Charlottesville: University Press of Virginia, 1996).

5. For scholarship on the domestic impact of overseas missionaries, see David A. Hollinger, *Protestants Abroad: How Missionaries Tried to Change the World but Changed America* (Princeton, NJ: Princeton University Press, 2017).

6. Mai Na M. Lee, *Dreams of the Hmong Kingdom: The Quest for Legitimation in French Indochina, 1850–1960* (Madison: University of Wisconsin Press, 2015); James Scott, *The Art of Not Being Governed: An Anarchist History of Upland Southeast Asia* (New Haven, CT: Yale University Press, 2009); Ma Vang, *History on the Run: Secrecy, Fugitivity, and Hmong Refugee Epistemologies* (Durham, NC: Duke University Press, 2021).

7. See Shone Yang's account in Lillian Faderman with Ghia Xiong, "Shamanism, Christianity, and Modern Medicine," in *I Begin My Life All Over: The Hmong and the American Immigrant Experience* (Boston: Beacon Press, 1999), 116. For overviews of traditional Hmong beliefs and practices, see Nusit Chindarsi, *The Religion of the Hmong Njua* (Bangkok: Siam Society, 1976); Gary Yia Lee and Nicholas Tapp, *Culture and Customs of the Hmong* (Santa Barbara, CA: Greenwood Press, 2010); and Nicholas Tapp, "Hmong Religion," *Asian Folklore Studies* 48, no. 1 (1989): 59–94.

8. For a discussion of "sacred presence," see Robert Orsi, *History and Presence* (Cambridge, MA: Harvard University Press, 2016). For a discussion of Hmong beliefs about the spirit world, see Lee and Tapp, *Culture and Customs of the Hmong*; Paja Thao and Dwight Conquergood, *I Am a Shaman: A Hmong Life Story with Ethnographic Commentary*, trans. Xa Thao, Southeast Asian Refugee Studies Occasional Papers, no. 8 (Minneapolis: Southeast Asian Refugee Studies Project, Center for Urban and Regional Affairs, University of Minnesota, 1989), 45.

9. Mai Neng Moua, *The Bride Price: A Hmong Wedding Story* (Saint Paul: Minnesota Historical Society Press, 2017), 107.

10. Dia Cha, interview by Paul Hillmer, October 5, 2005, Hmong Oral History Project, Concordia University (hereafter HOHPCU).

11. Lee and Tapp, *Culture and Customs of the Hmong*, 36.

12. Vincent Her, "Hmong Cosmology: Proposed Model, Preliminary Insights," *Hmong Studies Journal* 6 (2005): 2.

13. Other scholars have argued that the idea that religion should be efficacious is present in other Asian contexts. See Ian Reader and George J. Tanabe Jr., *Practically Religious: Worldly Benefits and the Common Religion of Japan* (Honolulu: University of Hawai'i Press, 1998).

14. Her, "Hmong Cosmology," 2–3; Lee and Tapp, *Culture and Customs of the Hmong,* 23, 35–38; Tapp, "Hmong Religion," 65–71; Thao and Conquergood, *I Am a Shaman,* 45.

15. Lee and Tapp, *Culture and Customs of the Hmong*, 24–30. See also Dia Cha, *Hmong American Concepts of Health, Healing, and Conventional Medicine* (New York: Routledge, 2003); Dia Cha, interview; Nusit Chindarsi, "Hmong Shamanism," in *Highlanders of Thailand,* ed. John McKinnon and Wanat Bhruksasri (Kuala Lumpur: Oxford University Press, 1983); Linda A. Gerdner and Shoua V. Xiong, *Demystifying Hmong Shamanism: Practice and Use* (Golden, CO: Bauu Press, 2015); Jacques Lemoine, "The Constitution of a Hmong Shaman's Powers of Healing and Folk Culture," *Shaman* 4, no. 1–2 (1996): 144–165; Jean Mottin, "A Hmong Shaman's Seance," *Asian Folklore Studies* 43, no. 1 (1984): 99–108; Tapp, "Hmong Religion," 71–80.

16. Thao and Conquergood, *I Am a Shaman,* 5.

17. Dia Cha, interview.

18. Mai Lee, interview by Mai Neng Vang, May 1, 2005, HOHPCU.

19. Boua Neng Moua, "Boua Neng Moua's Story," in *Hmong Means Free: Life in Laos and America,* ed. Sucheng Chan (Philadelphia: Temple University Press, 1994), 211.

20. Keith Vang, interview by Paul Hillmer, April 1, 2005, HOHPCU.

21. Chong Thao Xiong, "The Life of Chong Thao Xiong," in *Hmong Lives: From Laos to La Crosse,* ed. Wendy Mattison, Laotou Lo, and Thomas Scarseth (La Crosse, WI: The Pump House, 1994), 111. A *qeej* is a mouth organ of bamboo reed pipes often used in Hmong rituals.

22. Song Lee, "The Challenges and Contributions of Hmong American Elders: A Personal and Professional Perspective," in *Hmong and American: From Refugees to Citizens,* ed. Vincent Her and Mary Louise Buley-Meissner (Saint Paul: Minnesota Historical Society Press, 2012), 135–136.

23. Xiong, "The Life of Chong Thao Xiong," 101.

24. Xiong, "The Life of Chong Thao Xiong," 111; Nao Xue Vang, "The Life of Nao Xue Vang," in Mattison, Lo, and Scarseth, *Hmong Lives,* 29.

25. Moua, *The Bride Price.*

26. Vang, "The Life of Nao Xue Vang," 29.

27. On this point, I borrow from Laliberté's attention to religious establishment in Asian contexts. See André Laliberté, "The Five Worlds of Religious Establishment in Taiwan," in *Varieties of Religious Establishment,* ed.

Winnifred Fallers Sullivan and Lori Beaman (London: Routledge, 2016), 147–162.

28. Nao Thao, interview.

29. Siu-Woo Cheung, "Millenarianism, Christian Movements, and Ethnic Change among the Miao in Southwest China," in *Cultural Encounters on China's Ethnic Frontiers,* ed. Stevan Harrell (Seattle: University of Washington Press, 1997), 217–247; Lee and Tapp, *Culture and Customs of the Hmong;* Alison Lewis, "The Western Protestant Missionaries and the Miao in Yunnan and Guizhou, Southwest China," in *Turbulent Times and Enduring Peoples: Mountain Minorities in the Southeast Asian Massif,* ed. Jean Michaud (Richmond, UK: Curzon, 2000), 79–98; Tam T. T. Ngo, *The New Way: Protestantism and the Hmong in Vietnam* (Seattle: University of Washington Press, 2016); Tapp, "Hmong Religion."

30. Timothy Vang, "Coming a Full Circle: Historical Analysis of the Hmong Church Growth 1950–1998" (DMin diss., Fuller Theological Seminary, 1998).

31. For a discussion of the idea of world religions, see Tomoko Masuzawa, *The Invention of World Religions: Or, How European Universalism Was Preserved in the Language of Pluralism* (Chicago: University of Chicago Press, 2005). For a discussion of the relationship between the study of religion and imperialism, see Chidester, *Savage Systems;* David Chidester, *Empire of Religion: Imperialism and Comparative Religion* (Chicago: University of Chicago Press, 2014).

32. Yves Bertrais, ed., *Kab Ke Pam Tuag: Txheej Txheem (Les Funérailles, Ordonnance de La Cérémonie)* (Saint Paul, MN: Association Communauté Hmong, Hmong Pastoral Center, 1986); Hawj Tsav Xyooj and Yves Bertrais, eds., *Dab Neeg, Phau Ob (Contes et Légendes),* vol. 2 (Javouhey, French Guiana: Association Communauté Hmong, 1987).

33. Malcolm Maurice Sawyer, interview by Robert Shuster, November 14, 1983, Wheaton, IL, Collection 256, Archives of the Billy Graham Center (hereafter BGC).

34. Ted Andrianoff and Ruth Andrianoff, *Chosen by the God of Grace: The Story of the Birth of the Hmong Church through the Eyes of Ted and Ruth Andrianoff* (Camp Hill, PA: Christian Publications, 2000), 28.

35. Dia Cha, interview.

36. Andrianoff and Andrianoff, *Chosen by the God of Grace,* 6–7, 20.

37. Malcolm Maurice Sawyer, interview.

38. Andrianoff and Andrianoff, *Chosen by the God of Grace,* 10.

39. Daniel Chidester, "The Church of Baseball, the Fetish of Coca-Cola, and the Potlatch of Rock 'n' Roll: Theoretical Models for the Study of Religion in American Popular Culture," *Journal of the American Academy of Religion* 64, no. 4 (1996): 743–765.

40. For a discussion of Western missionaries and fetishes, see Chidester, *Savage Systems,* 12–13; Webb Keane, *Christian Moderns: Freedom and Fetish in the Mission Encounter* (Berkeley: University of California Press, 2007).

41. Chidester, *Empire of Religion;* Masuzawa, *The Invention of World Religions;* Wenger, *We Have a Religion.*

42. Helen Irvin Sawyer, interview by Stephanie Dixon, November 30, 1983, Wheaton, IL, Collection 256, Archives of the BGC.

43. Helen Irvin Sawyer, interview by Stephanie Dixon, November 22, 1983, Wheaton, IL, Collection 256, Archives of the BGC.

44. Helen Irvin Sawyer, interview, November 30, 1983.

45. Andrianoff and Andrianoff, *Chosen by the God of Grace*, 7.

46. Malcolm Maurice Sawyer, interview.

47. Helen Irvin Sawyer, interview, November 30, 1983.

48. Yong Kay Moua and Houa Vue Moua, interview by the author, September 12, 2012, Saint Paul, MN.

49. Wang Her, interview by Peter Chou Vang, June 1, 20018, HOHPCU.

50. Gary Yia Lee, interview by Paul Hillmer, December 30, 2005, HOHPCU.

51. Tapp, "The Impact of Missionary Christianity upon Marginalized Ethnic Minorities," 70–77; Lewis, "The Western Protestant Missionaries," 86–87.

52. Rev. Timothy Vang, interview by the author, September 12, 2012, Maplewood, MN.

53. Shong Yer Yang and Soua Lo, interview by the author, interpreted by Maile Vue, August 6, 2012, Saint Paul, MN.

54. Bee Yang, interview by the author, August 2, 2012, Saint Paul, MN. See also Kim Yang, interview by Mai Neng Moua, December 17, 1999, Hmong Women's Action Team Oral History Project (hereafter HWATOHP), MHS.

55. Wang Her, interview.

56. You Vang Yang, interview by May Hang, January 18, 2000, HWATOHP, MHS.

57. Joua Tsu Thao, interview by the author, September 19, 2012, Roseville, MN.

58. Joua Tsu Thao, interview.

59. Some Hmong people believed the United States had made a promise of independence if they defeated the Communists and sanctuary if they did not. See Chia Youyee Vang, *Hmong America: Reconstructing Community in Diaspora* (Urbana: University of Illinois Press, 2010), 26.

60. Vang, *Hmong America*, 23–43. For histories of the Hmong and the Secret War, see Sucheng Chan, "The Hmong Experience in Asia and the United States," in Chan, *Hmong Means Free*, 1–60; Jane Hamilton-Merritt, *Tragic Mountains: The Hmong, the Americans, and the Secret Wars for Laos, 1942–1992* (Bloomington: Indiana University Press, 1993); Paul Hillmer, *A People's History of the Hmong* (Saint Paul: Minnesota Historical Society Press, 2009); Seth Jacobs, *The Universe Unraveling: American Foreign Policy in Cold War Laos* (Ithaca, NY: Cornell University Press, 2012); Joshua Kurlantzick, *A Great Place to Have a War: America in Laos and the Birth of a Military CIA* (New York: Simon & Schuster, 2017); Gayle Morrison, *Sky Is Falling: An Oral History of the CIA's Evacuation of the Hmong from Laos* (Jefferson, NC: McFarland, 1998); Keith Quincy, *Hmong: History of a People* (Cheney: Eastern Washington University Press,

1988); and Keith Quincy, *Harvesting Pa Chay's Wheat: The Hmong and America's Secret War in Laos* (Spokane: Eastern Washington University Press, 2000).

61. Tong Pao Xiong, "The Life of Tong Pao Xiong," in Mattison, Lo, and Scarseth, *Hmong Lives*, 159.

62. See Nao Kao Xiong's account in Faderman with Xiong, "Shamanism, Christianity, and Modern Medicine," in *I Begin My Life All Over*, 109.

63. Pang Yang, "Pang Yang's Story," in Chan, *Hmong Means Free*, 218; Chou Nou Tcha, "Chou Nou Tcha's Story," in Chan, *Hmong Means Free*, 176.

64. Yang, "Pang Yang's Story," 219.

65. Shoua Vang and Nhia Vang, "The Sacred Drum," in *New Americans: An Oral History, Immigrants and Refugees in the U.S. Today*, ed. Al Santoli (New York: Viking Press, 1988), 310.

66. Vang, *History on the Run*.

67. See Doua Vang's account in Faderman with Xiong, "The Village," in *I Begin My Life All Over*, 28.

68. Neng Xiong, interview by the author, interpreted by Maile Vue, August 3, 2012, Minneapolis, MN.

69. Lynellyn Long, *Ban Vinai, the Refugee Camp* (New York: Columbia University Press, 1993), 39–53.

70. Jean Carlin, "Report of a Medical Consultant's Observations and Evaluations of and Recommendations for Indochinese (Southeast Asian) Refugee Camps," August 29–September 18, 1979, Orientation Manual, Box 4, American Refugee Committee (hereafter ARC) Records, MHS.

71. Melissa Borja and Jacob Gibson, "Internationalism with Evangelical Characteristics: The Case of Evangelical Responses to Southeast Asian Refugees," *Review of Faith and International Affairs* 17, no. 3 (2019): 80–93. For other scholarship on Christian missionary humanitarian work, see Heather D. Curtis, *Holy Humanitarians: American Evangelicals and Global Aid* (Cambridge, MA: Harvard University Press, 2018); Britt Halvorson, *Conversionary Sites: Transforming Medical Aid and Global Christianity from Madagascar to Minnesota* (Chicago: University of Chicago Press, 2018); David King, *God's Internationalists: World Vision and the Age of Evangelical Humanitarianism* (Philadelphia: University of Pennsylvania Press, 2019); Melani McAlister, *The Kingdom of God Has No Borders: A Global History of American Evangelicals* (New York: Oxford University Press, 2018); and Sarah Ruble, *The Gospel of Freedom and Power: Protestant Missionaries in American Culture after World War II* (Chapel Hill: University of North Carolina Press, 2012).

72. Mike Carroll, "Ban Vinai—Basic Information," Orientation Manual, Box 4, ARC Records, MHS.

73. The Thailand Report on Refugees: Report of the Consultation on World Evangelization Mini-Consultation on Reaching Refugees, June 16–27, 1980, Vietnam Refugees '75, Box 52, National Association of Evangelicals SC-113, Wheaton College Special Collections, Wheaton, IL.

74. For an overview of World Vision, see King, *God's Internationalists*.

75. "World Vision Foundation of Thailand Guidelines for Staff Assigned to Ban Vinai Displaced Persons Camp, Loei," Orientation Manual, Box 4, ARC Records, MHS.

76. Lois Visscher, Letter, April 1982, Lois Visscher Papers (hereafter LVP), Presbyterian Historical Society (hereafter PHS).

77. Committee for the Coordination of Services to Displaced Persons in Thailand (hereafter CCSDPT), Medical Subcommittee Minutes, May 12, 1983, CCSDPT: Minutes, January 5–July 7, 1983, Box 5, ARC Records, MHS.

78. Lois Visscher, Letter from Loei, Thailand, July 6, 1985, LVP, PHS.

79. Photo album, LVP, PHS.

80. Rudolph Skogerboe, "Ban Vinai Refugee Camp," Ban Vinai: Reports and Other Papers, 1980–1983, Box 5, ARC Records, MHS.

81. William Hutchison, *Errand to the World: American Protestant Thought and Foreign Missions* (Chicago: University of Chicago Press, 1987), 223.

82. Skogerboe, "Ban Vinai Refugee Camp."

83. CCSDPT, Open Session Minutes, June 3, 1983, CCSDPT: Minutes, January 5–July 7, 1983, Box 5, ARC Records, MHS.

84. Summary of Refugee Situation in Thailand, December 1979, February 1980, and October 1981, Box 5, ARC Records, MHS.

85. Ginny Ascensao to the ARC, Post Assignment Report, Ban Vinai: Reports and Other Papers, 1979–1980, Box 5, ARC Records, MHS.

86. CCSDPT, Medical Subcommittee Minutes, August 5, 1992, CCSDPT: Minutes, January 6–December 31, 1982, Box 5, ARC Records, MHS.

87. Shong Yer Yang and Soua Lo, interview.

88. True Xiong, interview by the author, interpreted by Maile Vue, August 9, 2012, Minneapolis, MN.

89. Neng Vang and Paj Ntaub Lis, interview by the author, March 25, 2012, Saint Paul, MN. The names have been changed upon the request of the narrators.

90. Yong Kay Moua and Houa Vue Moua, interview.

91. Cziasarh Neng Yang, interview by the author, September 17, 2012, Saint Paul, MN.

92. Tapp, "The Impact of Missionary Christianity."

93. True Xiong, interview.

94. Kao Kalia Yang, interview by Paul Hillmer, January 18, 2008, HOHPCU.

95. Dennis Grace, interview by Paul Hillmer and Tzianeng Vang, July 25, 2006, HOHPCU.

96. Long, *Ban Vinai, the Refugee Camp,* 59.

97. Lemoine, "Shamanism in the Context of Hmong Resettlement," 346.

98. Thao and Conquergood, *I Am a Shaman,* 68.

99. Ginny Ascensao to the ARC, Post Assignment Report, Ban Vinai: Reports and Other Papers, 1979–1980, Box 5, ARC Records, MHS.

100. Soua Sue Lee, interview by the author, July 2014, Saint Paul, MN.

101. Neng Vang and Paj Ntaub Lis, interview.

102. Nao Thao, interview.

103. Center for Applied Linguistics, *Cultural Orientation Resource Manual,* Vol. 1, 36.3, 46.16, Folders 4–6, Box 35, RSC, General/Multiethnic Collection, IHRC2968, IHRC, UMN.

104. Minnesota Governor State Advisory Council for Refugees, *Thailand Trip Report*, December 1986, State Refugee Advisory Council, 1981–1986, Administrative Files, Records of the RPO, MDPW, MHS.

105. Anne Farris Rosen, "A Brief History of Religion and the U.S. Census," *Pew Research Center* (blog), accessed June 5, 2022, https://www.pewresearch.org /religion/2010/01/26/a-brief-history-of-religion-and-the-u-s-census/. For an overview of the emergence of the principle of "religious privacy" in the postwar period, see Schultz, *Tri-Faith America*, 159–178.

106. In translating these Hmong terms, I relied on Yuepheng Xiong, *English-Hmong/Hmong-English Dictionary* (Saint Paul, MN: Hmongland Publishing, 2006); See also Vincent Her, "Reframing Hmong Religion," *Amerasia Journal* 44, no. 2 (August 1, 2018): 23–41.

107. Boxes 21–24 and 51–52, Case Files, IIM Records, IHRC3257, IHRC, UMN.

108. Shong Yer Yang and Soua Lo, interview.

2. Administering Resettlement

1. Gil Loescher and John Scanlan, *Calculated Kindness: Refugees and America's Half-Open Door, 1945 to the Present* (New York: Free Press, 1986), 130–135; Carl Bon Tempo, *Americans at the Gate: The United States and Refugees during the Cold War* (Princeton, NJ: Princeton University Press, 2008), 152, 172.

2. For an overview of the concept of "tri-faith" America in the second half of the twentieth century, see Kevin Schultz, *Tri-Faith America: How Catholics and Jews Held Postwar America to Its Protestant Promise* (New York: Oxford University Press, 2011).

3. Organizational Files: Correspondence and Miscellanea, 1979–1980, Box 1, ARC Records, MHS.

4. Anastasia Brown and Todd Scribner, "Unfulfilled Promises, Future Possibilities: The Refugee Resettlement System in the United States," *Journal on Migration and Human Security* 2, no. 2 (May 8, 2014): 101–120; Stephen R. Porter, *Benevolent Empire: U.S. Power, Humanitarianism, and the World's Dispossessed* (Philadelphia: University of Pennsylvania Press, 2016).

5. Geoffrey Cameron, *Send Them Here: Religion, Politics, and Refugee Resettlement in North America* (Montreal: McGill–Queen's University Press, 2021); Helen Fein, *Congregational Sponsors of Indochinese Refugees in the United States, 1979–1981: Helping beyond Borders* (Rutherford, NJ: Fairleigh Dickinson University Press, 1987); J. Bruce Nichols, *The Uneasy Alliance: Religion, Refugee Work, and U.S. Foreign Policy* (Oxford: Oxford University Press, 1988); Nicholas T. Pruitt, *Open Hearts, Closed Doors: Immigration Reform and the Waning of Mainline Protestantism* (New York: New York University Press, 2021).

6. Peter Beyer, "Deprivileging Religion in a Post-Westphalian State: Shadow Establishment, Organization, Spirituality and Freedom in Canada," in *Varieties of Religious Establishment*, ed. Winnifred Fallers Sullivan and Lori Beaman (London: Routledge, 2016), 75–91.

7. Bon Tempo, *Americans at the Gate,* 146.

8. Porter, *Benevolent Empire,* 216–217.

9. Bon Tempo, *Americans at the Gate,* 145–146.

10. Jana Lipman, "A Refugee Camp in America: Fort Chaffee and Vietnamese and Cuban Refugees, 1975–1982," *Journal of American Ethnic History* 33, no. 2 (2014): 57.

11. Sucheng Chan, *Survivors: Cambodian Refugees in the United States* (Urbana: University of Illinois Press, 2004), 80; Chia Youyee Vang, *Hmong America: Reconstructing Community in Diaspora* (Urbana: University of Illinois Press, 2010), 45–46.

12. Chan, *Survivors,* 39–80.

13. Erika Lee, *The Making of Asian America: A History* (New York: Simon and Schuster, 2016), 322–329.

14. Bon Tempo, *Americans at the Gate,* 149.

15. Paul Hillmer, *A People's History of the Hmong* (Saint Paul: Minnesota Historical Society Press, 2009), 181–234.

16. Lee, *The Making of Asian America,* 314.

17. Loescher and Scanlan, *Calculated Kindness,* 144; Susan B. Gall and Timothy L. Gall, eds., *Statistical Record of Asian Americans* (Detroit, MI: Gale Research, 1993).

18. Bon Tempo, *Americans at the Gate,* 173–179.

19. Norman Zucker and Naomi Zucker, *The Guarded Gate: The Reality of American Refugee Policy* (San Diego, CA: Harcourt Brace Jovanovich, 1987), 57–58; Porter, *Benevolent Empire,* 212–215.

20. Louis Harris & Associates, Louis Harris & Associates Poll: May 1975, Question 39, USHARRIS.062675.R2A, Louis Harris & Associates (Cornell University, Ithaca, NY: Roper Center for Public Opinion Research, 1975), Dataset, DOI: https://doi.org/10.25940/ROPER-31107850.

21. CBS News/New York Times, National Survey, June 1986, Question 38, USCBSNYT.063086.R35, CBS News/New York Times (Cornell University, Ithaca, NY: Roper Center for Public Opinion Research, 1986), Dataset, DOI: https://doi.org/10.25940/ROPER-31091243.

22. Loescher and Scanlan, *Calculated Kindness,* xvii–xviii.

23. Milton Benjamin, "The Crowd at the Exits," *Newsweek,* April 21, 1975.

24. *Indochina Migration and Refugee Assistance Act of 1975: Senate Report No. 94-119,* 94th Cong. 26 (May 12, 1975) (statement of David Stickney, American Friends Service Committee).

25. Bon Tempo, *Americans at the Gate,* 147, 143.

26. *Indochina Migration and Refugee Assistance Act of 1975: Senate Report No. 94-119,* 94th Cong. 3 (May 12, 1975).

27. "Pope Visits Indochinese Refugees and Calls for More Aid," *New York Times,* February 22, 1981.

28. *Indochina Migration and Refugee Assistance Act of 1975: Senate Report No. 94-119,* 94th Cong. 3 (May 12, 1975).

29. Hakon Torjesen, Karen Olness, and Erik Torjesen, *The Gift of the Refugees: Notes of a Volunteer Family at a Refugee Camp* (Eden Prairie, MN: The Garden, 1981), 157.

30. Gallup Organization, Gallup Poll # 1938-0139: Nazi Germany/Politics, Question 12, USGALLUP.38-139.Q03, Gallup Organization (Cornell University, Ithaca, NY: Roper Center for Public Opinion Research, 1938), Dataset, DOI: https://doi.org/10.25940/ROPER-31087123.

31. Douglas Kneeland, "Wide Hostility Found to Vietnamese Influx," *New York Times*, May 2, 1975. A May 1975 Harris poll found slightly more generous numbers—37 percent supported resettlement of Vietnamese refugees while 49 percent opposed. Another poll, in August 1977, found the split at 31–57 percent. See Louis Harris & Associates, Louis Harris & Associates Poll: May 1975, Question 38; Louis Harris & Associates, Louis Harris & Associates Poll: July 1977, Question 16, USHARRIS.082577.R1, Louis Harris & Associates (Cornell University, Ithaca, NY: Roper Center for Public Opinion Research, 1977), Dataset, DOI: https://doi.org/10.25940/ROPER -31103276.

32. Los Angeles Times, Los Angeles Times Poll # 1985-096: Poverty in America, Question 17, USLAT.96.R030, Los Angeles Times (Cornell University, Ithaca, NY: Roper Center for Public Opinion Research, 1985), Dataset, DOI: https://doi.org/10.25940/ROPER-31092830.

33. Mimi Thi Nguyen, *The Gift of Freedom: War, Debt, and Other Refugee Passages* (Durham, NC: Duke University Press, 2012). For another critical refugee studies perspective on the imperialist discourse of the grateful refugee, see Yen Le Espiritu, *Body Counts: The Vietnam War and Militarized Refugees* (Berkeley: University of California Press, 2014).

34. Louis Harris & Associates, Louis Harris & Associates Poll: May 1975, Question 41.

35. James Wooten, "The Vietnamese Are Coming and the Town of Niceville, Fla., Doesn't Like It," *New York Times*, May 1, 1975.

36. Louis Harris & Associates, Louis Harris & Associates Poll: May 1975, Question 42.

37. Los Angeles Times, Los Angeles Times Poll # 1985-096: Poverty in America, Question 18.

38. Kneeland, "Wide Hostility Found to Vietnamese Influx."

39. Wooten, "The Vietnamese Are Coming."

40. Bon Tempo, *Americans at the Gate*, 158–160.

41. Warren Brown, "Vietnamese Refugees Caught in Black-White Friction in New Orleans: A Different War," *Washington Post*, July 18, 1978.

42. Louis Harris & Associates, Louis Harris & Associates Poll: July 1977, Question 20.

43. Wooten, "The Vietnamese Are Coming."

44. Kneeland, "Wide Hostility Found to Vietnamese Influx."

45. Lutheran Immigration and Refugee Service (hereafter LIRS) Bulletin, Standing Committee, Protocol, and Minutes, September 6–7, 1978, LCUSA, DIRS, LCU 10/1, Archives of the ELCA, Elk Grove Village, IL.

46. Clare Booth Luce, "Refugees and Guilt," *New York Times*, May 11, 1975.

47. Louis Harris & Associates, Louis Harris & Associates Poll: July 1977, Question 18.

318 NOTES TO PAGES 89–91

48. Boxes 21–24 and 51–52, Case Files, IIM Records, IHRC3257, IHRC, UMN. See also Paul Levy, "Asian Refugees Find Life a Rough Ride in St. Cloud," *Minneapolis Star and Tribune,* April 12, 1982.

49. Margot Hornblower, "A Journey from Defeat to Success," *Washington Post,* July 5, 1980.

50. Dennis Williams, "The Newest Americans," *Newsweek,* September 10, 1979.

51. Paul Taylor, "Vietnamese Shrimpers Alter Texas Gulf Towns," *Washington Post,* December 26, 1984. See also Stephanie Hinnershitz, *A Different Shade of Justice: Asian American Civil Rights in the South* (Chapel Hill: University of North Carolina Press, 2017), 158–194.

52. Ellen Hume, "Ten Years After—Vietnam's Legacy: Indochinese Refugees," *Wall Street Journal,* March 21, 1985; Terry E. Johnson, "Immigrants: New Victims," *Newsweek,* May 12, 1986.

53. US Commission on Civil Rights, "Recent Activities against Citizens and Residents of Asian Descent" (Washington, DC: Commission on Civil Rights, 1986).

54. Cecilia M. Tsu, "'If You Want to Plow Your Field, Don't Kill Your Buffalo to Eat': Hmong Farm Cooperatives and Refugee Resettlement in 1980s Minnesota," *Journal of American Ethnic History* 36, no. 3 (2017): 38.

55. "Winona-Area Residents Oppose Hmong Jobs Training Proposal," *St. Paul Dispatch,* February 9, 1983.

56. Bill McAuliff, "Decision Planned in a Week on Relocating Hmong to Farm," *Minneapolis Star and Tribune,* March 10, 1983.

57. "Winona-Area Residents Oppose Hmong Jobs Training Proposal."

58. *Indochina Refugees: Hearings before the Subcommittee on Immigration and International Law of the Committee on the Judiciary, House of Representatives,* 94th Cong. 17 (May 5 and 7, 1975).

59. *Indochina Migration and Refugee Assistance Act of 1975: Senate Report No. 94-119,* 94th Cong. 13 (May 12, 1975) (statement of L. Dean Brown, Interagency Task Force on Indochina Refugees).

60. Douglas Kneeland, "Fears on Refugees Called Unfounded," *New York Times,* June 27, 1975.

61. *Indochina Refugee Children's Assistance Act Amendments of 1977: Hearings Before the Committee on Human Resources,* 95th Cong. 60 (September 22, 1977) (statement of Keith Comrie, Department of Social Services of the County of Los Angeles).

62. *Refugees from Indochina: Hearings before the Subcommittee on Immigration, Citizenship, and International Law of the Committee on the Judiciary, House of Representatives,* 94th Cong. 344 (July 22, 1975) (statement of Wells Klein, American Council for Nationalities Service). The pressure that the economic priorities placed on Southeast Asian refugees is discussed in Aihwa Ong, *Buddha Is Hiding: Refugees, Citizenship, the New America* (Berkeley: University of California Press, 2003); and Eric Tang, *Unsettled: Cambodian Refugees in the New York City Hyperghetto* (Philadelphia: Temple University Press, 2015).

63. *Refugees from Indochina: Hearings before the Subcommittee on Immigration, Citizenship, and International Law of the Committee on the Judiciary, House of Representatives*, 94th Cong. 465 (December 18, 1975) (statement of Julia Vadala Taft, Interagency Task Force on Indochina Refugees).

64. *Indochina Refugee Children's Assistance Act Amendments of 1977: Hearings before the Committee on Human Resources, United States Senate*, 95th Cong. 48–49 (September 22, 1977) (Senator Hayakawa).

65. *Indochina Refugees: Hearings before the Subcommittee on Immigration and International Law of the Committee on the Judiciary, House of Representatives*, 94th Cong. 24, 9 (May 5 and 7, 1975) (statement of L. Dean Brown, Interagency Task Force on Indochina Refugees).

66. *Indochina Refugees: Hearings before the Subcommittee on Immigration and International Law of the Committee on the Judiciary, House of Representatives*, 94th Cong. 10 (May 5 and 7, 1975) (statement of Julia Taft, Interagency Task Force on Indochina Refugees).

67. Vaughan Robinson, Roger Andersson, and Sako Musterd, *Spreading the "Burden"? A Review of Policies to Disperse Asylum Seekers and Refugees* (Bristol, UK: Policy Press, 2003).

68. Porter, *Benevolent Empire*, 198–201.

69. "Congress Approves Indochinese Refugee Aid," in *CQ Almanac 1975*, 31st ed. (Washington, DC: Congressional Quarterly, 1976), 317.

70. Vang, *Hmong America*, 46–49; David Haines, "Southeast Asian Refugees in the United States: The Interaction of Kinship and Public Policy," in *Asian American Family Life and Community*, ed. Franklin Ng (New York: Garland, 1998), 198–199.

71. Joe Rigert, "Refugee Resettlement: Experiences of Past Taught Us Little for Present," *Minneapolis Tribune*, June 26, 1975.

72. *Indochina Evacuation and Refugee Problems, Part III: Reception and Resettlement: Hearings before the Subcommittee to Investigate Problems Connected with Refugees and Escapees of the Committee on the Judiciary, United States Senate*, 94th Cong. 13–14 (May 13, 1975) (statement of John McCarthy, United States Catholic Conference [hereafter USCC]).

73. "More Church Involvement Urged in Refugee Programs," *Stockton (CA) Record*, October 17, 1980.

74. *Refugees from Indochina: Hearings before the Subcommittee on Immigration, Citizenship, and International Law of the Committee on the Judiciary, House of Representatives*, 94th Cong. 465 (1975) (statement of Julia Vadala Taft, Interagency Task Force on Indochina Refugees); *Indochina Migration and Refugee Assistance Act of 1975: Senate Report No. 94-119*, 94th Cong. 20 (May 12, 1975) (statement of L. Dean Brown, Interagency Task Force on Indochina Refugees).

75. For examples of the state and domestic religious voluntary aid, see Dorothy M. Brown and Elizabeth McKeown, *The Poor Belong to Us: Catholic Charities and American Welfare* (Cambridge, MA: Harvard University Press, 1997); Elisabeth Clemens and Doug Guthrie, *Politics and Partnerships: The Role of Voluntary Agencies in America's Political Past and Present*

(Chicago: University of Chicago Press, 2011); Maureen Fitzgerald, *Habits of Compassion: Irish Catholic Nuns and the Origins of New York's Welfare System, 1830–1920* (Urbana: University of Illinois Press, 2006); Alison Collis Greene, *No Depression in Heaven: The Great Depression, the New Deal, and the Transformation of Religion in the Delta* (New York: Oxford University Press, 2017); William Novak, "Public-Private Governance: A Historical Introduction," in *Government by Contract: Outsourcing and American Democracy,* ed. Martha Minow and Jody Freeman (Cambridge, MA: Harvard University Press, 2009), 23–40; and Beth S. Wenger, *New York Jews and the Great Depression: Uncertain Promise* (New Haven, CT: Yale University Press, 1996). For examples of the state and international religious voluntary aid, see Heather D. Curtis, *Holy Humanitarians: American Evangelicals and Global Aid* (Cambridge, MA: Harvard University Press, 2018); Nichols, *The Uneasy Alliance;* and Axel Schaefer, *Piety and Public Funding: Evangelicals and the State in Modern America* (Philadelphia: University of Pennsylvania Press, 2012).

76. David Daily, *Battle for the BIA: G. E. E. Lindquist and the Missionary Crusade against John Collier* (Tucson: University of Arizona Press, 2004); Jennifer Graber, *The Gods of Indian Country: Religion and the Struggle for the American West* (New York: Oxford University Press, 2018); Kathleen Holscher, "Separation," in *Religion, Law, USA,* ed. Joshua Dubler and Isaac Weiner (New York: New York University Press, 2019), 91–107.

77. During the Cold War, American evangelicals became increasingly interested in making use of expanded public funding opportunities for religious international aid and domestic social welfare programs. See Schaefer, *Piety and Public Funding.*

78. Brown and Scribner, "Unfulfilled Promises, Future Possibilities," 103–106. For an overview of how the federal government relied on voluntary agencies for refugee resettlement throughout the twentieth century, see Porter, *Benevolent Empire.*

79. David North, Lawrence Lewin, and Jennifer Wagner, *Kaleidoscope: The Resettlement of Refugees in the United States by the Voluntary Agencies* (Washington, DC: New TransCentury Foundation, 1982), 21–22.

80. American Council of Voluntary Agencies, 1978; January 1979–April 1980, Box 5, ARC Records, MHS.

81. Correspondence by Name, 1979–1981, Box 2, ARC Records, MHS.

82. Subject Files: San Francisco Meeting, July 12, 1979, Box 2, ARC Records, MHS.

83. North, Lewin, and Wagner, *Kaleidoscope,* 3–17.

84. *Indochina Refugees: Hearings before the Subcommittee on Immigration and International Law of the Committee on the Judiciary, House of Representatives,* 94th Cong. 18 (May 5 and 7, 1975) (statement of L. Dean Brown, Interagency Task Force on Indochina Refugees).

85. *Refugees from Indochina: Hearings before the Subcommittee on Immigration, Citizenship, and International Law of the Committee on the Judiciary, House of Representatives,* 94th Cong. 353 (July 22, 1975) (statement of John Schauer, Church World Service).

86. Zucker and Zucker, *The Guarded Gate,* 122.

87. North, Lewin, and Wagner, *Kaleidoscope,* 21, 41, 45.

88. North, Lewin, and Wagner, *Kaleidoscope,* 26–38.

89. North, Lewin, and Wagner, *Kaleidoscope,* 79.

90. That religious agencies pursued different objectives from government was especially apparent abroad, when there were differences of opinion about American foreign policy, particularly in regard to the Vietnam War. See Scott Flipse, "To Save 'Free Vietnam' and Lose Our Souls: The Missionary Impulse, Voluntary Agencies, and Protestant Dissent against the War, 1965–1971," in *The Foreign Missionary Enterprise at Home: Explorations in North American Cultural History,* ed. Grant Wacker and Daniel Bays (Tuscaloosa: University of Alabama Press, 2003), 206–222.

91. Letter from Wendell Anderson to Richard Friedman, November 5, 1975, Governor's Refugee Resettlement Office, 1976–1977, Governor's Indochinese Resettlement Office, RPO, MDPW, MHS.

92. Bruce Downing et al., *Hmong Resettlement Study Site Report: Minneapolis–St. Paul* (Minneapolis: Southeast Asian Studies Project, Center for Urban and Regional Affairs, University of Minnesota, 1984), 6.

93. State Plan for Refugees 1979, Program History Files, Records of the RPO, MDPW, MHS.

94. Downing et al., *Hmong Resettlement Study Site Report,* 7.

95. Tom Kosel, interview by the author, June 23, 2011, Saint Paul, MN.

96. "Voluntary Agencies," Governor's Refugee Resettlement Office, 1976–1977, Governor's Indochinese Resettlement Office, Administrative Files, Records of the RPO, MDPW, MHS.

97. Kay O'Loughlin, "Nun Teaching Hmong Refugees Refugees How to Find Jobs," *Catholic Bulletin,* July 22, 1982; Rosemary Schuneman, interview by the author, August 31, 2012, Saint Paul, MN.

98. Saint Mary's Catholic Church Records, MHS.

99. Southeast Asian Ministry, Folder 10, Box 10, RSC, UMN Records, General/Multiethnic Collection, IHRC2968, IHRC, UMN; Christ on Capitol Hill Lutheran Church Records, MHS.

100. Downing et al., *Hmong Resettlement Study Site Report,* 57.

101. "Regina Helps Hmong Brace for Winter's Cold," *Catholic Bulletin,* December 12, 1980.

102. Records of the Southeast Asian Ministry; Pearson Papers, MHS.

103. Shoua Vang and Nhia Vang, "The Sacred Drum," in *New Americans: An Oral History, Immigrants and Refugees in the U.S. Today,* ed. Al Santoli (New York: Viking, 1988), 303–332; Tsu, "'If You Want to Plow Your Field.'"

104. Southeast Asian Ministry, Folder 10, Box 10, RSC, UMN Records, General/Multiethnic Collection, IHRC2968, IHRC, UMN; "Charities Begin Hmong Helping Hmong Program," *Catholic Bulletin,* August 5, 1982.

105. Clint Eastwood, dir., *Gran Torino* (Warner Bros. Pictures/Village Roadshow Pictures, 2008).

106. Lutheran Immigration and Refugee Service, "The Real Cost of Welcome: A Financial Analysis of Local Refugee Reception" (Baltimore: Lutheran Immigration and Refugee Service, 2009), 9.

107. Brown and Scribner, "Unfulfilled Promises, Future Possibilities," 111. The USCC, one of the leading voluntary agencies involved with Southeast Asian refugee resettlement, combined with the National Conference of Catholic Bishops to form the United States Conference of Catholic Bishops in 2001.

108. Tom Gjelten, "U.S. Refugee Program 'On Life Support,' Facing Big Challenges," NPR, March 25, 2021, https://www.npr.org/2021/03/25/979723089/u-s-refugee-program-on-life-support-facing-big-challenges; Danielle DuClos, "Refugee Organizations Scramble to Settle Afghans after Years of Trump-Era Budget Cuts," ABC News, September 8, 2021, https://abcnews.go.com/Politics/refugee-organizations-scramble-settle-afghans-years-trump-era/story?id=79812415.

3. Ministering Resettlement

1. Kathleen Vellenga, interview by the author, September 14, 2011, Saint Paul, MN.

2. The idea of sponsorship is not new to refugee resettlement: Christian Americans have pursued other forms of sponsorship projects. See Hillary Kaell, *Christian Globalism at Home: Child Sponsorship in the United States* (Princeton, NJ: Princeton University Press, 2021).

3. Nancy Ammerman, *Studying Lived Religion* (New York: New York University Press, 2021); David Hall, ed., *Lived Religion in America: Toward a History of Practice* (Princeton, NJ: Princeton University Press, 1997).

4. *Refugees from Indochina: Hearings before the Subcommittee on Immigration, Citizenship and International Law of the Committee on the Judiciary House of Representatives,* 94th Cong. 370 (July 22, 1975) (statement of John McCarthy, United States Catholic Conference [hereafter USCC]).

5. *Refugees from Indochina: Hearings before the Subcommittee on Immigration, Citizenship and International Law of the Committee on the Judiciary House of Representatives,* 94th Cong. 316 (July 22, 1975) (statement of August Bernthal, LIRS). For other examples of refugees experiencing labor exploitation, see Stephen R. Porter, *Benevolent Empire: U.S. Power, Humanitarianism, and the World's Dispossessed* (Philadelphia: University of Pennsylvania Press, 2016), 102.

6. *Indochina Evacuation and Refugee Problems: Hearing before the Subcommittee to Investigate Problems Connected with Refugees and Escapees of the Committee on the Judiciary on the United States Senate,* 94th Cong. 33 (July 24, 1975) (statement of Donald Anderson, LIRS).

7. *Indochina Evacuation and Refugee Problems: Hearing before the Subcommittee to Investigate Problems Connected with Refugees and Escapees of the Committee on the Judiciary on the United States Senate,* 94th Cong. 638 (June 15, 1976) (Health, Education, and Welfare Task Force for Indochina Refugees, Report to the Congress).

8. "50 Viet Refugees on Way," *Catholic Bulletin,* July 11, 1975; David North, Lawrence Lewin, and Jennifer Wagner, *Kaleidoscope: The Resettlement of Refugees in the United States by the Voluntary Agencies* (Washington, DC: New TransCentury Foundation, 1982), 86–87.

9. "Suggested Proposal for Boat People," Oak Terrace Resettlement Plan, 1979–1980, Program History Files, Records of the RPO, MDPW, MHS.

10. Church World Service (hereafter CWS), *CWS Agreement Sponsor Form,* Pamphlets Relating to Refugee Relief and Assistance in Minnesota and the United States, MHS Pamphlet Collection, MHS.

11. Standing Committee, Protocol, Minutes, January 8–9, 1976, LCUSA, DIRS, LCU 10/1, Archives of the ELCA, Elk Grove Village, IL.

12. Tom Kosel, interview by the author, June 23, 2011, Saint Paul, MN.

13. North, Lewin, and Wagner, *Kaleidoscope,* 33.

14. Jeanne Luxem, "Gospel Verse Puts Parishes into Action," *Catholic Bulletin,* September 7, 1979; Peter Paula, "Fr. Thanh Builds Spiritual Refuge for Viet Refugees," *Catholic Bulletin,* January 9, 1979; Pat Westburg, "Parishes Join Resettlement Effort," *Catholic Bulletin,* June 13, 1975; "50 Viet Refugees on Way," *Catholic Bulletin,* July 11, 1975; "177 Refugees in Archdiocese," *Catholic Bulletin,* n.d.; "St. Cecilia Welcomes Hmong People; Special Masses to Be Set," *Catholic Bulletin,* December 3, 1982; "State Catholic 'Network' Expected to Settle 850 Viets," *Catholic Bulletin,* August 1, 1975; "Ten Hmong Initiated into Hastings Parish," *Catholic Bulletin,* April 7, 1983; "Viet Refugee Nun Settles in St. Paul," *Catholic Bulletin,* August 8, 1975.

15. Standing Committee, Protocol, Minutes, August 9, 1976, LCUSA, DIRS, LCU 10/1, Archives of the ELCA, Elk Grove Village, IL.

16. *Refugees from Indochina: Hearings before the Subcommittee on Immigration, Citizenship and International Law of the Committee on the Judiciary House of Representatives,* 94th Cong. 370 (July 22, 1975) (statement of John McCarthy, USCC).

17. Luxem, "Gospel Verse Puts Parishes into Action."

18. *Refugees from Indochina: Hearings Before the Subcommittee on Immigration, Citizenship and International Law of the Committee on the Judiciary House of Representatives,* 94th Cong. 325–328 (July 22, 1975) (statement of August Bernthal, LIRS). The fact that the actual cost of sponsoring refugees was much larger than the per capita grant was well documented. See Standing Committee, Protocol, Minutes, March 29–30, LCUSA, DIRS, LCU 10/1, Archives of the ELCA, Elk Grove Village, IL.

19. Box 51, Case Files, IIM Records, IHRC3257, IHRC, UMN.

20. Helen Fein, *Congregational Sponsors of Indochinese Refugees in the United States, 1979–1981: Helping beyond Borders* (Rutherford, NJ: Fairleigh Dickinson University Press, 1987), 59–73.

21. Ingrid Walter to Elmer Staats, January 24, 1978, Standing Committee, Protocol, Minutes, January 24–25, 1978, LCUSA, DIRS, LCU 10/1, Archives of the ELCA, Elk Grove Village, IL.

22. LIRS, *Face to Face: The Ministry of Refugee Resettlement—An Orientation Brochure for Congregations,* Pamphlets Relating to Refugee Relief and Assistance in Minnesota and the United States, MHS Pamphlet Collection, MHS.

23. Report on Phase II Follow Up Services, Indochina Resettlement Program, March 17, 1976, Standing Committee, Protocol, Minutes, March 29–30,

1976, LCUSA, DIRS, LCU 10/1, Archives of the ELCA, Elk Grove Village, IL.

24. Trinity Lutheran Church Records, Luther Seminary Archive (hereafter LSA).

25. Messiah Lutheran Records, LSA.

26. Luxem, "Gospel Verse Puts Parishes into Action."

27. Ann Baker, "Churches Rally to Refugees' Aid," *St. Paul Dispatch,* July 14, 1979.

28. "Priest's Neighbors Don't Share Zeal for Hmong Job Program," *Minneapolis Star and Tribune,* February 10, 1983.

29. *Refugees from Indochina: Hearings before the Subcommittee on Immigration, Citizenship and International Law of the Committee on the Judiciary House of Representatives,* 94th Cong. 370 (July 22, 1975) (statement of John McCarthy, USCC).

30. Health, Education, and Welfare Refugee Task Force, *Report to the Congress* (Washington, DC: The Task Force, 1976), 53.

31. Fein, *Congregational Sponsors of Indochinese Refugees,* 108.

32. Meeting Minutes for August 9, 1976, Standing Committee, Protocol, Minutes, August 9, 1976, LCUSA, DIRS, LCU 10/1, Archives of the ELCA, Elk Grove Village, IL.

33. Dayton Avenue Presbyterian Church (hereafter DAPC), "QATKCA (Quick Attempt to Keep Congregation Abreast)," *Dayton Parish News* (hereafter DPN), December 1975, MHS.

34. DAPC, "*QATKCA,*" DPN, February 1976, MHS.

35. DAPC, *All May Be One,* December 1975, MHS.

36. DAPC, *All May Be One.*

37. Vellenga, interview.

38. DAPC, DPN, September 1976, MHS.

39. Vellenga, interview.

40. DAPC, DPN, September 1976, MHS.

41. DAPC, DPN, March 1976, MHS.

42. DAPC, DPN, September 1976, MHS.

43. North, Lewin, and Wagner, *Kaleidoscope,* 72–74.

44. LIRS, *Face to Face: The Ministry of Refugee Resettlement,* LIRS Assorted Publications, LCUSA, DIRS, LCU 10//1, Archives of the ELCA, Elk Grove Village, IL.

45. CWS, *From Despair to Hope: How Sponsorship Brings New Life to Refugees,* n.d., Pamphlets Relating to Refugee Relief and Assistance in Minnesota and the United States, MHS Pamphlet Collection, MHS.

46. Joanne Karvonen, "Refugee Resettlement: One Congregation's Transforming Experience," *World and World: Theology for Christian Ministry* 29, no. 3 (2009): 243–245.

47. Mary Mergenthal, interview by the author, August 10, 2012, Saint Paul, MN.

48. Joanne Karvonen, interview by the author, August 10, 2012, Saint Paul, MN.

49. Mergenthal, interview.

50. Karvonen, interview. Helen Fein found that sponsors in her study also spoke of the Golden Rule. Fein, *Congregational Sponsors of Indochinese Refugees*, 65.

51. CWS Immigration and Refugee Program, Folder 15, Box 5, RSC, UMN Records, General/Multiethnic Collection, IHRC2968, IHRC, UMN.

52. Karvonen, interview.

53. Karvonen, "Refugee Resettlement," 249. "To show hospitality to strangers" is from Hebrews 13:2.

54. Dianne Anderson, interview by the author, September 19, 2012, Saint Paul, MN. The changing demographics of the neighborhood may be one reason why some urban churches have been able to stay afloat. Pointing to the example of Puerto Rican and Cuban Catholics who moved to Boston in the 1960s, Peggy Levitt has argued that recently arrived immigrants filled urban churches left nearly abandoned because of white flight. See Peggy Levitt, *The Transnational Villagers* (Berkeley: University of California Press, 2001), 168.

55. Bernice Heron, "The Adoption of the Thai Family," Lisalan Thai Oral History Interview, Vietnamese Oral History Project, MHS.

56. "Sponsors Sought to Help Refugees," *Catholic Bulletin*, August 8, 1980.

57. Karvonen, "Refugee Resettlement," 250.

58. Mergenthal, interview.

59. Bernard Casserly, "Welcome 'Boat People,'" *Catholic Bulletin*, July 6, 1979.

60. Karvonen, interview.

61. Karvonen, "Refugee Resettlement," 248–249.

62. Catherine Besteman, *Making Refuge: Somali Bantu Refugees and Lewiston, Maine* (Durham, NC: Duke University Press, 2016), 200.

63. Pearl Jones, interview by the author, August 29, 2012, White Bear Lake, MN. Interviewee's name has been changed at their request. Other congregations in the area also expressed the idea that working with refugees was a missionary opportunity at home. See Jim Adams, "Hope Parish Extends Missionary Hand to Hmong," *Minneapolis Star and Tribune*, November 4, 1982.

64. Jones, interview.

65. Dorothy Knight, interview by the author, August 6, 2012, Saint Paul, MN.

66. Observations on the 45-Day Reports, November 1, 1975, Standing Committee, Protocol, Minutes, November 6–7, 1975, LCUSA, DIRS, LCU 10/1, Archives of the ELCA, Elk Grove Village, IL.

67. Organizational Files: Correspondences and Miscellanea, 1979–1980, Box 1, ARC Records, MHS.

68. *LIRS Bulletin*, LCUSA, DIRS, LCU 10/1, Archives of the ELCA, Elk Grove Village, IL.

69. World Relief, *Christian Educational Materials for Indochinese Refugees*, Folder 31, Box 51, Case Files, IIM Records, IHRC3257, IHRC, UMN.

70. CWS, *Manual for Refugee Sponsorship*, CWS Records, PHS.

71. Prospectus for Project New Life, Standing Committee, Protocol, Minutes, January 8–9, 1976, LCUSA, DIRS, LCU 10/1, Archives of the ELCA, Elk Grove Village, IL.

72. Foreign missionaries often had an impact on domestic affairs. See David A. Hollinger, *Protestants Abroad: How Missionaries Tried to Change the World but Changed America* (Princeton, NJ: Princeton University Press, 2017).

73. Jones, interview.

74. Rosemary Schuneman, interview by the author, August 31, 2012, Saint Paul, MN.

75. Rev. Paul Tidemann, interview by the author, July 28, 2012, Saint Paul, MN.

76. Jones, interview.

77. *A Brief History of St. Anthony Park Lutheran Church,* Saint Anthony Park Lutheran Church Records, LSA.

78. Mergenthal, interview.

79. Paul Tidemann, "The Process of Trans-Cultural Change: One Congregation's Story," Saint Paul-Reformation Lutheran Church Records, LSA.

80. DAPC, "You Have to Work to Appreciate People," DPN, June–July 1978, MHS.

81. Kim Ode, "'He Has a Hmong Heart': Father Daniel Taillez, Now a Missionary to America," *Minneapolis Star Tribune,* January 12, 1989.

82. Malcolm Maurice Sawyer, interview by Robert Shuster, September 27, 1983, Wheaton, IL, Collection 256, Archives of the BGC.

83. Malcolm Maurice Sawyer, interview by Robert Shuster, November 14, 1983, Wheaton, IL, Collection 256, Archives of the BGC.

84. Helen Irvin Sawyer, interview by Stephanie Dixon, November 22, 1983, Wheaton, IL, Collection 256, Archives of the BGC.

85. Paul Tidemann, "I Have Called You Friends," May 16, 1982, in *Ordinary Moments: Ordinary People Blessed by God,* ed. Paul Tidemann (self-published, 2006), 42.

86. Tidemann, "I Have Called You Friends," 43.

87. Tidemann, interview.

88. William Hutchison, *Errand to the World: American Protestant Thought and Foreign Missions* (Chicago: University of Chicago Press, 1987); Sarah Ruble, *The Gospel of Freedom and Power: Protestant Missionaries in American Culture after World War II* (Chapel Hill: University of North Carolina Press, 2012); Grant Wacker, "Second Thoughts on the Great Commission: Liberal Protestants and Foreign Missions, 1890–1940," in *Earthen Vessels: American Evangelicals and Foreign Missions, 1880–1980,* ed. Joel Carpenter and Wilbur Shenk (Grand Rapids, MI: Eerdmans, 1990).

89. Fein, *Congregational Sponsors of Indochinese Refugees,* 59.

90. North, Lewin, and Wagner, *Kaleidoscope,* 88.

91. Schuneman, interview.

92. Knight, interview.

93. Schuneman, interview.

94. Anderson, interview.

95. True Xiong, interview by the author, interpreted by Maile Vue, August 9, 2012, Minneapolis, MN.

96. Neng Xiong, interview by the author, interpreted by Maile Vue, August 3, 2012, Minneapolis, MN. Hmong Christians sometimes did not remember

the names of the churches that sponsored them or even the names of the congregations they attended. Ruth Hammond, "New Faith, Old Belief," *St. Paul Pioneer Press,* September 16, 1984.

97. Yia Lee, interview by the author, July 29, 2012, Saint Paul, MN.

98. Yong Kay Moua and Houa Vue Moua, interview by the author, September 12, 2012, Saint Paul, MN.

99. Rev. Timothy Vang, interview by the author, September 20, 2012, Maplewood, MN.

100. Yong Kay Moua and Houa Vue Moua, interview.

101. Fong Her, interview by Peter Chou Vang, May 1, 2004, HOHPCU.

102. Bee Yang, interview by the author, translated by Maile Vue, August 2, 2012, Saint Paul, MN.

103. Yong Kay Moua and Houa Vue Moua, interview.

104. Neng Vang and Paj Ntaub Lis, interview by the author, March 25, 2012, Saint Paul, MN. Interviewees' names have been changed at their request.

105. Tzianeng Vang, interview by the author, September 5, 2012, Saint Paul, MN.

106. Cher Moua, interview by the author, September 6, 2012, Saint Paul, MN.

107. Rev. Timothy Vang, interview.

108. Sua Vu Yang, interview by MayKao Hang, January 22, 2000, HWATOHP, MHS.

109. Yia Lee, interview by the author, July 29, 2012, Saint Paul, MN.

110. Yen Le Espiritu, *Body Counts: The Vietnam War and Militarized Refugees* (Berkeley: University of California Press, 2014), 14.

111. North, Lewin, and Wagner, *Kaleidoscope,* 86.

112. Nicole Ives, Jill Witmer Sinha, and Ram Cnaan, "Who Is Welcoming the Stranger? Exploring Faith-Based Service Provision to Refugees in Philadelphia," *Journal of Religion & Spirituality in Social Work: Social Thought* 29, no. 1 (2010): 75.

113. Bruce Downing et al., *Hmong Resettlement Study Site Report: Minneapolis–St. Paul* (Minneapolis: Southeast Asian Studies Project, Center for Urban and Regional Affairs, University of Minnesota, 1984), 17.

114. Knight, interview.

4. Pluralizing Resettlement

1. Jim and Paula Nessa, interview by the author, August 28, 2012, Saint Paul, MN.

2. Joanne Karvonen, interview by the author, August 10, 2012, Saint Paul, MN.

3. Tom Kosel, interview by the author, June 23, 2011, Saint Paul, MN.

4. *Admission of Refugees into the United States, Part II: Hearings before the Subcommittee on Immigration, Citizenship, and International Law of the Committee of the Judiciary, House of Representatives,* 95th Cong. 48 (August 4, 1977) (testimony of Richard Holbrooke, Assistant Secretary of State for East Asian and Pacific Affairs).

5. Mary Mergenthal, interview by the author, August 10, 2012, Saint Paul, MN.

6. Joanne Karvonen, "Refugee Resettlement: One Congregation's Transforming Experience," *World and World: Theology for Christian Ministry* 29, no. 3 (2009): 248.

7. Quoted in Carl Bon Tempo, *Americans at the Gate: The United States and Refugees during the Cold War* (Princeton, NJ: Princeton University Press, 2008), 99.

8. *Christ Lutheran Bulletin,* May 3, 1975, MHS.

9. Geoffrey Cameron, *Send Them Here: Religion, Politics, and Refugee Resettlement in North America* (Montreal: McGill–Queen's University Press, 2021), 93. There were some Muslims and Buddhists resettled by Methodists earlier in the twentieth century. See Nicholas T. Pruitt, *Open Hearts, Closed Doors: Immigration Reform and the Waning of Mainline Protestantism* (New York: New York University Press, 2021), 146.

10. Ingrid Walter, transcript of an oral history conducted by Cordelia Cox, December 28, 1982, Oral History Collection of the Archives of Cooperative Lutheranism, LCUSA, 1984 (OH1), Archives of the ELCA, Elk Grove Village, IL.

11. For a discussion of how religious voluntary agencies shifted from resettling coreligionists to refugees of other religions, see Todd Scribner, "'Not Because They Are Catholic, but Because We Are Catholic': The Bishops' Engagement with the Migration Issue in Twentieth-Century America," *Catholic Historical Review* 101, no. 1 (Winter 2015): 74–99.

12. Peter Beyer, "Deprivileging Religion in a Post-Westphalian State: Shadow Establishment, Organization, Spirituality and Freedom in Canada," in *Varieties of Religious Establishment,* ed. Winnifred Fallers Sullivan and Lori Beaman (London: Routledge, 2016), 75–91.

13. On this point, I draw on the scholarship about the "Protestant secular." For an overview of the concept of the "Protestant secular," see Charles McCrary and Jeffrey Wheatley, "The Protestant Secular in the Study of American Religion: Reappraisal and Suggestions," *Religion* 47, no. 2 (April 3, 2017): 256–276.

14. For an overview of twentieth-century immigration reforms, see Mae M. Ngai, *Impossible Subjects: Illegal Aliens and the Making of Modern America* (Princeton, NJ: Princeton University Press, 2004); Aristide Zolberg, *A Nation by Design: Immigration Policy in the Fashioning of America* (Cambridge, MA: Harvard University Press, 2006).

15. For a history of the effort to end Asian exclusion, see Jane H. Hong, *Opening the Gates to Asia: A Transpacific History of How America Repealed Asian Exclusion* (Chapel Hill: University of North Carolina Press, 2019).

16. For examples of scholarship on Asian American religious communities before Hart-Celler, see Stephanie Hinnershitz, *Race, Religion, and Civil Rights: Asian Students on the West Coast, 1900–1968* (New Brunswick, NJ: Rutgers University Press, 2015); Duncan Ryūken Williams, *American Sutra: A Story of Faith and Freedom in the Second World War* (Cambridge, MA: Harvard University Press, 2019); and David Yoo, *Contentious*

Spirits: Religion in Korean American History, 1903–1945 (Stanford, CA: Stanford University Press, 2010).

17. Carolyn Chen, *Getting Saved in America: Taiwanese Immigration and Religious Experience* (Princeton, NJ: Princeton University Press, 2008); Kenneth Guest, *God in Chinatown: Religion and Survival in New York's Evolving Immigrant Community* (New York: New York University Press, 2003); Prema Kurien, *A Place at the Multicultural Table: The Development of an American Hinduism* (New Brunswick, NJ: Rutgers University Press, 2007); R. Stephen Warner and Judith Wittner, eds., *Gatherings in Diaspora Religious Communities and the New Immigration* (Philadelphia: Temple University Press, 1998); David Yoo, ed., *New Spiritual Homes: Religion and Asian Americans* (Honolulu: University of Hawai'i Press, in association with UCLA Asian American Studies Center, Los Angeles, 1999).

18. Thomas Banchoff, ed., *Democracy and the New Religious Pluralism* (Oxford: Oxford University Press, 2007); Charles L. Cohen and Ronald L. Numbers, eds., *Gods in America: Religious Pluralism in the United States* (New York: Oxford University Press, 2013); Diana Eck, *A New Religious America: How a "Christian Country" Has Now Become the World's Most Religiously Diverse Nation* (San Francisco: HarperSanFrancisco, 2001); Stephen Prothero, ed., *A Nation of Religions: The Politics of Pluralism in Multireligious America* (Chapel Hill: University of North Carolina Press, 2006); Robert Wuthnow, *America and the Challenges of Religious Diversity* (Princeton, NJ: Princeton University Press, 2005).

19. R. Stephen Warner, "The De-Europeanization of American Christianity," in *A Church of Our Own: Disestablishment and Diversity in American Religion* (New Brunswick, NJ: Rutgers University Press, 2005), 257–262.

20. Horace Kallen, "Democracy Versus the Melting-Pot," *The Nation*, February 25, 1915. See also William Hutchison, *Religious Pluralism in America the Contentious History of a Founding Ideal* (New Haven, CT: Yale University Press, 2003).

21. Putnam and Campbell wrote of the "Aunt Sally" effect, which contributes to religious tolerance. See Robert D. Putnam and David E. Campbell, *American Grace: How Religion Divides and Unites Us* (New York: Simon & Schuster, 2010).

22. Kevin Schultz, *Tri-Faith America: How Catholics and Jews Held Postwar America to Its Protestant Promise* (New York: Oxford University Press, 2011).

23. Ronit Stahl, *Enlisting Faith: How the Military Chaplaincy Shaped Religion and State in Modern America* (Cambridge, MA: Harvard University Press, 2017).

24. *Refugees from Indochina: Hearings before the Subcommittee on Immigration, Citizenship and International Law of the Committee on the Judiciary House of Representatives*, 94th Cong. 270 (July 17, 1975) (statement of Frank Wisner, Interagency Task Force on Indochina Refugees).

25. "ESL Survey Summary," Correspondence and Related Material, 1983–1985, Minnesota State Refugee Advisory Council (hereafter MSRAC), Administrative Files, Records of the RPO, MDPW, MHS.

26. St. Paul-Ramsey Medical Center to Steven Rhodes, November 18, 1982, MSRAC Minutes, Administrative Files, Records of the RPO, MDPW, MHS.
27. Tom Kosel, interview.
28. "Revised Report of the Special Committee on NCC Use of Government Resources," June 1967, CWS Papers, PHS.
29. David North, Lawrence Lewin, and Jennifer Wagner, *Kaleidoscope: The Resettlement of Refugees in the United States by the Voluntary Agencies* (Washington, DC: New TransCentury Foundation, 1982), 79.
30. Kosel, interview.
31. Standing Committee, Protocol, and Minutes, September 6–7, 1977, LCUSA, DIRS, LCU 10/1, Archives of the ELCA, Elk Grove Village, IL.
32. Wendy Tai, "Unsettling influences," *Minneapolis Star Tribune*, February 8, 1993.
33. Observations on the 45-Day Reports, November 1, 1975, Standing Committee, Protocol, and Minutes, November 6–7, 1975, LCUSA, DIRS, LCU 10/1, Archives of the ELCA, Elk Grove Village, IL.
34. Kosel, interview.
35. Kathleen Vellenga, interview by the author, September 14, 2011, Saint Paul, MN.
36. *World Relief Sponsorship Question and Answer Booklet,* World Relief, Folder 13, Box 11, RSC, UMN Records, General/Multiethnic Collection, IHRC2968, IRHC, UMN.
37. *Sponsorship: Access to a New Life,* Correspondence by Name, 1979–1981, Box 2, ARC Records, MHS.
38. *Face to Face: The Ministry of Refugee Resettlement,* LIRS Assorted Publications, LCUSA, DIRS, LCU 10/1, Archives of the ELCA, Elk Grove Village, IL.
39. *Manual for Refugee Sponsorship,* CWS Records, PHS. In Canada, the Mennonite voluntary agency adopted a similar approach, although Mennonite congregational sponsors had different beliefs about how to share Christianity with church-sponsored Hmong refugees. Voluntary agency officials insisted on not taking advantage of refugees' vulnerability, but sponsors objected to this approach, considering it "negative spiritually." See Daphne Winland, "The Role of Religious Affiliation in Refugee Resettlement: The Case of the Hmong," *Canadian Ethnic Studies* 24, no. 1 (1992): 102.
40. *Manual for Refugee Sponsorship.*
41. Rev. Jack O'Donnell to the LCUSA, August 10, 1977, Standing Committee, Protocol, and Minutes, September 6–7, 1977, LCUSA, DIRS, LCU 10/1, Archives of the ELCA, Elk Grove Village, IL.
42. *World Relief Sponsorship Question and Answer Booklet.*
43. Suggestions for Orientation, Standing Committee, Protocol, Minutes, January 8–9, 1976, LCUSA, DIRS, LCU 10/1, Archives of the ELCA, Elk Grove Village, IL.
44. *Face to Face.*
45. *World Relief Sponsorship Question and Answer Booklet.*
46. *Face to Face.*

47. Jim Adams, "Hope Parish Extends Missionary Hand to Hmong," *Minneapolis Star and Tribune*, November 4, 1982.

48. *Face to Face.*

49. "New Home, New Religion," *Atlanta Journal-Constitution*, August 18, 1996.

50. Wendy Tai, "Unsettling Influences," *Minneapolis Star Tribune*, February 8, 1993.

51. *The Hmong: Their History and Culture*, 18, LCUSA, DIRS, LCU 10/3, Archives of the ELCA, Elk Grove Village, IL.

52. *The Hmong*, 38, 40, 41.

53. *Religion of the Refugees*, Pamphlets Relating to Refugee Relief and Assistance, MHS.

54. *Religion of the Refugees.*

55. *A Guide to Two Cultures*, Pamphlets Relating to Refugee Relief and Assistance, MHS.

56. Refugee Core Committee Records, Archive of Saint Anthony Park Lutheran Church, Saint Paul, MN.

57. "Getting to Know You," *First Lutheran Herald*, August 1990, MHS.

58. Mahmood Mamdani, *From Citizen to Refugee: Uganda Asians Come to Britain* (London: Frances Pinter, 1973); Becky Taylor, *Refugees in Twentieth-Century Britain: A History* (Cambridge: Cambridge University Press, 2021).

59. Estelle Strizhak, "The Ugandan Asian Expulsion: Resettlement in the USA," *Journal of Refugee Studies* 6, no. 3 (1993): 260–264.

60. "Lutherans Welcome Ugandan Refugees into Minneapolis," *New York Times*, November 26, 1972.

61. Nizar Motani, *The Brown Diaspora*, LIRS Assorted Publications, LCUSA, DIRS, LCU 10/1, Archives of the ELCA, Elk Grove Village, IL.

62. Motani, *The Brown Diaspora.*

63. Motani, *The Brown Diaspora.*

64. Alice Bonner, "Presbyterians Aid Ugandans," *Washington Post*, June 22, 1973.

65. DAPC, DPN, September 1976, MHS.

66. Elaine Kirk, interview by the author, July 26, 2012, Saint Paul, MN.

67. Neng Vang and Paj Ntaub Lis, interview by the author, March 25, 2012, Saint Paul, MN. Interviewees' names have been changed at their request.

68. Refugee Core Committee Records, Archive of Saint Anthony Park Lutheran Church, Saint Paul, MN.

69. Boxes 21–24 and 51–52, Case Files, IIM Records, IHRC3257, IHRC, UMN.

70. Pat Westberg, "Viets 'Home' for First White Christmas," *Catholic Bulletin*, December 19, 1975.

71. Biloine Young, *My Heart It Is Delicious: Setting the Course for Cross-Cultural Health Care* (Afton, MN: Afton Historical Society Press, 2007), 23–24.

72. Pearl Jones, interview by the author, August 29, 2012, White Bear Lake, MN. Interviewee's name has been changed at their request.

73. Kosel, interview.

74. Dorothy Knight, interview by the author, August 6, 2012, Saint Paul, MN.

75. Paul Tidemann, "I Have Called You Friends," May 16, 1982, in *Ordinary Moments: Ordinary People Blessed by God,* ed. Paul Tidemann (self-published, 2006), 45.

76. Rev. Paul Tidemann, interview by the author, July 28, 2012, Saint Paul, MN.

77. Kosel, interview.

78. Knight, interview.

79. Nolan Zavoral, "Hmong Catholics Lose a Good Friend," *Minneapolis Star Tribune,* May 26, 2003.

80. Joanne Karvonen, interview by the author, August 10, 2012, Saint Paul, MN.

81. Bon Tempo, *Americans at the Gate,* 99.

82. *Refugees from Indochina: Hearings before the Subcommittee on Immigration, Citizenship and International Law of the Committee on the Judiciary House of Representatives,* 94th Cong. 331 (July 22, 1975) (statement of August Bernthal, LIRS).

5. Disrupting the Old Way

1. Paja Thao and Dwight Conquergood, *I Am a Shaman: A Hmong Life Story with Ethnographic Commentary,* trans. Xa Thao, Southeast Asian Refugee Studies Occasional Papers, no. 8 (Minneapolis: Southeast Asian Refugee Studies Project, Center for Urban and Regional Affairs, University of Minnesota, 1989), 24.

2. Eric Tang, *Unsettled: Cambodian Refugees in the New York City Hyperghetto* (Philadelphia: Temple University Press, 2015).

3. Yen Le Espiritu, *Body Counts: The Vietnam War and Militarized Refugees* (Berkeley: University of California Press, 2014), 18.

4. Oscar Handlin, *The Uprooted,* 2nd ed. (Boston: Little, Brown, 1973), 105.

5. Nao Thao, interview by the author, September 11, 2012, Saint Paul, MN.

6. Yaw Yang, interview by Marly Moua, December 1, 2007, HOHPCU.

7. Yong Kay Moua and Houa Vue Moua, interview by the author, September 12, 2012, Saint Paul, MN; Nao Thao, interview.

8. Cziasarh Neng Yang, interview by the author, September 17, 2012, Saint Paul, MN.

9. Paul Pao Herr, Mai Zong Vue, William Boua Yang, May Kao Yang, and United States Indochinese Refugee Resettlement Program, "Report on the Hmong-American Delegation Visit to Ban Napho Repatriation Center, Nakhon Phanom, Thailand: May 30th–June 7th, 1996," Special Collections and Archives, UC Irvine Libraries.

10. Kia Vue, interview by the author, interpreted by Maile Vue, September 8, 2012, Saint Paul, MN.

11. Center for Applied Linguistics, *Cultural Orientation Research Manual,* Vol. 1, Folders 4–6, Box 35, RSC Records, General/Multiethnic Collection, IHRC2968, IHRC, UMN.

12. Nao Thao, interview.

13. Nancy Shulins, "Hmong Refugees in U.S. Caught in a Time Warp," *Advocate* (Newark, OH), July 8, 1984. See also Peter H. King, "From Laos to Fresno: Hmong Try to Adjust," *Los Angeles Times,* April 7, 1985; and Margot Hornblower, "Hmongtana," *Washington Post,* July 5, 1980.

14. Stephen Morin, "Many Hmong, Puzzled by Life in the U.S., Yearn for Old Days in Laos," *Wall Street Journal,* February 16, 1983.

15. Lucia Mouat, "Hmong: Laotian Hill People Who Now Call St. Paul Home," *Christian Science Monitor,* July 12, 1982.

16. Bruce Downing et al., *Hmong Resettlement Study Site Report: Minneapolis–St. Paul* (Minneapolis: Southeast Asian Studies Project, Center for Urban and Regional Affairs, University of Minnesota, 1984), 20–55.

17. Karl Karlson, "We See Many Good Things for Us in St. Paul," *St. Paul Dispatch,* December 19, 1978.

18. Mimi Thi Nguyen, *The Gift of Freedom: War, Debt, and Other Refugee Passages* (Durham, NC: Duke University Press, 2012); Espiritu, *Body Counts.*

19. Tang, *Unsettled.*

20. Yer Moua, interview by Mai Neng Moua, January 20, 2000, HWATOHP, MHS.

21. Calvin Trillin, "US Journal: Fairfield, Iowa, Resettling the Yangs," *New Yorker,* March 24, 1980.

22. Box 21, Case Files, IIM Records, IHRC3257, IHRC, UMN.

23. Box 22, Case Files, IIM Records, IHRC3257, IHRC, UMN.

24. Box 21, Case Files, IIM Records, IHRC3257, IHRC, UMN.

25. Yaw Yang, interview.

26. Ses Boua Xa Moua's account in Lillian Faderman with Ghia Xiong, "To a Promised Land," in *I Begin My Life All Over: The Hmong and the American Immigrant Experience* (Boston: Beacon Press, 1999), 101.

27. For an overview of the relationship between immigration, citizenship, and white Christian identity, see Khyati Joshi, *White Christian Privilege: The Illusion of Religious Equality in America* (New York: New York University Press, 2020). For a discussion of the centrality of heathenness in the construction of racial difference, see Kathryn Gin Lum, *Heathen: Religion and Race in American History* (Cambridge, MA: Harvard University Press, 2022); Beth Lew-Williams, *The Chinese Must Go: Violence, Exclusion, and the Making of the Alien in America* (Cambridge, MA: Harvard University Press, 2018); and Joshua Paddison, *American Heathens: Religion, Race, and Reconstruction in California* (Berkeley: University of California Press, 2012).

28. Jean Seligmann, "The Curse of the Hmong," *Newsweek,* August 10, 1981. See also Nancy Shullins, "Hmong Refugees Undergo Severe Culture Shock, from Stone Age to the Space Age," *Los Angeles Times,* July 8, 1984; Evan Maxwell, "Refugees' Medical Mystery, Men of Hmong Dogged by Death," *Los Angeles Times,* July 12, 1981; Peg Meier, "Death Syndrome Fear Keeps Hmong Awake," *Minneapolis Star,* March 12, 1983.

29. Cher Vang, interview by Linda Rossi, February 3, 1992, Hmong Oral History Project (hereafter HOHP), MHS.

30. Khu Thao, interview by Kelly Vang, translated by Peter Chou Vang, July 1, 2004, HOHPCU.

31. Yong Kay Moua and Houa Vue Moua, interview.

32. Chia Youyee Vang, *Hmong America: Reconstructing Community in Diaspora* (Urbana: University of Illinois Press, 2010), 49.

33. Carl Bon Tempo, *Americans at the Gate: The United States and Refugees during the Cold War* (Princeton, NJ: Princeton University Press, 2008), 155–156.

34. Vang, *Hmong America,* 41.

35. Among other things, Hmong elders are essential for the practice and preservation of the Hmong way. According to Song Lee, they "provide guidance and support in the spiritual health and development of younger generations" and "play a role in passing on their knowledge of traditional rites, rituals, and the Hmong language." See Song Lee, "The Challenges and Contributions of Hmong American Elders: A Personal and Professional Perspective," in *Hmong and American: From Refugees to Citizens,* ed. Vincent Her and Mary Louise Buley-Meissner (Saint Paul: Minnesota Historical Society Press, 2012), 135–136.

36. Jacque Lemoine, "Shamanism in the Context of Hmong Resettlement," in *The Hmong in Transition,* ed. Glenn Hendricks, Bruce Downing, and Amos Deinard (New York: Center for Migration Studies and the Southeast Asian Refugee Studies Project of the University of Minnesota, 1986), 346.

37. Cziasarh Neng Yang, interview.

38. Bo Thao, interview by MayKao Hang, January 17, 2000, HWATOHP, MHS.

39. Kim Yang, interview by Mai Neng Moua, December 17, 1999, HWATOHP, MHS.

40. "A Conversation with Wang Kao Her," *Newsletter of the Southeast Asian Ministry,* March 1993.

41. Lao Family Community, Inc., University of Minnesota Center for Urban and Regional Affairs, and Northwest Regional Educational Lab, *The Hmong Resettlement Study, Volume I: Final Report* (Washington, DC: Office of Refugee Resettlement, 1985), 51.

42. Thao and Conquergood, *I Am a Shaman,* 33–34.

43. "A Conversation with Wang Kao Her."

44. Nao Khue Yang and Sarah Fang, interview by the author, interpreted by Maile Vue, September 5, 2012, Saint Paul, MN.

45. Nao Thao, interview.

46. Nao Khue Yang and Sarah Fang, interview.

47. Nao Thao, interview.

48. Nao Khue Yang and Sarah Fang, interview.

49. Cziasarh Neng Yang, interview.

50. "A Conversation with Wang Kao Her."

51. Nao Khue Yang and Sarah Fang, interview.

52. Yong Kay Moua and Houa Vue Moua, interview.

53. Rev. Timothy Vang, interview by the author, September 12, 2012, Maplewood, MN.

54. Shong Yer Yang and Soua Lo, interview by the author, interpreted by Maile Vue, August 6, 2012, Saint Paul, MN.

55. Rev. Pa Mang Her, interview by Peter Chou Vang, August 1, 2007, HOHPCU.

56. Tzianeng Vang, interview by the author, September 5, 2012, Saint Paul, MN.

57. Neng Vang and Paj Ntaub Lis, interview by the author, March 25, 2012, Saint Paul, MN. Interviewees' names have been changed at their request.

58. Xai Thao, interview by Mai Neng Vang, December 1, 2007, HOHPCU.

59. Cziasarh Neng Yang, interview. Hmong people over time did invoke the Constitution in defense of their practices, such as when one Hmong family cited the First Amendment in defense of creating a slaughterhouse in Grove Heights, MN. See Mark Brunswick, "Clash of Cultures," *Minneapolis Star Tribune*, February 23, 1997.

60. Ong Vang Xiong, interview by Mai Neng Moua, January 17, 2000, HWATOHP, MHS.

61. Nhia Yer Yang, interview by Linda Rossi, translated by May Herr, November 15, 1991, HOHP, MHS.

62. Thao and Conquergood, *I Am a Shaman,* 71.

63. Joua Tsu Thao, interview by the author, September 19, 2012, Roseville, MN.

64. Gary Yia Lee and Nicholas Tapp, *Culture and Customs of the Hmong* (Santa Barbara, CA: Greenwood Press, 2010), 32–35.

65. Chai Lee, interview by the author, July 21, 2014, Saint Paul, MN.

66. Nao Khue Yang and Sarah Fang, interview.

67. Keith Vang, interview by Paul Hillmer, April 1, 2005, HOHPCU.

68. Yia Lee, interview by the author, July 29, 2012, Saint Paul, MN.

69. Khu Thao, interview.

70. Nao Khue Yang and Sarah Fang, interview.

71. Soua Sue Lee, interview by the author, July 2014, Saint Paul, MN.

72. See Ghia Xiong's account in Faderman with Xiong, "Ghia," in *I Begin My Life All Over,* 252–253.

73. Shoua Vang and Nhia Vang, "The Sacred Drum," in *New Americans: An Oral History, Immigrants and Refugees in the U.S. Today,* ed. Al Santoli (New York: Viking Press, 1988), 327.

74. See Shone Yang's account in in Faderman with Xiong, "Shamanism, Christianity, and Modern Medicine," in *I Begin My Life All Over,* 116.

75. Sia Ly Thao, interview by Tou Thao, December 1, 2007, HOHPCU.

76. Mai Neng Moua, *The Bride Price: A Hmong Wedding Story* (Saint Paul: Minnesota Historical Society Press, 2017), 67.

77. Mai Lee, interview by Mai Neng Vang, May 1, 2005, HOHPCU.

78. Thao and Conquergood, *I Am a Shaman,* 18–19.

6. Following the New Way

1. Kia Vue, interview by the author, interpreted by Maile Vue, September 8, 2012, Saint Paul, MN.

2. Shari Rabin, *Jews on the Frontier: Religion and Mobility in Nineteenth-Century America* (New York: New York University Press, 2017), 7.

3. Catherine Albanese, "Exchanging Selves, Exchanging Souls: Contact, Combination, and American Religious History," in *Retelling U.S. Religious*

History, ed. Thomas Tweed (Berkeley: University of California Press, 1997), 200–226.

4. Linford Fisher, *The Indian Great Awakening: Religion and the Shaping of Native Cultures in Early America* (New York: Oxford University Press, 2014), 8.

5. Neng Vang and Paj Ntaub Lis, interview by the author, March 25, 2012, Saint Paul, MN. Interviewees' names have been changed at their request.

6. Tzianeng Vang, interview by the author, September 5, 2012, Saint Paul, MN.

7. Yia Lee, interview by the author, July 29, 2012, Saint Paul, MN.

8. Mai Vang Thao, interview by Bo Thao, November 14, 1999, HWATOHP, MHS.

9. Tzianeng Vang, interview.

10. Shong Yer Yang and Soua Lo, interview by the author, interpreted by Maile Vue, August 6, 2012, Saint Paul, MN.

11. Neng Xiong, interview by the author, translated by Maile Vue, August 3, 2012, Minneapolis, MN. See also Song Lo's experience shared in Thomas Collins and Les Suzukamo, "Dreams in Exile: The Hmong in St. Paul," *St. Paul Pioneer Press Dispatch,* November 26, 1989.

12. Bo Thao, interview by MayKao Hang, January 17, 2000, HWATOHP, MHS.

13. Kim Yang, interview by Mai Neng Moua, December 17, 1999, HWATOHP, MHS.

14. Rev. William Siong, interview by the author, September 11, 2012, Saint Paul, MN. Several scholars have identified the desire to be "American" as one of the reasons why Hmong and other Southeast Asian refugees have adopted Christianity. See Christine Desan, "A Change of Faith for Hmong Refugees," *Cultural Survival Quarterly* 7 (1983): 45–48; and Aihwa Ong, *Buddha Is Hiding: Refugees, Citizenship, the New America* (Berkeley: University of California Press, 2003), 205. In addition, Daphne Winland argued that Canadian Hmong refugees found that joining Mennonite churches facilitated that adjustment and adaptation to their new society. See Daphne Winland, "The Role of Religious Affiliation in Refugee Resettlement: The Case of the Hmong," *Canadian Ethnic Studies* 24, no. 1 (1992): 96–119; Daphne Winland, "Christianity and Community: Conversion and Adaptation among Hmong Refugee Women," *Canadian Journal of Sociology* 19, no. 1 (Winter 1994): 21–45; and Daphne Winland, "Revisiting a Case Study of Hmong Refugees and Ontario Mennonites," *Journal of Mennonite History* 24 (2006): 169–176.

15. Keith Vang, interview by Paul Hillmer, April 1, 2005, HOHPCU.

16. Mai Neng Moua, *The Bride Price: A Hmong Wedding Story* (Saint Paul: Minnesota Historical Society Press, 2017), 31.

17. Shong Yer Yang and Soua Lo, interview.

18. Rev. Bea Vue-Benson, interview by the author, September 5, 2012, Saint Paul, MN.

19. Rev. Pa Mang Her, interview by Peter Chou Vang, August 1, 2007, HOHPCU.

20. Cziasarh Neng Yang, interview by the author, September 17, 2012, Saint Paul, MN.

21. Yong Kay Moua and Houa Vue Moua, interview by the author, September 12, 2012, Saint Paul, MN. Several Hmong people explained the lack of family as the reason they converted to Christianity. As Yia Lee explained, "My husband has no brothers, [or] sisters, so he's the only one, and that is one of the reasons why we converted." Similarly, in her research on Hmong refugees resettled in the San Francisco Bay Area, the anthropologist Kay Taber found that Hmong refugees felt compelled to adopt Christianity because they were separated from kin whose participation was necessary for Hmong rituals. The absence of relatives made traditional ceremonies "impossible," she argued. See Kay Taber, "Hmong Kinship in Transition," *Treganza Anthropology Museum Papers* 16 (1994): 51.

22. Tzianeng Vang, interview.

23. Mao Yang, interview by the author, interpreted by Paj Ntaub Lis, August 12, 2012, Saint Paul, MN.

24. For an explanation of the *dab xwm kab,* see Gary Yia Lee and Nicholas Tapp, *Culture and Customs of the Hmong* (Santa Barbara, CA: Greenwood Press, 2010), 36.

25. Neng Vang and Paj Ntaub Lis, interview.

26. Joua Tsu Thao, interview by the author, September 19, 2012, Roseville, MN.

27. Rev. Timothy Vang, interview by the author, September 12, 2012, Maplewood, MN.

28. Paja Thao and Dwight Conquergood, *I Am a Shaman: A Hmong Life Story with Ethnographic Commentary,* trans. Xa Thao, Southeast Asian Refugee Studies Occasional Papers, no. 8 (Minneapolis: Southeast Asian Refugee Studies Project, Center for Urban and Regional Affairs, University of Minnesota, 1989), 24.

29. Vincent Her, "Hmong Cosmology: Proposed Model, Preliminary Insights," *Hmong Studies Journal* 6 (2005): 1; Lee and Tapp, *Culture and Customs of the Hmong,* 38.

30. Rev. Timothy Vang, interview.

31. Rev. Timothy Vang, interview. Many evangelical Christians believe that *dab,* or the spirits central to native Hmong beliefs, are malevolent and equivalent to demons or the devil, although this interpretation of *dab* may be a recent development due to contact with Christian missionaries. According to Dia Cha, Hmong people did not consider *dab* to be fundamentally evil until Christian missionaries introduced that interpretation. See Dia Cha, interview by Paul Hillmer, October 5, 2005, HOHPCU.

32. Rev. Timothy Vang, interview.

33. Cher Moua, interview by the author, September 6, 2012, Saint Paul, MN.

34. Tzianeng Vang, interview.

35. True Xiong, interview by the author, interpreted by Maile Vue, August 9, 2012, Minneapolis, MN.

36. Bee Yang, interview by the author, August 2, 2012, Saint Paul, MN.

37. Her, "Hmong Cosmology," 1; Winland, "Christianity and Community," 24.

38. Moua, *The Bride Price,* 57.

39. Ruth Hammond, "New Faith, Old Belief," *St. Paul Pioneer Press,* September 16, 1984. According to the article, "You a Vang Yang . . . learned that

NOTES TO PAGES 220–223

his sister in Ban Vinai refugee camp, Thailand, had gone back to the old religion after converting to Christianity. Alarmed, he mailed her a cassette on which he advised her not to sway back and forth, but to remain a Christian. 'You go to church, you have to stay in church all the time. Then the Lord will take care of you,' he told her on the tape. He himself does not attend a Christian church, but he says he might later."

40. Yang Cha Ying, interview by Linda Rossi, translated by May Herr, November 20, 1991, HOHP, MHS.

41. Cher Moua, interview.

42. Rev. William Siong, interview.

43. "Pom Siab Hmoob Theatre to Present 'The Garden of the Soul,'" *Asian Pages,* December 15, 1995.

44. Jaime Meyer et al., *The Garden of the Souls* (Saint Paul, MN: Pom Siab Hmoob Theatre, 1995), 4–5, 26. Others used theater to explore this religious schism, in a Hmong version of the classic "December dilemma," where Hmong new year is posed as the Hmong alternative to Christmas. See Doug Grow, "19-Year-Old Acts in His Own Success Story," *Minneapolis Star Tribune,* November 20, 1990.

45. Cher Moua, interview.

46. Lamin Sanneh, *Disciples of All Nations: Pillars of World Christianity* (New York: Oxford University Press, 2007), 56.

47. As Winland observed, "Part of the reason for the misapprehensions concerning religious differences is the assumption that religious change is unidirectional—from the missionary to the missionized. This process is thus frequently portrayed as an unbalanced process with exotic 'Other' capitulating to the forces of modernity." Her research on Hmong Mennonites indicated that Hmong religious change was "a complex and multi-dimensional process," and that it was necessary "to investigate how and in what ways they reconciled their new faith with the old." Her argument coincided with other scholars who have studied Hmong adoption of Christianity. See Winland, "Revisiting a Case Study of Hmong Refugees and Ontario Mennonites," 175. See also Nicholas Tapp, "The Impact of Missionary Christianity upon Marginalized Ethnic Minorities: The Case of the Hmong," *Journal of Southeast Asian Studies* 20, no. 1 (March 1989): 70–95.

48. Lu Vang with Phua Xiong, "Influence of Conversion to Christianity on a Hmong Woman's Decision about Hysterectomy: A Pastor's Perspective," in *Healing by Heart: Clinical and Ethical Case Stories of Hmong Families and Western Providers,* ed. Kathleen A. Culhane-Pera et al. (Nashville, TN: Vanderbilt University Press, 2003), 112.

49. For more discussion on the stakes of distinguishing between "religion" and nonreligious "culture," see Samira Mehta, *Beyond Chrismukkah: The Christian-Jewish Interfaith Family in the United States* (Chapel Hill: University of North Carolina Press, 2018).

50. Kim Ode, "'He Has a Hmong Heart': Father Daniel Taillez, Now a Missionary to America," *Minneapolis Star Tribune,* January 12, 1989.

51. Wendy Tai, "Hmong Families Torn by Collision of Old and New," *Minneapolis Star Tribune,* February 8, 1993. A Catholic Hmong New Year cele-

bration in 1982 at Saint Michael Parish in Providence, Rhode Island, indicates that Catholic worship services incorporated Hmong language and Hmong traditional song. A full recording of this Catholic Hmong New Year celebration is available in the Amy Catlin files, Ethnomusicology Library, University of California, Los Angeles.

52. David Schimke, "Devils and Shamans," *Twin Cities Reader,* August 21–27, 1996.
53. Moua, *The Bride Price,* 203; Sucheng Chan, "The Hmong Experience in Asia and the United States," in *Hmong Means Free: Life in Laos and America,* ed. Sucheng Chan (Philadelphia: Temple University Press, 1994), 55.
54. Hammond, "New Faith, Old Belief."
55. Schimke, "Devils and Shamans."
56. Moua, *The Bride Price,* 30.
57. Yia Lee, interview.
58. Chia Youyee Vang, *Hmong America: Reconstructing Community in Diaspora* (Urbana: University of Illinois Press, 2010), 94.
59. Moua, *The Bride Price,* 31.
60. Vang, *Hmong America,* 77–78; Winland, "The Role of Religious Affiliation in Refugee Resettlement," 106–107; Winland, "Christianity and Community," 33–41. Several scholars have demonstrated that religious institutions are important sites of ethnic community formation and of preservation and reformulation of ethnic identity, in addition to mutual aid. See, for example, Oscar Handlin, *The Uprooted,* 2nd ed. (Boston: Little, Brown, 1973); and Robert Orsi, *The Madonna of 115th Street: Faith and Community in Italian Harlem, 1880–1950,* 2nd ed. (New Haven, CT: Yale University Press, 2002).
61. Mao Yang, interview.
62. Winland, "Revisiting a Case Study of Hmong Refugees and Ontario Mennonites," 174.
63. Yong Kay Moua and Houa Vue Moua, interview.
64. Anne Fadiman, *The Spirit Catches You and You Fall Down: A Hmong Child, Her American Doctors, and the Collision of Two Cultures* (New York: Farrar, Straus and Giroux, 1998), 208; Yang, "Shone Yang's Story," 114–118. Similarly, Daphne Winland encountered Hmong Mennonites who continued to practice shamanism, although they preferred not to discuss the fact that they maintained these traditional practices. See Winland, "Christianity and Community," 22; and Winland, "The Role of Religious Affiliation in Refugee Resettlement," 111.
65. MayKao Hang, interview by May Hang, January 17, 2000, HWATOHP, MHS.
66. Rev. Bea Vue-Benson, interview. According to Mai Neng Moua, "Life after death is a very important issue for Hmong parents. Animist or Christian, it is hard for them to change these long-held values just because they now believe in different spirits." See Moua, *The Bride Price,* 58.
67. Rev. Bea Vue-Benson, interview. She also discussed how "shamanism allows room for other beliefs." See Brian Bonner, "Religious Divide," *St. Paul Pioneer Press,* December 17, 1995.

68. Yong Kay Moua and Houa Vue Moua, interview.
69. Even if many Hmong Christians renounced the practice of ancestor worship and other Hmong rituals, many continued to believe in traditional spirits and to maintain animist beliefs. See Winland, "Revisiting a Case Study of Hmong Refugees and Ontario Mennonites," 174.
70. Moua, *The Bride Price,* 34.
71. Other scholars have written about how the belief that religion should be efficacious is present in other Asian religious groups. See, for example, Ian Reader and George J. Tanabe Jr., *Practically Religious: Worldly Benefits and the Common Religion of Japan* (Honolulu: University of Hawai'i Press, 1998).
72. Vang and Xiong, "Influence of Conversion," 113.
73. Rev. Pa Mang Her, interview.
74. Vang and Xiong, "Influence of Conversion," 113.
75. Neng Vang and Paj Ntaub Lis, interview.
76. Yia Lee, interview.
77. Mary Her, interview by the author, interpreted by Maile Vue, August 1, 2012, Saint Paul, MN. Interviewee's name has been changed at their request.
78. True Xiong, interview. Similarly, Zai Xiong believed that becoming Mormon was the reason that he was able to regain his hearing, from 50 percent loss to only 15 percent loss. However, in his retelling of his conversion experience, he explained that after much praying, he received a message from God that he seek the help of a Western medical doctor rather than that of a shaman. In this sense, adoption of Christian beliefs and practices facilitated the adoption of Western medicine. See Zai Xiong's account in Lillian Faderman with Ghia Xiong, "Shamanism, Christianity, and Modern Medicine," in *I Begin My Life All Over: The Hmong and the American Immigrant Experience* (Boston: Beacon Press, 1999), 121–122.
79. See Lee, interview by MayKao Hang, January 23, 2000, HWATOHP, MHS.
80. Nao Thao, interview by the author, September 11, 2012, Saint Paul, MN.
81. Mao Yang, interview.
82. Neng Vang and Paj Ntaub Lis, interview.
83. Brian Bonner, "Religious Divide," *St. Paul Pioneer Press,* December 17, 1995. Dia Cha explained that Hmong people's pragmatic openness to many beliefs and practices means that "there is a lot of variation in Hmong behavior, belief, and values." See Dia Cha, interview.
84. Pacyinz Lyfoung, interview by MayKao Hang, December 17, 1999, HWATOHP, MHS.
85. Rev. Timothy Vang, interview.
86. Kia Vue, interview; Mao Yang, interview.
87. Bao Vang, interview by Kim Yang, December 8, 1999, HWATOHP, MHS.
88. Yia Lee, interview.
89. MayKao Hang, interview.
90. Moua, *The Bride Price,* 58.
91. Keith Vang, interview.
92. Rev. William Siong, interview.

7. Remaking the Hmong Way

1. The practice of putting government documents in the hand of the deceased at a funeral has been mentioned elsewhere. See Kao Kalia Yang, *The Latehomecomer: A Hmong Family Memoir* (Minneapolis: Coffee House Press, 2008), 253.

2. For overviews of First Amendment claims of different religious groups in the twentieth century, see Courtney Bender and Jennifer Snow, "From Alleged Buddhists to Unreasonable Hindus: First Amendment Jurisprudence after 1965," in *A Nation of Religions,* ed. Stephen Prothero (Chapel Hill: University of North Carolina Press, 2006), 181–208; and Sarah Barringer Gordon, *The Spirit of the Law: Religious Voices and the Constitution in Modern America* (Cambridge, MA: Belknap Press of Harvard University Press, 2010). For examples of how Native Americans have reconfigured their beliefs and practices as a religion in order to ensure rights and protections, see Tisa Wenger, *We Have a Religion: The 1920s Pueblo Indian Dance Controversy and American Religious Freedom* (Chapel Hill: University of North Carolina Press, 2009); and Gregory Johnson, *Sacred Claims: Repatriation and Living Tradition* (Charlottesville: University of Virginia Press, 2007). Native Americans have not limited themselves to using the First Amendent; they have used other categories, too. See Michael David McNally, *Defend the Sacred: Native American Religious Freedom beyond the First Amendment* (Princeton, NJ: Princeton University Press, 2020).

3. For examples of how other groups have adjusted their institutions to fit the Protestant norms, see Prema Kurien, *A Place at the Multicultural Table: The Development of an American Hinduism* (New Brunswick, NJ: Rutgers University Press, 2007).

4. Cziasarh Neng Yang, interview by the author, September 17, 2012, Saint Paul, MN.

5. Tzianeng Vang, interview by the author, September 5, 2012, Saint Paul, MN.

6. Cher Vang, interview by Linda Rossi, February 3, 1992, HOHP, MHS.

7. Cziasarh Neng Yang, interview.

8. Khu Thao, interview by Kelly Vang, translated by Peter Chou Vang, July 1, 2004, HOHPCU.

9. Lao Family Community Inc., University of Minnesota Center for Urban and Regional Affairs, and Northwest Regional Educational Lab, *The Hmong Resettlement Study, Volume I: Final Report* (Washington, DC: Office of Refugee Resettlement, 1985), 42–54; John Fincke, "Secondary Migration to California's Central Valley," in *The Hmong in Transition,* ed. Glenn Hendricks, Bruce Downing, and Amos Deinard (New York: Center for Migration Studies and the Southeast Asian Refugee Studies Project of the University of Minnesota, 1986), 184–186.

10. Mao Yang, interview by the author, interpreted by Paj Ntaub Lis, August 12, 2012, Saint Paul, MN.

11. Joua Tsu Thao, interview by the author, September 19, 2012, Roseville, MN.

12. Rev. Timothy Vang, interview by the author, September 12, 2012, Maplewood, MN.

13. Cziasarh Neng Yang, interview.

14. MayKao Hang, interview by May Yang Hang, January 17, 2000, HWATOHP, MHS.

15. Paja Thao and Dwight Conquergood, *I Am a Shaman: A Hmong Life Story with Ethnographic Commentary,* trans. Xa Thao, Southeast Asian Refugee Studies Occasional Papers, no. 8 (Minneapolis: Southeast Asian Refugee Studies Project, Center for Urban and Regional Affairs, University of Minnesota, 1989), 23.

16. Nao Thao, interview by the author, September 11, 2012, Saint Paul, MN.

17. Elizabeth Thao, "The Next Wave of Hmong Shamans: Sandy'Ci Moua's Story," *Twin Cities Daily Planet,* April 2, 2013; Elizabeth Thao, "The Next Wave of Hmong Shamans: Kuoa Fong Lo's Story," *Twin Cities Daily Planet,* April 2, 2013.

18. Nao Khue Yang and Sarah Fang, interview by the author, interpreted by Maile Vue, September 5, 2012, Saint Paul, MN.

19. Nao Thao, interview by the author, September 11, 2012, Saint Paul, MN.

20. J. Kou Vang, interview by the author, July 28, 2014, Maplewood, MN; Chu Wu, interview by the author, August 6, 2014, Saint Paul, MN.

21. Mai Neng Moua, *The Bride Price: A Hmong Wedding Story* (Saint Paul: Minnesota Historical Society Press, 2017), 225.

22. Soua Sue Lee, interview by the author, July 29, 2014, Saint Paul, MN.

23. Chu Wu, interview by the author, August 6, 2014, Saint Paul, MN.

24. J. Kou Vang, interview by the author, July 28, 2014, Maplewood, MN.

25. Chu Wu, interview.

26. J. Kou Vang, interview.

27. Chu Wu, interview.

28. J. Kou Vang, interview.

29. Mecca Bos, "Inside the Meat Market That Sells Animals for Sacrifice," *Vice* (blog), September 11, 2017, https://www.vice.com/en/article/a335q8/inside-one-of-americas-last-slaughterhouses-performing-ritual-sacrifice.

30. Soua Sue Lee, interview.

31. "Mission Statement," Hmong Cultural Center, Saint Paul, MN, 1993.

32. Soua Sue Lee, interview.

33. Chai Lee, interview by the author, July 21, 2014, Saint Paul, MN.

34. Cziasarh Neng Yang, interview. The creation of formal organizations to support the practice of traditional Hmong beliefs and rituals has not been limited to the Twin Cities; Hmong practitioners have created workshops to teach particular skills elsewhere in the United States. See Vincent Her, "Searching for Sources of Hmong Identity in Multicultural America," in *Hmong and American: From Refugees to Citizens,* ed. Vincent Her and Mary Louise Buley-Meissner (Saint Paul: Minnesota Historical Society Press, 2012), 31–46. Scholars have found that Southeast Asian refugees have not simply preserved their native rituals and beliefs but have innovated and reinvented their beliefs, practices, and institutions to meet new needs. See Hien Duc Do and Mimi Khuc, "Immigrant Religious Adaptation: Viet-

namese American Buddhists at Chua Viet Nam (Vietnamese Buddhist Temple)," in *Religion at the Corner of Bliss and Nirvana: Politics, Identity, and Faith in New Migrant Communities,* ed. Lois Ann Lorentzen et al. (Durham, NC: Duke University Press, 2009), 124–138.

35. Shoua Vang and Nhia Vang, "The Sacred Drum," in *New Americans: An Oral History; Immigrants and Refugees in the U.S. Today,* ed. Al Santoli (New York: Viking Press, 1988), 327.

36. Nengher Vang and Jeremy Hein, "Hmong American Leadership and Unity in the Post–Vang Pao Era," *Hmong Studies Journal* 16 (2015): 10.

37. Tzianeng Vang, interview. Other Asian immigrants, such as Japanese immigrants, have "Protestantized" their beliefs and practices. See Isao Horinouchi, *Americanized Buddhism: A Sociological Analysis of a Protestantized Japanese Religion* (Berkeley: University of California Press, 1973).

38. Poj Koob Yawm Ntxwv brochure.

39. Poj Koob Yawm Ntxwv brochure.

40. Poj Koob Yawm Ntxwv brochure.

41. "The Bylaws of Temple of Hmongism," Temple of Hmongism, accessed January 22, 2022, https://www.hmongism.org/bylaws.

42. "The Bylaws of the Temple of Hmongism." See also Weidong Zhang, "Revamping Beliefs, Reforming Rituals, and Performing Hmongness? A Case Study of Temple of Hmongism," *Hmong Studies Journal* 21 (2020): 1–28.

43. Gregory Plotnikoff et al., "Hmong Shamanism: Animist Spiritual Healing in Minnesota," *Minnesota Medicine* 85, no. 6 (2002): 29–34.

44. Much of the interest in Hmong shamanism owes to Anne Fadiman, *The Spirit Catches You and You Fall Down: A Hmong Child, Her American Doctors, and the Collision of Two Cultures* (New York: Farrar, Straus and Giroux, 1998). However, the book has been controversial. For a critique, see Monica Chiu, "Medical, Racist, and Colonial Constructions of Power: Creating the Asian American Patient and the Cultural Citizen in Anne Fadiman's *The Spirit Catches You and You Fall Down,*" *Hmong Studies Journal* 5 (2004–2005): 1–36.

45. Jean Hopfensperger, "Twin Cities Doctors Work to Bridge Gap with Hmong," *Minneapolis Star Tribune,* August 25, 1989.

46. Thomas Collins and Les Suzukamo, "Dreams in Exile: The Hmong in St. Paul," *St. Paul Pioneer Press Dispatch,* November 26, 1989.

47. Vang and Vang, "The Sacred Drum," 320.

48. Patricia Leigh Brown, "A Doctor for Disease, a Shaman for the Soul," *New York Times,* September 20, 2009.

49. Chai Lee, interview. Similarly, Mai Neng Moua observed, "For the Hmong, the lines between culture or traditions and religion were often blurry. That is, it is not always easy to separate culture from religion." See Moua, *The Bride Price,* 34.

50. David Schimke, "Devils and Shamans," *Twin Cities Reader,* August 21–27, 1996.

51. Cantwell v. Connecticut, 310 US 296 (1940); Everson v. Board of Education, 330 US 1 (1947). For an overview of the First Amendment and the relationship between church and state in the United States, see Winnifred

Fallers Sullivan, "The State," in *Themes in Religion and American Culture,* ed. Philip Goff and Paul Harvey (Chapel Hill: University of North Carolina Press, 2004), 225–259.

52. Sarah Barringer Gordon characterized the 1940s onward as "the new constitutional world." See Gordon, *The Spirit of the Law,* 3. For religious studies analysis of the relationship between religion and law in the twentieth-century United States, see Joshua Dubler and Isaac Weiner, eds., *Religion, Law, USA* (New York: New York University Press, 2019).

53. Bender and Snow, "From Alleged Buddhists to Unreasonable Hindus," 203.

54. You Vang Yang v. Sturner, 728 F. Supp. 845 (US District Court, D. Rhode Island, 1990); Yang v. Sturner, 750 F. Supp. 558 (US District Court, D. Rhode Island, 1990); State v. Tenerelli, 598 N.W.2d 668 (Minn. 1999).

55. Employment Division v. Smith, 494 US 872 (1990).

56. *You Vang Yang v. Sturner; Yang v. Sturner.*

57. United States v. Ballard, 322 US 78 (1994).

58. United States v. Seeger, 380 US 163 (1965).

59. Bender and Snow, "From Alleged Buddhists to Unreasonable Hindus," 198. The Hmong way also faces the challenge of overcoming the intellectual obstacle of being considered "idolatry" and thus a "false religion," a category that since early modern Europe has continued to shape judicial rulings on which groups are pursuing legitimately true religion. As Jakob de Roover argued, "Even where the state did not engage in explicit endorsement of any religious truth, the conceptual mechanism that allowed it to sift the religious (as the realm of toleration and freedom) from the secular (as the realm of state interference) always involved an implicit notion of false religion." See Jakob de Roover, "Secular Law and the Realm of False Religion," in *After Secular Law,* ed. Winnifred Fallers Sullivan, Robert Yelle, and Mateo Taussig-Rubbo (Stanford, CA: Stanford Law Books, 2011), 43–61.

60. Mai Neng Moua has emphasized the internal diversity of Hmong beliefs and practices across the diaspora. See Moua, *The Bride Price,* 108.

61. J. Kou Vang, interview.

Conclusion

1. Hmong Christian Church of God, Folder 27, Box 6, RSC, UMN Records, General/Multiethnic Collection, IHRC, UMN.

2. Paja Thao and Dwight Conquergood, *I Am a Shaman: A Hmong Life Story with Ethnographic Commentary,* trans. Xa Thao, Southeast Asian Refugee Studies Occasional Papers, no. 8 (Minneapolis: Southeast Asian Refugee Studies Project, Center for Urban and Regional Affairs, University of Minnesota, 1989), 18–19.

3. Hmong Christian Church of God, Folder 27, Box 6, RSC, UMN Records, General/Multiethnic Collection, IHRC, UMN.

4. Gary Yia Lee, interview by Peter Parkhill, March 10, 2000, National Library of Australia, Canberra.

5. Gary Yia Lee, "Culture and Adaptation: Hmong Refugees in Australia 1976–83," in *The Hmong in Transition,* ed. Glenn Hendricks, Bruce Downing, and Amos Deinard (New York: Center for Migration Studies and the

Southeast Asian Refugee Studies Project of the University of Minnesota, 1986), 65.

6. Gary Yia Lee, interview.

7. Gary Yia Lee, "Culture and Adaptation," 65.

8. Gary Yia Lee, interview.

9. Kou Her, interview by the author, July 6, 2015, Cairns, Queensland, Australia.

10. Fay Chia Lee and Jor Vue, interview by the author, July 7, 2015, Innisfail, Queensland, Australia.

11. Elizabeth Her, interview by the author, July 18, 2015, Sydney, New South Wales, Australia. Interviewee's name has been changed at their request.

12. Kou Her, interview.

13. Elizabeth Her, interview.

14. Pao Lee, interview by the author, July 14, 2015, Sydney, New South Wales, Australia.

15. Charles Saykao, interview by the author, July 27, 2015, Greensborough, Victoria, Australia.

16. Gary Yia Lee, interview.

17. Charles Saykao, interview.

18. "Reference: Indochinese Refugee Resettlement—Australia's Involvement," Senate Standing Committee on Foreign Affairs and Defence, Hansard Transcript of Evidence, vol. 1, March 18, 1981.

19. *Hmong Newsletter* 8, no. 2 (October 1986).

20. Ethnic Communities' Council of New South Wales, "Indochinese Refugee Situation and Australia's Role," October 1980, Submission to the Senate Standing Committee on Foreign Affairs and Defence.

21. Roberta Julian, Adrian Franklin, and Bruce Felmingham, *Home from Home: Refugees in Tasmania* (Canberra: Department of Immigration and Multicultural Affairs, Commonwealth of Australia, 1997), 103, 110.

22. Ethnic Communities' Council of New South Wales, "Indochinese Refugee Situation and Australia's Role."

23. Hmong-Australia Society Letter, November 5, 1986.

24. Gary Yia Lee, interview.

25. Gary Yia Lee, "Culture and Settlement: The Present Situation of the Hmong in Australia," in *The Hmong of Australia: Culture and Diaspora,* ed. Nicholas Tapp and Gary Yia Lee (Canberra: Australian National University Press, 2010), 20–21.

26. Xao Lor, interview by the author, July 19, 2015, Preston, New South Wales, Australia.

27. Nicholas Tapp, "Hmong Diaspora in Australia," in Tapp and Lee, *The Hmong of Australia,* 82.

28. Tapp, "Hmong Diaspora in Australia," 74. For more discussion of Hmong American missionaries, see Tam T. T. Ngo, *The New Way: Protestantism and the Hmong in Vietnam* (Seattle: University of Washington Press, 2016), 61–82.

29. Vang Yee Chang, interview by the author, July 6, 2015, Cairns, Queensland, Australia.

30. Gary Yia Lee, "Culture and Adaptation," 65.

31. Ethnic Communities' Council of New South Wales, "Indochinese Refugee Situation and Australia's Role."

32. Migration and Refugee Services, United States Catholic Conference, *Sponsorship: Access to a New Life,* Correspondence by Name, 1979–1981, Box 2, ARC Records, MHS.

33. DPCA Continuity File, September 15, 1975, Folder 1, Philip G. Johnson papers, US Army Heritage and Education Center, Carlisle, PA (hereafter Johnson papers, USAHEC).

34. *Indochina Evacuation and Refugee Problems, Part IV, Staff Reports Prepared for the Use of the Subcommittee to Investigate Problems Connected with Refugees and Escapees of the Committee on the Judiciary, United States Senate,* 94th Cong. 110 (June 9 and July 8, 1975).

35. DPCA Continuity File, September 15, 1975, Folder 1, Johnson papers, USAHEC; "Task Force New Arrivals Chaplain Program Summary," October 22, 1975, Folder 1, Johnson papers, USAHEC.

36. DPCA Continuity File, September 15, 1975, Folder 1, Johnson papers, USAHEC.

37. "Task Force New Arrivals Chaplain Program Summary," October 22, 1975.

38. "Task Force Chaplain Program Highlight Summary, 16 October–21 November 1975," November 24, 1975, Johnson papers, USAHEC.

39. Buddhist Volag Refugee Counseling Service, Johnson papers, USAHEC.

40. "Task Force New Arrivals Chaplain Program Summary," October 22, 1975.

41. "Task Force Chaplain Program Highlight Summary, 16 October–21 November 1975."

42. "Task Force New Arrivals Chaplain Program Summary," 22 October 22, 1975.

43. *Indochina Refugee and Evacuation Problems, Part 5, Conditions in Indochina and Refugees in the US: Hearing Before the Subcommittee to Investigate Problems with Refugees and Escapees of the Committee on the Judiciary,* 94th Cong. 38 (July 24, 1975) (statement of Donald Anderson, Lutheran Immigration and Refugee Service).

44. Hilary DeVries, "New Lives," *Christian Science Monitor,* December 21, 1984.

45. *A Guide to 3 Indochinese Cultures,* Minnesota Refugee Resettlement Office, Minnesota Department of Public Welfare, Folder 17, Box 115, RSC, IHRC, UMN.

46. John Moore, "Oriental Influence," *Wall Street Journal,* October 27, 1977.

47. James Wooten, "Vietnam Refugee Family Caught between Two Sponsors," *New York Times,* June 26, 1975.

48. Stephen Morin, "Many Hmong, Puzzled by Life in the U.S., Yearn for Old Days in Laos," *Wall Street Journal,* February 16, 1983.

49. Se Yang, "Shee Yee and the Evil Spirits That Ate People and Drank Blood," in *Myths, Legends and Folk Tales from the Hmong of Laos,* ed. Charles Johnson (Saint Paul, MN: Macalester College, 1985), 39–42.

Selected Primary Sources

Original Oral History Interviews

Anderson, Dianne. September 19, 2012. Saint Paul, MN.
Chang, Vang Yee. July 6, 2015. Cairns, Queensland, Australia.
Her, Elizabeth. July 18, 2015. Sydney, New South Wales, Australia.*
Her, Kou. July 6, 2015, Cairns, Queensland, Australia.
Her, Mary. Interpreted by Maile Vue. August 1, 2012. Saint Paul, MN.*
Jones, Pearl. August 29, 2012. White Bear Lake, MN.*
Karvonen, Joanne. August 10, 2012. Saint Paul, MN.
Kirk, Elaine. July 26, 2012. Saint Paul, MN.
Knight, Dorothy. August 6, 2012. Saint Paul, MN.
Kosel, Tom. June 23, 2011. Saint Paul, MN.
Kretzmann, Jane. September 10, 2010. Saint Paul, MN.
Lee, Chai. July 21, 2014. Saint Paul, MN.
Lee, Fay Chia, and Jor Vue. July 7, 2015. Innisfail, Queensland, Australia.
Lee, Gary Yia. July 14 and 15, 2015. Sydney, New South Wales, Australia.
Lee, Pao. July 14, 2015. Fairfield, New South Wales, Australia.
Lee, Soua Sue. July 29, 2014. Saint Paul, MN.
Lee, Yia. July 29, 2012. Saint Paul, MN.
Lor, Xao. July 19, 2015. Preston, New South Wales, Australia.
Mergenthal, Mary. August 10, 2012. Saint Paul, MN.
Moua, Cher. September 6, 2012. Saint Paul, MN.
Moua, Yong Kay, and Houa Vue Moua. September 12, 2012. Saint Paul, MN.

---

* Interviewee's name has been changed at their request.

Nessa, Jim, and Paula Nessa. August 28, 2012. Saint Paul, MN.
Saykao, Charles. July 27, 2015. Greensborough, Victoria, Australia.
Schuneman, Rosemary. August 31, 2012. Saint Paul, MN.
Siong, William. September 11, 2012. Saint Paul, MN.
Thao, Joua Tsu. September 19, 2012. Roseville, MN.
Thao, Nao. September 11, 2012. Saint Paul, MN.
Tidemann, Paul. July 28, 2012. Saint Paul, MN.
Vang, J. Kou. July 28, 2014. Maplewood, MN.
Vang, Neng, and Paj Ntaub Lis. March 25, 2012. Saint Paul, MN.*
Vang, Timothy. September 20, 2012. Maplewood, MN.
Vang, Tzianeng. September 5, 2012. Saint Paul, MN.
Vellenga, Kathleen. September 14, 2011. Saint Paul, MN.
Vue, Kia. Interpreted by Maile Vue. September 8, 2012. Saint Paul, MN.
Vue-Benson, Bea. September 5, 2012. Saint Paul, MN.
Xiong, Neng. Interpreted by Maile Vue. August 3, 2012. Minneapolis, MN.
Xiong, True. Interpreted by Maile Vue. August 9, 2012. Minneapolis, MN.
Yang, Bee. Translated by Maile Vue. August 2, 2012. Saint Paul, MN.
Yang, Cziasarh Neng. September 17, 2012. Saint Paul, MN.
Yang, Mao. Interpreted by Paj Ntaub Lis. August 12, 2012. Saint Paul, MN.
Yang, Nao Khue, and Sarah Fang. Interpreted by Maile Vue. September 5, 2012. Saint Paul, MN.
Yang, Shong Yer, and Soua Lo. Interpreted by Maile Vue. August 6, 2012. Saint Paul, MN.

Archived Oral History Collections

Billy Graham Center Archives, Wheaton, IL
    Malcolm Maurice and Helen Irvin Sawyer Collection 256
Concordia University, Saint Paul, MN
    Hmong Oral History Project
Evangelical Lutheran Church of America Archive, Elk Grove Village, IL
    Oral History Collection, Archives of Cooperative Lutheranism, Lutheran
        Council in the USA
Minnesota Historical Society, Saint Paul, MN
    Hmong Oral Histories Project, 1991–1993
    Hmong Women's Action Team Oral History Project, 1999–2000
    Vietnamese Oral History Project
National Library of Australia, Canberra
    Lee, Gary Yia, interview by Peter Parkhill, March 10, 2000

Archival Collections

Dayton Avenue Presbyterian Church Archive, Saint Paul, MN
    Church Records
Evangelical Lutheran Church of America Archives, Elk Grove Village, IL
    Lutheran Council in the USA Department of Immigration and Refugee Services
        (LCUSA/DIRS) 10/1: Standing Committee Minutes and Agenda, 1966–1987
        (LCUSA/DIRS) 10/3: Publications, 1975–1986

Immigration History Research Center, University of Minnesota, Minneapolis, MN
    International Institute of Minnesota Records
    Refugee Studies Center Records
Luther Seminary Archive, Saint Paul, MN
    Messiah Lutheran Church Records
    Saint Anthony Park Lutheran Church Records
    Saint Paul Reformation Lutheran Church Records
    Trinity Lutheran Church of Wanamingo Records
Minnesota Historical Society, Saint Paul, MN
    American Refugee Committee Records
    Christ Lutheran Bulletin
    Christ on Capitol Hill Records
    Dayton Avenue Presbyterian Church Records
    Minnesota State Refugee Program Records
    Pamphlets Relating to Refugee Relief and Assistance in Minnesota and the
        United States
Presbyterian Historical Society, Philadelphia, PA
    Church World Service Records
    Lois Visscher Papers
Saint Anthony Park Lutheran Church Archive, Saint Paul, MN
    Refugee Core Committee Records
Southeast Asian Archive, University of California, Irvine
    Bonner Files
United States Army History Education Center, Carlisle, PA
    Phillip G. Johnson Papers
Wheaton College Archives, Wheaton, IL
    National Association of Evangelicals Records

Acknowledgments

This book has its origins in a paper I wrote over two decades ago, as a nineteen-year-old college sophomore in a seminar on American immigration history. In the twenty-one years since, I have been grateful for the many people who have offered encouragement, guidance, wisdom, and love as I grew as a scholar, developed my ideas, and created a book from that humble seminar paper.

I must begin by thanking my teachers. I am forever grateful to have been advised by Mae Ngai, a paragon of scholarly excellence, generous mentorship, and public engagement. Thank you, Mae, for seeing my potential and investing in my success. At Columbia University, I was fortunate to have been advised not only by Mae, but also by Courtney Bender, Ira Katznelson, Mary Marshall Clark, and José Moya—a group I consider a dream team of academic mentorship.

Other teachers and mentors have supported me over the years. At the University of Chicago, Catherine Brekus fostered a love of American religious history. At Harvard University, Jane Rosenzweig taught me how to write, and Quenby Olmsted Hughes trained me in historical methods. I owe a special thanks to Lisa McGirr, who hired me as a research assistant in my first year of college, introduced me to archival research, and later served as my thesis advisor. Thank you to Ruth Feldstein, Sonia Lee, and Rebecca McLennan, whose comments on that thesis—which I consider the first full iteration of this book—shaped the direction of this project. I was fortunate to return to Harvard in 2020–2021 to develop my book manuscript as a faculty fellow at the Charles Warren Center for American History. Thank you to Catherine Brekus, James Kloppenberg, and David Holland for making that fellowship year possible, even during a global pandemic.

The research and writing of this book were possible due to several fellowships and research grants. I am grateful for the support I received from the Harvard Mellon Urban Initiative; the Charles Warren Center for Studies in American History; the Andrew Mellon Foundation; the American Council of Learned Societies; the University of Minnesota Immigration History Research Center; the Institute for Religion, Culture, and Public Life; the Southeast Asian Summer Institute (SEASSI); the Shawn family; and the Center for the Study of World Religions.

Being able to share this scholarship with the world by publishing with Harvard University Press has been a dream. Thank you to the staff of the Press, and especially to Kathleen McDermott, who saw promise in this project and nurtured it with great patience and editorial wisdom. Thank you also to the anonymous reviewers who provided generous and helpful suggestions for making this book better.

Chapter 2 builds on ideas first presented in "The Government Alone Cannot Do the Total Job," my contribution to *Shaped by the State,* edited by Brent Cebul, Lily Geismer, and Mason B. Williams and published by the University of Chicago Press in 2019.

Scholarship is best done in the context of community, and I have been fortunate to have been on the faculty of two universities that served as supportive intellectual homes during the development of this book. During my time on the faculty at the College of Staten Island, City University of New York, I received abundant support for research and writing. I am especially grateful to Eric Ivison and Susan Smith-Peter, who ensured I would be able to do the final research trips necessary for the completion of this book. In addition, the City University of New York's Faculty Fellowship Publication Program (FFPP) offered a valuable setting to workshop my writing and share ideas. I am thankful for the mentorship of Stephen Steinberg and the insight, advice, and encouragement of the brilliant people in my FFPP cohort: Kafui Attoh, Lawrence Johnson, Devin Molina, Emily Tumpson Molina, Seth Offenbach, and Susanna Rosenbaum.

At the University of Michigan, many kind and supportive colleagues played a direct role in developing both this book and my career as a scholar. Thank you to the program directors of the Asian/Pacific Islander American Studies program (Manan Desai, John Kuwada, and Hitomi Tonomura) and the chairs of American Culture Department (Greg Dowd, Lawrence LaFontaine-Stokes, and Alex Stern), who ensured I would have the time and resources to finish this book. Finally, thank you to Stephen Berrey, Miranda Brown, Farina Mir, and Lisa Nakamura for serving as wise, kind, and generous mentors.

Over the years, this book was improved through countless conversations with scholarly colleagues at workshops, seminars, and conferences. I am especially grateful that the University of Michigan organized a book manuscript workshop for me. Thank you to Jesse Hoffnung-Garskoff, Victor Mendoza, and Tisa Wenger for serving on the manuscript workshop panel and for the many colleagues who read my work and offered helpful ideas for improving it. Thank you to the research groups that invited me to share my work: the American Culture Workshop at the University of Michigan, the American Studies Foundation of Japan International Forum for Early Career Scholars, the Association for Asian American Studies Junior Faculty Workshop, the Center for the Study of Material and Visual Cultures of Religion at Yale University, the Miller Center at the University of Virginia, the Religion in America Seminar at Columbia University, and the Rocky Mountain Religion Seminar at the University of Utah. Thank you also to the colleagues who provided feedback at the following scholarly conferences: the American Academy of Religion, the American Historical Association, the American Society for Church History, the Association for Asian American Studies, the Biennial Conference on Religion and American Culture, the Henry Symposium at Calvin College, the International Conference on Hmong Studies at Concordia University, the Organization of American Historians, and the Society for Historians of American Foreign Relations.

Thank you to all the individuals who agreed to share their stories with me through oral history interviews. Listening to your stories was a powerful and humbling experience, and I continue to be awed by your generosity, hospitality, and openness. I did my best to honor your experiences in these pages.

Thank you to the many archivists and librarians who have provided research support, especially Haven Hawley, Daniel Necas, Mark Pfeifer, and Joel Thoreson.

This book would not have been possible without a small army of research assistants. I am thankful for Simon Huang, Tiffany Huang, and Jonah Wang for providing Minnesota-based research support, and for Christina Dellaventura, Matthew Dreher, Alzina Fok, Elina Grunkina, Monnique Johnson, and Julie Mizrahi, who served as research assistants when I was teaching at the College of Staten Island. Thank you to Ton Nu Nguyen-Dinh, who conducted research for me during my fellowship year at Harvard. Finally, I am grateful for my research assistants at the University of Michigan: Emily Bloom, Nick Colucci, Amelia Navins, and especially Jacob Gibson, who deserves special recognition as the most dedicated and diligent research assistant I have ever encountered.

I am grateful for the many Hmong studies scholars and colleagues who offered guidance throughout every stage of this project. Thank you especially to Paul Hillmer, Gary Yia Lee, Nue Lee, and Chia Youyee Vang for their practical advice and kind support. Thank you to my friends and colleagues at SEASSI for their encouragement. Thank you, most of all, to Maile Vue for serving as an interpreter and cultural guide.

One of the best opportunities of my scholarly career was participating in the Young Scholars in American Religion Program at the Center for the Study of Religion and American Culture at Indiana University. Thank you to Philip Goff for organizing this program and for Lauren Chism Schmidt for ensuring that our workshops were always a joy. This book and my life were both changed for the better thanks to the mentorship of Sally Promey and Sylvester Johnson and the friendship and scholarly community I found with Joseph Blankholm, Christopher Cantwell, Matthew Cressler, Sarah Dees, Jamil Drake, Katharine Gerbner, Samira Mehta, Shari Rabin, and Alexis Wells-Oghoghomeh.

Countless academic colleagues have shared ideas and supported me over the years. Thank you especially to Jessica Adler, Lisa Asedello, Bryan Averbuch, Rachel Bundang, Gabriel Catenus, David Chao, Katherine Clifton, Emily Conroy-Krutz, Heather Curtis, Joanna Dee, Joyce Del Rosario, Kristin Kobes Du Mez, Victoria Geduld, Aaron Gilbreath, Thai Jones, Helen Kim, Natalie Kimball, SueJeanne Koh, Scott Larson, Heather Lee, Jessica Lee, Tamara Mann, Linda Mehta, Monica Mercado, Michael Neuss, Meredith Oda, Yuki Oda, Arissa Oh, Catherine Osborne, Neal Presa, Swapnil Rai, Todd Scribner, Ian Shin, Aaron Shkuda, Matthew Spooner, Joseph Stuart, Jonathan Tran, Justin Tse, Dan Vaca, Matt Weiner, Andy Whitford, Mason Williams, and Ellen Wu.

Many kind friends housed me, fed me, took care of my child, listened to me talk through revisions, cheered me on, and showered me with love as I visited archives, traveled to conferences, and hunkered down to write. I cannot name you all, but thank you especially to Laurie Bramlage, Matt Bramlage, Bert Bratane, Sucie Chang, Leian Chen, Yasmeen Chism, Jane Cowan, Yolanda Davis, Jesse Gero, Jamie Hinson-Rieger, Susanne Hinson-Rieger, Christina Jenq, Denise Kim, Teri Kleinberg, Sophia Lai, Janet Lee, Jennifer Leung, Remy Lobo, Jane Moon, Jessica Son, Jordan Winfield, Vannie Ip Winfield, and Janet Yueh.

Finally, I would not have completed this book without the unfailing support of my family. Thank you to the extended Borja, Ledesma, Thomas, and Westin families for lifting me up with love and encouragement. I am especially grateful for my siblings—Christina, Michael, Jessy, Jeff, and

Alicia—for helping me believe in myself and stay grounded at the same time; my in-laws, Mary and George Westin, for offering boundless care and good humor; and my parents, Francisco and Eleanor Borja, for nurturing my lifelong passion for thinking and writing, and for being a steady source of wisdom, prayers, and comforting bowls of *arroz caldo*. Most of all, I am deeply grateful for my daughter, Beata Borja-Westin, and my spouse, Greg Westin, who have patiently tolerated both long research trips away from home and long-winded dinnertime commentary about historiographical interventions. They have taught me the importance of grounding my scholarship in joy and gratitude and reminded me of what matters most: creating a loving, just, and compassionate world. They continue to make me a better scholar and a better human, and for this, I am deeply blessed. Beata and Greg, this book is dedicated to you.

Index

Bible: and Hmong adoption of Christianity, 190, 204, 207, 209, 216–219, 238, 260–261; Hmong translation, 43, 49; and missionaries, 51, 59, 61; and resettlement work, 113, 117–118, 121–123, 135–136
Bible Christian movement, 43
Black Americans, 85, 125, 127
Blatz, Kathleen, 274
Breen, Stanley, 96
Brigl, Jim, 159
Brown, Anastasia, 104
Brown, Edmund Gerald "Jerry," 86
Brown, L. Dean, 90, 92, 97
Buddha, 46, 160, 215
Buddhism/Buddhists: in Australia, 288; and classifying religion, 23, 34–35, 46–47, 72; Festival of the Full Moon, 292; and Hmong religious life, 20; and immigration, 142–143; and refugee resettlement, 14–16, 29, 99, 124, 159, 192, 291–295; temple, 262
Buddhist Council for Refugee Rescue and Resettlement, 99
Bush, George W., 103
butchers/butcher shops, 187–188, 244, 250–251, 255–256, 278

Cambodia/Cambodians, 9, 13, 29, 56–57, 61, 75–80, 92, 112, 154, 159, 192, 291, 294
Canada, 174, 225
Cantwell v. Connecticut (1940), 268
Capitol Hill Refugee Project, 101
Carlin, Jean, 57–58
Carr, Robert, 87
Carter, Jimmy, 56, 75–80, 102
Catholic Charities, 94, 99–100, 138, 144, 159
Cha, Dia, 38, 40, 45
Chang, Vang Yee, 290
Charitable Choice, 14, 103
charities, 3, 9, 12, 15, 78, 94, 99–103, 138, 144, 159
China, 37, 48, 137, 180
China Inland Mission, 43
Christian and Missionary Alliance (CMA): handicraft sales program, 58; Hmong district, 4; and Hmong religion, 216–218, 223; missionaries, 43–49, 74, 125, 151–152, 221; and resettlement, 100, 189, 211
Christians/Christianity: as becoming American, 210; category of religion (*see* Protestants/Protestantism: idea of religion); Golden Rule, 116–118; Hmong, 1–4, 22, 48, 50, 54, 71, 74, 213, 218–227, 230, 239, 267, 280–281; as I-PASS token, 229.

See also specific voluntary agencies and Christian denominations
Christmas, 132, 159, 220, 225
Church of the Brethren, 294
Church World Service (CWS), 89, 97–101, 109–110, 113, 117–118, 123, 134, 144, 147–148, 152–153; *A Guide to Two Cultures,* 153–154; *Religion of the Refugees,* 152–153
CIA (Central Intelligence Agency), 1, 52–53, 183
Cold War, 58, 76, 81–87, 94, 143, 183, 291
Committee for the Coordination of Services to Displaced Persons in Thailand (CCSDPT), 64–65
Communism/Communists, 52–53, 81–83, 87–89, 143, 158: anti-Communism, 52, 81–83, 291
Consultation on World Evangelization (COWE), 59–60
conversion: Hmong ambivalence, 19; Hmong to Christianity, 7, 73–74, 147, 205–214, 229, 235–236, 248; Hmong understandings of, 217–225, 230–236, 239; in Laos, 44, 47–50; *lawb dab xwb tsis ntseeg* (some Hmong do away with the spirits but do not believe in God or Jesus), 231; and marriage, 236–237; and mission policies, 147, 153, 284; as spiritual migration, 17–22, 205–207, 210, 217, 220–222
Cooke, Terence (cardinal), 76
Cuba/Cubans, 77, 82–83, 92, 95
Cuban Refugee Program, 95

Dao, Yang, 223
Davis, Vincent, 87
Displaced Persons Act (1948), 94

Eastwood, Clint, 101
empire: and Christian missionaries, 36, 63, 128, 161; and refugee policies, 18, 35–36; religion as imperial project, 23, 46; and the Secret War, 73–74
Employment Division v. Smith (1990), 271
English as a Second Language (ESL) programs, 96, 99–100
Episcopalians, 4, 113, 161
Erickson, Ellen, 150
Ethnic Communities' Council of New South Wales, 288
Everson v. Board of Education (1947), 268

Fadiman, Anne, 226
Fang, Sarah, 175, 186